International Law in a Multipolar World

Since the creation of the United Nations in 1945, international law has sought to configure itself as a universal system. Yet, despite the best efforts of international institutions, scholars and others to assert the universal application of international law, its relevance and applicability has been influenced, if not directed, by political power. Today, the 'decline of the West' and ascent of China and India pose particular challenges for international law and institutions. The international system appears to be moving towards multipolarity, with various sites of power competing to exert influence in the world today. With contributors from a variety of countries providing perspectives from the disciplines of international law and international relations theory, *International Law in a Multipolar World* addresses the implications that multipolarity poses for the international legal system. Contributors including Jean d'Aspremont, Jörg Kammerhofer, Alexander Orakhelashvili, Christian Pippan and Nigel White explore issues such as the use of force, governance and democracy, regionalism and the relevance of the United Nations in a multipolar world, while considering the overarching theme of the relationship between power and law.

International Law in a Multipolar World is of particular interest to academics and students of public international law, international relations theory and international politics.

Matthew Happold is Professor of Public International Law at the University of Luxembourg

Routledge Research in International Law

Available:

International Law and the Third World
Reshaping Justice
Richard Falk, Balakrishnan Rajagopal and Jacqueline Stevens (eds.)

International Legal Theory
Essays and Engagements, 1966–2006
Nicholas Onuf

The Problem of Enforcement in International Law
Countermeasures, the Non-Injured State and the Idea of International Community
Elena Katselli Proukaki

International Economic Actors and Human Rights
Adam McBeth

The Law of Consular Access
A Documentary Guide
John Quigley, William J. Aceves and Adele Shank

State Accountability under International Law
Holding States Accountable for a Breach of *jus cogens* Norms
Lisa Yarwood

International Organisations and the Idea of Autonomy
Institutional Independence in the International Legal Order
Richard Collins and Nigel D. White (eds.)

Self-Determination in the Post-9/11 Era
Elizabeth Chadwick

Participants in the International Legal System
Multiple Perspectives on Non-State Actors in International Law
Jean d'Aspremont

Sovereignty and Jurisdiction in the Airspace and Outer Space
Legal Criteria for Spatial Delimitation
Gbenga Oduntan

International Law in a Multipolar World
Matthew Happold (ed.)

The Law on the Use of Force
A Feminist Analysis
Gina Heathcote

Forthcoming titles in this series include:

International Law, Regulation and Resistance
Critical Spaces
Zoe Pearson

The ICJ and the Development of International Law
The Lasting Impact of the *Corfu Channel* Case
Karine Bannelier, Théodore Christakis and Sarah Heathcote (eds.)

The Right to Self-determination Under International Law
'Selfistans', Secession and the Great Powers' Rule
Milena Sterio

The Cuban Embargo under International Law
El Bloqueo
Nigel D. White

Threats of Force
International Law and Strategy
Francis Grimal

Asian Approaches to International Law and the Legacy of Colonialism and Imperialism
The Law of the Sea, Territorial Disputes and International Dispute Settlement
Jin-Hyun Paik, Seok-Woo Lee, Kevin Y L Tan (eds.)

International Law in a Multipolar World

Edited by
Matthew Happold

Routledge
Taylor & Francis Group
LONDON AND NEW YORK

First published 2012
by Routledge
2 Park Square, Milton Park, Abingdon, Oxon, OX14 4RN

Simultaneously published in the USA and Canada
by Routledge
711 Third Avenue, New York, NY 10017

Routledge is an imprint of the Taylor & Francis Group, an informa business

British Library Cataloguing in Publication Data
A catalogue record for this book is available from the British Library

Library of Congress Cataloging in Publication Data
A catalog record has been requested

ISBN 978-0-415-56521-9 (hbk)
ISBN 978-0-203-80312-7 (ebk)

Typeset in Garamond
by Saxon Graphics Ltd, Derby

MIX
Paper from responsible sources
FSC® C004839

Printed and bound in Great Britain by the MPG Books Group

Contents

Notes on Contributors

Dr Jean d'Aspremont is Associate Professor of international law and Senior Research Fellow of the Amsterdam Center for International Law at the University of Amsterdam. He is Guest Professor of international humanitarian law at the University of Louvain in Belgium. He is senior editor of the *Leiden Journal of International Law*. He has acted as counsel in proceedings before the International Court of Justice. He is a member of the ILA Committee on Non-State Actors.

Dr Eric de Brabandere is Associate Professor of international law at Leiden University, the Netherlands and a visiting professor at the Faculté Libre de Droit of the Université Catholique de Lille, France. He is a senior editor of the *Leiden Journal of International Law*, and an editor of the *Revue belge de droit international*. He obtained his law degree from Ghent University, holds an LLM from the University of Geneva and a Ph.D. from Ghent University and previously worked as assistant lecturer at Ghent University, and as a barrister at the Brussels Bar. His areas of expertise include international dispute settlement and arbitration and general international law. He was recently awarded a VENI research grant from the Netherlands Organization for Scientific Research to conduct a three-year research project on the resolution of contemporary investment disputes.

Dr Carmen Draghici is a Lecturer in law at The City Law School, City University London, where she teaches human rights law, family and child law, and European Union law. Carmen holds a Ph.D. in international law and human rights, received in 2007 from the University of Rome 'La Sapienza', with a thesis on the international protection of family rights in Europe. Before joining City University London in 2009, Carmen was a Leverhulme visiting post-doctoral research fellow at the Centre on Human Rights in Conflict, School of Law, University of East London. Carmen also collaborates as a part-time lecturer in international law with the Open University of Catalonia (Barcelona). Her main research interests concern counter-terrorism and fundamental rights, the responsibility of states and international organizations, and the practice of the European Convention on Human Rights. She has contributed articles and chapters to UK and international journals and edited volumes, and is currently reworking her doctoral thesis into a monograph.

Prof. Matthew Happold (editor) is Professor of Public International Law at the University of Luxembourg. He previously taught at the universities of Hull, Nottingham and Sussex, and has been a visiting fellow at the Human Rights Program, Harvard Law School, and a visiting professional in the Office of the Prosecutor of the International Criminal Court. His publications include: *The Settlement of Investment Disputes under the Energy Charter Treaty* (CUP, 2011) (co-authored with Thomas Roe); *Child Soldiers in International Law* (MUP, 2005); and *Constitutional Human Rights in the Commonwealth* (BIICL, 2003) (co-edited with Michael Anderson).

Prof. Daniel H. Joyner is an Associate Professor of law at the University of Alabama School of Law. He has a BA in Japanese from Brigham Young University, a JD from Duke Law School, an MA in political science from the University of Georgia, and a Ph.D. in law from the University of Warwick. Prior to joining the Alabama Law faculty in 2007, Professor Joyner taught for four years on the faculty of the University of Warwick School of Law. He has also been a senior associate member of St Antony's College, Oxford University. His research interests are focused in public international law, with particular interest in the area of WMD proliferation and nuclear energy law; including non-proliferation treaties and regimes, issues of international trade, investment and export control law. His first book, *International Law and the Proliferation of Weapons of Mass Destruction* was published in 2009 (by OUP).

Dr Jörg Kammerhofer is currently a Senior Research Fellow at the Hans Kelsen Research Group at the University of Freiburg, Germany, which is publishing a collected works edition of all of Hans Kelsen's writings. He has written *inter alia* on customary international law, the law of the use of force under the Charter, on the procedure of the International Court of Justice and on Kelsen's conception of international law. His recent book deals with the intersection between theory and practice: *Uncertainty in International Law: A Kelsenian Perspective* (Routledge, 2010). He has given speeches on the problem of the conflicts of norms in connection with the fragmentation of international law and on the mythological use of the term 'constitutionalization' in international legal scholarship.

Dr Silviya Lechner is a Lecturer in the Department of War Studies, King's College London. Her primary interests lie in the area of moral and political philosophy and international ethics. She has published articles on diplomatic theory and on questions such as rights, rules and obligations. Her current work focuses on philosophical critiques of liberalism.

Dr Alexander Orakhelashvili is a Lecturer in law at the University of Birmingham. He obtained his master's degree (LLM *cum laude*) from Leiden University in 2000 and his Ph.D. from Cambridge University in 2005. He has been a fellow of Jesus College Oxford (2005–8), and has for several years taught public international law in the universities of Oxford, Cambridge and London. He is the author of *Peremptory Norms in International Law* (OUP, 2006); *The Interpretation of Acts and Rules in Public International Law* (OUP, 2008); and *Collective Security* (OUP, 2011), as well as of a number of articles in leading international law periodicals in Britain, Europe and the United States. His research interests encompass all areas of public international law. He has provided legal advice on international law matters arising in litigation before English and American courts, and is an editor of the *Journal of International Peacekeeping*.

Dr Pablo Pareja-Alcaraz is a Lecturer in international relations and coordinator of international affairs at the Faculty of Law of the University Pompeu Fabra, Barcelona. He teaches also at the Institut d'Educació Continua and the Institut Barcelona d'Estudis Internacionals, where he acts as the academic coordinator of the Erasmus Mundus Master Program in Public Policy. He obtained his bachelor degree in Political Science from the University Pompeu Fabra and holds a master's degree in European Studies from the London School of Economics and Political Science and a master's degree in foreign service from Georgetown University. His research and teaching interests focus on the international relations of East Asia, international relations theory and Chinese foreign policy.

Dr Christian Pippan is a Senior Lecturer in public international law at the Karl-Franzens University of Graz (Austria). He has been a visiting researcher at the Community Law Center of the University of the Western Cape (1999), an Erwin Schrödinger Scholar of the Austrian Science Fund (2002–3), an Emile Noël Fellow at the New York University School of Law (2002–4), a visiting fellow at the Max Planck Institute for Comparative Public Law and International Law in Heidelberg (2006), and a visiting fellow at the Lauterpacht Centre for International Law in Cambridge (2009). He also served as a European Union and OSCE Election Observer in EOMs to Egypt (2005), Belarus (2006) and Armenia (2007). His current research interests centre on issues of self-determination, secession and recognition; democracy and international law; and the internationalization of constitutional law.

Dr Isobel Roele has been a Lecturer in the Law School at Cardiff University since September 2008. She obtained her LLM and Ph.D. degrees from the University of Nottingham. She is an international law theorist and her research examines in particular the UN collective security system and the use of force between states. Her work draws on Habermas' concept of the criticizable validity claim and Foucault's notion of power.

Dr Katja Samuel is a Barrister who specializes in armed conflict, security, international human rights and international criminal law. Her research interests (upon which her doctoral research was based) also include Islamic law and the institutional law of the Organization of the Islamic Conference, especially their influence on international lawmaking. She has published previously on these themes.

Dr Aurel Sari is a Lecturer in law at the University of Exeter. He specializes in public international law and the legal aspects of European foreign and security policy and has published his work in the *European Journal of International Law*, *Human Rights Law Review* and the *International and Comparative Law Quarterly*. Aurel is currently working on a monograph examining the jurisdictional privileges and immunities of foreign armed forces under international law. He is a member of the editorial board of the *Military Law and the Law of War Review* and was a visiting fellow at the Lauterpacht Centre for International Law in Cambridge in 2009.

Dr James Summers is a Lecturer in law and director of postgraduate studies at the University of Lancaster Law School. He is the author of *Peoples and International Law* (Brill, 2007), several articles on the law of self-determination and editor of the book *Kosovo: A Precedent?* (Brill, forthcoming 2011).

Dr Dominika Švarc is a Legal Research Associate at the International Court of Justice. Previously, she worked as a research assistant to Prof. Christopher Greenwood at the London School of Economics (LSE) and as a guest research fellow at the Max Planck Institute for International Law. She received her LLM from LSE in 2005 and her Ph.D. from the University of Ljubljana in 2011. Her academic research focuses on international law on the use of force and the law of armed conflicts, particularly in the context of peace operations, and non-state violence. Her doctoral thesis studies the evolution and role of international law on the use of force in contemporary international politics from an interdisciplinary (IL/IR) perspective. She is also a co-author of a textbook on international humanitarian law for the Slovenian armed forces, and has been teaching international law on the use of force and armed conflict at the NATO Center of Excellence – Defence against Terrorism, in Ankara. Since 2008, she has served as a member of the ILA Committee on non-state actors.

Rima Tkatova is currently a Temporary Teaching and Research Assistant at the Jean Moulin Lyon 3 University. She is a graduate of the Kazakh National University (BA in international economic relations), the Adilet Higher Law School (LLB) and the Jean Moulin University Lyon III (LLM public international law), where she is a Ph.D. candidate, researching post-Soviet states and international law and the renewal of the international doctrine and practice. She is author of the following works: 'Le droit international post-sovietique en quête de son identite dans un monde hétérogene' in *Select Proceedings of the European Society of International Law*, Volume 2, 2008; 'Les particularités du développement de l'Etat de droit dans la Communauté des Etats indépendants' in *L'Etat de droit en droit international*: Colloque de Bruxelles/Société française pour le droit international, 2009; 'L'affaire relative à l'application de la Convention internationale sur l'élimination de toutes les formes de discrimination raciale (Géorgie c. Fédération de Russie)', *Journal du CDI*, No 3, 2009; 'Central Asian States and International Law: Between Post-Soviet Culture and Eurasian Civilization', *Chinese Journal of International Law*, vol. 9, 2010; and 'Organisations régionales post-soviétiques et l'énergie', in *Défis énergétiques et droit international*, LARCIER, 2010.

Prof. Nigel D. White is Professor of Public International Law at the University of Nottingham, formerly Professor of International Law at the University of Sheffield. In addition to publishing numerous articles and essays, he is author of several books including: *Keeping the Peace: The United Nations and the Maintenance of International Peace and Security* (2nd edn, MUP, 1997); *The Law of International Organisations* (2nd edn, MUP, 2005); *The UN System: Toward International Justice* (Lynne Rienner, 2002); and *Democracy Goes to War: British Military Deployments under International Law* (OUP, 2009). He is also editor of a number of leading collections, primarily *Collective Security Law* (Ashgate, 2004), and co-editor of *The UN, Human Rights and Post Conflict Situations* (MUP, 2005); *International Conflict and Security Law* (CUP, 2005); *European Security Law* (OUP, 2007); and *International Law and Dispute Settlement* (Hart, 2010). He is co-editor-in-chief of the *Journal of Conflict and Security Law*; and is co-editor of the UK's contribution to *International Law in Domestic Courts*.

Introduction

Matthew Happold

In his *Fragments upon the Balance of Power in Europe*, published in 1806, Friedrich von Gentz, looking back with nostalgia at *ancien régime* Europe, wrote that:

> What is usually termed a balance of power, is that constitution subsisting among neighbouring states more or less connected with one another; by virtue of which no one among them can injure the independence or the essential rights of another, without meeting with effectual resistance on some side, and consequently exposing itself to danger.[1]

Such a system had, in Gentz's view, been destroyed by France, which had imposed its hegemony over Europe; a hegemony which reached its apogee in between the writing and the publication of Gentz's *Fragments* with Napoleon's victory over Austria and Russia at Austerlitz in December 1805.

For international relations theorists, ideas of the balance of power and of multipolarity have been inextricably linked ever since. For many scholars, the existence of multiple sites of power within a system of states has been seen as leading towards a balance of power, as the members of the system enter into and change alliances to prevent any one of them from obtaining a predominance. Multipolar systems have, consequently, been seen as more stable and long-lasting than systems where one or two states predominate. International lawyers, however, have only recently began to consider the implications that multipolarity might have for the international legal system; or, perhaps, it might be more accurate to say that the issue has only recently regained their attention.

Since the creation of the United Nations in 1945, international law has sought to configure itself as a universal system. Yet, despite the best efforts of international institutions, scholars and others to assert the universal application of international law, its relevance and applicability has been influenced, if not directed, by political power. The Cold War saw a concentration on co-

1 Friedrich von Gentz, Fragments upon the Balance of Power in Europe (1806), 55. Originally published as *Fragmente aus der neusten Geschichte des politischen Gleichgewichts in Europa*, 2 vols. (1806). London: Printed for M. Peltier.

existence in a bipolar world, which many argued brought stability (or, perhaps, rather, statis) to the international legal system. The end of 'actually existing Socialism' in Central and Eastern Europe and the dissolution of the Soviet Union was seen as providing an opportunity for a truly universal system – a 'new world order' applicable regardless of power arrangements. However, it quickly became apparent that international law would have to address the dilemmas inherent in regulating a system dominated by a single global power: the USA. Over the past decade discourse has tended to focus on the implications for international law of a unipolar world, characterized by US hegemony and 'exceptionalism'.

At present, however, the international system appears to be experiencing a tendency towards multipolarity, with various sites of power able to exert a telling influence on international relations and international law. Events in recent years such as Russia's excursion into Georgia, the breakdown of the Doha round of trade negotiations, the USA's questionable actions (and even more questionable successes) in its 'war on terror', the prominence of emerging nuclear powers, China's assertions of its own interests on a global scale, and the rise of regional trading blocs all pose significant questions for international law and the international legal order. The perceived novelty of the current situation has meant that, at least among Western scholars, it has been seen largely as a threat rather than as an opportunity: as heralding the fragmentation of international law in an increasingly divided world. Can 'universal' international law exist in the absence of a global hegemon? To what extent can sovereign equality persist in a world of competing 'great powers' and 'spheres of influence'? What relevance will the United Nations retain? Is there an 'international community' and, if so, does it exist on a multilateral or a regional level? The fear has been of a move away from global international law administered by international organizations with universal or near-universal membership to discrete regional subsystems, and of the renewed privileging of state sovereignty and non-intervention over multilateralism and human rights.

To an extent such fears are unsurprising. The move towards multipolarity in global politics is a result of a growth in power of a number of non-Western states (in particular China and India), whose increasing economic, political and military clout threatens Western interests and presumptions. However, they cannot just be seen as originating from anxieties about a change in circumstances but also derive from current views about the structure and role of the international legal system, which multipolarity is thought to threaten. Indeed, the features of multipolarity which its proponents have exulted in are precisely those which many international lawyers now depreciate. Although not a static system, the balance of power is supposed to tend towards equilibrium. It is not a progressive system tending towards some higher goal. Rather, it serves to preserve a status quo, and the status quo which it seeks to preserve is the sovereignty (in fact and in law) of existing states. International law within such a system is a law between states, serving to smooth their interactions and permitting them better to pursue certain common aims. Such a view of international law is far from that held by many international lawyers today. Instead, international law is seen as based on institutions, reflecting community values and reaching into states to constrain their conduct internally. This is, of course, not the only narrative (there are many others) but it is an influential one, particularly as regards how international law is taught and in Western states. Recent events, however, have indicated how great a resonance ideas of sovereignty and independence continue to have for many states in the world today. And it may be, moreover, that a multipolar system has perhaps unappreciated advantages in terms of safeguarding international stability and the ability of individual states to pursue their own interests unhindered.

The chapters in the book seek to examine the implications of a more multipolar world for the international legal system. The majority of them originate in papers presented at the 2009 spring conference of the British Branch of the International Law Association, hosted by the University of Hull Law School in April 2009, with others commissioned to complete the selection. The chapters are written from a variety of perspectives. Some seek to bring to the issues insights derived from other disciplines – international relations, history or political theory (Lechner, Orakhelashvili, Pareja-Alcaraz, Švarc, Chapters 8, 6, 11 and 4); others argue for a rigorously legal approach (Kammerhofer, Chapter 7). Some look at the role of global organizations, in particular the United Nations, in the world today (Joyner, Roele, White, Chapters 3, 2, 1), others at regional organizations and regional groupings of states (Draghici, Pareja-Alcaraz, Samuel, Sari, Tkatova, Chapters 14, 11, 13, 15 and 12). Several look at particular incidents or areas of law (d'Aspremont and de Brabandere, Pippan, Summers, Chapters, 9, 10 and 5). Unsurprisingly, given their different backgrounds and approaches, the contributors come to a variety of conclusions. What can be said, however, is that together they provide valuable food for thought for those pondering the future of international law and international relations. The issues they cover are ones of real and pressing importance, not just to academics and commentators but to activists and policy makers.

I am grateful to the contributors, who kept to deadlines and responded generously to my suggestions, making my job as editor surprisingly easy. I am also grateful to Karen Grudzien Baston, Ph.D. candidate at the University of Edinburgh School of Law, for her expert editorial assistance. While organizing the conference which led to this publication, I was much assisted by my then-colleagues at the University of Hull Law School, in particular Richard Barnes, Richard Burchill and Lindsay Moir, as well as our School administrators Angie Mortimer and Ann Sweeney and Sarah Carter at the Wilberforce Centre for the Study of Slavery and Emancipation. I am also grateful to the British Branch of the International Law Association for giving us the opportunity to host the conference, and to our sponsors FCO Legal Advisers and Herbert Smith LLP, who provided much-needed financial assistance in a wintry economic climate.

1 The Security Council, the security imperative and international law

Nigel D. White

1.1 Introduction

The United Nations Security Council plays various roles on the international stage, which makes it difficult to prescribe the legal framework within which it should operate. It is wrong, however, to see the Council either as untrammelled by international law, or to see it as judge, jury and executioner – effectively a law unto itself. Its primary function according to the UN Charter is the maintenance of international peace and security. Just as governments act to protect the security of states from threats, so the Security Council performs a similar role in relation to the international order. Its constitution means that the Council's security function is both erratic and inconsistent; but that should not detract from its competence in tackling situations which threaten the security of states, groups or individuals. In so doing it may use powers that are mandatory, coercive and give rise to supreme duties, but the question this chapter addresses is whether this places the Council outside the international legal order, or whether it must, as a matter of law, still respect principles of the UN Charter and international law. Further, as a political organ that is central to the international legal order, its legitimacy is dependent upon it respecting the law. If it acts outside the international legal order, or its resolutions are susceptible of being interpreted in such a way, then the Security Council will be a divisive actor rather than a force for unity; its actions will be a cause of fragmentation and unilateralism rather than a source of cohesion and integration.

1.2 The many roles of the Security Council

Paul Kennedy in his recent work on the UN concludes that 'even if the world body is constitutionally one organism, there are in practice many UNs',[1] referring to the different elements of the UN system.[2] Indeed, this point can be taken

1 P. Kennedy, *The Parliament of Man: The Past, Present and Future of the United Nations* (Toronto: HarperCollins 2006), xvi.

2 For discussion of the different elements, see N. D. White, *The United Nations System: Toward International Justice* (Boulder, CO: Lynne Rienner, 2002), 3–22.

further when considering the most influential and powerful organ in the UN system – the Security Council. The Security Council has many facets, many roles and many functions in the international political and legal orders and this makes it difficult to prescribe the legal framework within which it should operate.

On the one hand, it is a 'corporate' organ of action taking coercive measures under Chapter VII to maintain or secure peace and security. On the other, it is an organ of 'diplomacy' recommending peaceful solutions to disputes under Chapter VI, or acting simply as a vehicle for powerful states to meet and discuss.[3] In taking measures to combat ruptures to international peace and security, the Security Council is seen as an 'executive' organ, but more recently, and controversially, it has also acted as a 'legislative' organ in requiring states to take measures to combat terrorism and prevent the spread of weapons of mass destruction (WMD).[4] Paul Szasz observes that when voting for Resolution 1373 in 2001 which legislated against terrorism, the members of the Council 'were most likely unaware...of the pioneering nature of what they were doing';[5] but as Roberto Lavalle states, when they adopted Resolution 1540 in 2004 legislating against the spread of WMD, they were 'fully ... aware of what they were doing'.[6] As well as acting as an 'executive' organ against states supporting terrorism,[7] and a 'legislative' organ against terrorism generally, the Security Council also appears to have acted in a 'judicial' or at least a 'quasi-judicial' way when putting in place a scheme of targeted measures whereby an individual whose name is placed on the Security Council's list of individual members or supporters of the Taliban or Al-Qaeda has his assets and funds frozen by relevant member states, as well as being subject to a travel embargo.[8] Though there is some debate as to whether these sanctions are 'administrative' rather than 'criminal', 'preventive' rather than 'punitive';[9] thereby causing uncertainty as to what human rights of the listed individuals are engaged, there seems to be

3 I. Claude, 'The Security Council', in E. Luard (ed.), *The Evolution of International Organizations* (London: Hudson, 1966), 68, 83–8.

4 UNSC Res. 1373 (28 September 2001) UN Doc. S/RES/1373 (on terrorism). For discussion, see M. Happold, 'Security Council Resolution 1373 and the Constitution of the United Nations' (2003) 16 LJIL 593; S. Talmon, 'The Security Council as World Legislature' (2005) 99 AJIL 175. UNSC Res. 1540 (28 April 2004) UN Doc. S/RES./1540 (on WMD).

5 P. C. Szasz, 'The Security Council Starts Legislating' (2002) 96 AJIL 910 at 904.

6 R. Lavalle, 'A Novel, if Awkward Exercise in International Law-Making: Security Council Resolution 1540' (2004) NILR 411, 435.

7 See, for example UNSC Res. 748 (31 March 1992) UN Doc. S/RES/748, which imposed sanctions against Libya for supporting terrorism.

8 Starting with UNSC Res. 1267 (15 October 1999) UN Doc. S/RES/1267 (against the Taliban) and UNSC Res. 1333 (19 December 2000) UN Doc. S/RES/1333 (against Al-Qaeda).

9 A. Bianchi, 'Assessing the Effectiveness of the UN Security Council's Anti-terrorism Measures: The Quest for Legitimacy and Cohesion' (2006) 5 EJIL 881, 905–7.

increasing judicial recognition that such measures, without any safeguards, violate the human rights of the individuals concerned.[10]

As well as exhibiting 'executive', 'legislative' and 'judicial' characteristics in an institutional sense, the Security Council is similarly multifaceted, or at least Janus-faced, when considering its place within the international legal order. When the Security Council acts under Chapter VI, to facilitate the peaceful settlement of disputes, it is required to respect the principles of sovereignty and consent,[11] but when it acts under Chapter VII, to take coercive measures against states (and individuals) it can bypass the principles of non-intervention (by the very terms of Article 2(7) itself)[12] and the non-use of force (by means of Article 42).[13] Furthermore, while it can be strongly argued (and this will be the line taken in this chapter) that, subject to the necessary competence to intervene in states and authorize the use of force, the Security Council is bound by international law. However, whenever it takes measures under the Charter it is accepted that its mandatory decisions are obligations of the UN Charter by virtue of Article 25,[14] which according to the terms of Article 103 prevail over any other inconsistent treaty provision.[15] The drafters of the UN Charter seemed to envisage the effects of Article 103 applying to the 'secondary' obligations imposed by the Security Council under Article 25,[16] and this was certainly the position of the International Court of Justice (ICJ) in its 1992 judgment on provisional measures in the Lockerbie cases brought by Libya against the United States and the United Kingdom.[17] Thus, while it will be argued that the Security Council is bound by international

10 See decision of the ECJ in Joined Cases C-402P and C-415/05P, *Yassin Abdullah Kadi and Al Barakaat International Foundation* v. *Council of the European Union and the Commission of the European Communities* [2008] ECR I-6351 and the decision of the Human Rights Committee in *Sayadi and Vinck* v. *Belgium* (2009) 16 IHRR 16. For discussion, see H. Keller and A. Fischer, 'The UN Anti-Terror Sanctions Regime under Pressure' (2009) 9 *Human Rights Law Review* 257.

11 The heart of Chapter VI, Art. 36(1) states that the 'Security Council may, at any stage of a dispute of the nature referred to in article 33 or of a situation of a like nature, recommend appropriate procedures or methods of adjustment'.

12 Art. 2(7) states that:

> [n]othing in the present Charter shall authorize the United Nations to intervene in matters which are essentially within the domestic jurisdiction of any State or shall require the Members to submit such matters to settlement under the present Charter; but this principle shall not prejudice the application of enforcement measures under Chapter VII.

13 In the Charter scheme there are two exceptions to the prohibition on the threat or use of force in Art. 2(4) of the Charter; individual or collective self-defence in response to an armed attack under Art. 51; and the empowerment of the Security Council to 'take such action by air, sea or land forces as may be necessary to maintain or restore international peace and security' in Art. 42.

14 Art. 25 states that 'Members of the United Nations agree to accept and carry out the decisions of the Security Council in accordance with the present Charter'.

15 Art. 103 states that '[i]n the event of a conflict between the obligations of the Members of the United Nations under the present Charter and their obligations under any other international agreement, their obligations under the present Charter shall prevail'.

16 UNCIO, vol. XIII 707.

17 *Questions of Interpretation and Application of the 1971 Montreal Convention Arising from the Aerial Incident at Lockerbie* [1992] ICJ Rep. 114, 126.

law, Article 103 suggests that it can free itself from that law by means of creating overriding obligations.

This makes the Security Council very difficult to quantify and reform, and very difficult to control.[18] It appears that the main controls are political ones so that any controversial decision needs to avoid the veto, to gain a majority in the Council, and arguably in the Assembly if the measure is to be sustainable. Though international law in theory might apply to decisions of the Security Council, the application of that law to control those decisions seems to be non-existent, or rather is dependent upon self-regulation, by the Security Council recognizing, for instance, that its listing procedure for suspected members of the Taliban and Al-Qaeda must become more human rights compliant, which it has done to an extent.[19] There is certainly no system of independent judicial review of such decisions as the saga of the Lockerbie trials shows.[20]

It can be strongly contended that a legal order that has at its heart such a multifarious, many-tentacled actor, able to act in the most coercive, devastating manner in one situation, but unable to act at all in another very similar situation, is not really a 'legal order' at all, but simply a set of uncertain standards, rules of thumb, which can be potentially overridden by a politically motivated organ. Arguably, because of this, the rule of politics and not the rule of law thus prevails in international relations.

1.3 The Security Council unbound?

It is wrong, however, to see the Council (or for the Council to see itself) either as untrammelled by international law, or to see it as judge, jury and executioner – effectively a law unto itself. Difficulties in application, in enforcement and in compliance should not disguise the fact that international law is applicable to the Security Council. In other words the Security Council is not somehow outside of, or exceptional to, the international legal order: rather, it is an exceptional body within the international legal order. In any political and legal order there must be room for executive discretion that enables the executive or government to take emergency action to protect society from genuine imminent threats to its very existence. However, such a power is not placed outside the system, but is exceptional within it. Although the idea of an effective government being the essential component of the state is still part of the international legal criteria for statehood,[21] 'effectiveness' is no longer the sole criterion. A state is bound by international laws protecting the rights

18 On reform debate, see N. Schrijver, 'Reforming the UN Security Council in Pursuance of Collective Security' (2007) 12 *Journal of Conflict and Security Law* 127.

19 See I. Johnstone, 'The UN Security Council, Counterterrorism and Human Rights', in A. Bianchi and A. Keller (eds.), *Counterterrorism: Democracy's Challenge* (Oxford: Hart, 2008), ch. 10.

20 N. D. White, 'To Review or Not To Review? The *Lockerbie* Cases Before the World Court' (1999) 12 LJIL 401; A. Aust, 'Lockerbie: The Other Case' (2000) 49 ICLQ 278.

21 M. Shaw, *International Law* (6th edn, Cambridge: Cambridge University Press, 2008), 197–204.

of minorities and the right to participate in government, as well as other customary, and where applicable, treaty rights and duties. Kelsen's precondition for a national legal order that it must be 'by and large effective', can be viewed, if his monist thesis is accepted, as a principle of international law that was dominant in his time,[22] but which now would be a more complex principle of international law encompassing respect for human rights and self-determination. Similarly, rather than being simply an untrammelled organ of action, it will be argued below that the Security Council is subject to international law, in the shape of the UN Charter, peremptory norms of international law (*jus cogens*), non-derogable human rights and customary international law.

It can only be by arguing that the Security Council should respect the basic laws of that order – derived from its constitution (the UN Charter), *jus cogens*, non-derogable human rights and basic customary laws – that it is possible to reconcile the presence of such an organ with the existence of a legal order. The Security Council must be seen by other international actors – states, organizations and individuals – as operating within the international legal order – and as importantly, see itself as so doing. The consequences of not doing this are unlikely to be in the form of judicial censure, though the decision in *Kadi* shows this is possible, but more likely in criticism and in lack of compliance with its decisions.

The Security Council does possess exceptional powers that enable it to disregard the norms prohibiting intervention and the use of force that bind other international legal actors, but even when using these exceptional powers it is required to act within the purposes and principles of the UN Charter, after determining the existence of a threat to the peace, breach of the peace or act of aggression.[23] The principles of the UN Charter are contained in Article 2 and include the sovereign equality of members, good faith, the peaceful settlement of disputes, the non-use or threat of force, and non-intervention. The purposes are found in Article 1 and include the maintenance of international peace and security (and to that end 'to take effective collective measures for the prevention or removal of threats to the peace'); the development of friendly relations basic of respect for equal rights and self-determination of peoples; the achievement of cooperation in economic, social, cultural and humanitarian issues; and the promotion of respect for human rights. In the case of the Security Council, its function, according to Article 24(1) is to maintain or restore international peace and

22 'According to international law, the constitution of a state is valid only if the legal order established on the basis of the constitution is, by and large effective. It is this general principle of effectiveness, a positive norm of international law, which, applied to an individual national legal order, provides the basic norm of this national legal order' (H. Kelsen, *Principles of International Law* (2nd edn, London: Stevens, 1967), 562).

23 Art. 39 of the UN Charter.

security[24] as one of the purposes of the UN, but it must, according to Article 24(2), also act in accordance with the whole range of purposes and principles of the UN, which includes respect for human rights.[25]

In considering the international legal responsibility of intergovernmental organizations, the International Law Commission (ILC) identified that responsibility only attaches to organizations with an objective international legal personality.[26] Given that the ICJ determined in 1949 that the UN has this attribute, it has both rights and duties under international law.[27] A rhetorical organization, one discussing matters and adopting recommendations, will not normally violate international law. In contrast, an organization such as the UN, that is operational with missions in the field and with those missions performing functions such as peacekeeping and peace building, will be bound by those general norms of international law that are customary as well as *jus cogens* – those peremptory rules of international law that could be said to underpin the international legal order – prohibiting gross violence on the international stage.[28] The ILC's Special Rapporteur Giorgio Gaja recognized the applicability of the latter by stating that the failure of the UN to prevent genocide in Rwanda in 1994 constituted a breach of an international obligation. He stated further that 'difficulties relating to the decision-making process could not exonerate the United Nations'.[29] Furthermore, it is clear that 'omissions are wrongful when an international organization is required to take some positive action and fails to do so',[30] and that both states and organizations are under a duty to suppress and prevent the commission of genocide.

The Security Council is thus bound by *jus cogens* so that it should not commit acts in violation of these norms. But there is also an expectation that it should take action to combat serious violations of peremptory norms committed by states and individuals, such as genocide and crimes against humanity, or where there are systematic war crimes being committed. Bearing in mind that the primary obligation in the Convention on the Prevention and Suppression of the Crime of Genocide of 1948 is to 'prevent and punish' the crime of genocide, and this norm has become not only custom but *jus cogens*, the Security Council is under this obligation as well as states. There is an

24 Art. 24(1) states that '[i]n order to ensure prompt and effective action by the United Nations, its members confer on the Security Council primary responsibility for the maintenance of international peace and security, and agree that in carrying out its duties under this responsibility the Security Council acts on their behalf'.

25 Art. 24(2) states that '[i]n discharging these duties the Security Council shall act in accordance with the Purposes and Principles of the United Nations'.

26 ILC, 'Report on the Work of its 55th Session' (2003) UN Doc. A/58/10, 33. See also UNGA, 'First Report on Responsibility of International Organizations by Mr Giorgio Gaja, Special Rapporteur' (26 March 2003) UN Doc. A/ CN.4/532, 11.

27 *Reparations for Injuries Suffered in the Service of the United Nations* [1949] ICJ Rep. 174, 179.

28 A. Orakhelashvili, *Peremptory Norms in International Law* (Oxford: Oxford University Press, 2006), 114.

29 UNGA 'Third Report on Responsibility of International Organizations by Mr Giorgio Gaja, Special Rapporteur' (13 May 2005) UN Doc. A/CN.4/553, 4.

30 *Ibid.* 3.

increasing recognition that the Security Council has a duty to act in these situations,[31] as opposed to the older view that it has complete discretion as to when to take Chapter VII action.[32] This creates complexities regarding the Security Council's uneasy relationship with the International Criminal Court and more widely between peace and justice.[33] The 'responsibility to protect' debate represents the progress made in reconciling peace and justice when protecting civilians.[34] However, the inadequacies of the Security Council's response to the situations in Darfur and the Congo reflect the reality of the progress that has been made.

Though there is general recognition that institutions are bound by *jus cogens*,[35] there may still be doubt about whether organizations are bound by customary law which, in the traditional ethos of international law, is made by states for states. The flat-earth view of international law is exemplified by the Permanent Court's statement in the *Lotus* case of 1927.[36] But even by that date such an approach was not fully accurate given the existence of international organizations, principally the League of Nations whose creation challenged the contractual model of international law.[37] Though it stated in 2005 that 'for an international organization most obligations are likely to arise from the rules of the organization' or the internal law deriving from the constituent treaty as developed by practice, the ILC did concede that the same sort of obligations that apply to states can apply to organizations, namely 'a customary rule of international law, a treaty or a general principle within the international legal order'.[38] Simply put, being a separate legal person in an international context signifies the possession of rights and duties. This means that international organizations should respect the basic human rights that are found in customary law when making judgments about states and individuals.

According to Article 103, the so-called supremacy clause in the UN Charter, in the case of conflicting obligations between those in the Charter and those in other international agreements, the obligations in the Charter should prevail.

31 N. D. White, 'Responses of Political Organs to Crimes by States', in A. Nollkaemper and H. Van der Wilt (eds.), *System Criminality in International Law* (Cambridge: Cambridge University Press, 2009), 314, 330–3.

32 H. Kelsen, *The Law of the United Nations* (London: Stevens, 1950), 294.

33 N. D. White and R. Cryer, 'The ICC and the Security Council: An Uncomfortable Relationship', in J. Doria, H.-P. Gasser and M. C. Bassiouni (eds.), *The Legal Regime of the International Criminal Court* (Leiden: Martinus Nijhoff, 2009), 455.

34 High Level Panel Report (2004), para. 203. See a more qualified version in the World Summit Outcome document at UNGA Res. 60/1 (24 October 2005) UN Doc. A/RES/60/1, para. 139. For discussion of responsibility to protect, see E. McLean, 'The Responsibility to Protect: The Role of International Human Rights Law' (2008) 13 *Journal of Conflict and Security Law* 123; C. Focarelli, 'The Responsibility to Protect Doctrine and Humanitarian Intervention: Too Many Ambiguities for a Working Doctrine' (2008) 13 *Journal of Conflict and Security Law* 191.

35 ILC Report (n. 26), 47.

36 *The Case of the SS Lotus*, PCIJ Series A, No. 10 (1927) 18.

37 A. McNair, 'The Functions and Differing Character of Treaties' (1930) 11 BYIL 100, 112; H. Lauterpacht, 'The Covenant as the Higher Law' (1936) 17 BYIL 54.

38 ILC, 'Report on the Work of its 57th Session' (2005) UN Doc. A/60/10, 87–8.

While accepting that this covers Charter obligations imposed by the Security Council under Chapter VII and Article 25,[39] those obligations, by the terms of Article 103 itself, only specifically override inconsistent treaty obligations.

To argue that Article 103 should be interpreted to override customary duties as well on the basis that the Charter is a global constitution and Article 103 is evidence of this,[40] fails to recognize that the Charter is an imperfect constitution that creates a powerful organ with weak constitutional constraints. To argue the supremacy of Security Council-imposed obligations over any inconsistent duty under such a constitution will further the dominance of politics over law and thus in reality weaken the claim made that the Charter is a world constitution.[41] Care should be taken in interpreting Article 103 too widely. Further, when deciding which treaty obligations can be overridden by Security Council-imposed duties, a resolution should not be interpreted with too broad a footprint. As the Council acts within the purposes and principles of the UN, a resolution must allow states to uphold their human rights obligations, for instance, as far as is possible.

Article 103 was intended to allow UN obligations to displace those treaty obligations directly in their path, for instance, an arms embargo requires a state to suspend any agreement it has to supply arms to the target government.[42] Article 103 should not be used as an excuse to override any treaty obligation that might simply prevent the most efficient application of the sanctions. For instance, states should freeze the assets of individuals as required by the Security Council under its targeted measures, but should still as far as possible protect the human rights of those individuals in accordance with their international treaty obligations.[43] To accept that human rights obligations can be overridden by apparently inconsistent Security Council obligations, as was the approach of the House of Lords (though with plenty of misgivings and

39 Article 25 of the UN Charter provides that '[t]he Members of the United Nations agree to accept and carry out the decisions of the Security Council in accordance with the present Charter'. The combination of Arts. 25 and 103 seems to have been accepted by the drafters of the UN Charter at San Francisco in 1945. See UNCIO (n. 16), 707. See also L. M. Goodrich, E. Hambro and A. P. Simons, *Charter of the United Nations* (3rd edn, New York, NY: Columbia University Press, 1969), 616.

40 R. Bernhardt, 'Article 103', in B. Simma (ed.), *The Charter of the United Nations: A Commentary* (2nd edn, Oxford: Oxford University Press, 2002), 1299.

41 See R. St J. MacDonald, 'Fundamental Norms in Contemporary International Law' (1987) 25 *Canadian Yearbook of International Law* 115, 125. MacDonald states that in debates leading to the drafting of Article 30 of the Vienna Convention on the Law of Treaties (which addresses Article 103 of the UN Charter), states 'took the view that Article 103 was an early forerunner of the *jus cogens* doctrine', in that the Charter contained 'peremptory norms', or 'incontestable norms', or 'a quasi-universal set of norms', rendered binding upon states by virtue of Article 103. In this context Article 103 is seen as supporting the fundamental rules of the UN and international systems, including the protection of fundamental human rights, and not as a means of undermining them.

42 N. Bentwich and A. Martin, *A Commentary on the Charter of the United Nations* (London: Routledge & Kegan Paul, 1950), 179.

43 *Kadi* (n. 10), paras. 331–76; R. Liivoja, 'The Scope of the Supremacy Clause of the United Nations Charter' (2008) 57 ICLQ 583, 586.

some caveats) in the *Al-Jedda* case,[44] is conceding too much to the executive. Surely the effect of executive orders within any legal order must be interpreted cautiously and narrowly. It would be unimaginable for courts to accept the argument that when the Security Council authorizes states to use 'necessary measures', meaning military force, against another state, it would be in effect overriding the states' obligations under humanitarian law not to target civilians or their property.[45] So the question arises, why should it be any different with regard to basic human rights?

Although some governments (and domestic courts) have interpreted Articles 25 and 103 quite broadly, it is not clear that this is the intention of the Security Council as a whole. In its declaration on combating terrorism (Resolution 1456, 2003) the Security Council, meeting at the level of foreign ministers, declared that states 'must ensure that any measure taken to combat terrorism comply with all their obligations under international law, and should adopt measures in accordance with international law, in particular international human rights, refugee, and humanitarian law'.[46] This is hardly institutional *opinio juris* to the effect that its resolutions enable states to bypass their human rights obligations. Indeed later Council resolutions on terrorism tend to reinforce the view that the Security Council is directing states to make their implementing measures human rights compliant, not only by reiterating the general statement that such measures must comply with applicable human rights law, but also by specifically requiring that states, in accordance with their own domestic laws, notify the listed individual of his or her listing, the reasons for it, and the process for seeking delisting.[47] Although there is still room for improvement in achieving a truly human rights-compliant regime, the Security Council is certainly making steps towards this, but more importantly, it realizes that it should do this as a matter of obligation as well as legitimacy.

44 *R (Al-Jedda)* v. *Secretary of State for Defence* [2007] UKHL 58 [39] (Lord Bingham).

45 Liivoja (n. 43), 589.

46 UNSC Res. 1456 (20 January 2003) UN Doc. S/RES/1456.

47 In UNSC Res. 1822 (30 June 2008) UN Doc. S/RES/1822, the Security Council reaffirmed the need 'to combat by all means, in accordance with the Charter of the United Nations and international law, including applicable international human rights, refuges, and humanitarian law, threats to international peace and security caused by terrorist acts'. The resolution reaffirmed the listing procedure and demanded in operative para. 17 that:

> Member States receiving notification [of a listed individual or entity] above take, in accordance with their domestic laws and practices, all possible measures to notify or inform in a timely manner the listed individual or entity of the designation and to include with this notification a copy of the publicly releasable portion of the statement of case, any information on reasons for listing available on the Committee's website, a description of the effects of designation, as provided in the relevant resolutions, the Committee's procedures for considering delisting requests, and the provisions of Resolution 1452 (2002) regarding available exemptions.

In UN SC Res. 1904 (17 December 2009) UN Doc. S/RES/1904, the Security Council created an Ombudsperson to assist the Committee with delisting requests.

1.4 The security imperative

The Security Council's primary function according to the Charter is the maintenance of international peace and security.[48] Just as governments act to protect the security of states from threats, so the Security Council performs a similar role in relation to the international order. Its constitution means that the Council's security function is both erratic and inconsistent; but that should not detract from its competence to tackle situations that threaten the security of the international community, states, or indeed of groups and individuals, if such threats have international repercussions.

In so doing it may use powers that are mandatory, coercive and give rise to supreme duties, but the question this chapter addresses is whether this places the Council outside the international legal order, or whether it must, as a matter of law, still respect principles of the UN Charter and international law. More specifically, given that it relies on the duty of member states to follow decisions of the Security Council under Article 25 of the Charter, the question is how far can the Security Council go in terms of creating superior obligations for states in order to fulfil the security imperative?

There is a growing tendency in some writers, albeit often a reluctant one, to accept the Security Council as increasingly omnipotent, especially when dealing with global threats such as Al-Qaeda, so that a combination of Articles 25 and 103 of the UN Charter will even override human rights obligations,[49] if they are seen as hampering counter-terrorist techniques such as rendition, administrative detentions and coercive interrogation methods.[50] In effect, supposedly constitutional provisions of the UN Charter (especially Article 103) are being used to override constitutional rights, found in instruments that are derived from the Charter. This seemed, until the ECJ's judgment in *Kadi* in 2008,[51] to be the orthodoxy emerging in a number of judgments from regional and domestic courts (the English House of Lords in *Al-Jedda*,[52] and the European Court of Human Rights in *Behrami*).[53] It is argued here that this doctrinal position is not clearly established in international law.

48 Art. 24(1) of the UN Charter. On the secondary responsibility for peace and security of the General Assembly, see N. D. White, *The Law of International Organisations* (2nd edn, Manchester University Press, 2005), 75–80, 102–6.

49 See for example J. E. Alvarez, *International Organizations as Lawmakers* (Oxford: Oxford University Press, 2005), 207.

50 See generally B. Fassbender, 'The UN Security Council and International Terrorism', in A Bianchi (ed.), *Enforcing International Law Norms against Terrorism* (Oxford: Hart, 2004), ch. 6.

51 *Kadi* (n. 10).

52 *Al-Jedda* (n. 44). Lord Bingham stated that Article 103 applied to give supremacy to the obligations created in SC Res. 1546 of 2004, and that the meaning of 'obligations' in Article 103 should not be given a 'narrow, contract-based, meaning' [33].

53 Grand Chamber Decision as to the Admissibility of *Behrami and Behrami* v. *France* (App. no. 71412/01) and *Saramati* v. *France, Germany and Norway* (App. no. 78166/01) EHRR (2 May 2007). Though the case was decided on the basis that the acts and omissions in question were attributable to the UN and not to a state party to the ECHR, the Court accepted the supremacy of Security Council decisions (paras. 147–8).

It is recognized in most domestic legal orders that when the life of the state is at stake, the government may derogate from certain human rights obligations contained in treaties to which it is a party.[54] Under the International Covenant on Civil and Political Rights a government may derogate from its obligations only to the extent required by the exigencies of the emergency but rights such as the right to life, freedom from torture, freedom from slavery and freedom of thought, conscience and religion are non-derogable rights.[55]

While the Security Council is not bound directly by the International Covenants (which only allow states to become parties), it still is prohibited from overriding the non-derogable human rights obligations of states, since this would be acting contrary to the purposes and principles of the UN Charter, which, as has been seen, includes the promotion of, and respect for, human rights. Furthermore, when implementing the obligations created by Security Council resolutions, governments should be left to judge, within the parameters of human rights jurisprudence, whether they must derogate from treaty-based human rights if the life of the nation is truly threatened. A largely rhetorical 'war' on terrorism should not be seen as sufficient for such derogations, though the imminent threat of a terrorist attack might be. In reporting to the Security Council on compliance with any decision, a government should show how it has reconciled its obligations to the Security Council with its obligations as a state under the Charter and under general international law.[56]

54 For a general discussion, see J. Oraa, *Human Rights in States of Emergency in International Law* (Oxford: Clarendon, 1992).

55 Art. 4 International Covenant on Civil and Political Rights 1966.

56 In this regard the Counter-Terrorism Committee (CTC) set up by UNSC Res. 1373 (28 September 2001) issued a Policy Guidance document, 'Conclusions for Policy Guidance regarding Human Rights and the CTC' (25 May 2006) S/AC.40/2006/PG.2, to its Counter-Terrorism Committee Executive Directorate (CTED), which provides that:

> In its comprehensive review report of 16 December 2005 (S/2005/800), which was endorsed by the Council, the Committee reiterated that States must ensure that any measure taken to combat terrorism should comply with all their obligations under international law and that they should adopt such measures in accordance with international law, in particular human rights law, refugee law and humanitarian law. It also stressed that the CTED should take this into account in the course of its activities. The Committee has agreed on the following guidance to CTED in this regard:
>
> > When analysing States' implementation of resolution 1373, preparing draft letters to States, and organising visits, the CTED should, as appropriate:
> >
> > a. provide advice to the CTC, including for its ongoing dialogue with States on their implementation on resolution 1373 (2001), on international human rights, refugee and humanitarian law, in connection with identification and implementation of effective measures to implement resolution 1373 (2001).
> > b. advise the CTC on how to ensure that any measures States take to implement the provisions of resolution 1624 (2005) comply with their obligations under international law, in particular international human rights law, refugee law, and humanitarian law.
> > c. liaise with the Office of the High Commissioner for Human Rights and, as appropriate, with other human rights organizations in matters related to counter-terrorism.

Indeed, there is a danger that many repressive states might see a Security Council resolution as an excuse to clamp down on dissidents under the guise that they are terrorists. This may have been particularly so in the period 2001 to 2004 before the Security Council incorporated a definition of terrorism into its decisions.[57] In such cases it is up to the Security Council to ensure that a state does not apply the resolution in such a draconian way. In this way the Security Council can uphold the purposes and principles of the UN Charter, which include the promotion of human rights. Rather than only ensuring that a state has seriously implemented the counter-terrorist measures required by UNSC Resolution 1373 and its successors, the Security Council should also make sure that in so doing basic human rights remain intact.[58] As an actor within the international legal order, the Security Council can and should carry out its primary purpose within the framework of international law.

The Security Council must be content that each state, or indeed regional legal organization, will incorporate its decisions while respecting the states' human rights obligations under both treaty and customary law. In its *Kadi* judgment of 2008 the European Court of Justice (ECJ) found that the European Union's incorporation of obligations under the targeted sanctions regime initiated by UNSC Resolution 1267 (1999) violated European fundamental rights of Mr Kadi, who had been listed by the Council's 1267 Committee and therefore had his assets frozen without recourse to a remedy. The Court gave the European bodies the chance to redraft the regulations in a way that was human rights compliant.[59]

Furthermore, although states may, if a state of emergency exists, derogate from certain treaty rights such as the right to liberty and security of the person, they are still bound by customary law. Though there may be some disagreement over what constitutes customary human rights obligations, Brownlie authoritatively identifies genocide; slavery or the slave trade; the murder or causing the disappearance of individuals; torture or cruel, inhuman or degrading treatment or punishment; prolonged arbitrary detention; systematic racial discrimination; and a 'consistent pattern of gross violations of internationally recognised human rights' as constituting breaches of core rights.[60] The Committee on Economic, Social and Cultural Rights has also

> The CTC and CTED, under direction of the Committee, should incorporate human rights into their communications strategy, as appropriate, noting the importance of States ensuring that in taking counter-terrorism measures they do so consistent with their obligations under international law, in particular human rights law, refugee law and humanitarian law, as reflected in the relevant Security Council resolutions.

57 J. Friedrichs, 'Defining the International Public Enemy: The Political Struggle Behind the Legal Debate on International Terrorism' (2006) 19 LJIL 69, 70. The Security Council included a definition of terrorism in UNSC Res. 1566 (8 October 2004) UN Doc. S/RES/1566.

58 On the significant progress made in this regard see E. J. Flynn, 'The Security Council's Counter-Terrorism Committee and Human Rights' (2007) 7 *Human Rights Law Review* 371.

59 *Kadi* (n. 10).

60 I. Brownlie, *Principles of Public International Law* (7th edn, Oxford: Oxford University Press, 2008), 563.

identified certain core economic rights,[61] which, upon any test, must be customary. Furthermore, none of these rights can be overridden by the Security Council, since, as has been established above, Article 103 only applies to treaty obligations.

Prolonged arbitrary detention was an issue before the UK House of Lords in the *Al-Jedda* case of 2007,[62] but the Court did not consider custom, only the extent to which the right to liberty and security of person under the European Convention on Human Rights was overridden by Security Council Resolution 1546 of 2004 on Iraq. Mr Al-Jedda had been detained without charge or trial for several years for 'imperative reasons of security' in that he was a suspected terrorist. This was an undeniable breach of his rights under Article 5(1) of the European Convention on Human Rights (ECHR).[63] The Court felt that the only way of interpreting Resolution 1546 was to permit the UK, for imperative reasons of security, to override Mr Al-Jedda's right to liberty, but only to the extent necessary to achieve security.[64] Lord Carswell gave the most far-reaching judgment in this regard when he stated that the power to intern may lawfully be exercised by the UK but only in such a way 'to minimise the infringement of the detainee's rights' under the ECHR;[65] in particular he identified the following 'safeguards':

> The compilation of intelligence about such persons which is accurate and reliable as possible, the regular review of the continuing need to detain each person and a system whereby that need and the underlying evidence can be checked and challenged by representatives on behalf of the detained persons, so far as is practicable and consistent with the needs of national security and the safety of other persons.[66]

Lord Carswell's approach shows that the security imperative does not have to be incompatible with the protection of an individual's human rights – a balance can be achieved whereby the Security Council and its security imperative can be incorporated within the international legal order.

61 'The Committee is of the view that a minimum core obligation to ensure the satisfaction of, at the very least, minimum essential levels of each of the rights is incumbent upon every State Party. Thus, for example, a State Party in which any significant number of individuals is deprived of essential foodstuffs, of essential primary health case, of basic shelter and housing, or the most basic forms of education is, prima facie, failing to discharge its obligations under the Covenant. If the Covenant were to be read in such a way as not to establish such a minimum core obligation, it would largely be deprived of its raison d'être' (in UNCHR Fifth Session, 'The Nature of Parties Obligations (Art. 2, para. 1): CESCR General Comment 3' (14 December 1990) UN Doc. E/1991/23, para. 10).

62 *Al-Jedda* (n. 44) [58].

63 Ibid. Lord Bingham [2] and [27].

64 *Ibid*. Lord Bingham [39].

65 *Ibid*. Lord Carswell [136].

66 *Ibid*. Lord Carswell [130].

1.5 Unilateral interpretations of the collective will

Despite Lord Carswell's and other of their Lordships' misgivings, the House of Lords in *Al-Jedda* ultimately accepted the UK government's interpretation of Resolution 1546, but the question must be asked whether this was the meaning intended by the Security Council as a whole, bearing in mind that power to detain was only mentioned in a letter annexed to the Resolution from US Secretary of State Colin Powell to the Interim Prime Minister of Iraq agreeing to the continuation of the multinational force.[67] As dangerous as the Security Council acting unlawfully is, of equal peril is that its decisions are interpreted by states in ways that violate basic principles of international law, hiding behind the supremacy of the Security Council to protect themselves. Such unilateral interpretations of the collective will are considered here.[68]

Once the Cold War ended and the Security Council started taking copious amounts of action expressing its 'corporate will' there was potentially more danger to the UN Charter scheme than when the Council was deadlocked. Of course, the emergence of a powerful executive within the international order has a number of potential advantages. Powerful states have realized the potential of the Security Council given the huge range of its powers and the limited forms of accountability for their exercise. In general terms of legality and legitimacy, Security Council approval is the key that powerful states seek to unlock coercive non-defensive action. For instance, all the doubts that exist about whether a state can unilaterally undertake humanitarian intervention, or anticipatory action, are swept away if the Security Council authorizes it as a response to a threat to the peace.[69]

Whatever its weaknesses, recent conflicts in Kosovo and Iraq, and even Afghanistan, show the unique authority of the Council in collective security matters, since the states using force attempted to justify their actions as coming under Security Council resolutions.[70] If powerful states manage to persuade the Council to adopt resolutions tackling threats to or breaches of the peace within the meaning and purposes of the Charter as developed by practice, then the international community generally accepts the legitimacy of such actions and will support the Council. In this regard simply witness the support for the Coalition in the Gulf Conflict of 1991.[71]

67 A. E. Cassimatis, 'International Humanitarian Law, International Human Rights Law, and Fragmentation of International Law' (2007) 56 ICLQ 623, 626.

68 See also N. Krisch, 'Unilateral Enforcement of the Collective Will' (1999) 3 *Max Planck Yearbook of United Nations Law* 59.

69 C. Greenwood, 'International Law and the Pre-Emptive Use of Force: Afghanistan, Al-Qaida, and Iraq' (2003) *San Diego International Law Journal* 7, 36.

70 UNSC Res. 1244 (10 June 1999) UN Doc. S/RES/1244 (authorizing the UN/NATO administration of Kosovo); UNSC Res. 1368 (12 September 2001) UN Doc. S/RES/1368 (seemingly endorsing the right of self-defence in response to 9/11); UNSC Res. 1483 (22 May 2003) UN Doc. S/RES/1483 (accepting the occupation of Iraq by the US/UK).

71 P.-M. Dupuy, 'The Constitutional Dimension of the Charter of the United Nations Revisited' (1997) 1 *Max Planck Yearbook of United Nations Law* 20.

But the Security Council is a political body and this is not only reflected in its chequered history in the realm of collective security, but also by its make-up and the wide discretion given to it by the UN Charter. In such a body it is inevitable that a member or group of members wanting it to act in a certain way must persuade the remaining members to its way of thinking. While the United States with British support won the argument in the case of Resolution 678 of November 1990, which authorized necessary measures against Iraq early in 1991, they lost it when trying to gain the Security Council's authority to invade Iraq in March 2003.

Consensus among the five permanent members (P5) is clearly crucial for the effectiveness of the Council. Each permanent member has a veto power and can block a decision of the Council by casting a negative vote. But each permanent member will also look to the Council to endorse any course of action it wants legalized and legitimated. Britain and the US will often combine, sometimes with France, to push for a decision, while Russia and China are cast as the sceptics that have to be convinced by dint of diplomacy and persuasion. While the US and the UK (and to a lesser extent France) are liberal interventionists, Russia and China are seen as non-interventionists, though the reality is these are only positions taken when it protects each state's own interests. So, for example, Russia is prepared to intervene in its own backyard (shown recently by its intervention in Georgia in September 2008), just as the United States historically has.

But powerful states do not always get what they want from the Council. In such conditions there has been a trend towards powerful states interpreting previously adopted Council decisions in ways that breach the understanding underlying the resolution. In these cases other member states, while not necessarily accepting the interpretations given to the decision, will view the Council warily since it appears that action is being taken in its name. This must affect the authority of the Council. If it appears that resolutions can be pulled this way and that, or can be resurrected after a number of years, or can be enforced even though there is no provision in them for coercion, then the wider UN membership will rightly view resolutions with a great deal of scepticism. If this trend continues, then member states will no longer respect the authority of the Council. Its unique position in the international system as the primary body for collective security will be undermined.

1.5.1 Iraq 2003

However, the Iraq crisis of 2003 does seem to suggest that the majority of the Council and member states are not prepared to acquiesce in unilateral interpretations of Council resolutions. In one sense the failure of the Security Council in its diplomatic function to solve the Iraq crisis in early 2003 did not undermine its authority. This was because the Council had agreed on the executive action to be taken in the shape of an inspection process,[72] and it was the American and British rupture of this consensus that the membership did not accept. The Americans and British pointed to Security Council decisions that could sustain a legal case for the use of force,[73] but their cleverly constructed legal arguments did not hold sway. They ignored the clear political and legal consensus in the Council and in the wider membership – in effect they ignored the will of the Council. Bearing in mind that the Security Council acts on behalf of the whole membership in collective security matters,[74] in effect the US and the UK ignored the will of the UN.

While there are some ambiguities in Resolution 1441 of 2002, in particular its reference to Resolution 678 of 1990, and its statement of the position that Iraq was in 'material breach' of Resolution 687 (1991) and would therefore face the 'severest consequences', it did not contain the formula that is accepted by UN members, namely an 'authorization' to use 'necessary measures' to tackle a threat to or breach of the peace under chapter VII of the UN Charter. More importantly the members of the Security Council did not agree to this resolution on the basis that it authorized the use of force without any further resolution. This was made clear in statements made by Council members in the meeting at which Resolution 1441 was adopted, when the US representative made it clear that it saw no 'automaticity' in the resolution, while Sir Jeremy Greenstock stated that it contained no hidden triggers.[75] Thus even those states that subsequently argued for and undertook unilateralist military action seemed to accept the collective understanding. Furthermore, the later attempt by the US and UK to revive Resolution 678 also ignored the consensus behind

72 UNSC Res. 1441 (8 November 2002) UN Doc. S/RES/1441 in para. 2 decided 'to afford Iraq, by this resolution, a final opportunity to comply with its disarmament obligations under relevant resolutions of the Council; and accordingly decides to set up an enhanced inspection regime with the aim of bringing to full and verified completion the disarmament process established by resolution 687 (1991) and subsequent resolutions of the Council'.

73 In the UK the legal case for invasion was given by the Attorney General in a parliamentary written answer of 17 March 2003 immediately prior to the invasion to the effect that the basis for the use of force was Resolution 678 which was reactivated by material breach of the disarmament provisions of Resolution 687 of 1991 and all resolutions up to and including Resolution 1441 of 2002. The Attorney General concluded that 'all that resolution 1441 requires is reporting to and discussion by the Security Council of Iraq's failures, but not an express further decision to authorise force' (in (2003) 52 ICLQ 819). The full advice given by the Attorney General was not released until 28 April 2005, in which he was much more equivocal saying that if the 'matter ever came before a court' such a body 'may well' conclude that Resolution 1441 did require a 'further Council decision in order to revise the authorization in resolution 678' (see N. D. White, *Democracy Goes to War* (Oxford: Oxford University Press, 2009), 262–5).

74 Art. 24(1) of the UN Charter (n. 24).

75 Other members spoke about the lack of an automatic right to use force in the resolution (Mexico, Russia, Bulgaria, Syria, Cameroon, China), labelled the 'two-stage approach' by France. The mood of the meeting was summed up by the representative of Ireland when he thanked the sponsors of the resolution (US and UK) for their assurances that the purpose of the resolution was 'to achieve disarmament through inspections, and not to establish the basis for the use of force' (UNSC 4644th Meeting (8 November 2002) UN Doc. S/PV.4644).

that resolution, with UK Foreign Secretary Douglas Hurd reassuring the Council in the Security Council meeting in November 1990 that a vote for 678 did not give the Coalition carte blanche against Iraq, and was only designed to authorize the force necessary to push Iraq out of Kuwait.[76]

1.5.2 Kosovo 2008

The very idea, consistently advocated by the British government as part of its support for humanitarian intervention, namely that military action should be limited to protecting the endangered civilians,[77] is also undermined by the fact that NATO's intervention in Kosovo produced a chain of events that resulted in Kosovo's controversial declaration of independence from Serbia on 17 February 2008, thereby changing the very nature and make-up of the country being intervened in, and also leading to calls for independence for other putative micro-states, including the breakaway regions in Georgia. The idea that such interventions should not undermine the territorial integrity and political independence of the target states (understandably – given the fears of China and Russia) underpinned the Security Council's approach to Kosovo, therefore making it unlikely that the declaration of independence was compatible with the will of the Security Council. The forthcoming Advisory Opinion of the International Court of Justice may shed different light on this.

Security Council Resolution 1244 adopted in 1999 after the withdrawal of Serb forces, clearly reaffirmed the 'commitment of all Member States to the sovereignty and territorial integrity of the Federal Republic of Yugoslavia', as well as calling for 'substantial autonomy and meaningful self-administration for Kosovo'. The resolution authorized an international civil presence (UNMIK) to promote the 'establishment, pending a final settlement, of substantial autonomy and self-government in Kosovo'.[78] It seems impossible

76 UNSC 2963rd Meeting (29 November 1990) UN Doc. S/PV.2963.

77 In 1999, after the Kosovo bombings and the withdrawal of Serb forces, the UK submitted a 'framework to guide intervention by the international community' to the UN secretary general. In a speech to the American Bar Association on 19 July 2000, the Foreign Secretary Robin Cook outlined six of the principles upon which intervention should be based. First, intervention should be reduced by more effective conflict prevention; second, armed force should only be used as a last resort; third, 'the immediate responsibility for halting violence rests with the state in which it occurs'; fourth 'when faced with an overwhelming humanitarian catastrophe, which a government has shown it is unwilling or unable to prevent or is actively promoting, the international community should intervene. Intervention in internal affairs is a sensitive issue. So there must be convincing evidence of extreme humanitarian distress on a large scale, requiring urgent relief. It must be objectively clear that there is no practicable alternative to the use of force to save lives'. Fifth, 'any use of force should be proportionate to achieving the humanitarian purpose and carried out in accordance with international law'; and sixth 'any use of force should be collective'. The latter signifies that the authority of the Security Council should be secured 'whenever possible', but if not then action by regional bodies such as NATO was sufficiently collective (G. Marston (ed.), *United Kingdom Materials on International Law, 1975–2001* (Oxford: Oxford University Press, 2004), pt. 16.IV, item 82 (see also item 90)).

78 UNSC Res. 1244 (10 June 1999) UN Doc. S/RES/1244.

to read this resolution to accommodate a unilateral declaration of independence by Kosovo as a form of 'settlement', in the absence of any enabling Security Council resolution, which was not forthcoming.[79] Indeed, the meeting at which Resolution 1244 was adopted reveals the lack of transformatory intent in that decision – the idea was to preserve the sovereignty of Serbia not to undermine it, while achieving substantial self-government for Kosovo.[80]

For the Foreign Secretary, David Miliband, in explaining the UK's recognition of the new state of Kosovo, to argue that Resolution 1244 did not preclude independence,[81] would seem to be another example of the British government reading a UN resolution in the face of its clear meaning – a technique that had already been used unconvincingly in the arguments put forward to justify the invasion of Iraq in 2003. Despite the huge controversy that this provoked, it seems the British government cannot resist the temptation to place reliance on unsupported interpretations, and furthermore to display immense hubris in claiming their correctness.

1.6 Conclusion

The separate will or autonomy of the Security Council suggests that its corporate decisions should have a certain 'objective' existence, beyond them being a decision of the Security Council binding on members of the Security Council under Article 25 of the UN Charter. On occasions the content may have clear meaning reflecting without further interpretation the will of the Security Council, as when 'necessary measures' are authorized, but often because of the political nature of the Security Council, ambiguous content reflects the compromises that are inevitable if consensus is to be achieved. But clarity is possible in certain key resolutions – Resolution 1441 on Iraq and

79 A. Orakhelashvili, 'Statehood, Recognition and the United System: A Unilateral Declaration of Independence in Kosovo' (2008) 12 *Max Planck Yearbook of United Nations Law* 32–6.

80 See UNSC 4011th Meeting (10 June 1999) UN Doc. S/PV.4011 in which Russia stated that the resolution affirmed the sovereignty and territorial integrity of the FRY. China stated 'we are also opposed to any act that would create division between different ethnic groups and undermine national unity. Fundamentally speaking, ethnic problems within a State should be settled in a proper manner by its own Government and people, through the adoption of sound policies. They must not be used as an excuse for external intervention, much less used by foreign States as an excuse for the use of force'. The US ambassador stated that the FRY 'must provide credible assurance of its willingness to engage in a political process aimed at the establishment of an interim political framework agreement providing for substantial self-government for Kosovo, taking full account of the Rambouillet accords'. The UK representative declared that 'this resolution applies also in full to the Kosovo Albanians, requiring them to play their full part in the restoration of normal life to Kosovo and in the creation of democratic, self-governing institutions'. France stated that the 'Security Council will remain in control of the implementation of the peace plan for Kosovo because it is requesting the Secretary-General to report to it regularly on the implementation of the resolution and to include reports from the leadership of the civil and security presences. Those of us who wish to recall the primacy of the Security Council for the maintenance of international peace and security, as established by the Charter, have been satisfied'.

81 Interview with David Miliband, *Today Programme* (BBC Radio 4, 19 February 2008). See also his more cautious answer to the House of Commons. Hansard HC vol. 472, col. 21W (19 February 2008).

Resolution 1244 on Kosovo are examples – if the collective view of the Security Council is gained by reading the statements of the Council members at the time of the adoption of the resolution.[82] From these it is clear that Resolution 1441 did not authorize the use of force against Iraq in 2003 or unlock Resolution 678, and that Resolution 1244 did not permit the independence of Kosovo without a further resolution of the Security Council. Unfortunately member states tend to ignore this consensus when it suits and argue for unilateral interpretations. For instance, the British government, even having had its fingers burnt over Iraq, could not resist repeating its unilateralist approach in relation to Kosovo. Furthermore, there is evidence of the British courts accepting such arguments, as in the House of Lords' decision in *Al-Jedda*, where the Court accepted the British interpretation that Resolution 1546 of 2004 on the security situation in Iraq and allowed for the detention of suspected terrorists without charge or trial, and held that this security imperative overrode the right to liberty enshrined in Article 5 of the ECHR.

As a political organ that is central to the international legal order, the Security Council's legitimacy is dependent upon it respecting the law. If it acts outside the international legal order, or its resolutions are susceptible to being interpreted in such a way, then the Security Council will be a divisive actor rather than a force for unity. Its actions will be a cause of fragmentation and unilateralism rather than a source of cohesion and integration.

82 What Ian Johnstone would call 'inter-subjective interpretation' ('Treaty Interpretation: The Authority of Interpretive Communities' (1991) 12 *Mich.J.Int'l L.* 371, 381).

2 Ascertaining inchoate threats to international peace and security

Isobel Roele

This chapter deals with the ability of the United Nations Security Council (UNSC) to determine the existence of a threat to international peace and security. It looks at the measures the Security Council has taken that have both responded to and pre-empted the findings of the Secretary-General's High Level Panel on Threats, Challenges and Change (HLP) in 2004.[1] This report emphasized both the new security environment to which the Council must adapt itself and the legitimacy of the Council's operation as elements of the Council's continuing credibility.

De facto limits on the Council's discretion have been eroded by the security environment in which it makes decisions. This environment may be said to be characterized by uncertainty.[2] Coupled with the destructive potential of threats from terrorists and rogue states with weapons of mass destruction (WMD) that are thought to arise in such a context, the Council faces an imperative to act. Effective action has required a change in tactics. In practice this has meant, *inter alia*, taking preventive measures designed to prevent distant threats realizing their destructive potential.[3]

A particular sort of proactive measure is the focus of this chapter: the gathering of information about the conditions in which terrorists can operate from the territory of a sovereign state or of the conditions in which a state could obtain nuclear weapons. Information gathering is a proactive strategy that seeks to reduce uncertainty in the security climate. In theory, knowing more, sooner, makes it possible to manage distant threats before a point of crisis is reached. However, the Council can only act under Chapter VII of the UN Charter – which enables it to impose binding obligations on UN member states – once it has found a threat to international peace and security. These

1 Report of the High Level Panel on Threats, Challenges and Change, *A More Secure World: Our Shared Responsibility* (2004) (at: www.un.org/secureworld).

2 See UN Secretary-General Ban Ki-moon's remarks to the Summit of the League of Arab States (Doha, Qatar, 30 March 2009) (at: www.un.org/News/Press/docs/2009/sgsm12158.doc.htm; accessed 10 December 2009); L. Amoore, 'Risk before Justice: When the Law Contests its Own Suspension' (2008) 21(4) LJIL 847, 852.

3 *More Secure World* (n. 1), 2–3.

'non-imminent but nonetheless real' threats[4] are identified in this chapter as 'inchoate' threats.

Managing threats in a world of uncertainty requires a multilateral response.[5] This is particularly the case when such management necessitates intrusion into the domestic sphere of states. Such intrusion may be particular to given states, as in the cases of Iran and Lebanon,[6] or more general, as in the case of 'legislative' Resolutions such as 1373 and 1540.[7] We might question how far the structure and politics of the Council permit such responses. Aside from issues of composition, the Security Council needs to reform its decision-making processes. The less stable its assumptions and the less clear the facts on which it makes its judgments, the more necessary it is to involve others in the process and to publicize the process so the Security Council's reasons for its decisions are apparent. This chapter emphasizes the importance of meaningful procedural reform to accompany the shift from material to inchoate threats.

The chapter is divided into three parts. In the next section, the High Level Panel's report is discussed in the light of the new strategic environment. In the second section, the notion of inchoate threats is explored and particular examples given. In the final section, the chapter identifies the generalized threats from international terrorism and the proliferation of WMD as inchoate threats and questions the Council's approach to managing them. Such generalized threats are the epitome of the inchoate threat and measures to tackle them are accordingly wide-ranging. If managing such inchoate threats is a multilateral exercise that demands the cooperation of all states, processes of identifying and responding to such threats should involve more international actors.

2.1 The Security Council and the new strategic environment

The Security Council makes decisions about international peace and security on behalf of the UN member states.[8] When acting under Chapter VII of the Charter, the Council is empowered to make decisions about the maintenance of international peace and security that bind all member states.[9] Furthermore, actions under Chapter VII are exceptions to the usual rule that the UN shall not intervene in matters 'essentially within the domestic jurisdiction of any state'.[10] Since the vast majority of states are members of the UN,[11] the Council

4 *Ibid.* 3.

5 *Ibid.* 9.

6 See sections 2.1 and 2.2.

7 See section 2.3.2.

8 UN Charter, Article 24(1).

9 UN Charter, Article 25.

10 UN Charter, Article 2(7).

11 Former Secretary-General of the UN, Kofi Annan, once confessed his envy of the Fédération Internationale de Football Association (FIFA) which counted 207 states as members against the UN's 192. S. Aust, H. Hoyng and G. Mascolo, 'Interview with Kofi Annan' *Der Spiegel* (18 July 2006) (at: www.spiegel.de/international/spiegel/0,1518,427239,00.html; accessed 10 December 2009).

is sometimes seen as a beacon of multilateralism. Such an impression is especially strong when Security Council action is compared to unilateral actions of powerful states.[12] However this dichotomy between multilateral and unilateral action does not tell the whole story.

The Council is subject to fluctuations in activity. After many fallow years, it made energetic use of its Chapter VII powers during the early 1990s, only to be quieted by bad experiences later that decade. The terrorist attacks of 11 September 2001 might be seen to have sparked a renewed consensus on action in the light of the unprecedented 'legislative' Resolutions 1373 and 1540.[13] It is not unusual, during periods of inaction, for the Security Council to be reviled as ineffective. Conversely, when the Council is active, international lawyers worry about the limits of its authority.[14] It has been said that:

> The dominant role of the permanent five, the secrecy of the Council's procedures, the lack of a clearly delimited competence and the absence of what might be called a legal culture within the Council hardly justify enthusiasm about its increased role in world affairs.[15]

Nevertheless, in 2004 the HLP affirmed its faith in the propriety of Security Council action and, in the light of the immensity of potential threats to international peace and security, encouraged the Security Council to adapt itself to the new strategic environment. This environment, it will be argued, is characterized by uncertainty. The Council has adapted itself by taking action against inchoate threats – threats that remain distant, diffuse and uncertain. It is argued that such action requires increased transparency, accountability and inclusiveness on the part of the Security Council to prevent its providing a veil for the policies of individual states.

2.1.1 The High Level Panel Report

The HLP Report, *A More Secure World: Our Shared Responsibility*, emphasized that the Council's credibility depended on the perception that it was effective, efficient and equitable.[16] This requires the Security Council to both make the most of its broad discretion to act under Chapter VII and to create consensus on 'the nature of today's threats'.[17] Underlying *A More Secure World* was the feeling that the Council operates in a 'different world' to the one envisaged by

12 A similar point has recently been made; see C. Miéville, 'Multilateralism as Terror: International Law, Haiti and Imperialism' (London: Birkbeck ePrints, 2009), 2 (at: http://eprints.bbk.ac.uk/783; accessed 10 December 2009).

13 See text accompanying (n. 102).

14 See e.g. W. M. Reisman, 'The Constitutional Crisis in the United Nations' (1993) 87 AJIL 83.

15 M. Koskenniemi, 'The Police in the Temple – Order, Justice and the UN: A Dialectical View' (1995) 6 EJIL 325, 327.

16 *A More Secure World* (n. 1), 17–19.

17 *Ibid.* 80, para. 248.

the Charter drafters in 1945.[18] Specifically, the Panel found that '[t]he attacks of 11 September 2001 revealed that States, as well as collective security institutions, have failed to keep pace with changes in the nature of threats'.[19] The 'fundamentally different security climate' is one in which there is 'unprecedented scope for destruction'.[20] It is argued that the magnitude of this potential harm should be seen in the light of a security environment characterized by uncertainty.

The HLP report argued that these days 'threats are interrelated and a threat to one is a threat to all'.[21] It found that 'all States have an interest in forging a new comprehensive collective security system that will commit all of them to act cooperatively in the face of a broad array of threats'.[22] However, in order to do this, it would be necessary to come to a consensus on the nature of today's threats. Although the HLP suggested that today's threats are as diverse as 'poverty, infectious disease and environmental degradation', this chapter intends to focus on the widening of the concept of violence-based threats. The diffuse nature of such threats emphasizes the importance of adopting a multilateral response.

2.1.2 A security climate characterized by uncertainty

The uncertainty of the current security climate was perhaps most famously expressed by former US Secretary of Defense, Donald Rumsfeld. He said:

> There are known knowns. There are things we know we know. We also know there are known unknowns. That is to say we know there are some things we do not know. But there are also unknown unknowns, the ones we don't know we don't know.[23]

In so saying, Rumsfeld encapsulated the tangled and confused nature of a security environment characterized by uncertainty. Security threats can no longer be managed by scientific–realist prediction, as it was sometimes said they could be during the Cold War.[24] So-called 'rogue states and their terrorist clients',[25] in the words of the former US President George W. Bush's National Security Strategy, neither resemble, nor play by the same rules as, the Soviet

18 *Ibid.* 10, para. 1.
19 *Ibid.* 13, para. 16.
20 *Ibid.* 14, para. 16.
21 *Ibid.* 14, para. 17.
22 *Ibid.* 16, para. 28.
23 Secretary of Defense Rumsfeld Speech (NATO HQ, Brussels, 6 June 2002) (at: www.nato.int/docu/speech/2002/s020606g.htm; accessed 10 December 2009).
24 See e.g. J. L. Gaddis, 'International Relations Theory and the End of the Cold War' (1992–3) 17(3) *International Relations* 5, 56.
25 *US National Security Strategy* (Washington, DC: USGPO, 2002), 14.

Union.[26] Indeed, it might be said that terrorists and rogue states, by their very nature, reject the rules of the game.

It is to be emphasized that apprehension of the new actors and their capabilities was not limited to those involved in President Bush's 'war on terror'. The UN's High Level Panel found that rapid developments in technology mean that 'smaller and smaller numbers of people are able to inflict greater and greater amounts of damage, without the support of any State'.[27] Changes to the security environment in which the UN operates have meant that threats are 'more diverse, less visible and less predictable'.[28] Such threats are uncertain both in terms of whether and how they manifest themselves. Perhaps the core example of such a threat is the 'nightmare scenario' of the terrorist armed with WMD.[29] Thus, UN Secretary-General, Ban Ki-moon, told the Security Council that terrorism is 'a faceless enemy that knows no boundaries' and that WMD 'present a unique existential threat to...humanity'.[30]

A fear of devastation without warning means that the Security Council may need to extend its reach beyond the merely obvious in order to maintain international peace and security. This is because when the stakes are so high, it cannot wait until it is certain to act if, by then, it would be too late. The uncertainty of the security environment might be thought to flow from the lack of indicators, or 'knowns', from which predictions can be made. It would seem that the Security Council has, broadly, two options: to adopt a 'precautionary principle' approach, whereby action does not depend on confident prediction,[31] or to attempt to find out more about the threats it faces.

2.2 Inchoate threats in an uncertain world

Owing to the uncertainty of the security environment, the Council has been forced to adopt a creative conception of what counts as a threat to international peace and security. The HLP emphasized that the 'Council may well need to be prepared to be much more proactive'.[32] The Council must take action before a threat can manifest itself. To this end, it has pursued various strategies to prevent terrorists getting hold of funds and to prevent WMD or related

26 *Ibid.* 13.

27 *More Secure World* (n. 1), 13–14.

28 *A Secure Europe in a Better World* (12 December 2003) (European Security Strategy, Brussels 2003) (at: www.consilium.europa.eu/showPage.aspx?id=266&lang=EN; accessed 10 December 2009, 3).

29 *More Secure World* (n. 1), 64.

30 UNSC Provisional Record (8 January 2007) UN Doc. S/PV.5615 (2007) 23.

31 F. Johns and W. G. Werner, 'The Risks of International Law' (2008) 21 LJIL 783, 784; R. Suskind, in Amoore (n. 2), 852; R. Urueña, 'Risk and Randomness in International Legal Argumentation' (2008) 21(4) LJIL 787, 809.

32 *More Secure World* (n. 1), 64, para. 194.

technology becoming available to them.[33] A potential problem for the Council is that there are states which are unable or unwilling to fulfil these obligations. In its report, the HLP warned of 'nightmare scenarios combining terrorists, weapons of mass destruction and irresponsible States'.[34] These states pose inchoate threats to international peace and security.

The dictionary definition of inchoate is 'just begun, incipient; in an initial or early stage'.[35] This seems to resonate with the HLP's idea of threats that are 'non-imminent but nonetheless real'. Indeed, one of the concerns of the HLP was that 'distant' threats should not become 'imminent' and that 'imminent' threats should not become 'destructive'.[36] The HLP drew the boundaries of the threats covered in Chapter VII very broadly indeed. It found that the Security Council may take action:

> whether the threat is occurring now, in the imminent future or more distant future; whether it involves the State's own actions or those of non-State actors it harbours or supports; or whether it takes the form of an act or omission, an actual or potential act of violence or simply a challenge to the Council's authority.[37]

Inchoate threats are not potential threats in the sense that they already come within the Article 39 definition. On the other hand, they lack a determinate form because they are acts that are merely initial or partial in terms of the threat faced by the international community. The desire to tackle inchoate threats to international peace and security flows from the desire to minimize uncertainty about major threats like international terrorism and the proliferation of WMD.

The word 'inchoate' is also to be found in English criminal law.[38] It refers to a set of offences that can be committed even though no harm is actually caused.[39] They include encouraging or assisting crime, conspiracy and attempt.[40] In English criminal law, 'inchoate offences always relate to a substantive offence': an attempt or a conspiracy relates to some specific offence rather than criminality in general.[41] While no direct analogy between domestic law and international law is intended, it may prove interesting to consider some of the SC's innovations through this lens. It could be useful to think of

33 See e.g. UNSC Res. 1373 (28 September 2001) UN Doc. S/RES/1373 and UNSC Res. 1540 (28 April 2004) UN Doc. S/RES/1540.

34 *More Secure World* (n. 1), 64, para. 194.

35 *Oxford English Dictionary*, Online.

36 *More Secure World* (n. 1), 23.

37 *Ibid.* 64, para. 193.

38 In using the terminology of inchoate offences, it is not claimed that threats and offences are the same thing as the Security Council enforcing the law.

39 A. Ashworth, *Principles of Criminal Law* (6th edn, Oxford: Oxford University Press, 2009), 437.

40 Serious Crime Act 2007, Pt 2; Criminal Law Act 1977, s. 1; Criminal Attempts Act 1981, s. 1.

41 D. Ormerod, *Smith and Hogan: Criminal Law* (12th edn, Cambridge: Cambridge University Press, 2008), 379.

substantive threats to international peace and security such as the proliferation of nuclear weapons[42] or the spread of international terrorism,[43] as being attended by certain inchoate offences. These inchoate offences, just as occurs in domestic legal systems,[44] make it possible for the Council to move away from a purely reactionary approach to threats to international peace and security.

2.2.1 Do weak states encourage or assist terrorism?

A weak state could be seen as encouraging or assisting international terrorism by omission if it fails to maintain law and order in its territory, enabling terrorists to use it as a base from which to operate.[45] The HLP Report warned that 'in signing the Charter of the United Nations, States not only benefit from the privileges of sovereignty but also accept its responsibilities', which include external responsibilities to the international community as well as internal ones to its own people.[46] Indeed, the European Union Security Strategy singles out state failure as one of the key threats to security on the grounds that it is associated, *inter alia*, with terrorism.[47] Likewise, the UK's National Security Strategy lists 'failed and fragile states' in a specific category of concern.[48] As the Australian Defence Update puts it, '[f]ailing states are a significant concern because the insecurity they face can easily move beyond their borders'.[49] The approach can also be glimpsed in general obligations such as those contained in Security Council Resolutions 1373 and 1540.[50]

The Security Council has already intervened directly in cases where a state's failure to maintain control of its territory has resulted in violence. One example of this is Lebanon. In July 2006, Israel launched an attack on Lebanon in response to rocket attacks from the south of the country that had been perpetrated by Hezbollah. The Israeli government asserted that 'responsibility for this belligerent act of war lies with the Government of Lebanon, from whose territory these acts have been launched into Israel'.[51] While expressing concern about the use of violence in Lebanon, the Council's response seems to

42 Note by the President of the Security Council (31 January 1992) UN Doc. S/23500; UN Doc. S/RES/1540 (2004).

43 UN Doc. S/RES/1373 (2001).

44 Ormerod (n. 41), 380.

45 UNGA Res. 60/288 (20 September 2006) UN Doc. A/RES/60/288, 5.

46 *More Secure World* (n. 1), 17.

47 *Secure Europe* (n. 28), 4.

48 The National Security Strategy of the United Kingdom, *Security in an Interdependent World* (March 2008), 13–14 (at: www.cabinetoffice.gov.uk/reports/national_security_strategy.aspx; accessed 10 December 2009).

49 Australia's National Security: *A Defence Update 2005* (at: www.defence.gov.au/update2005/docs.cfm; accessed 10 December 2009, 3).

50 See section 2.3.2.

51 UNGA Identical Letters from the Permanent Representative of Israel to the UN (12 July 2006) UN Docs. A/60/937 and S/2006/515.

have acknowledged that the Lebanese authorities bear responsibility for ensuring that terrorist groups cannot operate out of its territory.

In Resolution 1701 the Council found that the situation constituted a threat to international peace and security, and emphasized 'the importance of the extension of the control of the Government of Lebanon over all Lebanese territory' and the importance of its exercising its full sovereignty to prevent non-governmental groups obtaining weapons.[52] While the issue came to a head in the summer of 2006, 'the importance of the extension of the control of the Government of Lebanon over all Lebanese territory' had been an issue in the Security Council since 2004.[53]

Lebanon was listed as the 29th of over 170 states in *Foreign Policy's* index of failed states.[54] The continuing insecurity of Lebanon constitutes an inchoate threat to international peace and security insofar as this state of affairs enables Hezbollah to launch terrorist attacks from its territory. Accordingly, the Security Council decided to remain actively involved in the matter[55] and Lebanon's domestic sphere remains public international property.

2.2.2 *Are rogue states engaged in attempt?*

Assuming that it is possible to identify so-called 'rogue states', it may be interesting to view the Security Council's actions with respect to the acquisition of nuclear technology by certain states as responding to attempt. In English criminal law, the definition of attempt is to be found in section 1 of the Criminal Attempts Act 1981.[56] It specifies that an act must be 'more than merely preparatory' if the defendant is to be found guilty of attempting to commit a given offence. Here, we are particularly interested in rogue states who attempt to engage in the development, acquisition or use of nuclear weapons.

The main problem with the law of attempt is that the *actus reus* is not, per se, illegal and nor does it necessarily appear to be dangerous or against the law. The key element for the law of attempt is to establish the defendant's *mens rea*, the mental element of the offence. In the international arena, where there is no formal 'jury' to determine the *mens rea* of a state, such a judgment would depend on whether the state that had acquired nuclear technology was viewed as a rogue or a responsible state. This is because, notoriously, nuclear technology and installations are 'dual-use'. When a state, for instance, develops a nuclear fuel cycle, it may be doing so in a manner entirely commensurate

52 UNSC Res. 1701 (11 August 2006) UN Doc. S/RES/1701, operative para. 33.

53 UNSC Res. 1559 (17 May 2004) UN Doc. S/RES/1559.

54 'The Failed States Index 2009' *Foreign Policy* (at: www.foreignpolicy.com/articles/2009/06/22/the_2009_failed_states_index; accessed 10 December 2009).

55 UNSC Res. 1884 (27 August 2009) UN Doc. S/RES/1884.

56 Section One reads: 'If, with intent to commit an offence to which this section applies, a person does an act which is more than merely preparatory to the commission of the offence, he is guilty of attempting to commit the offence'.

with its right to pursue peaceful purposes under Article IV of the Treaty on the Non-Proliferation of Nuclear Weapons 1968.[57]

The idea of the 'rogue state', if not exactly embraced in the terminology of the UN, is present in spirit. The High Level Panel held that:

> If confronted by States that have the capacity to undertake their obligations but repeatedly fail to do so, *the Security Council* may need to take additional measures to ensure compliance, and *should devise a schedule of predetermined sanctions for State non-compliance*.[58]

The Security Council's ability to claim that a state is not in compliance with its resolutions is a way of holding a state responsible for something it has not yet done, insofar as a non-compliant attitude can be said to evidence the existence of a 'rogue state'.

A good example of this is the Council's approach to Iran's nuclear programme. Iran appeared in the Bush administration's infamous 'axis of evil'[59] and its President, Mahmoud Ahmadinejad, is sometimes quoted as having threatened to 'wipe Israel off the face of the earth'.[60] Less hyperbolically, it was also found to have been concealing parts of its nuclear programme from the International Atomic Energy Agency (IAEA) for nearly twenty years.[61] Iran has been asked to indefinitely suspend the enrichment of uranium until the IAEA inspectors have confirmed that its programme is used for exclusively peaceful purposes.[62] Iran has continued to develop its enrichment programme and, while it is cooperating with inspectors in many respects,[63] still suffers from what Mohammed El Baradei has called a 'confidence deficit'.[64] Others' lack of confidence in Iran, as argued above, supplied the *mens rea* element crucial to distinguishing criminal attempts from innocent activities.

If Iran is to be found to be engaged in an attempt to develop and use nuclear weapons, it should be shown that it has done a 'more than merely preparatory act'. Although nuclear technology is, by its nature, dual-use, it has been suggested that the existence of oil reserves in Iran indicates that its

57 Article IV(1) reads: 'Nothing in this Treaty shall be interpreted as affecting the inalienable right of all the Parties to the Treaty to develop research, production and use of nuclear energy for peaceful purposes without discrimination and in conformity with Articles I and II of this Treaty'.

58 *More Secure World* (n. 1), 50–1, para. 156 (emphasis in original).

59 US President G. W. Bush, State of the Union Address (29 January 2002) (at: http://archives.cnn.com/2002/ALLPOLITICS/01/29/bush.speech.txt; accessed 10 December 2009).

60 National Security Strategy of the United States of America (September 2006), 20.

61 See e.g. UNSC Provisional Record (24 March 2007) UN Doc. S/PV.56478 (comments of US Ambassador Wolff).

62 UNSC Res. 1696 (31 July 2006) UN Doc. S/RES/1696 and UNSC Res. 1737 (23 December 2006) UN Doc. S/RES/1737.

63 Report by the Director General of the IAEA (28 August 2009) IAEA Doc. GOV/2009/55, 6.

64 Transcript of Q&A with Director General on Activities in Iran (22 February 2008) (at: www.iaea.org/NewsCenter/Transcripts/2008/transcr220208.html; accessed 10 December 2009).

nuclear programme is not for civilian fuel purposes.[65] Against this, Iran has argued that it exports its oil and that it needs back-up options.[66] In order to determine whether Iran's progress with its uranium enrichment programme is more than merely preparatory, it would be necessary to know whether Iran was attempting to develop nuclear weapons. This circular state of affairs underlines the uncertainty aspects of the Iran problem.

One way that the Security Council has attempted to tackle the circularity is to acquire indicators of Iran's state of mind in the form of its record of compliance with both IAEA and Security Council resolutions. In this way, and to the extent that the resolutions reflect the so-called 'will of the international community', Iran can be said to demonstrate its 'rogue' nature. Thus, although the pursuit of a nuclear programme per se does not constitute a threat to international peace and security, in the light of Iran's record of compliance with international resolutions and its poor public image in Western states, it might be said that its enrichment of uranium constitutes an attempt to commit the 'offence' of nuclear proliferation. In this case, the enrichment of uranium is an inchoate, or incipient, threat to international peace and security.

While this part of the chapter has focused on inchoate threats that can be tied to specific threats, it is worth emphasizing that the concept of inchoate threat to international peace and security can be seen in the Council's recently conceived practice of identifying general threats to international peace and security. The inchoateness of general threats such as those arising from 'international terrorism',[67] or 'proliferation of nuclear, chemical and biological weapons, as well as their means of delivery'[68] is more pronounced than that surrounding the threats discussed above in relation to Lebanon and Iran.

2.3 Critiquing the Council's information-gathering practices

The concept of the inchoate threat to international peace and security may impugn the credibility of the UN Security Council. There are two main reasons for this. The first flows from the HLP's call for a consensus on the nature of today's threats and the need for preventive action.[69] It is difficult to gain consensus about what constitutes a threat when threats are imbued with uncertainty. The second reason is that recognizing the existence of weak and rogue states undermines the fundamental principle of sovereign equality contained in the UN Charter.[70] On the one hand, the finding of an inchoate threat to international peace and security may allow the Security Council to

65 UN Doc. S/PV.56478, 9 (comments of US Ambassador Wolff).

66 UNSC Provisional Record (3 March 2008) UN Doc. S/PV.5848, 6 (comments of Iranian Ambassador Khazaee).

67 UN Doc. S/RES/1373 (2001).

68 UN Doc. S/RES/1540 (2004).

69 *More Secure World* (n. 1), 80, para. 248.

70 UN Charter, Article 2(1).

impose effective obligations on states, enabling it to reduce the probability of a threat or to find out more about a threat. On the other hand, the finding that a situation is a threat also involves the possibility of coercive enforcement action. This is particularly the case in the light of certain states' views that they are entitled to take unilateral action to enforce compliance with a Chapter VII resolution.[71]

The credibility of Security Council decisions depends on the feeling that the proponents of a given action have properly made out their case and, consequently, on the transparency and inclusiveness of the process of decision making. If coercive or invasive action is to flow from the identification of an inchoate threat, it is likely to look less selective or self-serving where it is based on firm evidence and where the consideration of such evidence has involved a broad cross-section of states. Owing to the incomplete or unrealized nature of inchoate threats, it is arguable that they should be subject to a higher standard of procedural rigour and a more careful application of safeguards. Such a standard is doubly justified as it may prevent mistakes as well as iniquity.[72]

To the extent that inchoate threats to international peace and security remain cloaked in uncertainty because of their incipient or partial nature, it makes sense that Security Council action to tackle such threats should be centred on knowledge gathering. A fact-finding approach also makes sense as regards inchoate threats because, it might be argued, time is not so much of the essence as in the case of an imminently realizable threat.[73] The Council does not have an exemplary track record when it comes to considering facts.[74] The position taken here is that the Security Council must improve its consideration of factual issues if it is to be able to credibly deal with inchoate threats. This would involve a better use of intelligence in Security Council debates and more transparent and accountable means of decision making. In this part of the chapter, we will examine the Security Council's approach to reducing uncertainty and its consequent efforts to manage inchoate threats. Two main ways in which the Security Council gathers information will be touched on: reports of the Secretary-General and UN sub-agencies and the Council's own sub-committees' databases.

It is argued that the way the Council has gone about managing uncertainty and identifying problem states is flawed. In cases of both 'weak' and 'rogue' states, the *modus operandi* of the Council has been to impose obligations on the

71 See T. M. Franck, 'Inspections and their Enforcement: A Modest Proposal' (2002) 96(4) AJIL 899, 899.

72 The Security Council was used as a forum to air 'evidence' of the USA's case against Iraq in February 2003. UNSC Provisional Record (5 February 2003) UN Doc. S/PV.4701.

73 See criticisms acknowledged by Quigley. J. Quigley, 'Security Council Fact-Finding: A Prerequisite of Effective Prevention of War' (1992) 7 *Fla.J.Int'l L.* 191, 244.

74 See e.g. T. O'Donnell, 'Security Council Resolution 1530, Evidence and the United Nations Security Council' 100 ASIL PROC. (2006) 47; J. Quigley, 'The United Nations Security Council: Promethean Protector of Helpless Hostage?' (2000) 35 *Tex.Int'l LJ* 129.

states and use them as a measure for the threat posed by the situation. This can be seen as a means of reducing uncertainty. By holding states to certain obligations, the Council effectively concretizes the inchoate threat posed by the situation in the state by tying it to specific norms. It enables the Council to say that the allegedly weak state has failed to meet standards and that the alleged rogue state has demonstrated its contempt for the common policy. However, such an approach places a premium on legitimacy.

2.3.1 UN Secretary-General and sub-agency reports

The UN Secretary-General has reported to the Security Council about threats to international peace and security on many occasions. Successive Secretary-Generals have interpreted their Charter powers broadly to include fact-finding.[75] However, the UN Charter also contains the seeds of the Secretary-General's authority to do so: the Secretary-General 'shall perform such other functions as are entrusted to him by these organs'.[76] The Council has often requested that the Secretary-General assemble a commission of experts to enable him to carry out this task. Such panels of experts considered the situation in Darfur,[77] the Rwandan genocide,[78] violations of humanitarian law in the former Yugoslavia[79] and the assassination of the President of Burundi,[80] to name but a few.

The case of Lebanon, mentioned above,[81] is a case where the Security Council used reports of the Secretary-General as a means of dealing with the threat posed by the lack of confidence in Lebanon's ability to prevent Hezbollah operating within its borders. It is noteworthy that the Secretary-General was specifically asked to report on 'the implementation...of this resolution'.[82] Similarly, in the case of Iran, IAEA inspectors report on Iran's compliance with its obligations under its Comprehensive Safeguards Agreement and under the Council's Chapter VII resolutions. The major difficulty with this approach is that until the Security Council acts under Chapter VII, it cannot compel states to open themselves to scrutiny. This was affirmed by the General Assembly's 1991 Declaration on Fact-finding by the United Nations in the

75 M.-C. Bourloyannis, 'Fact-Finding by the Secretary-General of the United Nations' (1989–90) 22(4) *NYUJ Int'l Law & Pol*. 641, 646.

76 UN Charter, Article 98.

77 UNSC Res. 1564 (1 October 2004) UN Doc. S/RES/1564.

78 UNSC Res. 935 (1 July 1994) UN Doc. S/RES/935; UNSC 'Letter from the Secretary-General to the President of the UN' (9 December 1994) UN Doc. S/1994/1405.

79 UNSC Res. 780 (6 October 1992) UN Doc. S/RES/780; UNSC 'Letter from the Secretary-General to the President of the UN' (2 May 1994) UN Doc. S/1994/674.

80 UNSC Res. 1012 (28 August 1995) UN Doc. S/RES/1012; UNSC 'Letter from the Secretary-General to the President of the UN' (25 July 1996) UN Doc. S/1996/682.

81 See section 2.1.

82 UNSC Res. 1559 (2 September 2004) UN Doc. S/RES/1559.

Field of the Maintenance of International Peace and Security.[83] A second problem with the approach is that such reports are often not publicly debated.

Sovereign states may be wary of welcoming fact-finders appointed by international organizations.[84] In so doing, they lose control of the flow of information about domestic matters and, potentially, open themselves up to accusations.[85] On the other hand, one way for a state to clear its name is to open its borders to fact-finders.[86] It should be remembered that even where a state is compelled to allow fact-finders access to key sites, witnesses and documentation, as is the case with Iran at present, the success of the fact-finding mission still depends on the cooperation of the host state.[87] This factor was underlined by the Compendium report of the UN Monitoring and Verification Inspections Agency (UNMOVIC).[88] The report noted that this depended on Iraq's perception that the inspectors were impartial and not merely the puppets of a few powerful states.[89] These limitations on fact-finding missions do not seem confined to the case of Iraq.

Iran's cooperation with the IAEA inspectors has been undermined by its perception that the Security Council campaign of 'incremental pressure' is illegal.[90] While the Secretariat of the IAEA is a technical body, its Board of Governors is a political body which is composed of those states 'most advanced in the technology of atomic energy'.[91] The extent of the cooperation of the host state will depend on how far it feels that it leaves itself vulnerable to hostile parties. Where the Security Council is seen as a hostile party, it is unlikely that fact-finding missions that have been requested by it or those that have been brought within its control will tempt the host state to be open.

Aside from the practicalities of acquiring facts and the necessity of encouraging the host state to cooperate, the Security Council's eventual handling of them should be mentioned. In the first place, it should be noted that any engagement with the facts of a given situation is to be applauded. It

83 UNGA Res 46/59 (9 December 1991) UN Doc. A/RES/46/59.

84 E. L. Kerley, 'The Powers of Investigation of the United Nations Security Council' (1961) 5 AJIL 892, 892.

85 Quigley (n. 73), 245.

86 For instance, in 1998 the Sudanese government attempted to do this following the US bombing of the El Shifa pharmaceutical plant in Khartoum. UNSC 'Letter from the Permanent Representative of the Sudan to the President of the Security Council' (21 August 1998) UN Doc. S/1998/786, para. 4.

87 Former Director General of the IAEA, Mohammed El Baradei, had been urging Iran to increase IAEA inspectors' access to key sites by signing an Additional Protocol. Transcript of the IAEA Director General's Remarks at the Joint Press Conference with the Atomic Energy Organization of Iran (4 October 2009) (at: www.iaea.org/NewsCenter/Transcripts/2009/transcript051009.pdf; accessed 10 December 2009).

88 UN Monitoring and Verification Inspection Commission, *Compendium of Iraq's Proscribed Weapons Programmes in the Chemical, Biological and Missile Areas* (2007) (at: www.unmovic.org; accessed 10 December 2009, 1059).

89 *Ibid.* 1060.

90 UNSC Provisional Record (3 March 2008) UN Doc. S/PV.5848, 5–6 (comments of Iranian Ambassador Khazaee).

91 IAEA Statute, Article VI(A)(1).

has been aptly noted that the Council's track record in the matter is far from perfect. There have been cases where the Council has jumped to conclusions, emotionally reacting to a given situation.[92] There have also been cases where the Council has acted solely on the information of the complainant.[93] In some ways, simply appointing a committee of third parties to investigate can be seen as a step forward.

However, to obtain a collection of facts is not necessarily the same thing as understanding a given situation. It has been suggested by various scholars that the Security Council develop the ability to analyse facts.[94] This is particularly the case where there are competing accounts and explanations of certain facts. The dispute over Iran's nuclear programme mentioned in the last section is a case in point.[95] In order to get the best out of the facts, it is suggested that a more inclusive process is necessary whereby interested states can contribute what they know or counter information given by other states. As well as enabling the Council to be more fully informed, an inclusive process would also aid the transparency of the process and, consequently, the accountability of the Council. If debates occurred, if not in public, then at least in advertised sessions, states that are not members of the Council could attend them.

Relatively small alterations to the Council's working methods could vastly improve the access of non-Council members to debates.[96] One such reform would be to ensure that all meetings were advertised in advance so that smaller states had time to prepare a contribution to them.[97] Furthermore, it has been argued that the decision on what format a particular meeting will take should include non-Security Council members.[98] Apparently, 'experts' meetings are now the key focus of interaction between Council members.[99] This can mean that draft resolutions are formed into completed documents before they even get to the informal consultation stage.

Another important reform would be to ensure that such meetings were a real part of decision making and not mere window-dressing. While the use of

92 T. O'Donnell, 'Naming and Shaming: The Sorry Tale of Security Council Resolution 1530 (2004)' (2006) 17 EJIL 945, 951.

93 Quigley (n. 74), 133.

94 See e.g. S. Chesterman, *Shared Secrets: Intelligence and Collective Security* (New South Wales: Lowry Institute for International Policy, 2006), 4.

95 See section 2.2.

96 The Council's Informal Working Group on Documentation and Other Procedural Questions, revived by Japan in 2006, is based on just this point.

97 The necessity of this has been acknowledged by the President of the Council. UNSC 'Note by the President of the Security Council' (19 July 2006) UN Doc. S/2006/507, para. 11.

98 Security Council Report, 'Update Report No. 1: Security Council Working Methods' (12 August 2008) (at: www.securitycouncilreport.org/site/c.glKWLeMTIsG/b.4420143; accessed 10 December 2009).

99 Security Council Report, 'Special Research Report: Security Council Transparency, Legitimacy and Effectiveness' (18 October 2007) No. 3 (at: www.securitycouncilreport.org/site/c.glKWLeMTIsG/b.3506555; accessed 10 December 2009).

Arria-formula meetings has become more widespread,[100] it is still the case that many Security Council meetings are mere pro forma affairs: at a meeting about Council working practices, one delegate complained that:

> Too often we turn up at open debates and merely read out what our capitals have sent us, rather than responding to the interventions that have gone before and that have been the product of very careful consideration.[101]

In order to improve its consideration of facts, it would seem that a significant culture shift is required from the Council. If the Council's findings as regards the existence of inchoate threats in specific cases are not to be seen as the pursuit of its national agenda by one of its permanent members, its *modus operandi* will have to change. It is emphasized that identifying inchoate threats often requires states to infer intention from the facts. The malleability of such processes of inference means that the credibility of the Council would benefit from the body being open to scrutiny.

2.3.2 Sub-committee databases

The two sub-committees referred to in this part of the chapter are the 1540 Committee and the Counter Terrorism Committee (CTC) established pursuant to Security Council Resolution 1373. Both bodies were established in Chapter VII resolutions which impose mandatory, 'legislative',[102] obligations on all states to tackle the threats of international terrorism and the proliferation of weapons of mass destruction.[103] These abstract threats are inchoate threats in the sense that they do not point to any particular future manifestation of international terrorism or use of WMD. The idea of the inchoate threat to international peace and security gels particularly well with the Security Council device of setting up committees to monitor and record states' compliance with their obligations. Indeed, unlike the examples explored in the second section of this chapter, the inchoate nature of the threats from 'international terrorism' and proliferation of WMD are so unsubstantiated that it is not even possible to point to specific state actors.

In this section of the chapter, although the issues focused on are different, many of the criticisms of Security Council practice looked at in the previous section also apply. The Security Council is insufficiently transparent and inclusive, which renders its practice difficult to scrutinize and, potentially,

100 T. G. Weiss and K. E. Young, 'Compromise and Credibility: Security Council Reform?' (2005) 36(2) *Security Dialogue* 131, 135 n. 4.

101 UNSC Provisional Record (27 August 2008) UN Doc. S/PV.5968, 31.

102 P. C. Szasz, 'The Security Council Starts Legislating' (2002) 96 AJIL 901; M. Happold, 'Security Council Resolution 1373 and the Constitution of the United Nations' (2003) 16 LJIL 593; S. Talmon, 'The Security Council as World Legislature' (2005) 99 AJIL 175.

103 UN Doc. S/RES/1373 (2001); UN Doc. S/RES/1540 (2004).

subject to abuse. The lack of scrutiny is all the more pronounced where its sub-committees are concerned,[104] although it should be noted that both bodies play up their commitment to transparency at least rhetorically.[105] The sub-committees can be seen as the general equivalent of the Secretary-General reports dealt with in the previous section. While those reports relate to specific states and are often triggered by specific incidents, the work of the sub-committees flows from obligations imposed on all UN member states to counter general threats to international peace and security.

As was the case with reports into specific incidents discussed above,[106] the Security Council sub-committees also rely on the cooperation of UN member states.[107] However, the issues as regards cooperation differ significantly. First, the fact that the monitoring is aimed at all states and not isolated individual states is important. It may be that the formal equality of the burden prevents states feeling victimized or being afraid of accusation. Second, and correspondingly, there is the issue of 'reporting fatigue'. Today numerous sub-committees demand report after report from states, many of whom feel that the resources involved would be better spent tackling the problem directly.[108]

The problems pertaining to Security Council credibility with the creation of databases can be grouped in two broad categories: those that render the exercise futile and those that create the potential for the process to be abused. As to the latter point, while the Security Council has not considered a state's failure to carry out its obligations a threat to international peace and security, the trend noted above for the Security Council to anchor inchoate threats to international peace and security to specific obligations suggests that it is a not inconsiderable danger. The importance of the implementation regimes not being an excuse for undue 'pressure or interference in the internal affairs of states' has also been raised in Security Council debates.[109]

As to the futility of the reporting exercise, it has been said that reporting requirements are often fulfilled perfunctorily. For instance, it has also been noted that many states use their 1373 reports as an opportunity to underline their 'good standing in the international fight against terrorism'.[110] The patchy quality of the reports is indicated by the fact that states have not

104 J. Alvarez, 'Hegemonic International Law Revisited' (2003) 97 AJIL 873, 875.

105 UNSC Provisional Record (6 May 2008) UN Doc. S/PV.5886, 3 (CTC Chairman Jurica); UNSC 'Letter from the Chairman of the Security Council Committee to the President of the Security Council' (25 April 2006) UN Doc. S/2006/257, para. 125.

106 See section 2.

107 Briefing by Mr Ranko Vilović, Chairman of the Security Council Committee established pursuant to Resolution 1373 (2001) concerning counterterrorism (13 November 2009) (at: www.un.org/sc/ctc/pdf/CTC_Briefing_to_SC_13nov_2009.pdf; accessed 10 December 2009). See also the 'Report of the 1540 Committee' (30 July 2008) UN Doc. S/2008/493, 2.

108 Talmon (n. 102), 191.

109 UNSC Provisional Record (23 February 2007) UN Doc. S/PV.5635, 9 (Russian Ambassador Churkin).

110 A. Bianchi, 'Assessing the Effectiveness of the UN Security Council's Anti-Terrorism Measures: The Quest for Legitimacy and Cohesion' (2006) 17 EJIL 881, 893.

included relevant information. For instance, of the 96 states that participate in the IAEA database on illicit trafficking of nuclear material, 23 failed to mention this in their reports to the 1540 Committee.[111] This may signal a lack of enthusiasm brought on by so-called 'reporting fatigue'.[112]

Another issue compounding accusations that the reports are a futile exercise is that it may be difficult to decide whether a state is in compliance with its obligations or not.[113] This is particularly the case as regards the wording of Resolution 1540 which requires states to take 'appropriate effective measures'.[114] The ambiguity of this phrase suggests that either the 1540 Committee or individual member states will have to take responsibility for interpreting it. If the latter, there is a risk that Resolution 1540 may be ineffective. If the former, it may be argued that states' internal affairs are at the mercy of a Security Council sub-committee whose accountability can by no means be taken for granted.

Since the sub-committees have made it clear that they do not expect to see perfect compliance immediately,[115] and since the 1540 Committee, at least, has emphasized the 'urgency' of the exercise,[116] the standard for compliance is far from straightforward. In this connection, it has been suggested that when reports list measures that have been taken, they do not tend to tackle the way they are implemented in practice, thus suggesting the whole time-consuming process is merely a cosmetic measure.[117] Additionally, both Iran and Syria – formerly said to be part of the 'Axis-of-Evil' – have submitted reports to the 1540 Committee.

The danger of the abuse of these committees can be seen in the drafting of the resolutions. It has frequently been pointed out that Security Council resolutions are usually the result of political compromise and, consequently, can mean all things to all men.[118] Legislative resolutions are not as detailed as treaties and may therefore be very ambiguous or unclear.[119] Indeed, one of the key concepts of Resolution 1373, terrorism, was not defined by the Security Council until 2004.[120] Furthermore, it has been pointed out that the

111 UNSC 'Letter from the Chairman of the Security Committee to the President of the Security Council' (30 July 2008) UN Doc. S/2008/493 (2008), para. 38.

112 UNSC Provisional Record (30 May 2006) UN Doc. S/PV.5446; UN Doc. S/PV.5635 (2007) 16; Talmon (n. 102), 191; Bianchi (n. 110), 897.

113 P. Crail, 'Implementing UN Security Council Resolution 1540: A Risk-Based Approach' (2006) 13(2) *Nonproliferation Review* 355, 358.

114 UN Doc. S/RES/1540 (2004), operative para., paras. 2 and 3.

115 See e.g. UNSC Provisional Record (4 October 2002) UN Doc. S/PV.4618, 5.

116 UN Doc. S/2008/493 (2008), 3.

117 But cf. text to nn. 120–1.

118 M. Wood, 'The Interpretation of Security Council Resolutions' (1998) 2 *Max Plank Yearbook of United Nations Law* 73, 89; M. Byers, 'Agreeing to Disagree: Security Council Resolution 1441 and Intentional Ambiguity' (2004) 10(2) *Global Governance* 165, 165.

119 Talmon (n. 102), 188.

120 UN Doc. S/RES/1566 (2004), operative para. 3.

Resolution does not require states to adopt the definition when implementing their obligations.[121] This makes for considerable interpretative discretion.

A particular area of concern is the move from monitoring the existence of abstract legislation in UN member states to monitoring the practical enforcement of such legal obligations. In order to facilitate this move from the formal to the practical, the sub-committees have had to rethink their methods. For instance, owing to the limitations of relying solely on documents submitted by states, the operation of the CTC has evolved since 2001. While a past chairperson of the CTC has said that 'without reports…we cannot do our work', she also played up the importance of its ability to undertake visits to member states.[122] As a tactic to avoid futility, the move makes sense; however, it increases the intrusiveness of the monitoring process. Accordingly, states may feel reluctant to allow experts access.

The sub-committees play a role not only in identifying gaps in counter-terrorism and counter-proliferation, but also in plugging those gaps. In resolutions following on from 1373, the Security Council has suggested that the CTC look into best practices, codes and standards.[123] The 1540 Committee is less well developed in this regard. However, it has begun, through 'experience sharing' to create a model of best practice against which states' implementation might be measured.[124] The sub-committees are, rightly, aware of the potential sensitivity of producing best practice models for universal implementation.[125] Encouragingly, both bodies point to the importance of creating a 'dialogue' with member states.[126] Nevertheless, it is worth emphasizing that – whatever the formal limits of Security Council authority – the requirement that UN member states change their domestic law is not negligible. Where such requirements involve the export of a certain model of obligation enforcement, questions may be raised about the colonial overtones of the practice. This impression might be compounded because the states helping less-developed nations to build capacity are mostly well-developed Western nations.[127]

It has been written that under the initial chairmanship of Jeremy Greenstock, the enabling work of the CTC was deliberately emphasized over its monitoring role in order to avoid frightening states in the light of the novel sort of obligations imposed on them in Resolution 1373.[128] However,

121 B. Saul, 'Definition of "Terrorism" in the UN Security Council: 1985–2004' (2005) 4(1) *Chinese Journal of International Law* 141, 165.

122 UN Doc. S/PV.5446 (2006), 6.

123 See e.g. UN Doc. S/RES/1377 (2001); UN Doc. S/RES/1466 (2003); UN Doc. S/RES/1566 (2004).

124 UN Doc. S/2008/493 (2008), para. 81.

125 *Ibid.* para. 86.

126 See e.g. UNSC Provisional Record (13 November 2009) UN Doc. S/PV.6217, 4 (CTC) and 8 (1540 Committee).

127 See the CTC's Technical Assistance Matrix (at: www.un.org/sc/ctc/matrix/mindex.html; accessed 10 December 2009).

128 Ambassador Greenstock said that the 'CTC is not a tribunal and does not judge States' (UN Doc. S/PV.4618 (2002), 5).

some scholars nevertheless perceive a threat to states in the activities of the committee. It has been said that 'the CTC can count on the threat of economic sanctions or military action to buttress its efforts'.[129] Indeed, it is not unreasonable to suggest that states that consistently refuse to provide reports or to implement the obligations contained in Resolutions 1373 or 1540 will be judged to have failed to comply with Council resolutions. To the extent that such failure to comply would be a step closer to the realization of the threat posed by WMD or international terrorism, it could be branded as a threat to international peace and security analogous to that posed by Iran's nuclear programme, for instance. The finding of an Article 39 situation opens the door to the range of more directly coercive measures contained in Chapter VII.

2.4 Conclusion

In order for the Council to better deal with inchoate threats to international peace and security, it should improve its capacity for both the collection and consideration of facts. The HLP found that 'whether there is credible evidence of the reality of the threat in question' is an important factor in the legitimacy of the Security Council's enforcement action.[130] Inchoate threats require a fact-finding capacity for two reasons. The first pertains to the existence of the threat: characteristic of inchoate threats is that they are not necessarily obvious on the face of things. The second pertains to the management of the threat: until more is known about the specifics of a given situation, it is difficult to tailor a response to it. This opens the door to mistake and overreaction in the sensitive area of the inviolability of sovereign states' domestic spheres. The objection could also be expressed less formalistically as a manifestation of 'hegemonic international law',[131] or as facilitating imperialism.[132]

At present the UN Security Council treats facts as intelligence rather than evidence. By this, it is meant that in many cases the facts on which it proceeds are not publicized and, in some cases, are used more 'for support than illumination'.[133] This problem is compounded by the fact that the Council relies on intelligence offered to it by states.[134] It is suggested that the credibility of the Council in dealing with inchoate threats will depend on its willingness to become a more effective arena for inclusive and engaged discourse. This is even more apparent when the Security Council tackles general inchoate threats with 'legislation' aimed at members of the UN as a

129 Alvarez (n. 104), 875.

130 *More Secure World* (n. 1), 64, para. 195.

131 Alvarez (n. 104), 875.

132 A. Anghie, *Imperialism, Sovereignty and the Making of International Law* (Cambridge: Cambridge University Press, 2005), 274.

133 T. L. Hughes, quoted in S. Chesterman, 'The Spy Who Came in from the Cold War: Intelligence and International Law' (2006) 27 *Mich.J.Int'l L.* 1071, 1100.

134 T. M. Franck, *Fairness in International Law and Institutions* (Oxford: Clarendon, 1995), 292.

whole.[135] Not only would the participation of a broader range of states at an earlier, pre-decision, stage of discussion provide the Council with more information, it would also inject an element of scrutiny into the process. It seems that effective action to manage inchoate threats to international peace and security must be reconciled with states' willingness to support such action outside the Council in order to guarantee the multilateral nature of that action.

135 Talmon (n. 102), 186.

3 Nuclear non-proliferation and the UN Security Council in a multipolar world

Can international law protect states from the Security Council?

*Daniel H. Joyner**

In this chapter I would like to discuss the United Nations Security Council's efforts to implement, preserve and universalize the obligations of the 1968 Nuclear Non-Proliferation Treaty (NPT). This discussion will lead to questions regarding the Security Council's role and authority in the international legal system, and ultimately to a consideration of how international law can better guarantee that the Council does not exercise an unwarranted degree of legal power at the expense of the member states of the United Nations.

First, however, a word on how this chapter fits in with the title of this volume: *International Law in a Multipolar World*. I take 'multipolarity' as used in this book's title to mean the state of international relations in which there is a distribution of power at the top of the power pyramid, whereby more than two states have relatively equal, or at least not significantly disproportional, amounts of military, cultural, and economic influence. It is likely that this concept of multipolarity has significant explanatory power with reference to the state of international relations today. The United States is the most powerful state in the world by almost any measure. However, it does not enjoy the almost unlimited influence over other states which classic hegemons, or states at the apex of unipolar systems, have historically. A number of other states are either emerging or re-emerging as powers challenging US influence, particularly within their geographical regions. These include China, Russia, India and the European Union.

The first way in which this chapter fits in with the theme of this volume, is that the move from the Cold War system of bipolarity between the US and the USSR, to the modern multipolar reality, was the geopolitical shift which enabled the Security Council to begin the period of relatively effective

* I would like to dedicate this chapter to the memory of Professor Sir Ian Brownlie, who died in a tragic automobile accident in Egypt on 3 January 2010 as this chapter was being written. I never had the opportunity to know Sir Ian personally, a fact which I now regret. However, his authoritative presence at the centre of the discipline of international law has been of great value to me, and will endure long after his passing.

functioning which it has enjoyed for almost twenty years. Thus, the Security Council can truthfully be said currently to play a meaningful role in international law only because of the multipolarity of the modern state of international relations.

This chapter's focus on the Security Council's efforts in the area of nuclear weapons proliferation is also relevant to the theme of this volume because, quite ironically, the multipolarity of the modern system of international relations – i.e. the dispersal of power among many states and not centralized in one or a few – at the selfsame time makes the Security Council's core mission of maintaining international peace and security, including in the issue area of nuclear weapons proliferation, next to impossible. The arm of the Security Council has been proved over and over again to be of quite limited length, particularly in the face of a recalcitrant target state.

In either blissful or wilful ignorance of these limitations, however, the Security Council continues to see itself at the apex of authority in international security law, and capable of significantly influencing the policies and behaviours of states which its controlling permanent members determine to be a threat to international peace and security. An even more recent phenomenon is the Council's apparent determination that it is empowered not only to act as an executive body, authorizing uses of force to restore international peace and security on an ad hoc basis, but also to act as a legislative body crafting proactive and permanent legal edicts covering important areas of international relations, such as terrorism (Resolution 1373) and weapons of mass destruction (WMD) proliferation (Resolution 1540). Indeed, as we will see in the case studies below on Resolution 1540, Iran and North Korea, the Security Council appears to consider itself to possess ultimate and essentially unlimited legal authority – i.e. to represent something of a legal hegemon – within its broad mandate to maintain and restore international peace and security. Authority, for example, to command a state to re-accede to treaties from which that state has duly withdrawn according to the treaties' terms. Authority to command a state not to take action which is recognized by a broadly subscribed treaty to be that state's 'inalienable right'. Indeed, the Security Council has for the past few years been so bullish in its attitude towards its own authority, and has ostensibly used that authority to trample on so many of the most important underlying principles of the international legal system, that we may need to begin seriously considering how international law can protect states from the authoritarian Security Council which multipolarity has unleashed.

The chapter will proceed with three case studies in the nuclear weapons proliferation issue area in which the Security Council has arguably demonstrated its determination of its own unlimited legal authority by acting in disharmony with fundamental principles of the international legal system. These case studies include the passage of Security Council Resolution 1540 in 2004, and the respective cases of the North Korean and Iranian nuclear programmes. The chapter will then conclude with a consideration of how international law should respond to the Security Council's demonstrated claim to being essentially *legibus solutus* (above the law) in its exercise of its Chapter VII authority to maintain and restore international peace and security.

3.1 Resolution 1540

On 28 April 2004 the Security Council passed Resolution 1540. This resolution was passed, not coincidentally, shortly after the revelation in February 2004 of the existence of a long-standing clandestine nuclear materials-smuggling ring headed by the father of Pakistan's gas centrifuge programme, Dr Abdul Qadeer Khan.[1] In Resolution 1540, the Security Council undertook to address a number of fundamental limitations of the existing WMD non-proliferation treaties and regimes system. In the Security Council meetings leading up to the passage of Resolution 1540, some of which were opened to comment from non-Council members, many states noted the need for such a resolution to close 'gaps' in the coverage of existing non-proliferation treaty instruments. One such gap identified by states during these meetings was the problem of the non-universality of the system, a result of the fact that non-proliferation treaties, as all treaties, have been adopted only voluntarily by states, and that for a variety of reasons many states, including some of significant proliferation concern, have remained outside the non-proliferation system.[2]

A second major challenge to the non-proliferation treaties and regimes system is the fact that all existing restrictions within the regimes upon manufacture, possession and trafficking in weapons-related technologies are addressed to states themselves.[3] Thus at the international level there is no substantive restriction on private parties, including business entities as well as other non-state actors, engaging in any of these activities. The utility of Resolution 1540 in addressing this non-state actor gap in the non-proliferation treaties and regimes system was noted by numerous states, particularly in the context of international efforts to combat terrorism.

The resolution addresses the non-state actor problem described above in operative paragraph 1 in which it provides that 'all States shall refrain from providing any form of support to non-state actors that attempt to develop, acquire, manufacture, possess, transport, transfer or use nuclear, chemical or

1 See D. H. Joyner, 'International Legal Responses to WMD Proliferation', in C. W. Hughes and R. Devetak (eds.), *The Globalization of Political Violence: Globalization's Shadow* (London: Routledge, 2007).

2 See S. Gahlaut and V. Zaborsky, 'Do Regimes Have the Members They Need?' (February 2003) Center for International Trade and Security Working Paper (Athens, GA: Center for International Trade and Security, 2003).

3 M. Asada, 'WMD Terrorism and Security Council Resolution 1540: Conditions for Legitimacy in International Legislation', IILJ Working Paper 2007/9 (at: www.iilj.org/publications/2007–9Asada.asp); J. du Preez, 'The 2005 NPT Review Conference: Can It Meet the Nuclear Challenge?' (April 2005) *Arms Control Today* 5.

biological weapons and their means of delivery'. Furthermore, operative paragraph 2 provides that:

> all States, in accordance with their national procedures, shall adopt and enforce appropriate effective laws which prohibit any non-State actor to manufacture, acquire, possess, develop, transport, transfer or use nuclear, chemical or biological weapons and their means of delivery, in particular for terrorist purposes, as well as attempts to engage in any of the foregoing activities, participate in them as an accomplice, assist or finance them.

It then addresses in operative paragraph 3 the problem of the non-universality of non-proliferation law by directly imposing an obligation upon states to establish and maintain effective export control laws and regulations at the national level:

> including appropriate laws and regulations to control export, transit, trans-shipment and re-export and controls on providing funds and services related to such export and trans-shipment such as financing...as well as establishing end-user controls; and establishing and enforcing appropriate criminal or civil penalties for violations of such export control laws and regulations.

As in Resolution 1373 on international terrorism, passed in 2001, Resolution 1540 in operative paragraph 4 establishes a Committee of the Security Council to monitor the implementation by states of the obligations imposed by the resolution. Although Resolution 1373 and Resolution 1540 were adopted in very different contexts and are meant to cover quite different, although of course related, areas of law, they share important similarities in structure as well as in legal import. These two resolutions have been claimed by some commentators to have ushered in a new age of Security Council jurisprudence and to have signalled intent by the Council to act as a legislative body, in supplementation of its executive functions.[4]

There had before the passage of Resolution 1373 been other controversial acts of the Security Council which had caused debate on the topic of the proper role and powers of the Council.[5] Notable in this regard were the actions before the International Court of Justice arising out of the explosion of Pan Am flight 103 over Lockerbie, Scotland in 1988. However, although in the *Lockerbie* cases there was an allegation that the Council had overstepped its

4 See M. Happold, 'Security Council Resolution 1373 and the Constitution of the United Nations' (2003) 16 LJIL 593; P. Szasz, 'The Security Council Starts Legislating' (2002) 96 AJIL 901–2.

5 See M. Koskenniemi, 'The Police in the Temple: Order, Justice and the UN – A Dialectical View' (1995) 6 EJIL 325; K. Harper, 'Does the United Nations Security Council Have the Competence to Act as a Court and Legislature?' (1994) 27 *NYU J.Int'l Law & Pol.* 103; B. Martenczuk, 'The Security Council, the International Court and Judicial Review: What Lessons from Lockerbie?' (1999) 10 EJIL 517.

prerogatives under the Charter, there was no hint of legislative aspirations in the Council's actions. The resolutions involved were clearly targeted against the acts and omissions of one state, Libya, and they set clear demands which, if met, would bring about the end of the mandate for exercise of Council authority. Thus they were in keeping with the Council's understood role, if perhaps excessively bold in construction.

Because of the predominantly non-legislative characteristics of this and virtually all other Security Council decisions, it can be concluded that at the end of the 1990s, the Security Council had not yet passed a true piece of international legislation.[6] However, in the swelling of outrage and concern following the attacks of 11 September 2001, and, as has been alleged, with little foresight of the legal import of what they were doing, the Council passed Resolution 1373.[7] The Council passed this resolution not only to respond to the 11 September acts of terror themselves, or to mete out any measure of punishment upon its perpetrators, or to target them or those states that aided and abetted them. The attacks served as a backdrop and a catalyst for the establishment of a much broader and temporally indefinite normative regime addressing the issue of international terrorism.

The context of the passing of Resolution 1540 offers even less evidence of a specific situation of threat to international peace and security to which the resolution can be regarded as responding. Again, the revelation of the Khan network provided a circumstantial pretext which seemed to explain the prioritization of the subject of WMD proliferation and its address by the Council in Resolution 1540, but the resolution itself went far beyond simply responding to the existence of this network. It newly imposed a broad set of obligations upon all UN member states which had the purpose of permanently changing the structure and content of national legal systems.

These resolutions, simply put, cannot be described as ad hoc responses to events urgently arising in international politics. They were rather calculated, proactive, forward-looking normative creations. In each case, the Security Council determined that an entire class of actions which had been, and which might in the future be, committed potentially by any state, constituted a threat to international peace and security. The Council then decided in each case that all UN member states should take extensive measures, broadly prescribed in the resolutions, including changes to their national legal systems, in order to combat these ill-defined present and future threats. The obligations imposed under both Resolutions 1373 and 1540 are not temporally limited, either explicitly or implicitly. Their duration is clearly meant to be indefinite. Moreover, there are no specifically targeted states. The obligations imposed in the resolutions are stated in an abstract manner, so as to make their application universal.

6 Szasz (n. 4); Happold (n. 4); M. Koskenniemi, 'International Legislation Today: Limits and Possibilities' (2005) 23 *Wisconsin International Law Journal* 61.

7 Happold (n. 4).

3.2 The UN Charter and WMD non-proliferation law

The United Nations Charter makes no mention of the term 'proliferation' and makes no distinction in the language of its provisions as between conventional and non-conventional (i.e. nuclear, chemical and biological) weapons. The Charter rather uses the terms 'disarmament' and the 'regulation of armaments' in three of its articles: Article 11(1), Article 26 and Article 47. These provisions address the subject of the regulation of military armaments generally through international law, as such technologies existed and were maintained in national arsenals at the time of the drafting of the Charter.[8] The UN Charter system which these provisions comprise was constructed to address issues of international arms control and to facilitate the generation of international law to regulate this issue area.

Article 11(1) is a further specification of the general powers of consideration and recommendation granted to the General Assembly in Article 10.[9] The General Assembly under Article 11(1) is to consider 'general principles of cooperation in the maintenance of international peace and security', a power which should be read to include consideration of abstract, general ideas about how member states should work together, and fundamental principles which should underpin the legal relationships which bind states in this area.[10] This power is apposite to the General Assembly because of its character as the deliberative organ of the United Nations and as the only UN body comprising all members of the organization, thus allowing the broadest possible spectrum of interests and perspectives to have input into the formulation of basic principles governing state cooperation in international arms control efforts.[11]

The role of the Security Council in this system is specified in Article 26, which provides:

> In order to promote the establishment and maintenance of international peace and security with the least diversion for armaments of the world's human and economic resources, the Security Council shall be responsible for formulating, with the assistance of the Military Staff Committee referred to in Article 47, plans to be submitted to the Members of the United Nations for the establishment of a system for the regulation of armaments.

A number of points regarding the Security Council's role under Article 26 bear mention. First is to observe that Article 26, in addition to conferring powers and function upon the Security Council, also establishes responsibilities

8 D. Cheever, 'The UN and Disarmament' (1965) 19 *Int'l Org.* 453.

9 B. Simma *et al.* (eds.), *The Charter of the United Nations: A Commentary* (2nd edn, Oxford: Oxford University Press, 2002), 277–8.

10 *Ibid.* 277–80.

11 L. Sohn, 'Enhancing the Role of the General Assembly of the United Nations in Crystallizing International Law', in J. Makarczyk (ed.), *Theory of International Law at the Threshold of the 21st Century: Essays in Honour of Krzysztof Skubiszewski* (The Hague: Kluwer Law International, 1996), 549–61.

for the Council in carrying out its complementary role with the General Assembly in the exercise of its Article 11(1) powers. The Council is given the responsibility, on the basis of the recommendations of 'general principles of cooperation' it receives from the General Assembly, and with the assistance of the Military Staff Committee, to formulate concrete plans in order to implement the general principles recommended by the Assembly. These plans are to compose a coherent 'system' for the regulation of armaments, which would imply that the plans to be authored by the Council using this power are not to be situation specific, as in the case of an ad hoc response to a discrete event in international affairs. Rather, these plans are to form the basis for a universally applicable, enduring system of 'practical and effective' international arms control.[12]

The Security Council under Article 26 only has the power to formulate plans. It must then submit those plans to the member states of the United Nations for their approval and for establishment through multilateral treaty as actual legal principles governing their relationships with each other. The Security Council's plans in and of themselves have no binding force upon members, and are merely hortatory offerings, although endowed with the gravitas of having been generated through the Charter system for creation of arms control law.[13] Members may, however, choose either to accept or reject these plans, in analogous fashion to the ratification of UN-approved treaties by member states. As Hans Kelsen has observed:

> With respect to Article 26 of the Charter . . . the 'plans' formulated by the Security Council 'for the establishment of a system for the regulation of armaments' may provide for reduction of armaments; they must be 'submitted to the members of the United nations'. That means that they are binding upon the members only if accepted by them. The obligation is established by a treaty concluded by the members with the organization. Unlike Article 8, paragraph 4 of the [League of Nations] Covenant, Article 26 does not provide expressly for the 'adoption' of the plan by the members, but if the plan of the Security Council is to be submitted to the members, it can be only for the purpose of being adopted by them.[14]

Thus under the Charter system, member states retain their full sovereignty over decisions to enter into legal relationships in the area of international arms control. This right is not presumptively subsumed under the Council's binding decision-making powers under Article 25, nor under its broad powers

12 B. Bechhoefer, *Postwar Negotiations for Arms Control* (Washington, DC: Brookings Institution, 1961); O. Bogdanov, 'Outlawry of War and Disarmament' (1971–2) 133 *Recueil des Cours* 15–42; Simma (n. 9), 466–8.

13 Simma (n. 9), 466–8.

14 H. Kelsen, *Collective Security under International Law* (1957; Union, NJ: Lawbook Exchange, 2001, repr.), 214.

to maintain international peace and security under the articles of Chapter VII.[15]

3.3 The limits of Chapter VII

The UN Charter in Article 24 confers upon the Security Council 'primary responsibility for the maintenance of international peace and security'. In the same paragraph the members of the United Nations 'agree that in carrying out its duties under this responsibility, the Security Council acts on their behalf'. This statement is the closest the Charter comes to attempting to remedy the non-democratic reality, made requisite by geopolitical circumstances in 1945, that the most powerful organ of the United Nations and the only organ capable of issuing decisions binding upon all UN members, is composed of only 15 of those members (who now total 191), five of whom are given permanent status and have an effective veto power over every decision of the Council.

In this language seeming to imply a representative relationship between the Council and the rest of the UN membership, the Charter attempts to legitimize the declaration in Article 25 by the membership, that all UN members 'agree to accept and carry out the decisions of the Security Council in accordance with the present Charter'. Thus, Article 25 establishes the binding character of Security Council decisions upon the entirety of the UN membership.[16]

Although the specific powers granted to the Security Council under the Charter, and particularly in the articles of Chapter VII, are both broadly and vaguely worded, the Charter does however provide limits upon the discretion of the Council in its exercise of these powers. As the Council derives its powers from the Charter's terms, it is by the same process bound by those terms. As the Appeals Chamber of the International Criminal Tribunal for the former Yugoslavia (ICTY) has observed:

> The Security Council is an organ of an international organization, established by a treaty which serves as a constitutional framework for that organization. The Security Council is thus subjected to certain constitutional limitations, however broad its powers under the constitution may be. Those powers cannot, in any case, go beyond the limits of the jurisdiction of the organization at large, not to mention other specific limitations or those which may derive from the internal division of power within the organization. In any case, neither the text

15 H. Kelsen, *The Law of the United Nations: A Critical Analysis of Its Fundamental Problems* (London: Stevens, 1951).

16 See the discussion of Article 24 as an independent source of authority for binding decisions of the Security Council in Happold (n. 4), 604–5.

nor the spirit of the Charter conceives of the Security Council as *legibus solutus* (unbound by law).[17]

One such limiting provision upon the Council's power is Article 24(2), which provides that 'In discharging these duties the Security Council shall act in accordance with the purposes and principles of the United Nations'.[18] The purposes and principles of the United Nations are to be found in Articles 1 and 2 of the Charter, and include the right of states to self-determination, respect for human rights, the principle of sovereign equality, an obligation to act in good faith and an obligation not to intervene in matters 'essentially within the domestic jurisdiction' of member states. As the International Court of Justice stated in the *Certain Expenses* advisory opinion in 1962: 'When the organization takes action which warrants the assertion that it was appropriate for the fulfilment of one of the stated purposes of the United Nations, the presumption is that such action is not *ultra vires* the organization'.[19]

Another limiting provision is Article 25. As previously stated, perhaps the greatest import of the text of this article is the establishment of the universally binding character of Security Council decisions.[20] However, the fact that, under this provision, members agree to accept and carry out the decisions of the Security Council 'in accordance with the present charter' suggests that the measure of this obedience should be contingent upon the validity of the Council's decisions and actions as held up to the standard of the provisions of the Charter, and further that it is conceivable that other provisions of the Charter might in some cases take precedence over conflicting Security Council decisions.[21] To paraphrase the article's meaning in this regard, UN members are not obligated to comply with the decisions of the Council one wit further than those decisions themselves comply with the provisions of the Charter.[22]

Although the general purposes and principles of the United Nations are difficult to apply in a meaningful way so as to provide justifiable limitations on the powers of the Security Council under Article 24(2), in the non-proliferation issue area the process for creation of new non-proliferation law contained in Articles 11(1) and 26 described above does provide a clear, authoritative lawmaking procedure which can properly be called the UN Charter system for the creation of non-proliferation law. As this system

17 *Prosecutor* v. *Tadić* (Jurisdiction) ITC-Y94-1-AR72, para. 28 (2 October 1995).

18 See D. Schweigman, *The Authority of the Security Council Under Chapter VII of the UN Charter* (London: Kluwer Law International, 2001), 29–33.

19 *Certain Expenses of the United Nations*, ICJ Reports (1962), 151, 168.

20 See R. Higgins, 'The Advisory Opinion on Namibia: Which UN Resolutions are Binding under Article 25 of the Charter?' (1972) 32 ICLQ 269–86.

21 J. Delbruck, 'Article 25', in B Simma *et al.* (eds.), *The Charter of the United Nations: A Commentary* (Oxford: Oxford University Press, 1994) 455; E. de Wet, *The Chapter VII Powers of the United Nations Security Council* (Oxford: Hart, 2004), 375–8; P. Rösgen, 'Rechtsetzungakte der Vereinten Nationen und ihrer Sonderorganisationen: Bestandsaufnahme und Volzug in der Bundesrepublik Deutschland' (Ph.D. thesis, University of Bonn, 1985), 157.

22 De Wet (n. 21), 377.

involves a clearly delineated division of roles and authorities between the organs of the UN, it thus comprises a limitation upon the authority of the Security Council deriving from 'the internal division of power within the organization'.[23] This limitation is therefore a part of the substantive law of the Charter in accordance with which, under Article 25, the Security Council is bound to act.[24]

Thus, while the provisions of the Charter in many instances provide limitations upon the powers of the Council which, though valid, are difficult to apply unambiguously, because of the presence of the lawmaking system contained in Articles 11(1) and 26, the non-proliferation law creation issue area does not labour under the same difficulty. I would argue that the Article 25 limitations on the Council's powers can be applied in the non-proliferation law issue area because of the presence of the criteria for legitimate lawmaking by UN bodies contained in Articles 11(1) and 26 of the UN Charter. Accordingly, any act by the Security Council which attempts to create 'a system for the regulation of armaments' outside of the Article 11(1) and Article 26 institutional process is in breach of Article 25, and is thus an act *ultra vires* the Council's authority.[25]

Security Council Resolution 1540 meets this test precisely. The resolution clearly attempts to establish a system for the regulation of WMD, which includes a universalized export control law requirement and a universalized requirement to enact laws on the subject of non-state actors. Therefore, to be valid as a source of binding obligation upon UN member states, I argue that this system of obligations cannot be established through the Council's use of its Chapter VII powers, but must rather be constructed through the procedures provided for in Articles 11(1) and 26.

My essential argument is that in passing what can only be viewed as an ostensible piece of international legislation in Resolution 1540, the Security Council confused the proper scope of its enforcement powers under Chapter VII, with the proper scope of its long unused, limited lawmaking powers under Article 26. Consequently, the Council, by unilateral exercise of its Chapter VII powers, has taken to itself a role which, under the Charter system, it is to share both with the General Assembly in the exercise of its Article 11(1) powers, as well as with the general membership of the United Nations, to whom it is directed under Article 26 to submit proposals for the creation of new international laws in the area of weapons proliferation.

The added political, legal and chronological efficiency of the path chosen by the Security Council is not denied. For the members of the Security Council, the long unused Charter system for the creation of non-proliferation law would certainly have looked less attractive, particularly as the amount of control they would have been able to exercise over the outcome of the approval

23 *Prosecutor* v. *Tadić* (n. 17).

24 *Ibid.*

25 Happold (n. 4), 593.

process under the Charter system would have been severely diluted from that they would wield through the Chapter VII process.

However, none of these reasons of expedition and control sufficiently justifies going around the Charter system and assuming a lawmaking authority which was never intended to be exercised by the Council under the Charter. The Charter system in Articles 11(1) and 26 is the authoritative system for the creation of new non-proliferation law for good reasons. The system in Articles 11(1) and 26 divides roles among the political organs of the UN, leaving the final and most important role of actual establishment as law of the principles generated through this institutional process, to the UN member states themselves. This system was created by the Charter framers in maintenance of the classical principles of state sovereignty and sovereign equality in international lawmaking, and was consistent with the positivist tradition that the consent of states to be bound underlies the validity of all of the sources of international law. This system was informed by the understanding that the consent given to Council authority in the first instance by states in Article 25 of the Charter does not equate to direct consent of states at the second instance to every substantive decision of the Council. And while this distinction is less troublesome in the domestic context under most theories of the positivist social compact, it is troubling to states in the international legal system which more jealously guard their sovereign autonomy under the sometimes maligned, but still quite virile Westphalian sovereignty paradigm.

In adopting Resolution 1540, the Security Council, whose role in the Charter system for non-proliferation law creation is really a facilitative and definitional one, effectively bypassed the steps assigned to the General Assembly and to the member states by taking the issue to itself and acting both in the deliberative role assigned to the General Assembly, as well as the law creation role assigned to the members collectively. In doing so, the Council acted in disharmony with the fundamental international legal principle of state sovereignty, and the derivative principle of the consensual foundation of the sources of international law. In short, it acted as a legal hegemon, unbound by the fundamental rules and principles of international law, and the limited nature of its own authority under the Charter.

3.4 Iran

In late 2002, the world learned from Iranian opposition groups in exile that Iran had concealed from the International Atomic Energy Agency (IAEA) the existence of facilities at Natanz and Arak engaged in experiments involving uranium enrichment and plutonium separation for eighteen years. Upon a report by IAEA inspectors detailing their findings of the undeclared activities, the IAEA Board of Governors reached the conclusion in a Resolution passed on 26 November 2003 that, because of this concealment and other reporting omissions, Iran had 'failed in a number of instances...to meet its obligations under its Safeguards Agreement with the agency'.[26] The Board further recognized that Iran had a particular onus of cooperation and transparency in order to 'provide and maintain the assurances required by Member States' and to 'restore confidence'.[27] Iran subsequently agreed upon a temporary suspension of its uranium enrichment activities and in December 2003 signed the IAEA Additional Protocol.

Despite these concessions, Iran has consistently maintained that all of its work with fissile materials and related technologies, including work at these undeclared sites, has been aimed at furthering its capacity to produce civilian nuclear energy. Iran has argued that despite its failure to comply with reporting requirements under its safeguards agreement, it has always been in compliance with its substantive obligations under the NPT. In this argument, Iran has relied specifically upon the 'inalienable right' of all states to engage in peaceful uses of nuclear technologies recognized in Article IV, paragraph 1, of the NPT.[28]

However, suspicions have become widespread, particularly among Western states and Israel, that Iran does indeed have nuclear weapons ambitions, and, in particular, that the uranium enrichment work which Iran has carried out is intended not solely for use in peaceful energy production, but for the creation of nuclear weapons. Notwithstanding these suspicions, IAEA inspectors have to date found no conclusive evidence to support allegations of a clandestine nuclear weapons programme in Iran.[29]

3.5 Resolution 1737

Despite this lack of evidence of a weapons programme, the IAEA Board of Governors took the decision on 4 February 2006 to refer Iran's case to the UN Security Council. This referral, without a supporting report by IAEA inspectors providing evidence that Iran was in breach of its substantive NPT obligations, or that it was in continuing breach of its safeguards agreement, has led some to criticize the Board's decision as premature.[30] Notwithstanding these concerns, on 31 July 2006 the Security Council passed Resolution 1696 in which, acting under Article 40 of Chapter VII of the UN Charter, it demanded that Iran suspend all uranium enrichment-related and reprocessing

26 IAEA, 'Implementation of the NPT Standards Agreement in the Islamic Republic of Iran', Doc. GOV/2003/81 (26 November 2003), 2.

27 *Ibid.*

28 For an analysis of the legal arguments surrounding Iran's nuclear programme, see D. H. Joyner, *International Law and the Proliferation of Weapons of Mass Destruction* (Oxford: Oxford University Press, 2009), 50–5.

29 For a fuller discussion of the question of evidence of an Iranian nuclear weapons programme see D. H. Joyner, 'Why Less is More: Law and Policy Considerations on the Iranian Nuclear Issue', *Harvard Law and Policy Review* (Online) (2010). See also US National Intelligence Estimate, 'Iran: Nuclear Intentions and Capabilities' (November 2007) (at: www.dni.gov/press_releases/20071203_release.pdf).

30 Joyner (n. 29).

activities, and requested a report from the IAEA director-general by 31 August to confirm this suspension. The Council followed up Resolution 1696 on 23 December 2006 with Resolution 1737, in which it acted under Article 41 of the Charter and made binding the demands of Resolution 1696.

Iran's failure to abide by the terms of these resolutions, insisting that its activities are firmly within its rights under NPT Article IV, has led to the adoption of further Security Council resolutions under Chapter VII, including a number of resolutions imposing trade restrictions and other economic sanctions upon Iran and upon specified Iranian individuals and business entities.

3.6 Resolution 1929

Tensions between Iran and Western powers were aggravated by Iran's disclosure in September 2009 that it had for some years been constructing a facility near Qom intended as an additional uranium enrichment facility to supplement its primary enrichment facility at Natanz. Since this disclosure by Iran, one of the points of debate among international observers has been whether in the timing of this disclosure, Iran violated its obligations under its legal agreements with the IAEA.

Iran has argued that its disclosure was perfectly consistent with its legal obligations under its Safeguards Agreement with the IAEA (INFCIRC/214), as implemented through a Subsidiary Arrangements agreement which Iran entered into with the IAEA in 1976.[31] Under the provisions of this Subsidiary Arrangements agreement known as 'Code 3.1', Iran has argued that it is only obligated to disclose the existence of new enrichment facilities 'normally not later than 180 days before the facility is scheduled to receive nuclear material for the first time'.

Some observers, however, argue that Iran did in fact violate its international obligations by not disclosing the existence of the Qom facility earlier.[32] They argue that Iran agreed by exchange of letters with the IAEA in 2003 to a new and revised set of Subsidiary Arrangements, known as 'modified Code 3.1', which provide that preliminary design information on new enrichment facilities is to be provided 'as soon as the decision to construct or to authorize construction has been taken, whichever is earlier'.

The crux of the dispute regarding which of the versions of Code 3.1 is applicable to Iran's actions in and around September 2009 centres on Iran's 29 March 2007 letter to the IAEA in which Iran declared its intention to 'revert' to the original 1976 Code 3.1 formulation. The IAEA Legal Adviser's office issued an opinion in March 2009 in which it rejected Iran's unilateral declaration of reversion, and maintained that the agreed modified Code 3.1

31 'IAEA: Iran broke law by not revealing nuclear facility', CNN.com, 30 September 2009.

32 See James Acton, 'Iran Violated International Obligations on Qom Facility' (at: www.carnegieendowment.org/publications/index.cfm?fa=view&id=23884).

provisions remained in force between Iran and the IAEA. As the Legal Advisor's office concluded:

> The implementation of the provisions of Subsidiary Arrangements can only be amended or suspended with the agreement of both parties to them. . . The provisions cannot be amended or suspended unilaterally by the state. Thus Iran's failure to provide design information in accordance with the modified Code 3.1 as agreed to by Iran in 2003 is inconsistent with Iran's obligations under the Subsidiary Arrangements to its Safeguards Agreement.

The UN Security Council entered the fray of this essentially legal debate on 9 June 2010 with the passage of Resolution 1929, in which it acted under Article 41 of the Charter and decided that Iran:

> shall without delay comply fully and without qualification with its IAEA Safeguards Agreement, including through the application of modified Code 3.1 of the Subsidiary Arrangement to its Safeguards Agreement . . .

3.7 Legal analysis of Resolution 1737

In consideration of the legal merits of Iran's claim of justification of its activities by reference to Article IV of the NPT, it is important first to note that uranium enrichment, when declared, is not a NPT violation per se. Certainly when uranium is enriched to a U-235 presence of less than 20 per cent, and can thus still be classified as low-enriched uranium (LEU), that enrichment activity is one that falls within the Article IV inalienable right to engage in peaceful uses of nuclear technologies. This understanding was clear at the time of the drafting of the NPT. As the Director of the US Arms Control and Disarmament Agency told the Senate Foreign Relations Committee in 1968:

> It may be useful to point out, for illustrative purposes, several activities which the United States would not consider per se to be violations of the prohibitions in Article II. Neither uranium enrichment nor the stockpiling of fissionable material in connection with a peaceful program would violate Article II so long as these activities were safeguarded under Article III. Also clearly permitted would be the development, under safeguards, of plutonium fuelled power reactors, including research on the properties of metallic plutonium, nor would Article II interfere with the development or use of fast breeder reactors under safeguards.[33]

33 W. Foster, 'Extension of Remarks By Mr Foster in Response To Question Regarding Nuclear Explosive Devices' (10 July 1968) US Senate Foreign Relations Committee, Ninetieth Congress, Second Session, Executive H, Treaty on the Non-proliferation of Nuclear Weapons (10, 11, 12, 17 July 1968), 39. Also available from P. K. Kerr, 'Iran's Nuclear Program: Tehran's Compliance with International Obligations' Congressional Research Report for Congress R40094 (31 March 2009), 2.

Japan and a number of other Non-nuclear Weapon State (NNWS) parties to the NPT have carried out enrichment of uranium for the purpose of nuclear power generation for many years without complaint from the IAEA Board of Governors. Japan has in fact separated and stockpiled at least 43.1 tons of plutonium, as well as having a robust and productive gas centrifuge programme for uranium enrichment at its facility in Rokkasho, thus illustrating that even the overproduction and stockpiling of fissile materials is deemed permissible by the IAEA.[34] It is only when this enrichment activity by an NNWS is undeclared to the IAEA that a violation of an IAEA safeguards agreement results. Even this, however, is not a violation of the NPT per se. Only if enrichment proceeds to the production of highly enriched uranium (HEU), at approximately 20 per cent presence of U-235, does it produce weapons-usable material. Undeclared enrichment of weapons-usable HEU would create a prima facie case of breach of Article II of the NPT and such activity would not be justifiable by reference to Article IV.

As a matter of law, therefore, Iran was quite correct in its interpretation that its uranium enrichment activities were covered by Article IV of the NPT at least until 23 December 2006. The basis of its case was not altered by previous IAEA urgings that Iran cease uranium enrichment, as the IAEA's only legal competence is in the administration of safeguards agreements, and the continuation of uranium enrichment in declared sites, under IAEA safeguards, posed no challenge to the provisions of Iran's safeguards agreement. The legal landscape did change, however, on 23 December 2006 with the passage of Security Council Resolution 1737, under which the Council exercised its authority under Chapter VII of the UN Charter to order Iran to cease uranium enrichment.

Regardless of the prudence or other merit of this demand by the Council, in passing this resolution the Council likely did change the legal underpinnings of Iran's case for justifying its enrichment activities by reference to NPT Article IV.[35] This issue can be approached legally under a number of different theories. The most often cited theory focuses on the provisions of the UN Charter, which in Article 103 specifies that 'In the event of a conflict between the obligations of the Members of the United Nations under the present Charter and their obligations under any other international agreement, their obligations under the present Charter shall prevail'. By virtue of Article 103, in conjunction with the already-mentioned Article 25, therefore, the obligations of the Charter are declared superior to all other treaty rights and obligations.

34 See report from Kyodo news agency (at: www.redorbit.com/news/science/231519/japans_separated_plutonium_stockpile_increases_to_43_tons/index.html). Uranium enrichment through centrifuge cascade is also carried out, for example, at the Almelo facility in the Netherlands, and at the Gronau facility in Germany.

35 See the discussion of the limits of the Security Council's Chapter VII authority below.

Under this analysis, with the passage of Resolution 1737, the Council invoked Iran's obligation as a UN member to abide by the Council's decisions under Article 25, which is an obligation superior to all other treaty obligations pursuant to Article 103, including the rights and duties contained in the NPT. Iran thus became legally obligated to comply with Resolution 1737, as well as with all other resolutions passed by the Security Council under its Chapter VII authority, and unable to rely upon its right to peaceful use of nuclear technologies in NPT Article IV to justify actions in disharmony with such Council decisions.

The problem with this analysis, however, is that it would empower the UN Security Council to trump any of the rights held by states by virtue of their statehood. The implications of this theory are far-reaching and unsettling. Article IV of the NPT, to which 187 states are currently parties, recognizes the residual entitlement of NNWS treaty parties to possess and use nuclear technologies and materials for peaceful purposes, notwithstanding the obligations not to pursue nuclear weapons which they undertook in Article II. This residual entitlement is termed by the treaty to be an 'inalienable right'. This is strong language intended to convey deep legal meaning, analogous to the recognition in Article 51 of the UN Charter of an 'inherent right' of self-defence.[36] The phrasing characterizes the right guaranteed by Article IV not simply as a right created by the NPT, but rather as a pre-existing right independent of the treaty and only recognized by its terms.[37] Like the inherent right to self-defence recognized by the UN Charter, this inalienable right to possess and use nuclear technologies and materials for peaceful purposes would appear to be recognized by the 187 states party to the NPT as comprising one of the bundle of rights inuring to a state by virtue of its statehood, and recognized in both customary and conventional international law.

It can be argued (as I have done elsewhere)[38] that one theory for the superiority of Chapter VII resolutions over the rights of NPT Article IV is to be found in the reasoning that, as noted above, the rights defined in Article IV are not creations alone of the treaty terms of the NPT, but are, rather, rights recognized by the terms of the treaty yet existing independently within the bundle of rights inherent in the attributes of a state. Under this argument, while the Article IV rights are important features of the sovereign character of all NPT parties, they are nonetheless classifiable along with all other general

36 On the recognition of the customary right of self-defence in UN Charter Article 51, see D. Bowett, *Self-Defence in International Law* (Manchester University Press, 1958), 185. ('It is...fallacious to assume that members have only those rights which the Charter accords to them; on the contrary they have those rights which general international law accords to them except in so far as they have surrendered them under the Charter...The view of Committee I at San Francisco was that this prohibition [Article 2(4)] left the right of self-defence unimpaired.')

37 See S. Hall, 'The Persistent Spectre: Natural Law, International Order and the Limits of Legal Positivism' (2001) 12 EJIL 269. On the question of the relationship between this right and Articles I and II of the NPT, see Joyner (n. 28), 45–50.

38 Joyner (n. 28), 54–5.

state rights which are, by a state's consent to the terms of Article 25 of the Charter, made surmountable by and subject to the authority of the Security Council acting under Chapter VII. Thus far this theory may be correct, but it does not fully deal with the central question of the ambit of the Charter's Article 39 grant of authority to the Security Council. Over which of their rights did states contract discretion to the Security Council in exercise of its Article 39 authority, and over which did they not? Space here only permits a superficial answer. However, I will argue that there must be limits to the Council's Article 39 'powers of appreciation' and resulting authoritative discretion, lest the Council become a legal hegemon, unbound by law in the exercise of its Chapter VII powers.[39] The idea of the Security Council, with its unrepresentative make-up and proprietary rights system comprising such a legal hegemon is unlikely to be acceptable to most of the nations of the world.

In summary, then, by trampling upon a right of states recognized in a broadly subscribed treaty to be an 'inalienable right', the Security Council has in its NPT-related dealings with Iran arguably overstepped the bounds of its Chapter VII authority. It has at least, in doing so, pushed the limits of that authority to a point at which serious questions must be asked about what those limits are, and how international law should respond in order to guarantee that there are legal limits placed upon the power of the Security Council, preventing it from becoming a legal hegemon unbound by law.

3.8 Legal analysis of Resolution 1929

Returning to the discussion above in the context of Resolution 1540, of the limits on the Security Council's authority expressed particularly in Article 25 of the Charter, I argue that Resolution 1929 represents yet another occasion on which the Council has acted *ultra vires* its Chapter VII authority. The analysis here is very similar to that conducted above in the case of Resolution 1540. In the case of Resolution 1929, the Security Council considers what is essentially a legal question – i.e. the obligations of Iran under its Safeguards Agreement with the IAEA – and whether those obligations include either the original or the modified Code 3.1 formulation with regard to the disclosure of the existence of new nuclear facilities. The Council makes what can only be

39 The term 'powers of appreciation' is taken from Judge Shahabuddeen's searching query in his opinion in the *Lockerbie* case: 'The question now raised…is whether a decision of the Security Council may override the legal rights of states, and, if so, whether there are any limitations on the power of the Council to characterize a situation as one justifying the making of a decision entailing such consequences. Are there any limits to the Council's powers of appreciation? In the equilibrium of forces underpinning the United Nations within the evolving international order, is there a conceivable point beyond which a legal issue may properly arise as to the competence of the Security Council to produce such overriding results? If there are any limits, what are those limits, and what body, if other than the Security Council, is competent to say what those limits are?' *Questions of Interpretation and Application of the 1971 Montreal Convention Arising from the Aerial Incident at Lockerbie (Libyan Arab Jamahiriya* v. *United Kingdom).* (Request for the Indication of Provisional Measures: Order of 14 April 1992), ICJ Reports [1992], 3, 142.

described as a judicial decision, accepting one legal argument or interpretation as more persuasive than another. In unmistakably judicial form, the Council then rules on the legal question by issuing an order that the party in the dock before it must abide by its determination of the law.

Again, under the UN Charter Article 25 analysis adopted above, notwithstanding the Council's broad mandate in Articles 39, 40 and 41, there are limits to the Council's authority to act under Chapter VII. Such limitations can be most clearly determined when the Charter itself provides for an alternative decision-making process or forum. And the Charter is quite clear on the question of which forum, or organ within the institutional structure it creates, is to decide legal disputes, and perform judicial functions.

In Article 92, it provides that the International Court of Justice 'shall be the principal judicial organ of the United Nations'. And even more specifically, in Article 36 it provides this explicit directive and reminder to the Security Council itself:

> In making recommendations under this Article the Security Council should also take into consideration that legal disputes should as a general rule be referred by the parties to the International Court of Justice in accordance with the provisions of the Statute of the Court.

As discussed above the Security Council does have broad authority to act under the Articles of Chapter VII when it determines the existence of a threat to international peace and security. But this authority is not without bounds. The Security Council itself is bound by Article 25 to act in accordance with the Charter. The Council is in this way bound to observe the order and delegations of roles provided for by the instrument from which it draws its own authority. Where, as in Articles 36 and 92, the Charter clearly delegates a role and type of authority to a separate UN organ, the Security Council cannot legally usurp the authority so delegated, and arrogate it to its own use.

I argue that in passing Resolution 1929, the Council did just that. It usurped the role of the International Court of Justice in settling a legal dispute among UN member states, and in exercising an essentially judicial interpretive/determinative function to do so. This is a role which was never intended by the Charter framers for the Security Council to fulfil. The Council has neither the mandate nor the qualifications to act as an international judicial body. In passing Resolution 1929, therefore, the Council acted in contravention of Article 25 of the Charter. The operative paragraphs in Resolution 1929 which express the determinations of the Council acting in this judicial role, notably paragraph 5 quoted above, are therefore *ultra vires* the Council's authority and, like Resolution 1540, are as a result void *ab initio*.[40]

However, the fact that the Security Council, notwithstanding its lack of authority in the Charter do so, nevertheless is convinced that it can act as an

40 Joyner (n. 28), 195.

international judiciary, in addition to its newly assumed legislative role, gives rise to grave concern that the Council considers itself above the law – a legal hegemon.

3.9 North Korea

United Nations Security Council Resolution 1874 was adopted on 12 June 2009 in response to the nuclear weapon test which had been conducted by the Democratic People's Republic of North Korea (DPRK) on 25 May 2009. This was the second nuclear weapon test conducted by the DPRK, its first having been held on 9 October 2006. The Security Council had responded to the first nuclear test by the adoption of Resolution 1718 on 14 October 2006. Resolution 1874 essentially reiterates the Security Council's previous condemnation of the DPRK's first nuclear test, and further builds upon and supplements the sanctions imposed upon the DPRK in Resolution 1718.

Resolution 1874 represented the latest in a long line of Security Council resolutions focused on the problem of the DPRK's nuclear weapons programme.[41] Long-standing international concern about the DPRK's nuclear weapons programme had been aggravated by three principal events: the first was the DPRK's announcement on 10 January 2003 that it was withdrawing from the NPT, and the second and third were the 2006 and 2009 nuclear weapon tests.

The DPRK's withdrawal from the NPT was significant on a number of levels. It represented the first and only time that a state has withdrawn its membership from the treaty, which is the cornerstone legal instrument in the nuclear non-proliferation normative regime. It also exempted the DPRK from any obligation under either conventional or customary international law prohibiting it from developing or possessing, or even proliferating, nuclear weapons. It is within this context of the DPRK's withdrawal from the NPT, and its evidencing to the world its possession of nuclear weapons, that Resolution 1874 must be understood.

In Resolution 1874, acting under Article 41 of its Chapter VII authority, the Council first condemns 'in the strongest terms' the 25 May 2009 nuclear test. It then demands that the DPRK not conduct any further nuclear weapon tests, or launch of any ballistic missile technology. These injunctions are clearly aimed at reiterating the prohibitions placed upon the DPRK by Resolution 1718, and at addressing the immediate symptoms of the problem of its nuclear weapons programme. The Council then, however, goes on to address the more fundamental legal problem relating to the DPRK's nuclear weapons programme – the current absence of international law prohibiting the DPRK from developing, possessing and proliferating nuclear weapons. In operative paragraphs 5 and 6, the Council demands that North Korea retract

41 E.g. UNSC Res. 825 (11 May1993) UN Doc. S/RES/825, UNSC Res. 1695 (4 July 2006) UN Doc. S/RES/1695 and UNSC Res. 1718 (14 October 2006) UN Doc. S/RES/1718.

its statement of withdrawal from the NPT, and return 'at an early date' to membership in the NPT and to a safeguards agreement with the IAEA.

Following its demand that the DPRK rejoin the NPT, the Council proceeds in operative paragraph 8 to 'decide' – thus using its most binding and determinative language – that the DPRK shall abandon its nuclear weapons and related development programme, and shall submit itself to the terms of a safeguards agreement administered by the IAEA. The DPRK concluded a safeguards agreement with the IAEA on 30 January 1992 (INFCIRC/403). However, pursuant to the safeguards agreement, its continuance in force was limited to the term of the DPRK's membership in the NPT.[42] Thus, the DPRK's withdrawal from the NPT had as a consequence its simultaneous withdrawal from its safeguards agreement with the IAEA.[43] Operative paragraph 8 of Resolution 1874 thus purports to reverse both the DPRK's withdrawal from the NPT and its withdrawal from its IAEA safeguards agreement, by commanding the state to abide by one of the central obligations of the NPT – i.e. the obligation of non-nuclear weapons States not to develop or possess nuclear weapons – and to abide by the terms of its IAEA safeguards agreement.

This demand and these decisions by the Security Council are singular. First made in Resolution 1718 and then reiterated in Resolution 1874, the Council's demand that the DPRK rejoin the NPT is the only example, to my knowledge, of a Security Council demand that a state re-accede to a treaty from which that state had duly withdrawn according to the treaty's terms. As if that were not enough, the Council in operative paragraph 8 goes one step further, essentially deciding that the DPRK continues to be bound by the central obligation of the NPT and by the terms of its former IAEA safeguards agreement. One might think that there is an element of hypocrisy in a Council decision that a particular state is not allowed, apparently *in perpetuam*, to develop and possess the same weapons technologies which at least eight other states – five of whom have permanent seats on the Council itself – are known to possess.

In its NPT-related decisions concerning North Korea, therefore, the Security Council has determined that it has the authority to contravene a state's decision to withdraw from treaty obligations, according to those treaties' terms. It has further determined that, regardless of the will or contrary actions of the state, it has the authority to impose permanent, substantive obligations on a state with regard to its military capabilities.

These actions of the Security Council would seem to carry serious implications with regard to the consensual nature of all of the sources of international law, which is in turn intimately linked to the sovereign character

42 Article 26 of the DPRK's safeguards agreement provides, 'This Agreement shall remain in force as long as the Democratic People's Republic of Korea is party to the Treaty [the NPT]'.

43 See F. Kirgis, 'North Korea's Withdrawal from the Nuclear Nonproliferation Treaty' (January 2003) *ASIL Insight* (at: www.asil.org/insigh96.cfm).

of states in the international legal system. If the Security Council can order a state to enter into, or at least maintain *jus dispositivum* obligations against the will of the state concerned, what indeed can the Security Council not do? From a jurisprudential perspective, by asserting its power over the consent of states to be bound by international law, the Council's actions regarding North Korea represent an even more fundamental 'authority grab' by the Council than do its actions regarding Iran. In its Resolutions 1718 and 1874, the Council appears to consider itself unbound by the fundamental rules and principles of international law and the sovereign character of the member states of the United Nations, and empowered to do anything it deems expedient to bring about international peace and security. In short, it appears to consider itself a legal hegemon.

3.10 How can international law protect states from the Security Council?

The case studies above in the nuclear non-proliferation law issue area show, what I argue to be, several examples of the Security Council demonstrating its recent determination that it is essentially unbound by law, whether UN Charter law or otherwise, in its fulfilment of its mandate to maintain and restore international peace and security. I would further argue that it is also clear from the context of these case studies, that in each case it was the permanent five members of the Council, who are also not coincidentally the five Nuclear Weapon State parties to the NPT, who took the initiative in having the relevant Security Council resolutions adopted. This fact has led some in the developing world to charge that the permanent five have hijacked the Security Council in order to use it as an instrument of unbridled legal authority for carrying out their own desires for international lawmaking in this area.[44] As the representative from Indonesia stated at the April 2008 NPT Preparatory Committee meeting:

> [T]he tendency for the Security Council to judge compliance and to act as an enforcer of the NPT needs to be urgently rectified. There is no doubt this inclination has a political motivation, as the Council will not in any way act in a similar manner on non-compliance to Article VI. It has also become a source of concern that the expansion of the Security Council involvement in this field risks to undermine the authority of the IAEA.[45]

44 See, e.g., the statements of Egypt, Iran, Mexico, Cuba, India and Namibia in the meetings leading up to the adoption of Resolution 1540 in 2004. In UNSC 4950th Meeting (22 April 2004) UN Doc. S/PV/4950 and UNSC 4950th Meeting (22 April 2004) UN Doc. S/PV/4950 (Resumption 1).

45 IGAW Puja, 'Statement …at the Second Session of the Preparatory Committee for the 2010 Review Conference of the State Parties to the treaty on the Non-proliferation of Nuclear Weapons, Geneva' (29 April 2008) (at: www.un.org/NPT2010/SecondSession/statements.html).

Interestingly, the Indonesian Ambassador here argues specifically that the permanent five have used the Security Council to accomplish their own political interests in the name of enforcing NPT law, yet have hypocritically ignored very significant issues of disarmament law under NPT Article VI,[46] because this would not serve their political interests.

This realization of the permanent five's adoption of the Security Council as an instrument for carrying out their own political agendas through international lawmaking in this area, is likely to be quite disconcerting to many smaller, developing countries, who might legitimately worry whether they will be the next target of the Council's attentions. It thus becomes necessary to consider what international law, and the international legal system, can or should do to protect states, particularly smaller and developing states, from the UN Security Council and its demonstrated bullish, near hegemonic attitude towards its own legal authority? I would like to explore one vein of thinking in the remainder of this chapter.[47]

In addition to the hierarchically equal *jus dispositivum* sources of international law (treaties, customs and general principles) it has come to be generally accepted that there are a few 'higher obligations' which are universal and non-derogable for states in the international legal system. These higher-order peremptory rules are termed *jus cogens*. As Ian Brownlie has written:

> In the recent past both doctrine and judicial opinion have supported the view that certain overriding principles of international law exist, forming a body of *jus cogens*...They are rules of customary law which cannot be set aside by treaty or acquiescence but only by the formation of a subsequent customary rule of contrary effect. The least controversial examples of the class are the prohibition of the use of force, the law of genocide, the principle of racial non-discrimination, crimes against humanity, and the rules prohibiting trade in slaves and piracy.[48]

Jus cogens rules are the closest that the current international legal system comes to constitutional or higher-order system rules. As this enumerated list demonstrates, however, the most widely accepted rules of *jus cogens* are prohibitions of certain conduct by states, and in a very few cases by individuals, deemed universally unacceptable by the international community. There have been some indications of principles of law constituting state entitlements, or

46 Article VI provides that: 'Each of the Parties to the Treaty undertakes to pursue negotiations in good faith on effective measures relating to cessation of the nuclear arms race at an early date and to nuclear disarmament, and on a Treaty on general and complete disarmament under strict and effective international control.'

47 In a similar vein and from an institutional perspective, I recently argued for a renaissance of attention to the International Court of Justice's role as a judicial check upon the Security Council. To avoid redundancy, I will not pursue that line of thought here. See Joyner (n. 28), ch. 5.

48 I. Brownlie, *Principles of Public International Law* (7th edn, Oxford: Oxford University Press, 2008), 510–11.

rights, in customary international law having attained *jus cogens* status, but they are considerably more controversial. These include the principle of permanent sovereignty over natural resources, and the principle of self-determination.[49] Indeed, the status and substance of these principles, even as rules of customary international law, is disputed.[50] Thus, to date, clear *jus cogens* status has been attained almost exclusively by rules of international law which prevent states from using their authority and power to harm individuals.

However, an important new data point was created in this area by the European Court of Justice (ECJ) in its 2008 decision in the *Kadi* case.[51] In this case, the ECJ struck down an EU Council regulation which had frozen the financial assets of Mr Kadi and Mr Al Barakaat. This EU regulation was in direct implementation of UN Security Council resolutions requiring the enforcement by UN member states of financial sanctions against persons designated by the Council's Sanctions Committee as being involved in international terrorism. The ECJ struck down the regulation because it determined that it violated certain fundamental due process rights guaranteed to EU nationals under EU law.

The *Kadi* decision is important because, *inter alia*, it stands for the proposition that the UN Security Council cannot override domestic law when that domestic law contains fundamental legal rights. The case thus establishes an important persuasive precedent of the principle that the power of the Security Council is not, in fact, unlimited.

This landmark case may mark the beginning of attempts by states to create and apply principles of international law which limit the Security Council's Chapter VII authority, and secure to them and their citizens a measure of legal protection from overly aggressive uses of the Council's authority. If so, one avenue to pursue would be the clarification of the basic rights which inure to states by virtue of their sovereignty, and the establishment of these rights as rules of *jus cogens* – supplementing the existing corpus of *jus cogens* rules which, as noted above, currently consist almost exclusively of rules prohibiting state conduct.

This notion of delineating the basic rights which states possess by virtue of their statehood is not new. As Sir Arthur Watts has explained:

49 On natural resources, see UNGA Resolutions 3171 (XXVIII) (17 December 1973) and 3281 (XXIX) (12 December 1974). On self-determination, see Judge Ammoun, *Barcelona Traction Case* (Second Phase) (Separate Opinion, 5 February 1970), ICJ Reports 304. The concept of self-determination is not strictly speaking a right of states, but more precisely the right of a people in a particular geographical place to constitute a state. However, it is sufficiently similar to a state entitlement for the analytical purposes herein.

50 On natural resources see, e.g. the Interlocutory Award in the case concerning *SEDCO, Inc.* v. *National Iranian Oil Company and the Islamic Republic of Iran*, Iran–U. Claims Tribunal, 10 Iran–US Cl. Rep. 180 (1986). On self-determination, see, e.g. *Reference re Secession of Quebec* (1998) 2 SCR 217 (Supreme Court of Canada).

51 Joined Cases C-402P and C-415/05P, *Yassin Abdullah Kadi and Al Barakaat International Foundation* v. *Council of the European Union and the Commission of the European Communities* [2008] ECR I-6351.

> As international law developed in the second half of the nineteenth century and the first half of the twentieth it was thought useful, and perhaps even necessary, to consider whether there were some fundamental legal principles which were inherent in the relations of States as members of the international community. The search for some hierarchical structure to the many particular rules of international law seemed to require no less. The idea grew that there were certain fundamental rights which were essential and self-evident attributes of Statehood, together with certain fundamental duties.[52]

In 1949 the newly established International Law Commission (ILC) adopted a draft Declaration on Rights and Duties of States. This draft Declaration consisted of 14 draft articles which enunciated, in broad terms, some of the basic rights and duties of states. The 1949 draft Declaration was never adopted by the General Assembly, and largely fell by the wayside as geopolitical shifts over the subsequent decades – notably including the process of decolonization and the communist–capitalist rivalry between East and West – made agreement on a statement of states' 'fundamental' rights increasingly difficult. In 1970, however, a successor statement to the 1949 draft articles was adopted by the General Assembly, entitled the Declaration on Principles of International Law concerning Friendly Relations and Cooperation among States.[53] This 1970 Declaration predominantly discussed states' obligations, such as the obligation not to use or threaten force against other states, or otherwise to intervene in the affairs of other states. However, in its discussion of the principle of the sovereign equality of states, it does delineate some of the most basic rights of states, including the right of any state 'freely to choose and develop its political, social, economic and cultural systems'.

Both the 1949 draft Declaration, and the 1970 Declaration can be described as something of a jumble of proclamations of the rights and duties of states, with no clear systematic approach to either subject, and certainly no claim to an exhaustive listing of either rights or duties. The lack of progress since 1970 on a clear and definitive statement of the rights of states inuring to them by virtue of their statehood is likely explained by a number of factors. The first is simply the enormity of the task of getting agreement by states as to which rights are 'fundamental' among the bundle of rights which states inherently possess. The very notion of fundamental rights of states is likely to be seen quite differently by developing and developed states, and by states with different approaches to economics and government.

The second factor is the concern, often present in delineation of entitlements, that the listing of some rights will appear to prejudice others not listed, and have a limiting effect upon the subject. This dynamic was analogously present

52 A. Watts (ed.), *The International Law Commission: 1949–1998*, vol. 3 (Oxford: Oxford University Press, 1999), 1645.

53 UNGA Res. 2625 (XXV) (24 October 1970).

in the deliberations surrounding the drafting of the United States Constitution, and resulted in a compromise approach whereby nine amendments were added to the original document listing the rights of the constituent states of the United States, or in some cases the people of those states, yet a tenth amendment was added to make clear that the enumerated rights were not an exhaustive rendering, and that '[t]he powers not delegated to the United States by the Constitution, nor prohibited by it to the States, are reserved to the States respectively, or to the people'.

However, the Security Council's new interpretation of the extent of its authority, and the arguable use of the Council by the permanent five as an instrument for promoting their own political interests, may make a return to this normative effort advisable. The ILC spent the better part of fifty years developing its Draft Articles on State Responsibility for Internationally Wrongful Acts, which it finally adopted in 2001. The development of a similar set of Draft Articles on the Fundamental Rights of States would seem to be a naturally complementary project for the ILC to now pursue. Such a normative delineation and clarification of the rights of states inherently inuring to them by virtue of their statehood, and recognized in customary international law, would be the first evolutionary step towards those rights eventually achieving *jus cogens* status and thereby constituting a set of needed limitations on the currently seemingly unlimited authority of the United Nations Security Council.

Thus, to return to the case study of Iran, if the inalienable right to peaceful nuclear energy technologies recognized in Article IV of the NPT were to be recognized as among the fundamental rights of states, and thereby achieve the status of a rule of *jus cogens*, this would form an effective legal curtailment of the authority of the Security Council to restrict this fundamental right, and would serve to protect developing countries in their exercise of this right. Other fundamental rights relative to the case studies reviewed herein might include the right not to be bound by international legal obligations to which a state has not expressly or impliedly consented. Such a delineation of the fundamental rights of states and their establishment as rules of *jus cogens* would constitute something of an international 'bill of rights' for states, which could be structured, as the bill of rights in the US Constitution, to expressly provide for the non-exhaustive nature of the delineated rights.

This notion of an international bill of rights for states is of course only one avenue whereby states can begin to draw lines in the sand, setting limits upon the authority of the Security Council. Others include the more ad hoc approach adopted by the ECJ in the *Kadi* case, as well as the strengthening of the authority of the International Court of Justice to more effectively act as a co-equal judicial check upon the Council. However it is pursued, it appears that the international legal system must develop effective limits upon the authority of the Security Council, lest the Council become an effective legal hegemon, unbound by law.

4 Using force in international affairs

The role of international law in contemporary international politics

Dominika Švarc

It is the harshest test of international law, perhaps an unfair test, to ask whether and how it affected the decisions and acts of men who saw themselves as grappling with issues of national survival.[1]

International law works in mysterious ways.[2]

4.1 Introduction

Questions about the role and relevance of international law in international politics are not new. They have, however, acquired new intensities and dimensions in our increasingly complex world, particularly when it comes to the use of force in international relations. Recent military interventions in Kosovo, Afghanistan, Iraq, Southern Lebanon and Georgia have been accompanied by polarized debates about the role of law in decision making on the use of force. Authors such as Glennon[3] and Arend[4] have interpreted the lack of compliance (or less-than-perfect compliance) in these situations, especially in the case of the Iraq War in 2003, as evidence of impotence, irrelevance and even 'death' of international legal rules and institutions designed to regulate the use of force in international affairs. Similarly, Franck alluded to his long-held doubts about the viability of the UN Charter Article 2(4) prohibition on the use of force by bitterly remarking that on 19 March 2003, this quintessential principle of international legal order was merely

1 A. Chayes, *The Cuban Missile Crisis: The Cuban Missile Crisis, International Crisis and the Role of Law* (Lanham, MD: University Press of America, 1974) 1.

2 G. Simpson, 'Duelling Agendas: International Relations and International Law (Again)' (2005) 1(1–2) *Journal of International Law and International Relations* 61, 72.

3 M. J. Glennon, 'Why the Security Council Failed' (2003) 82(3) *Foreign Affairs* 16, 24.

4 A. C. Arend, 'International Law and the Preemptive Use of Military Force' (2003) 26(2) *Washington Quarterly* 89, 101.

killed again.[5] Others, such as Charlesworth[6] and Falk,[7] have seen in these events, and in the use of legal arguments that accompanied them, a confirmation of the validity and weight of the international law on the use of force in the contemporary world.

This chapter contributes to the ongoing debates by looking at some of the pathways through which international law may affect the political processes and outcomes in this sensitive area of international political life. In order to do so, the chapter builds on different perspectives of both international law (IL) and international relations (IR) scholarship on the role of international law in international politics.

The predominant positivist IL scholarship has largely neglected the need for explanatory models for the functioning of international law. The American transnational legal process school is practically the only theoretical approach in legal theory that offers some assumptions and theoretical suggestions regarding the functioning of international law in the broader context of international politics, based primarily on the empirical analysis of specific cases.[8] However, more general elaborated models about the role of international law in international affairs are rare. One example is Falk's categorization of the different functions of international law as that of constraint, coordination of different political preferences, stabilization of international interaction, facilitating cooperation and shaping of shared expectations about the appropriate behaviour in international relations.[9] From a different perspective, Henkin has distinguished between three main functions of international law: coordination, reputation and communication.[10] More recently, Onuma categorized the general functions of international law in international society as the binding, communicative, value-declaratory and justifying and legitimating functions of international law.[11]

Apart from these examples, the search for explanatory models of the role of international law in international politics has traditionally remained in the domain of IR scholarship, which in turn has centred mainly on the direct constraining effect (or the lack thereof) on a state's behaviour. When viewed from this angle, the role of international law is reduced to that of a source of

5 See T. M. Franck, 'Who Killed Article 2 (4)? Or: The Changing Norms Governing the Use of Force by States' (1970) 64 AJIL 809; Cf. T. M. Franck, 'The Use of Force in International Law' (2003) 11 *Tulane Journal of International and Comparative Law* 7.

6 H. Charlesworth, 'Saddam Hussein: My Part in His Downfall' (2003) 23 *Wis.Int'l L.J.* 127.

7 R. A. Falk, *The Costs of War: International Law, the UN, and World Order* (London: Routledge, 2008).

8 See e.g. Chayes (n. 1); F. A. Boyle, *World Politics and International Law* (Durham, NC: Duke University Press, 1985).

9 R. A. Falk, 'The Relevance of Political Context to the Nature and Functioning of International Law: An Intermediate View', in K. W. Deutsch and S. Hoffman (eds.), *The Relevance of International Law: Essays in Honor of Leo Gross* (Cambridge, MA: Schenkman Publishing Company, 1968).

10 L. Henkin, *How Nations Behave: Law and Foreign Policy* (New York, NY: Columbia University Press, 1979).

11 Y. Onuma, 'International Law in and with International Politics: The Functions of International Law in International Society' (2003) 14 EJIL 105.

ex post facto justifications for political decisions taken on the basis of extra-legal factors such as national interest and power politics[12] or to a functional instrument influencing states' strategic calculations regarding the most efficient ways of maximizing their particular interests.[13] Recently, post-positivist critical approaches in IR, particularly constructivism, have opened up space for a broader and more dynamic understanding of the functioning and the relevance of international legal norms and institutions in international politics, by looking at the more subtle, indirect ways in which they may affect the course and outcomes of international politics.[14]

These different understandings are all taken into account in this chapter, the subjects of which, however, are not the classic questions of whether, to what extent and under what conditions, international law 'matters' in states' decision making with respect to the use of force. Instead, this chapter explores how international law operates in the broader context of international politics and in what ways it may (or may not) structure, shape and alter the processes and outcomes of contemporary international politics in this area.

The analysis is divided into two parts. Drawing from the existing theoretical explanations of IL and IR theories, the first part develops a set of theoretical propositions concerning two important mechanisms through which international law may affect the political processes with respect to the use of force: first, as a regulatory framework, providing a set of legal parameters delimiting the range of acceptable policy choices; and second, as a framework for legitimation, providing an authoritative, relatively autonomous, and most commonly shared source and measure of legitimacy of political action. In order to illustrate these theoretical propositions, the second part looks at the role of international law on the use of force in the processes of shaping, justifying and evaluating the decision of the US, the UK and their allies, to invade Iraq in March 2003. This example provides a powerful manifestation of the complexity of pathways through which international law may (or may not) affect the course of contemporary international politics.

12 See e.g. H. J. Morgenthau, *Politics among Nations: The Struggle for Power and Peace* (7th edn, Boston, MA: McGraw-Hill Higher Education, 2006); J. L. Goldsmith and E. A. Posner, *The Limits of International Law* (New York, NY: Oxford University Press, 2005).

13 See e.g. R. O. Keohane, 'Compliance with International Commitments: Politics within a Framework of Law' (1992) 85 ASIL PROC. 176; R. O. Keohane, 'International Relations and International Law: Two Optics' (1997) 38 HILJ 487.

14 See e.g. F. Kratochwil, *Rules, Norms, and Decisions: On the Conditions of Practical And Legal Reasoning in International Relations and Domestic Affairs* (Cambridge: Cambridge University Press, 1989); N. Greenwood Onuf, 'Constructivism: A User's Manual', in V. Kubálková, N. Onuf and P Kowert (eds.), *International Relations in a Constructed World* (Armonk, NY: ME Sharp, 1998); M. Finnemore and K. Sikkink, 'International Norm Dynamics and Political Change' (1998) 52 *Int'l Org.* 887; J. Brunnée and S. J. Toope, 'International Law and Constructivism: Elements of an Interactional Theory of International Law' (2001) 39 CJTL 19.

4.2 Theorizing the role of international law in international politics

4.2.1 International law as constraint: transcending causality

In a basic sense, international law operates as the regulatory framework of international politics. It provides a set of formalized and legally binding substantive and institutional rules, which prohibit, request, or allow certain behaviours. The primary purpose of these rules is to constrain choices by excluding certain policy options as legally unacceptable, but they also enable action by creating and defining relevant categories of behaviour and by permitting certain conduct.[15]

In relation to the use of force in international relations, the UN Charter-based paradigm primarily constrains states' freedom of action by outlawing military force as a tool of international relations.[16] At the same time, this legal framework also enables military action by determining when, in what manner, and for what purposes, states may resort to military force in the international arena. It allows them to act differently from the 'normal' course of action in exceptional circumstances with a Security Council mandate or in the exercise of their inherent right of self-defence.[17] International legal rules on the use of force thus delimit the range of acceptable policy choices in international relations and constrain states' freedom of action as parameters within which they may individually or collectively shape their political decisions about the use of force in order to pursuit their political objectives, values and interests.[18]

This basic understanding of international law as constraint has always been the focus of both IL and IR scholarship. IR theorists, in particular, have struggled to find ways to prove or measure this constraining effect or the lack thereof in real-life situations. In so doing, the prevailing rationalist IR approaches have centred almost exclusively on the direct, causal impact of international legal rules and institutions on political outcomes, that is to say on the question whether, to what extent, and under what conditions, international law and institutions directly determine actual political decisions and actions of states in international relations. The answers have been sought mainly through standard causal models based on empirical analysis of the extent of compliance between the international legal rules and actual state

15 See A. J. Hurrell, '"There are no Rules" (George W. Bush): International Order after September 11' (2002) 16(2) *International Relations* 185, 186.

16 Mainly under Arts. 2(3) and 2(4) and Chapter VII of the UN Charter.

17 See Chapter VII of the United Nations Charter, esp. Arts. 39, 42 and 51.

18 See e.g. D. W. Coplin, *The Functions of International Law: An Introduction to the Role of International Law in the Contemporary World* (Chicago, IL: Rand McNally, 1966); Chayes (n. 1), 25; Henkin (n. 10), 43; Hurrell (n. 15), 186; A. Björkdahl, 'Norms in International Relations: Some Conceptual and Methodological Reflections' (2002) 15(1) *Cambridge Review of International Affairs* 9, 15 and 22.

action in a concrete situation, i.e. by identifying correlations between the normative and empirical in international life.[19]

While it may seem the closest one can get to a 'scientific' explanation of the constraining effect of international law, this approach is plagued by many conceptual and methodological flaws which significantly reduce its analytical value. Although a thorough exploration of these problems would exceed the scope of this chapter, a few basic observations can be made. To start with, the standard causal analysis builds on the assumption that causes are responsible for effects[20] and requires as a precondition a clear definition of the dependent and independent variables, in this case of international law and international politics. Yet, international law and international politics cannot truly be conceived as categorically separate spheres of social action.[21] International law is only one of many factors that may (or may not) influence states' political decisions in given situations. Its impact always needs to be evaluated in connection with non-legal rationales for political action, such as economic, national-security and moral.[22] Even if one could separate these factors, it would be practically impossible to 'measure' the relative weight of each factor on the final political outcome.

Moreover, the fundamental flaw of the causal analysis is that it can only serve to prove the absence of any direct constraining effect of international law. Where state conduct is incompatible with the international legal rule(s), the causal approach leads to a conclusion that other, non-legal factors prevailed in the decision-making process, that is to say that international law did not determine the political outcome.[23] However, when a state acts in compliance with international legal rules, the conclusion is less clear: a state may have complied either because it felt legally obliged to do so or simply because the relevant legal rule complemented its national interests, that is to say, there was no conflict between the legal and non-legal considerations relevant to the particular decision-making process. Any claim about the positive direct effect of international legal rules on actual behaviour is thus unavoidably exposed to a powerful counter-argument that compliance is merely a result of coincidence.[24] An analysis based on a comparison between the normative and

19 R. O. Keohane, 'Rational Choice Theory and International Law: Insights and Limitations' (2002) 31 JLS s. 307, s. 313.

20 A. S. Yee, 'The Causal Effects of Ideas on Policies' (1996) 50(1) *Int'l Org.* 69, 70.

21 This has been elaborated elsewhere, see e.g. F. Kratochwil, 'How Do Norms Matter?', in M. Byers (ed.), *The Role of Law in International Politics: Essays in International Relations and International Law* (Oxford: Oxford University Press, 2000), 37–43; C. Reus-Smit, 'Introduction', in C Reus-Smit (ed.), *The Politics of International Law* (Cambridge: Cambridge University Press, 2004), 2.

22 Onuma (n. 11), 125–6.

23 Morgenthau (n. 12), 282; S. Hoffman, 'International Law and the Control of Force', in K. W. Deutsch and S. Hoffman (eds.), *The Relevance of International Law: Essays in Honor of Leo Gross* (Cambridge, MA: Schenkman Publishing Company, 1968), 38.

24 See e.g. Goldsmith and Posner (n. 12), 39 claiming that states never act out of a feeling of 'legal obligation', but rather always on the basis of rational calculations of their own particular interests. For a similar assertion see Hoffman (n. 23), 37.

actual behaviour of states can prove the irrelevance of international legal rules and institutions but it cannot prove beyond doubt any constructive, positive effect of these rules and institutions on international political processes and outcomes.[25] With this being the prevailing approach in IR theory, it is not surprising that for decades it was almost 'anachronistic to suggest that law might have something to do with the high politics of international security'.[26]

The regulatory role of international legal rules and institutions can (and should) be understood in a broader sense, as transcending the limited image of causal relationships and deterministic effects. It is quite possible to accept that international rules and institutions may not (always) directly cause or prevent certain conduct or that these effects simply cannot be empirically proved without altogether negating any constraining impact of international law in the overall decision-making concerning the use of force. As observed by Puchala and Hopkins, leaders almost always feel constrained by principles, norms and rules, prescribing and prohibiting different forms of behaviour; they try, for most part, to stay within this normative framework.[27] Leaders will try, at least at the outset, to avoid options which are clearly incompatible with the existing international legal parameters of the use of force. They will, even in extreme situations, seek to shape their political decisions and actions regarding the use of force through existing normative options, frequently different from the available political options.[28] Eventually, these considerations may lead to a rejection of certain policy alternatives as (legally) unacceptable for the furtherance of particular political objectives, or they might at least encourage the decision makers to direct their choice from a legally clearly unacceptable measure to more acceptable options.[29]

In adopting and exploring this broader understanding of the indirect constraining power of international law, institutionalist and constructivist IR literature often compares it with that of traffic rules: although these rules cannot directly determine state behaviour, they operate as behavioural standards that can guide actors in their decision making[30] and may indirectly affect their political choices through various pathways.

In the institutionalist reading, international law may affect actors' rational calculations of the relationship between their particular objectives and alternative political strategies and means for the realization of these objectives.[31] According to this understanding, international law on the use of

25 See also Chayes (n. 1), 35.

26 M. Koskenniemi, 'The Place of Law in Collective Security' (1996) 17 MJIL 455, 455.

27 D. J. Puchala and R. F. Hopkins, 'International Regimes: Lessons from Inductive Analysis' 36(2) *Int'l Org.* 245, 270. See also T. M. Franck, *The Power of Legitimacy among Nations* (New York, NY: Oxford University Press, 1990), 3–4.

28 Franck (n. 27).

29 See Björkdahl (n. 18), 23.

30 See Boyle (n. 8), 80–1and Björkdahl (n. 18), 15.

31 Chayes (n. 1), 102.

force functions as some sort of a 'shadow of future'[32] (the likelihood and importance of future interactions). Aware of the relatively regular and durable nature of their mutual relations and the benefits of cooperation, states seek to shape their political decisions within the limits imposed by international law. Two main factors shape this attitude: the risks of negative consequences of non-compliant behaviour for their future international interactions,[33] and the positive expectation that other states will likewise act in accordance with international law in order to make international interactions more predictable, more stable and thus more effective.[34] In this way, international law on the use of force may indirectly constrain the choice between alternative strategies for realization of their individual or collective political goals, values, interests and preferences,[35] while simultaneously facilitating the pursuit of such goals through stabilization and greater predictability of international political life.[36]

This does not necessarily imply that legal considerations will prevail over the non-legal ones. As with any legal system, states can choose to act in violation of international law if they are willing to risk the negative consequences of non-compliant behaviour. Nonetheless, states (even the most powerful ones) understand that the existence and implementation of international law normally brings about more benefits than the absence of any international legal constraints.[37] In his study of the role of international law on the use of force in the context of the 1962 Cuban Missile Crisis, Chayes aptly captured this understanding by describing how international law on the use of force 'promotes or discourages conduct by a subtle intermixture of a broad range of inducements and penalties' and through a cautious allocation of 'benefits and burdens, opportunities and risks, often in ways whose relation to the activity to be influenced seems remote or subterranean'.[38] In sum, viewed from the institutionalist perspective, compliant behaviour is simply in the rational interest of all states, searching for the most effective ways of long-term maximization of their individual or collective interests.[39]

Through a constructivist theoretical lens, however, international rules and institutions can have an even deeper, constitutive effect, expanding beyond the rational–institutionalist functionalist explanation. Not only can rules influence the way states rationally calculate the most effective ways to maximize their interests and preferences, but they may also affect the way

32 R. Axelrod, *The Evolution of Cooperation* (New York, NY: Basic Books, 1984), 174–5.

33 Such as reputational costs, diplomatic or economic sanctions and other negative consequences that almost inevitably follow legally incompatible actions; see K. W. Abbott and D. Snidal, 'Hard and Soft Law in International Governance' (2000) 54 *Int'l Org.* 421, 427.

34 See K. A. Oye, 'Explaining Cooperation Under Anarchy: Hypotheses and Strategies' (1985) 38(1) *World Politics* 1, 12–18. See also A. T. Guzman, 'A Compliance-based Theory of International Law' (2002) 90 CLR 1823, 1844–51.

35 See e.g. Falk (n. 7), 145; Finnemore and Sikkink (n. 14), 891; Onuf (n. 14), 59; Hurrell (n. 15), 186.

36 Boyle (n. 8), 80.

37 *Ibid.* 80–1.

38 Chayes (n. 1), 25.

39 *Ibid.*

states shape their own individual and/or collective preferences in a given situation, even in such sensitive area as the use of force.[40] As a specific social structure, international law articulates shared expectations about the very nature of international political life, defines standards of appropriate behaviour which guide social action, and shapes the space within which states perceive their own identities and interests, and within which they connect these identities and interests with the available political alternatives for their realization in specific circumstances.[41] Specifically, the UN-based paradigm on the use of force is an eloquent expression of the virtually universally shared belief that peace is the central common value of the international community. Peace is to be preserved if at all possible, whilst force may only be employed as a last resort and 'in the common interest'.[42]

As an expression of such inter-subjective values and objectives, international law on the use of force fulfils another important aspirational function in contemporary international politics. According to Gray, it 'set[s] out the goal to be aimed at, the ideal that states adhere to'.[43] In this way, international law further indirectly affects the way states perceive situations and how they shape and perceive their own identities and interests in these situations, as well as the way they perceive the means available to them for the furtherance of their interests.[44] Its rules signal a shared normative understanding that 'peace-loving states' do not use force to pursue their interests.[45] International law on the use of force inevitably affects states' self-perception of their interests and identities and thus indirectly constrains their political choices, even when it cannot define and predict more than a range of possible choices.

4.2.2 International law as the source and measure of legitimacy

International law also operates as the main framework of 'legitimization discourse',[46] in which states shape, communicate and evaluate claims and

40 For further discussions on this see Hurrell (n. 15) and C. Reus-Smit, 'The Politics of International Law', in C Reus-Smit (ed.), *The Politics of International Law* (Cambridge: Cambridge University Press, 2004) 21.

41 See among others Kratochwil (n. 14); Onuf (n. 14); Finnemore and Sikkink (n. 14); Björkdahl (n. 18), 22; Hurrell (n. 15), 186.

42 United Nations Charter, Preamble.

43 C. Gray, *International Law and the Use of Force* (3rd edn, Oxford: Oxford University Press, 2008), 27.

44 See e.g. R. K. Herrmann and V. P. Shannon, 'Defending International Norms: The Role of Obligation, Material Interest, and Perception in Decision Making' (2001) 55 *Int'l Org.* 621, 623; Hurrell (n. 15), 186; Reus-Smit (n. 40), 21.

45 Save in extreme circumstances and primarily on the basis of a collective decision taken within the Security Council.

46 A. Chayes and A. Handler Chayes, *The New Sovereignty: Compliance with International Regulatory Agreements* (Cambridge, MA: Harvard University Press, 1995); T. M. Franck, *Fairness in International Law and International Institutions* (New York, NY: Oxford University Press, 1995); Ian Johnstone, 'Security Council Deliberations: The Power of the Better Argument' (2003) 14 EJIL 437, 437; Reus-Smit (n. 41), 19–21.

counter-claims about the acceptability of their particular policies and actions regarding the use of force. The UN Charter-based rules on the use of force serve as the expression of the prevailing shared understandings about the appropriate behaviour in international relations. As such, they offer accepted standards, on the basis of which states and other relevant actors can evaluate the legitimacy of the political decisions and behaviour of other states and decide which states' political decisions and behaviour must be justified in order to be perceived as legitimate.[47] The rules of international law on the use of force provide the most widely accepted source and measure of legitimacy of actions that involve the use of force.

In practice states regularly rationalize and justify their political decisions concerning the use of force by reference to the key substantive and institutional rules on the use of force, as codified in the UN Charter: either as an exercise of self-defence or as an exercise based on the Security Council authorization or both.[48] According to Gray,[49] it rarely happens that states do not offer any legal explanation of their policies or actions.[50] As Franck[51] has pointed out, this is true even with respect to the most powerful states. It is important to emphasize that states regularly offer legal justifications even though there is no international legal rule obliging them to do so.[52] This need for the legal justification of political decisions and actions confirms the relevance of international law on the use of force in international politics.[53] Among the range of instrumental or non-instrumental factors that may explain this need for finding some legal justification for action,[54] one important reason is what Westra called the 'expectation of compliance'.[55] Acting states are aware that other states expect them to be able to justify their behaviour in terms of international law and that they will normally evaluate this behaviour as either acceptable or unacceptable on the basis of its formal legal validity, that is to

47 See R. A. Falk, 'The Interplay of Westphalia and Charter Conceptions of International Legal Order', in R. A. Falk and CE Black (eds.), *The Future of the International Legal Order* (Princeton, NJ: Princeton University Press, 1969), 33–54; see also Chayes (n. 1), 43–4; Boyle (n. 8), 177; S. V. Scott, 'International Law as Ideology: Theorizing the Relationship between International Law and International Politics' (1994) 5 EJIL 313, 324.

48 See O. Schachter, 'The Right of States to Use Armed Force' (1984) 82 *Mich.L.Rev.* 1620, 1623; Gray (n. 43), 22–3.

49 Gray (n. 43).

50 Rare examples include the Turkish cross-border incursions into Northern Iraq in the 1990s and in 2007, and the NATO intervention in Kosovo in 1999.

51 Franck (n. 27), 196–204.

52 This need to justify actions on the basis of international law has been highlighted by authors in both IR and IL literature as a sign that state action cannot be adequately explained only in terms of national interest and power politics; see e.g. Chayes and Chayes (n. 46), 118; A. J. Hurrell, 'International Society and the Study of Regimes: A Reflective Approach', in Volker Rittberger (ed.), *Regime Theory and International Relations* (Oxford: Clarendon Press, 1993), 61.

53 See Chayes and Chayes (n. 46); Franck (n. 46); Gray (n. 43), 22–3.

54 For a broader discussion, see Johnstone (n. 46) 441–3.

55 J. H. Westra, *International Law and the Use of Armed Force: the UN Charter and the Major Powers* (New York, NY: Routledge, 2007), 21.

say its compatibility with the established standards of international law on the use of force.[56]

States apparently believe that by acting within the frameworks of international legal rules and institutions they can strengthen the perceived legitimacy and acceptability of their actions regarding the use of force in ways that the mere observation of non-legal (political, moral or other social) norms cannot secure.[57] Of course, states also regularly offer non-legal justifications but they rarely claim that such non-legal factors can legitimize otherwise illegal behaviour.[58] As Bjola pointed out, 'moral and political justifications represent a necessary step for building up the legitimacy of an intervention, but the main challenge is to find the proper way to translate them into legally sound arguments'.[59] The limits of legitimacy are ultimately the limits articulated in international legal concepts and standards determining the scope of appropriate use of force, such as 'armed attack', 'breach of the peace', 'self-defence', 'necessity' or 'proportionality'. Despite their inherently political origin and certain interpretative openness, these concepts and standards offer a different objective and authoritative basis for the justification and evaluation of political decisions and actions than the non-legal (political, ethical or other social) factors that prevailed in the period when international law had not yet limited the discretion of states to use force in their international relations.[60]

All this inevitably provokes the realist response that states, particularly the most powerful ones, merely use international law as a tool for the attainment of their own particular political objectives, values and preferences.[61] According to realism, concepts and rules of international law, particularly those regulating the use of force, are fundamentally indeterminate and immensely adjustable; through creative interpretation and reinterpretation of these rules they may be ultimately invoked to legitimize almost any form of behaviour and provide a 'veil of legitimacy' for otherwise questionable political decisions.[62] This is a serious accusation. It would be unrealistic to ignore the impressive creativity of some governments and their legal advisers in composing more or less

56 See Henkin (n. 10), 41.

57 See e.g. Chayes and Chayes (n. 46); Franck (n. 46); C. Bjola, 'Legitimating the Use of Force in International Politics: A Communicative Action Perspective' (2005) 11 EJIL 266, 283.

58 With the obvious exception of NATO's intervention in Kosovo in 1999. For discussion of the conflation of legal, political and ethical arguments in that context, see e.g. N. Krisch, 'Legality, Morality and the Dilemma of Humanitarian Intervention after Kosovo' (2002) 13 EJIL 323.

59 Bjola (n. 57), 283.

60 See Falk (n. 47), 62–3.

61 See Morgenthau (n. 12), 288; see also J. L. Goldsmith and E. A. Posner, 'Moral and Legal Rhetoric in International Relations: A Rational Choice Perspective' (2002) 31(1) JLS s. 115, ss. 119–20; J. Mearsheimer, *The Tragedy of Great Power Politics* (New York, NY: WW Norton, 2001), 23.

62 See Bjola (n. 57), 275 and 283; S. V. Scott and O. Ambler, 'Does Legality *Really* Matter? Accounting for the Decline in US Foreign Policy Legitimacy Following the 2003 Invasion of Iraq' (2007) 13 EJIL 67, 73. M. Koskenniemi also criticized this 'over-legitimizing' nature of international law (*From Apology to Utopia: The Structure of International Legal Argument* (Cambridge: Cambridge University Press, 1989), 48).

persuasive legal justifications for their controversial policies and decisions with regard to the use of force. Sometimes, as in the case of the 2003 Iraq invasion, this 'creativity' turns into an open and shameless manipulation and stretching of the established legal rules, or their widely accepted interpretation, in an attempt to bestow legitimacy on controversial military action.[63]

To an extent, this instrumentalization is inherent in the very nature of international legal discourse, its relative indeterminacy and interpretative openness and susceptibility to pragmatic argumentation. As with any legal or normative system, this space of epistemological uncertainty provides the actors with a certain degree of freedom as they construct justifications for their behaviour, and enables political manoeuvring in international relations under the mask of the 'alleged objectivity of legal analysis'.[64] This is further intensified by the horizontal and decentralized nature of the international legal order, which implies an even broader range of interpretative discretion by the principal actors (states). In the absence of an effective supranational body with the ultimate authority to pass judgments on the validity of political actions and the legal arguments used to support them, acting states remain the primary interpreters of the legal rules they seek to apply and invoke.[65]

Nonetheless, this space for political manipulation in legitimation discourse is not unlimited. One of its most important limitations is what Falk called an 'imperfect measure of symmetry'[66] in the international legal order; that is to say an awareness that the claims of right that one nation asserts must be, at least in principle, available for evaluations by an external 'jury of peers',[67] comprising other states as well as other relevant actors, such as international political and judicial institutions,[68] legal experts and the general public. The reactions of these external jurors in almost all cases of dubious military excursions into other states' territories show that regardless of their 'good' or 'bad' intentions, states cannot do and say whatever they please when it comes to using force.[69] Not every possible interpretation of an international legal rule will be accepted as a valid legal argument by other states, epistemic communities or the general public, who will ultimately evaluate the legal nature and legitimacy of any given political decision or action on the basis of

63 See Boyle (n. 8), 60; Falk (n. 7), 140; N. Krisch, 'Unilateral Enforcement of the Collective Will: Kosovo, Iraq, and the Security Council' (1999) 3 *Max Planck Yearbook of United Nations Law* 59; Bjola (n. 57), 267.

64 A. L. Paulus, 'International Law After Postmodernism: Towards Renewal or Decline of International Law?' (2001) 14 LJIL 727, 732.

65 See Falk (n. 7), 138–9.

66 *Ibid.* 139.

67 Franck (n. 5), 15–16; see also O. Schachter, 'Self-Defense and the Rule of Law' (1989) 83 AJIL 259, 264.

68 E.g., the Security Council, the General Assembly and other political bodies, as well as the International Court of Justice.

69 See Y. Dinstein, *War, Aggression, and Self-defence* (Cambridge: Cambridge University Press, 2004), 89.

widely accepted and established standards and concepts of international law.[70] The argument of implied (or revived) authorization in the case of Iraq, the stretched interpretations of the self-defence standards in the cases of Southern Lebanon, Georgia, and others – whatever 'instrumental' or 'manipulative' or 'pragmatic' arguments and justifications were put forth, they were normally met by powerful counter-claims of the invasions' 'formal illegality'. Such 'external' evaluation importantly strengthens the autonomous normative value of international legal arguments and reduces the risks arising out of attempted political manipulation of these arguments in order to justify otherwise illegitimate behaviour. That the language of international law leaves room for some interpretative flexibility and political discretion does not lead to the conclusion that states can politically (ab)use any rule of international law or that with support of sufficiently creative legal advisers, any political decision or action could be successfully justified on the basis of international law.

These propositions do not purport to overlook the important role of power in the legitimation discourse. As Falk pointed out, both de facto and institutionalized 'inequalities of power introduce some asymmetry'[71] into this process, which to some extent may strengthen the normative claims of powerful state(s) in comparison with their weaker counterparts and in principle allows for 'arguments of power' to prevail over the 'power of arguments'.[72] Nonetheless, even the relative power position cannot on its own guarantee successful legitimization of the state's political decisions and actions. Authors of both IL and IR literature have emphasized that the persuasiveness of arguments used in justification of states' military action ultimately hinges on their perceived legal validity, based on shared beliefs about the scope and content of international legal rules on the use of force.[73]

Therefore, while power and national interests inevitably affect the use of legal arguments in the legitimization process, international legal arguments retain their relatively autonomous normative power and offer an independent, objective measure for evaluating the legitimacy of any given policy or action with respect to the use of force, even in relation to the most powerful states. Even 'instrumental' or 'manipulative' reasoning takes place within the 'formal' structures of international institutional and material legal norms which ultimately constrain it. Henkin wrote: 'The fact that nations feel obliged to justify their actions under international law, that justifications must have

70 See e.g. D. Kristiotis, 'When States Use Armed Force', in C. Reus-Smit (ed.), *The Politics of International Law* (Cambridge: Cambridge University Press, 2004), 63; Falk (n. 7), 151.

71 Falk (n. 7), 139–40.

72 This can be observed in a number of Security Council debates on controversial unilateral military actions which never led to a condemning resolution because of a veto exercised by one or more of the permanent members. For discussion, see Johnstone (n. 46).

73 See among others Chayes (n. 1), 42; T. Risse, '"Let's Argue!": Communicative Action in World Politics' (2000) 54 *Int'l Org.* 1, 9–10; Onuma (n. 11), 131 and 136; S. J. Toope, 'Emerging Patterns of Governance and International Law', in M. Byers (ed.), *The Role of Law in International Politics: Essays in International Relations and International Law* (Oxford: Oxford University Press, 2000).

plausibility, that plausible justifications are often unavailable or limited, inevitably affects how nations will act'.[74] Even the most powerful states will normally refrain from invoking unpersuasive normative arguments, the rejection of which could seriously damage not only the perceived legitimacy of their action(s) but also their broader international credibility.

In any case, regardless of the (un)persuasiveness of specific legal arguments used by states to justify their political decisions, the very use of these arguments in the legitimization discourse confirms that states perceive international law as an important structural framework of their international behaviour when it comes to the use of force. It is important that states 'feel' the need to find some plausible legal justification for their actions, even when they are not legally obliged to do so. For good or ill, states apparently prefer power in a legal guise to power without it.[75] In Henkin's words: 'When a nation claims to observe international law to create an image of itself, either in its own eyes or in its neighbors' eyes, it is significant that this is the image which nations value'.[76] When states offer legal arguments to justify their actions, they not only seek to persuade other actors about the legitimacy of their political choice; they also signal their belief that at least in principle, they remain committed to the rule of law and the basic shared principles and values of the international legal order.

4.3 International law and the use of force against Iraq in March 2003

4.3.1 The road to war

The decision to use force against Iraq in March 2003 was officially motivated by the US administration's concerns about Iraq's alleged weapons of mass destruction (WMD) programmes.[77] These concerns, which intensified after the 11 September 2001 terrorist attacks, became the leitmotif of the official US narrative which accused Iraq of continuously violating its international obligations under the relevant international agreements and a series of Security Council resolutions requiring that Iraq fully declare and eliminate its WMD.

In November 2002, the Security Council members, acting at US urging, unanimously adopted Resolution 1441, which confirmed that Iraq 'remains in

74 Henkin (n. 10), 45.

75 See also Hurrell (n. 15), 188–9.

76 Henkin (n. 10), 45.

77 The circumstances and events that led to the decision to attack Iraq in 2003 have been extensively covered elsewhere. See e.g. R. W. Copson, 'Iraq War: Background and Issues Overview' (Congressional Research Service – Report for Congress, April 2003) (at:www.fas.org/man/crs/RL31715.pdf; accessed 18 June 2009); D. M. Malone, *The International Struggle over Iraq: Politics in the UN Security Council, 1980–2005* (Oxford: Oxford University Press, 2006); R. Thakur and W. Pal Singh Sidhu (eds.), *The Iraq Crisis and World Order: Structural, Institutional and Normative Challenges* (Tokyo: United Nations University Press, 2006).

material breach of its obligations'[78] and giving Iraq a final opportunity to 'comply with its disarmament obligations' or 'face serious consequences'.[79] Although the resolution left open to interpretation the question of whether a further Council decision would be needed for military action against Iraq to be lawful,[80] the US and UK administrations used these words as the final brick in building the case for a more aggressive attitude towards Iraq. During January and February 2003, President Bush, other top US officials and UK Prime Minister Tony Blair repeatedly indicated that time was running out for Iraq to voluntarily disarm[81] and that military coercive action was becoming unavoidable.[82] Their speeches fuelled speculation that the US (and the UK) might soon act against Iraq even without a second Security Council resolution. On 26 January 2003, the US Secretary of State Colin Powell told the World Economic Forum in Davos that 'multilateralism cannot be an excuse for inaction' and that the United States 'continues to reserve [its] sovereign right to take military action against Iraq alone or in a coalition of the willing'.[83] Similarly, the UK Prime Minister increasingly considered the military option unavoidable, although he felt less comfortable with the idea of a unilateral strike. He thus continued to advocate a major UN role and kept pushing for a new Security Council resolution which would make it 'absolutely clear' that Iraqi non-compliance was 'unacceptable'.[84] The momentum for such an authorizing resolution seemingly came on 5 February 2005, after Powell detailed to the UN Security Council what he described as Iraq's 'web of lies' in denying that it continued to run WMD programmes in defiance of its international obligations.[85]

These allegations did not increase international support for military action. The majority of Security Council members opposed it, most notably France, Germany, Russia and China who were not convinced by evidence presented by Secretary Powell and urged that international inspections be allowed more time.[86] The split over the necessity of military action deepened after the main international inspector Hans Blix confirmed in his 14 February 2003 report to the Security Council that Iraq had started to cooperate with the inspectors.

78 UNSC Res. 1441 (8 November 2002) UN Doc. S/RES/1441, op. para. 1.

79 *Ibid.* op. para. 13.

80 The resolution did not authorize states to use 'all necessary means' to implement its requirements nor did it imply such authorization.

81 Quoted by Copson (n. 77).

82 *Ibid.*

83 *Ibid.* 2.

84 White House Office of the Press Secretary, 'President Bush Meets with Prime Minister Blair' (31 January 2003) (at: http://georgewbush-whitehouse.archives.gov/news/releases/2003/01/20030131-23.html; accessed 18 June 2009).

85 White House Office of the Press Secretary, 'Transcript: US Secretary of State Colin Powell Addresses the UN Security Council' (5 February 2003) (at: http://georgewbush-whitehouse.archives.gov/news/releases/2003/02/20030205-1.html; accessed 15 June 2009).

86 *Ibid.* 2 and 7.

Unsurprisingly, the US administration rejected the Blix report as a 'farce'[87] and accelerated its efforts to secure international support for an immediate military disarmament of Iraq.

On 24 February 2003, the US, the UK and Spain introduced to the Security Council a draft 'second resolution' stating that Iraq had failed 'to take the final opportunity afforded to it by Resolution 1441' to disarm.[88] The proponents of the draft made it clear that the text of the proposed resolution authorized immediate military action to disarm Iraq by way of 'reviving' the previous authorization to use force against Iraq spelled out in Resolution 678 of 1990.[89] In response, France, Germany and Russia filed a memorandum at the Security Council, warning that the conditions to use force against Iraq had not been fulfilled.[90] On 10 March 2003, President Chirac warned that his government would veto the resolution, and Russian officials said that their government would likely do the same.[91] In any case, the draft had little chance of succeeding. Only four Security Council members (the US, the UK, Spain and Bulgaria) supported it, far from the nine votes required under Article 27 of the UN Charter.

This was the end of diplomatic efforts to resolve the situation. On 17 March 2003, the proposed second resolution was taken off the table and the same evening, President Bush issued an ultimatum to Saddam Hussein. On 19 March 2003, the US–UK coalition forces[92] launched a military strike against Iraq.

4.3.2 International law as constraining factor in the context of the use of force against Iraq

Even though the coalition invaded Iraq without a definitive Security Council authorization and thus in violation of international law,[93] this does not mean that

87 See J. Tuchman Matthews, 'UN Inspection in Iraq Was No Sham' (26 March 2004) (at: www.carnegieendowment.org/publications/index.cfm?fa=view&id=1500; accessed 7 October 2009).

88 United States Department of State, 'Iraq: US/UK/Spain Draft Resolution' (24 February 2003) (at: www.globalsecurity.org/wmd/library/news/iraq/2003/iraq-030224-usia02.htm; accessed 15 June 2009).

89 See Malone (n. 77), 199.

90 See P. Sands, *Lawless World: America and the Making and Breaking of Global Rules* (London: Penguin Books, 2005), 185.

91 Reported by Copson (n. 77), 7.

92 With the support of smaller contingents from Australia, Denmark, Poland and Spain.

93 This chapter adopts the position that the use of force against Iraq in 2003 violated the UN Charter-based paradigm of international law on the use of force; for elaboration of this view, see: R. Singh and A. Macdonald, 'Legality of use of force against Iraq: Opinion' (Matrix Chambers, London, 10 September 2002) (at: http://lcnp.org/global/IraqOpinion10.9.02.pdf; accessed 17 July 2005); R. Singh and C. Kilroy, 'In the Matter of the Potential Use of Armed Force by the UK against Iraq and the Draft US/UK Resolution Published on 24 February 2003: Opinion', repr. in G. Farebrother and N. Kollerstrom (eds.), *The Case against War: The Essential Legal Inquiries, Opinions and Judgments Concerning War in Iraq* (Nottingham: Spokesman, 2003); Sands (n. 90), 174–203; P. Shiner, 'The Iraq War, International Law and the Search for Legal Accountability', in P. Shiner and A. Williams (eds.), *The Iraq War and International Law* (Oxford: Hart Publishing, 2008).

international legal considerations had no constraining influence in the decision-making process. Whereas in the classic causal sense, it may not have determined (prevented) the final decision to use force, international law on the use of force rules and institutions played an important regulatory role in the build-up to war.

It might seem naive to expect that in such radical and politically tense circumstances as those of March 2003 legal arguments could prevail. But international legal considerations in fact were not pushed aside; rather, they were a constant feature of the policy- and decision-making processes, both internationally and domestically, both within states who launched the attack and within those who refused to take part. As Sands observes,[94] the legality of the use of force against Iraq was a headline topic around the world, not only among decision-makers and legal experts, but also among the general public.

Coalition members went through lengthy processes of choosing among more or less legally acceptable alternative political options. They apparently considered international law on the use of force to be the relevant framework to delimit the range of available options. They generally sought to bring their military action against Iraq under the umbrella of the international law on the use of force, particularly by consistently insisting that the safest legal course was to secure Security Council authorization.[95] In any case, none of the participating states was willing to admit that it was acting outside of the international legal framework or that the question of the international legality of the invasion was irrelevant in light of other pressing non-legal factors. Leaders and their legal advisers desperately tried at least to give the impression that they were trying to act within the limits of international law. They spent much time and paper on persuading their domestic contingencies and the rest of the world that they were legally entitled to go to war even without a second (post-1441) Security Council resolution, on the basis of 'revived authorization' from the earlier resolutions. In a peculiar way, this attitude confirms the importance of the deeper, constitutive and aspirational effects of international law. All the participating states sought to preserve their identities as law-abiding states, purportedly seeking to further international law and normative ideals of justice and peace through their military action.

The extent of this commitment to the rule of law, however, varied significantly among the coalition members. The US administration was much less concerned with issues of international legality than its coalition partners, especially once it was given the green light to act at the national level.[96] This

94 Sands (n. 90), 174.

95 The attempts to get the Council's authorization cannot be explained merely in terms of power politics and national narrow interest. At least for the UK Prime Minister Blair, one of the main reasons 'to go down the UN route was...the legal advice that [the UK government] got'. See the informal transcript of Tony Blair's oral evidence given on 29 January 2010 (at: www.iraqinquiry.org.uk/media/43909/100129–blair.pdf; accessed 1 February 2010, 150).

96 See US Public Law 107–243: Authorization for Use of Military Force Against Iraq Resolution of 2002. HJ Res. 114, 116 Stat. 1498 (16 October 2002) (at: http://cspan.org/Content/PDF/hjres114.pdf; accessed 8 October 2008).

attitude was reflected in a statement of John Bolton, the US Under-Secretary of State at the time, who rejected assertions that international law could in any way restrain American action taken consistently with the US constitutional requirements.[97] The White House Chief of Staff Andrew Card was even more blunt in his comment on the adoption of the Resolution 1441: 'The UN can meet and discuss, but we don't need their permission [to attack Iraq]'.[98]

The UK government, meanwhile, was much more committed to compliance with international law and the issue of legality. Not only the legal advisers, but also the relevant senior policy makers paid much attention to the legal questions and kept stressing the importance of keeping the final political choice in line with the requirements of the UN Charter.[99] As Sands observes, the Prime Minister as well as his cabinet members 'missed no opportunity [in the run-up to war] to stress that any decision to go to war would have to be justified under the United Nations Charter'.[100] The Foreign Secretary Jack Straw repeatedly promised that any decision of the UK government would be taken in accordance with UK's obligations under international law.[101] The Prime Minister Tony Blair recently confirmed in his oral evidence before the UK Iraq Inquiry that he always considered 'the legal question…very important'; so important, in fact that the government 'would have been unable to take action' had the main governmental legal adviser, Attorney General Lord Goldsmith advised at the end that '[t]his [action] cannot be justified lawfully'.[102] Parliament certainly conditioned its approval of the military action on the attorney general's advice that the use of force by the UK against Iraq without a new Security Council resolution would still be compatible with international law.[103] International law on the use of force featured prominently in the internal deliberations of the UK government, at

97 J. R. Bolton, '"Legitimacy" in International Affairs: The American Perspective in Theory and Operation' (Remarks to the Federalist Society, 13 November 2003) (at: www.america.gov/st/washfile-english/2003/November/20031113180557yakcm0.8482935.html; accessed 8 October 2009).

98 Quoted in 'US Will Attack without Approval' *Guardian* (11 November 2002) (at: www.guardian.co.uk/world/2002/nov/11/iraq.usa; accessed 8 October 2009).

99 The UK Iraq Inquiry, launched in July 2009 to examine the UK government's involvement in the war, has released many previously classified internal documents further confirming that there was much discussion about the legality of the use of force against Iraq within the government (see: www.iraqinquiry.org.uk; accessed 1 February 2010).

100 Sands (n. 90), 180.

101 For example, in his speech before the House of Commons in November 2002; see UK Foreign and Commonwealth Office, 2002, 'Opening Speech by the Foreign Secretary, Jack Straw, in a debate on Iraq. House of Commons' (25 November 2002) (at: www.fco.gov.uk/resources/en/news/2003/10/fco_nst_252202_strawiraq; accessed 8 October 2009). The Australian Prime Minister made a similar promise; see A. Byrnes and H. Charlesworth, 'The Illegality of the War Against Iraq' 22(1) *Dialogue* 4.

102 See Tony Blair's oral evidence before the Iraq Inquiry (n. 95), 99, 150.

103 Similarly, the UK military considered it necessary to secure compatibility with international law of the proposed military action against Iraq; see the informal transcript of the oral evidence given by David Brummel (then Legal Secretary to the Law Officers) on 26 January 2010 (at: www.iraqinquiry.org.uk/media/43620/100126pm-brummell.pdf; accessed 1 February 2010).

least in the process of policy formation, even if it was not decisive for the ultimate decision to go to war.

The popular impression that international law had little constraining relevance in the decision-making process regarding Iraq partly reflects the focus on the coalition members, particularly the US. But looking at those states that did not take part in the military action and/or openly opposed it, international legal considerations were often one of the main constraining factors behind their decisions. The majority of the Security Council members opposed any premature military action taken before all peaceful means had been exhausted as incompatible with international law. Similarly, many states outside the Security Council explicitly refused to participate in the initial strike owing to the legal ambiguities surrounding action taken without a fresh Security Council determination.[104] Similar legal reservations were expressed, among others, by the representatives of the Arab states and the Organization of Islamic Conference,[105] as well as by the President of the European Commission, Romano Prodi, who on several occasions confirmed the Commission's insistence on a second, explicit, Security Council resolution as a legal basis for action.[106]

4.3.3 International law as a framework for the legitimization of military action against Iraq

The troubled case of Iraq also shows how international law operates as the fundamental source and measure of the legitimacy of political decision and actions in concrete situations. The extent to which international legal arguments were used in the processes of justification and legitimization of the military action against Iraq is unprecedented and defies the realist expectation that debates surrounding the decision to go to war in such a sensitive political and security momentum will be free from legal arguments. Although a wide range of non-legal (security, political and moral) arguments were also deployed to justify the use of force in this case, none of the participating states suggested that these non-legal factors could legitimize an action that was otherwise incompatible with international law.

Knowing that their decisions and actions would be exposed to evaluation by other states and other relevant actors, the US and UK invested vast resources into trying to find persuasive legal explanations and started very early to develop a complex set of arguments to rationalize their planned military action. On the eve of the attack, all three main coalition members – the US,

104 Reported by A. Göl, 'A Turkish Perspective', in R. Thakur and W. Pal Singh Sidhu (eds.), *The Iraq Crisis and World Order: Structural, Institutional and Normative Challenges* (Tokyo: United Nations University Press, 2006), 116.

105 See A. Saikal, 'Reactions in the Muslim World to the Iraq Conflict', in Thakur and Pal Singh Sidhu (n. 104), 190.

106 'President Prodi regrets the divisions on Iraq' (17 March 2003) (at: www.europa-eu-un.org/articles/en/article_2142_en.htm; accessed 9 October 2009).

the UK and Australia – sent a letter to the Security Council, offering not only political and security arguments, but also legal justifications for their action. They apparently believed that through the use of legal arguments, they could increase the perceived legitimacy of their decision in a way that neither their privileged geopolitical position nor the previously offered subjective security, ethical or other non-legal justifications were able to do.[107]

Coalition states were also aware that the spectrum of available legal arguments that could be successfully deployed was extremely narrow. Accordingly, they never officially invoked arguments that would be clearly unconvincing, either because of their incompatibility with the established standards of the international law on the use of force (such as the arguments of regime change and preventive self-defence) and/or with the facts on the ground (such as the argument of self-defence against an imminent attack or an argument of humanitarian intervention). Instead, the choice of the final official legal argument for action was determined by the traditional, UN Charter framework for the resort to force, although based on somewhat peculiar interpretations of the law. All three main coalition members eventually invoked the argument of the 'combined' or 'revived' effect of previous Security Council Resolutions 678 (1990), 687 (1991) and 1441 (2002).[108] The reasoning of this argument has been sufficiently explained elsewhere,[109] but in brief, the 'revival' argument posits that the finding in Resolution 1441 that Iraq was in material breach of previous Security Council resolutions, and Iraq's failure to take the final opportunity to comply, itself constituted the decision of the Council to revive the authorization, given in Resolution 678, to use force in order to restore international peace and security in the region.

Although this argument is not patently false, it is still quite unpalatable and it was rejected by the majority of legal experts around the world. Sands rightly mocks its deeply weak and instrumental nature: 'The [combined effects] argument is well spun and could, at a pinch, win the prize for the most plausible response to the question: what is the best possible argument to justify the use of force in Iraq in March 2003?'.[110] But at its very best, this argument was the least bad among the bad arguments, 'and very few states and virtually no established international lawyers see its merits'.[111] Even in the UK, a number of prominent government officials and legal advisers

107 Ultimately, the inability to justify the action in Iraq in terms of the international law on the use of force created a whole range of costs for the participating states. See e.g. Falk (n. 7), 145.

108 UNSC, 'Letter from the Permanent Representative of Australia to the United Nations' (20 March 2003) UN Doc. S/2003/352; UNSC, 'Letter from the Permanent Representative of the United Kingdom of Great Britain and Northern Ireland to the United Nations' (20 March 2003) UN Doc. S/2003/350; UNSC, 'Letter dated 20 March 2003 from the Permanent Representative of the United States of America to the United Nations' (20 March 2003) UN Doc. S/2003/351.

109 See Sands (n. 90), 188–9. See also the transcript of Sir Michael Wood's oral evidence to the Iraq Inquiry (at: www.iraqinquiry.org.uk/media/43614/100126am-wood.pdf; accessed 29 January 2010).

110 Sands (n. 90), 189.

111 *Ibid.*

rejected it as unconvincing and legally invalid. Among them, Michael Wood (the Foreign and Commonwealth Office Legal Adviser at the time) confirmed in his testimony before the UK Iraq Inquiry[112] that the FCO legal team consistently advised, right up to the war, that there was no legal basis for military action without a fresh Security Council determination.[113] In his provisional advice to the Prime Minister on 7 March 2003, even Attorney General Lord Goldsmith warned that the revival argument, while not unreasonable, was controversial and would not provide a watertight legal justification.[114] He did, however, change his view soon after, and in his parliamentary answer of 17 March 2003 advised Parliament that Resolution 1441 provided a sufficient legal basis to use force against Iraq and a second resolution was not legally required.[115]

This argument was clearly deployed in an instrumental manner, in order to provide a 'veil of legitimacy' for a dubious political decision motivated by other, non-legal factors, such as regime change. Nonetheless, this does not confirm the realist assertion that international law has no autonomous normative power and is only used as a tool in the hands of powerful states. One argument that confirms this view is that despite its clearly privileged geopolitical position, the US–UK coalition completely failed to legitimize its military action against Iraq through creative legal advice and the invention of pragmatic arguments. This was precisely because the external 'adjudicators' (other states and other relevant actors) had evaluated and condemned this action as illegitimate primarily on the basis of its compatibility with the established standards and interpretations of international law. A few examples suffice to illustrate the point at hand.

On the state level, the prevailing position of states opposing the invasion is well reflected in the official statement issued by the Legal Department of the Ministry of Foreign Affairs of the Russian Federation, denying any normative value to the revival argument:

> As the legal basis for the military action against Iraq references are made to Security Council resolutions 678 (1990), 687 (1991) in 1441 (2002). In our view...neither the interpretation of the combination of resolutions 678, 687 and 1441 per se, nor their interpretation in the context of provisions of the UN Charter gives occasion to declare that the states now using force against Iraq had the right to decide upon such action. In this

112 See Wood's oral evidence to the Iraq Inquiry (n. 109). This was further confirmed before the Iraq Inquiry by Elizabeth Wilmshurst, who in 2003 was FCO Deputy Legal Adviser; (at: www.iraqinquiry.org.uk/media/43474/wilmshurst-statement.pdf; accessed 29 January 2010).

113 Elizabeth Wilmshurst resigned in March 2003 because she disagreed with the government about the legality of the use of force.

114 'Lord Goldsmith to the Prime Minister on the legality of the use of force, 7 March 2003' 29 April 2005) *Guardian* (at: http://image.guardian.co.uk/sys-files/Guardian/documents/2005/04/28/legal.pdf; accessed 15 June 2005).

115 *Ibid.*

> case for the use of force against Iraq a new decision of the UN Security Council was needed. In the absence of such a decision the use of force against Iraq is unlawful.[116]

Similar analyses and critiques of the coalition's arguments can be found in numerous writings of international legal scholars.[117] Some of these took the form of a collective uprising against the blatant violation of international law and the shameless political manipulation of legal arguments. For example, on 18 March 2003, the International Commission of Jurists issued a public statement warning that the US–UK military action in Iraq lacked a valid legal basis and constituted an 'outright illegal invasion of Iraq, which amounts to a war of aggression'.[118] In the UK, a group of sixteen international law professors sent an open letter to Downing Street, arguing that taking part in military action without a new Security Council decision would be unlawful. The letter was published in the *Guardian* on 7 March 2003. A similar letter was sent to the *New York Times* by a group of American international lawyers, but the editors declined to publish it. Australian academics Byrnes and Charlesworth also issued an open letter rejecting the coalition arguments of the combined effect and condemning the military action against Iraq as unlawful.[119]

These examples demonstrate that while the use of legal arguments in legitimization discourse always oscillates between the normative and instrumental, the independent normative power of these arguments remains significant. The coalition's claims of legitimacy based on the revival argument were confronted by powerful counter-claims of the invasion's 'formal illegality'. In the end, the latter arguments prevailed, proving that international legal rules cannot be instrumentalized at will to legitimize any political solution; rather, they operate as a relatively independent, objective and authoritative source and measure of the legitimacy of political action.

4.4 Conclusion

This chapter has shown how international law may affect the processes and outcomes of international politics with respect to the use of force by providing

116 Legal Department of the Ministry of Foreign Affairs of the Russian Federation, 'Legal Assessment of the Use of Force against Iraq' (2003) 52 ICLQ 1059, 1059 and 1062–3.

117 See Singh and Macdonald (n. 93); Singh and Kilroy (n. 93); Shiner (n. 93), 22–8. Among the rare exceptions were C. Greenwood, 'The Legality of Using Force against Iraq' (Memorandum to the Select Committee on Foreign Affairs) (at: www.publications.parliament.uk/pa/cm200203/cmselect/cmfaff/196/2102406.htm; accessed 25 June 2007) and R. Wedgwood, 'Comment & Analysis: Legal Authority Exists for a Strike on Iraq' (14 March 2003) *Financial Times*.

118 International Commission of Jurists, 'Iraq – ICJ Deplores Moves Toward a War of Aggression on Iraq' (18 March 2003) (at: www.icj.org/IMG/pdf/Iraq_war_18_03_03_.pdf; accessed 17 September 2009).

119 A. Byrnes and H. Charlesworth, 'No, This War is illegal' (19 March 2003) *The Age* (at: www.theage.com.au/articles/2003/03/18/1047749770379.html; accessed 21 June 2009).

the fundamental regulatory and legitimization framework within which states shape, justify and evaluate their decisions regarding the use of force in international relations.

International law on the use of force operates as the fundamental regulatory framework for resort to force in international relations, by providing a legalized and formalized set of substantive and institutional rules which constrain and enable states' decisions in this respect. These rules delimit the parameters within which states may individually or collectively pursue their particular or common political interests and objectives. While they may not always be decisive for the ultimate political decision(s) regarding the use of force, they can significantly influence and constrain the policy formation in this area through more subtle mechanisms, such as by affecting a state's rational balancing between the benefits and risks of (non-)compliant behaviour or by affecting the way states shape and perceive their political interests, identities, and objectives. Even the ultimate test case of military action against Iraq in 2003 confirms that international law is a significant constraining factor in international politics when it comes to the use of force. Although the constraints of international law did not prevent the US–UK coalition from invading Iraq, legal considerations were a constant and significant element of the policy- and decision-making process and the participating states went out of their way to bring their decision to use force against Iraq under the umbrella of international law, primarily by trying to secure Security Council authorization. In addition, international law was a significant factor in shaping the decisions of those states that rejected participation in or support for this military adventure.

International law on the use of force provides the most commonly accepted source and measure of the legitimacy of political action. Being aware that their political solutions will inevitably be exposed to evaluation by 'external' jurors who expect that actions will be taken in accordance with international law, states feel obliged to provide reasonably persuasive legal justifications for their political choices. Despite the relative indeterminacy and openness to pragmatic interpretation of international law, the independent normative power of legal arguments remains significant. Any (instrumental) claim on the part of the acting state(s) will be met by powerful counter-claims on the part of the evaluating states and other actors, who will evaluate the original claims primarily on the basis of their formal (in)compatibility with the generally accepted standards and interpretations of international law on the use of force. International law on the use of force, therefore, inevitably affects the ways states rationalize and justify their political solutions and may thus indirectly influence the choice between alternative policy options. As the analysis in this chapter reveals, international law was the main framework within which states and other actors signalled, exchanged and evaluated their arguments about the (il)legality of the use of force against Iraq. The intense efforts of the coalition states to find the most acceptable, persuasive legal rationale for their decision, indicate their awareness that they had to be able to justify their political choices on the basis of generally accepted international legal norms, and that within that framework, the range of arguments that can be effectively deployed is inherently limited. In the end, the coalition states failed to legitimize their controversial political decision through a pragmatic innovative argument of 'combined effect', precisely because other states and other actors evaluated the value of this argument against the generally accepted legal framework on the use of force, and on this basis considered the argument as legally invalid and the military action against Iraq as unlawful and illegitimate.

Therefore, although international legal rules may not be decisive to the final outcomes of international politics, they importantly affect the processes of policy and decision making, as well as the process of the legitimization of political action. They alter the space within which the 'game' of international politics is played: they determine the rules of the game, shape the nature, identity and interests of the players, define the purposes for which force may be used and the conditions under which it may be employed, and shape the considerations of legitimacy of political choice. Even the ultimate test case of the use of force against Iraq in March 2003 confirms that international law on the use of force plays a significant role in contemporary international politics, albeit not always in the sense in which it has been traditionally explained or expected.

5 Russia and competing spheres of influence

The case of Georgia, Abkhazia and South Ossetia

James Summers

5.1 Introduction

In 1999 the Russian representative to the UN Security Council Sergei Lavrov commented on NATO's intervention in Kosovo: 'It highlights the urgent need to form a truly multipolar world order based on the Charter of the United Nations, a world order in which there will be no room for unilateral diktat or attempts at domination by force'.[1]

However, rather than this benign image of a multipolar world, the theme of this chapter is how multiple poles can challenge the UN Charter and international law through territorial spheres of influence. The notion of 'multipolarity' itself sits uneasily with the principle of sovereign equality, as, unless there are more than 192 poles, it assumes the dominance of some states over others. Such inequality is inevitable in the interstate system, but how does it impact on international law?

The UN Charter institutionalizes a multipolar world, giving five states (the P5) a permanent seat on the Security Council and a veto on questions of international peace and security. Thus, there are two models for a legal multipolar world. The first works within the collective framework of the Security Council. The second is where states pursue and defend their spheres of influence through unilateral doctrines on the use of force, such as expansive interpretations of self-defence or humanitarian intervention. This chapter focuses on the position of Georgia in relation to Abkhazia and South Ossetia and Russia's assertion of a 'near abroad', which Russia has sought to assert both within and outside the UN system.

The Caucasus have historically been a location for competing spheres of influence, with Russia, the Ottomans and Persia competing among the diverse ethnic mix of Christian and Muslim peoples. Those powers promoted their influence through support for different groups, often with devastating effects for nations perceived as disloyal, from the Tsarist expulsion of the Circassians, to repeated Ottoman and Turkish massacres of the Armenians, to Stalin's deportations of Chechens, Ingush and other nationalities. Russia has seen the

1 UNSC Verbatim Record (10 June 1999), UN Doc. S/PV.4011, 8.

area as part of its sphere of influence and has stated this quite explicitly in the Security Council: 'Historically, Russia was the guarantor of the security of the peoples of the Caucasus, and it will remain so'.[2]

5.2 The break-up of the Soviet Union

The legal context for the conflict between Georgia, Russia and South Ossetia and Abkhazia is the break-up of the Soviet Union. The USSR was arranged as a multinational federation of fifteen Union Republics (SSRs), two of which were the Russian Socialist Federal Soviet Republic (RSFSR) and the Georgian SSR. Each Union Republic represented a large and (except Russia) peripheral nation with a right to self-determination. They were considered to be sovereign states,[3] with a (theoretical) right to secede[4] and had many of the trappings of statehood such as flags, parliaments, educational and scientific institutions and ministries.[5] Smaller or more centrally located nations were represented by autonomous republics (ASSRs), most of which were located in Russia. These included Abkhazia in Georgia; and North Ossetia, the Chechen–Ingush Republic and Tatarstan in Russia. These were not sovereign but they had their own constitutions and institutions.[6] Further down in the national hierarchy were autonomous *oblasts*, or regions (AOs), of which examples include South Ossetia and Adjaria in Georgia.[7]

This hierarchical nationality structure caused considerable resentment, as large central nations, such as the Tatars, were located in ASSRs, while smaller, peripheral ones, such as Estonians had SSRs. Moreover, the status of republics was not fixed. For example, the Karelian-based Karelo–Finnish Republic was elevated to an SSR in 1940 (in anticipation of the annexation of Finland) but then reduced to an ASSR within Russia in 1956.[8] Abkhazia too was for a brief period an SSR in 1921 before being demoted to an ASSR within Georgia in 1931.[9] Moreover, the status of a republic proved decisive in the break-up of the Soviet Union. Only Union Republics were recognized as independent states: autonomous republics or regions were not.

2 UNSC Verbatim Record (8 August 2008), UN Doc. S/PV.5952, 5; UNSC Verbatim Record (28 August 2008), UN Doc. S/PV.5969, 17.

3 Article 76, Constitution of the USSR 1977, in H. Hannum (ed.), *Documents on Autonomy and Minority Rights* (Dordrecht: Martinus Nijhoff, 1993), 745.

4 Article 72, Constitution of the USSR 1977 (n. 3).

5 G. Smith, 'The Soviet State and Nationalities Policy', in G Smith (ed.), *The Nationalities Question in the Post-Soviet States* (London: Longman, 1996), 18; A. Kagedan, 'Territorial Units as Nationality Policy', in H. R. Huttenbach (ed.), *Soviet Nationality Policies* (London: Mansell, 1990), 165.

6 Article 82, Constitution of the USSR 1977 (n. 3).

7 Z. Gitelman, 'Nationality and Ethnicity in Russia and the Post-Soviet Republics', in S. White, A. Pravda and Z. Gitelman (eds.), *Developments in Russian and Post-Soviet Politics* (London: MacMillan, 1994), 240.

8 J. N. Hazard, 'Codification of Soviet Nationality Policies', in H. H. Huttenbach (ed.), *Soviet Nationality Policies* (London: Mansell, 1990), 55, 57.

9 T. Potier, *Conflict in Nagorno-Karabakh, Abkhazia and South Ossetia* (The Hague: Kluwer, 2001), 9.

The collapse of the Soviet Union was the result of an internal power struggle between central authorities in Moscow and the leaderships of the fifteen Union Republics that made up the Soviet federation. Superficially the USSR was a union of sovereign republics, though this was largely a veneer for a highly centralized state based on the Communist party.[10] Nonetheless, the leaderships in the republics were able to consolidate power at their local level.[11] Moreover, as the republics, each representing a nation, usually represented the limit of political advancement for non-Russians, their political elites became national ones, who could advance self-determination to increase their powers.[12] Most union republics were led by national communist elites which sought to increase their powers within the Soviet system.[13] The culmination of this struggle between the republics and the centre was a new Union Treaty, which would restructure the Soviet state as a looser federation of sovereign states.[14] However, in Georgia and the Baltic Republics, in elections in 1990, national communists were replaced by opposition nationalists who pressed bolder claims to separate from the USSR.[15]

The Soviet response was a law on secession passed on 3 April 1990, which prescribed the procedure by which a republic could secede from the USSR, intending to make it as difficult as possible. A referendum had to be held in the republic, which required a two-thirds majority, followed by a minimum five-year transition period, followed by another referendum. Moreover, minorities within the republic had a right to choose in referendums whether they wished to remain with the republic or separate and remain part of the Soviet Union.[16] As all the Union Republics had significant minorities, this was calculated to make secession prohibitively costly for them. As a result, no republic ever seceded under this law. The Baltic Republics, which were recognized before the dissolution of the USSR, based their independence on their previous de jure statehood.[17] The Soviet Union was ultimately dissolved by agreement.

10 R. J. Hill, 'Ideology and the Making of a Nationalities Policy', in A. J. Motyl (ed.), *The Post-Soviet Nations: Perspectives on the Demise of the USSR* (New York, NY: Columbia University Press, 1992), 59.

11 A. J. Motyl, *Sovietology, Rationality, Nationality: Coming to Grips with Nationalism in the USSR* (New York, NY: Columbia University Press, 1990), 64–5; R. E. Ericson, 'Economic Structure and the National Question', in A. J. Motyl (ed.), *The Post-Soviet Nations* (New York, NY: Columbia University Press, 1992), 253; J. Hutchinson, *Modern Nationalism* (London: Fontana Press, 1994), 105.

12 G. Gleeson, 'Leninist Nationality Policy: Its Source and Style', in H. H. Huttenbach (ed.), *Soviet Nationality Policies* (London: Mansell, 1990), 18.

13 Motyl (n. 11), 175–6, 179–82; A. Wilson, *Ukrainian Nationalism in the 1990s* (Cambridge: Cambridge University Press, 1997), 24–5; V. Vujacic and V. Zaslavsky, 'The Causes of the Disintegration in the USSR and Yugoslavia' (1991), 88 *Telos* 132.

14 S. White, *After Gorbachev* (Cambridge: Cambridge University Press, 1993), 179; Smith (n. 5), 18–19.

15 S. Jones and R. Parsons, 'Georgia and the Georgians', in G. Smith (ed.), *The Nationalities Question in the Post-Soviet States* (London: Longman, 1996), 302–5.

16 J. N. Hazard, 'Managing Nationalism: State, Law and the National Question in the USSR', in A. J. Motyl (ed.), *The Post-Soviet Nations* (New York, NY: Columbia University Press, 1992), 122–3.

17 R. Mullerson, 'The Continuity and Secession of State, by Reference to the Former USSR and Yugoslavia' (1993), 42 ICLQ 480–3

However, in addition to providing a legal basis for irredentism and secessionism in Union Republics, Soviet authorities also backed separatist movements. An example was Transdniestr, a Russophone region on the east bank of the Dniestr River in Moldova. On 2 September 1990 authorities in the region declared it a separate republic within the USSR. Transdniestrian separatists subsequently enjoyed support from elements within the Soviet 14th Army stationed there, and then open intervention from the army itself, allowing them to establish a de facto state separate from Moldova.[18]

Mikhail Gorbachev's attempts to secure a new union treaty, which would have preserved a restructured Soviet Union, however, led to a hard-line coup against him. When this failed, the power of the central government collapsed and the republics further increased their power. Ultimately, this led to independence.[19] On 8 December 1991, in the Minsk Declaration, the leaders of the republics of Russia, Byelorussia and the Ukraine, which were the original signatories to the 1922 treaty establishing the Soviet Union, dissolved the USSR. In its place, they established the Commonwealth of Independent States (CIS).[20] On 23 December CIS membership was extended to other former union republics.[21] Nonetheless, despite independence, in most cases the political leaderships did not change, nor did their political culture, which remained authoritarian and oriented towards Moscow. The great exceptions to this were the Baltic Republics, which were geographically and culturally aligned with central Europe and the Nordic countries, and had a recent history of independence. They were able to move into the Western sphere of influence, refusing to join the CIS and successfully acceding to NATO and the EU. Georgia was also a leading republic in seeking independence, and on independence refused to join the CIS. However, its attempts to distance itself from Russia were less successful and marred by ethnic conflict.

5.3 Georgia, Abkhazia and South Ossetia

Georgia was a Union Republic within the Soviet Union with a population of 5.4 million, of whom 68.8 per cent were ethnic Georgians.[22] The largest-sized minorities in the republic were Armenians (8 per cent), Russians (6 per cent) and Azerbaijanis (6 per cent). However, the focus of Georgia's struggle for

18 S. J. Kaufman, 'Spiraling to Ethnic War: Elites, Masses, and Moscow in Moldova's Civil War', in M. Brown *et al.* (eds.), *Nationalism and Ethnic Conflict* (Cambridge, MA: MIT Press, 1997), 169–99; J. Eyal and G. Smith, 'Moldova and the Moldovans', in G. Smith (ed.), *The Nationalities Question in the Post-Soviet States* (London: Longman, 1996), 240–2.

19 Smith (n. 5), 19; P. J. S. Duncan, 'Ukraine and the Ukrainians', in G Smith (ed.), *The Nationalities Question in Post-Soviet States* (London: Longman, 1996), 198–9.

20 'The Minsk Declaration, 8 December 1991' (1992), 31 ILM 142–6. See A. Wilson, 'Post-Soviet States and the Nationalities Question', in G Smith (ed.), *The Nationalities Question in the Post-Soviet States* (London: Longman, 1996), 24–5.

21 'The Alma Alta Declaration, 21 December 1991' (1992), 31 ILM 147.

22 B. G. Hewitt, 'Abkhazia: A Problem of Identity and Ownership', in J. F. R. Wright, S. Goldenberg and R. Schofield (eds.), *Transcaucasian Boundaries* (London: UCL Press, 1996), 192.

independence and Russia's attempts to assert its dominance over the country centred on Abkhazia and South Ossetia. The Abkhaz and Ossetians were two small minorities within Georgia, who inhabited the Abkhazia ASSR and South Ossetia AO, respectively. The Abkhaz, distant relatives of the Circassians, constituted less than 2 per cent of Georgia's population, while the Ossetians, a group loosely related to the Persians, constituted 3 per cent.[23]

Abkhazia, on Georgia's north-west coast, was the larger of the two autonomies, with 524,000 inhabitants, and, on the face of it, an unlikely candidate for a separatist bid. Ethnic Abkhaz only formed 17 per cent of its population. The largest group (46 per cent) were ethnic Georgians. Others included Russians, Armenians and Greeks. South Ossetia was a small mountainous region with a population of 98,000, about two-thirds of whom were Ossetian, the rest ethnic Georgian. Ossetian nationalists dreamed of uniting with North Ossetia, an autonomous republic, which lay across the border in Russia. This was a larger entity, with 632,000 people, but was heavily integrated into Russia. Ossetians formed only a bare majority of its population.[24] Both autonomies had considerable strategic value. Abkhazia was adjacent to Russia's Black Sea coastline, with port facilities, and the main railway line connecting Russia to Georgia and the south Caucasus ran through it. South Ossetia had other important communication links. The Roki tunnel, and main highway through the Caucasus, connecting Russia and Georgia, ran through the autonomous region.[25]

Ethnic tensions had long been present in those autonomies. The Abkhaz lost their majority status in Abkhazia in the late nineteenth century,[26] becoming an embattled minority and suffering forced assimilation under Stalin.[27] However, the autonomies' institutions were disproportionately filled with Abkhaz and Ossetian officials, who were well placed to challenge Georgia. Ethnic Georgians living in Abkhazia and South Ossetia complained about discrimination from local authorities.[28]

Abkhazia and South Ossetia were already pursuing a separatist agenda under Georgia's national communists. In 1988 Ossetian and Abkhaz nationalist movements formed, allegedly aided by Soviet agencies to create a pro-Moscow counterweight to Georgian nationalism.[29] On 10 November

23 S. Goldenberg, *The Pride of Small Nations* (London: Zed Books, 1994), 101.

24 G. Joffé, 'Nationalities and Borders in Transcaucasia and the Northern Caucasus', in J. F. R. Wright, S. Goldenberg and R. Schofield (eds.), *Transcaucasian Boundaries* (London: UCL Press, 1996), 26–8; J. F. R. Wright, 'The Geopolitics of Georgia', in J. F. R. Wright, S. Goldenberg and R. Schofield (eds.), *Transcaucasian Boundaries* (London: UCL Press, 1996), 160.

25 Goldenberg (n. 23), 102, 105; J. Birch, 'The Georgian/South Ossetian Territorial and Boundary Dispute', in J. F. R. Wright, S. Goldenberg and R. Schofield (eds.), *Transcaucasian Boundaries* (London: UCL Press, 1996), 173; T. Dragadze, 'Report on Chechnya' (1995), 14 *Central Asian Survey* 466.

26 Joffé (n. 24), 26.

27 Goldenberg (n. 23), 102–3.

28 Jones and Parsons (n. 15), 300; Potier (n. 9), 13.

29 R. Seely, *Russo-Chechen Conflict, 1800–2000: A Deadly Embrace* (London: Frank Cass, 2000), 191–2.

1989 the South Ossetian regional parliament demanded that the autonomous region be upgraded to an autonomous republic. This was refused by the Georgian Soviet. In August 1990 the Georgian parliament, attempting to restrict separatist movements, passed a law preventing parties participating in forthcoming elections unless they operated throughout the territory of Georgia. In response, both the Abkhaz and South Ossetian Soviets passed declarations of sovereignty, on 25 August and 20 September respectively, thereby proclaiming themselves separate Soviet Republics.[30]

Georgia's first free election resulted in the national communists being replaced on 28 October 1990 by the nationalist Round Table-Free Georgia Bloc led by Zviad Gamsakhurdia. Gamsakhurdia was a human rights activist, who had once been called the Vaclav Havel of the Caucasus. Such accolades stopped once he came to power.[31] Gamsakhurdia promoted a narrow ethnic nationalism that alienated Georgia's minorities, for example, condemning mixed marriages as a threat to the nation. In a heavy-handed response to South Ossetia's declaration of sovereignty on 11 December 1990, he abolished its autonomy and imposed an economic blockade.[32] Fighting broke out between South Ossetian and Georgian militias in which civilians were targeted and atrocities committed.[33]

While fighting took place in South Ossetia, Gamsakhurdia's government engaged in negotiations with the Abkhaz authorities over the political status of Abkhazia. The result was a settlement close to the Soviet system in which ethnic Abkhaz remained disproportionately represented in parliament under a quota system, with 28 deputies to 26 for ethnic Georgians and 11 for others. However, this settlement was condemned by local Georgians as apartheid.[34]

Abkhazia's and South Ossetia's alignment with Russia against Georgian separatism was underlined in the Soviet referendum of 17 March 1991. Georgia boycotted this referendum and held its own vote on independence on 31 March 1991. However, Abkhazians and South Ossetians participated in the USSR referendum and voted clearly in favour of the preservation of the Soviet Union. Of votes in Abkhazia, 99 per cent were in favour. The results in South Ossetia were never published.[35]

Georgia declared independence on 9 April 1991, but was not recognized by any state. The same month, Soviet troops were sent into South Ossetia to pacify the conflict there.[36] The Soviet Union was dissolved on 9 December 1991 and Georgia was admitted to the United Nations on 31 July 1992.[37]

30 Independent International Fact-Finding Mission on the Conflict in Georgia, *Report* (Independent International Fact-Finding Mission on the Conflict in Georgia, 2009), II, 71, 73.

31 Goldenberg (n. 23), 82.

32 Birch (n. 25), 166, 179.

33 Goldenberg (n. 23), 106; Report (n. 30), II, 71.

34 Report (n. 30), II, 74.

35 *Ibid.* 72–4.

36 *Ibid.* 71.

37 UNGA Res. 46/241 (31 July 1992), UN Doc. A/RES/46/241.

However, at this stage, even leaving aside South Ossetia and Abkhazia, it scarcely fitted the criteria of a government in control of a territory. In January 1992 Gamsakhurdia was deposed in a violent coup. Eduard Shevardnadze, Gorbachev's former foreign minister, was invited to succeed him.[38] This also represented Georgia returning to the post-Soviet model, with members of the national communist elite taking control. However, the government had lost control not only of South Ossetia and Abkhazia, but also of the western region of Mingrelia, where Gamsakhurdia's supporters held out, and the south-western Muslim autonomy of Adjaria. It did not even have a properly constituted national army and was dependent on rival paramilitary groups.[39]

South Ossetia had previously sought to be part of the USSR outside Georgia. However, after the disintegration of the Soviet Union, it held a referendum on independence on 19 January 1992 and its parliament declared independence on 29 May 1992, subsequently appealing for union with Russia, which Russia refused.[40] On 24 June 1992 the presidents of Georgia and Russia, and representatives from South and North Ossetia signed the Sochi Agreement on a ceasefire and the deployment of a peacekeeping force in South Ossetia.[41]

Russia seemed to have supported the South Ossetian separatists, but the degree of that assistance remains unclear.[42] The legal status of this assistance varied. On 7 January 1991 Gorbachev issued a decree ordering Georgian interior ministry troops out of South Ossetia. Soviet troops, however, were not sent until April 1991, after Georgia declared independence, when they engaged Georgian units and irregulars.[43] However, this might also be seen as an attempt by a state (the Soviet Union) to maintain law and order in a secessionist region (Georgia). The Georgian government was then an unrecognized secessionist entity. There is some evidence that Soviet troops supplied arms, including heavy weapons, to South Ossetian militias, and reports that they allowed South Ossetian irregulars to engage in ethnic cleansing against local Georgians.[44] Only after the break-up of the Soviet Union on 8 December could this support be considered an intervention in the internal affairs of another state.

In May 1992 political tensions in Abkhazia over ethnic Abkhaz dominance led to a split in the autonomy's government, with Georgian deputies establishing a parallel administration. In July, the now Abkhaz-dominated parliament replaced the autonomous republic's 1978 constitution with the

38 S. F. Jones, 'Georgia: The Trauma of Statehood', in I. Bremmer and R. Taras (eds.), *New States and New Politics: Building the Post-Soviet Nations* (Cambridge: Cambridge University Press, 1997), 521–3; Jones and Parsons (n. 15), 297.

39 Jones and Parsons (n. 15), 305.

40 Report (n. 30), II, 72.

41 *Ibid.* 72.

42 Jones and Parsons (n. 15), 308–9.

43 Joffé (n. 24), 16.

44 Birch (n. 25), 174–6.

1925 version, declaring itself a separate republic from Georgia, and demanding a new union treaty between them.[45]

On 14 August 1992 Georgian troops were dispatched to Abkhazia, officially to protect the railway line connecting Russia and Georgia and to rescue kidnapped government ministers, but more likely to subdue the Abkhaz independence movement.[46] Fighting with Abkhaz militias erupted. Georgian forces initially controlled the majority of Abkhazia, holding the east and west of the territory, while Abkhaz forces were boxed in the central region around the town of Gudauta. Russian-led peace negotiations brought the parties to an accord on 3 September 1992. However, this was soon breached. The Russians mediated a second peace agreement (the Sochi Agreement) on 27 July 1993.[47] On 24 August 1992 the United Nations established the United Nations Mission in Georgia (UNOMIG) to police this agreement.[48] However, as the Georgians began withdrawing under the terms of the agreement, they were again attacked by the Abkhaz. At the same time, supporters of Gamsakhurdia launched an offensive in the neighbouring Georgian province of Mingrelia. In two weeks Georgian forces were expelled from Abkhazia, with the exception of the Kodori Valley, where fighting continued until April 1994. There were 300,000 people forced from their homes, including 250,000 ethnic Georgians.[49] This represented the systematic ethnic cleansing of the Georgian population of Abkhazia.

5.4 Russian military assistance

Russia is believed to have provided substantial support to the Abkhaz separatists, though its precise nature remains obscure.[50] It is claimed that Russia gave air support. A UN military observer invited to inspect a Su-27 fighter-bomber shot down by Georgians on 19 March 1993 found that papers held by the dead pilot identified him as a major in the Russian air force.[51] In addition, Russia was alleged to have sent a battalion of troops, as well as military equipment for the separatists, including tanks, armoured personnel carriers, rocket launchers and artillery pieces, together with Russian commanders for their crews.[52] An additional element is the Confederation of Caucasian Mountain People, a paramilitary group composed of Caucasians,

45 Report (n. 30), II, 74–6.

46 Goldenberg (n. 23), 107.

47 Potier (n. 9), 11–12; Goldenberg (n. 23), 107–8.

48 UNSC Res. 858 (24 August 1993), UN Doc. S/RES/858.

49 Report (n. 30), II, 76–9.

50 T. Goltz, 'The Hidden Russian Hand' (1993), 92 *Foreign Affairs* 92–116; Jones and Parsons (n. 15), 308–9; Gitelman (n. 7), 255; Dragadze (n. 25), 466; V. Tishkov, *Ethnicity, Nationalism and Conflict in and After the Soviet Union* (London: Sage, 1997), 226, Goldenberg (n. 23), 108–9; D. E. Mark, 'Russia and the New Transcaucasus' (1996–7), 105 *Foreign Policy* 151.

51 Goltz (n. 50), 108.

52 Seely (n. 29), 193.

mostly Chechens, as well as Russians. Its relationship with the Russian state is ambiguous, but there have been allegations that the group was set up with support from the KGB as a front organization for assisting the Abkhaz separatists.[53] Ironically, its members included Chechens who would later fight against Russia in the Chechen secession.[54] The Abkhaz conflict began in August 1992 after Georgia had been admitted to the United Nations. Russian support for separatists in Abkhazia was, therefore, a violation of the prohibition on the use of force and non-intervention in the internal affairs of another state.

On 14 May 1994 the two sides, again under Russian mediation, signed the Agreement on a Ceasefire and Separation of Forces (the Moscow Agreement).[55] Under the terms of the agreement, a CIS peacekeeping force, essentially of Russian troops, was deployed between the two sides. On a Russian initiative, the deployment of CIS peacekeepers was endorsed by the Security Council on 30 June,[56] despite reservations expressed by members about ambiguities in relation to its role.[57]

Russia also provided assistance for the Georgian government's suppression of Gamsakhurdia's insurrection. In return Georgia was required to join the CIS and to allow the expansion of four Russian bases on its territory. This clearly brought it back within Russia's sphere of influence.[58]

Russia has repeatedly asserted its dominant role in the Caucasus as part of its 'near abroad'. There is considerable debate over the precise role of individuals and organs in supporting separatism in Georgia. However, several interests may have led Russia to intervene. First, there may have been a desire to make an example of Georgia as a leading secessionist republic. Second, Russia had concerns over the stability of the south Caucasus in relation to its own north Caucasian republics. The conflict in South Ossetia led to an influx of refugees into North Ossetia, which in turn led to conflict and the ethnic cleansing of Ingush in North Ossetia.[59] A Russian presence south of the Caucasus might be considered important for Russia's own stability.[60] Third, possession of Abkhazia and South Ossetia allowed Russia to expand its territory, especially after its loss of control of large sections of the Black Sea coastline with Ukrainian independence.[61] Fourth, the Russian presence

53 *Ibid.* 90.

54 *Ibid.* 191–2; A. Lieven, *Chechnya: Tombstone of Russian Power* (New Haven, CT: Yale University Press, 1998), 33–4, 59, 244.

55 UNSC Letter from the Permanent Representative of Georgia to the UN (17 May 1994), UN Doc. S/1994/583, annex I.

56 UNSC Res. 934 (30 June 1994), UN Doc. S/RES/934.

57 UNSC Verbatim Record (30 June 1994), UN Doc. S/PV.3398, 3–4.

58 Mark (n. 50), 151; Report (n. 30), I, 13; Goldenberg (n. 23), 113.

59 Seely (n. 29), 131–2.

60 S. Littlefield, 'Citizenship, Identity and Foreign Policy: The Contradictions and Consequences of Russia's Passport Distribution in the Separatist Regions of Georgia' (2009), 61 *Europe–Asia Studies* 1469; S. Markedonov, 'The Paradoxes of Russia's Georgia Policy' (April–June 2007), 2 Russia in Global Affairs (at: http://eng.globalaffairs.ru/numbers/19/1116.html; accessed 4 January 2010).

61 Dragadze (n. 25), 466.

allowed Russia to continue to apply pressure to keep rival powers out of the Caucasus.

5.5 Unrecognized states and peacekeeping

The conflict in Abkhazia and South Ossetia allowed Russia to extend its control within those territories and its influence over Georgia. Russia was the major contributor to the peacekeeping forces that formed the buffer between the separatist regions and Georgia. Russia was explicitly recognized as the facilitator for any political solution, which meant that any settlement had to be agreeable to it.[62] It also exercised considerable internal political control within the regions themselves and this increased as it extended its own nationality to the population of the territories.

The peacekeeping mission in Abkhazia had two aspects: the UN peacekeeping mission UNOMIG and the CIS peacekeepers. Legally the deployment of both was based on the consent of Georgia.[63] UNOMIG, established in July 1993 to police the ceasefire line between Georgia and Abkhazia, was a small force dependent on the CIS peacekeepers for operational support. Its mandate had to be renewed by the Security Council twice a year,[64] and this allowed Russia to exert pressure over its mandate. For example, in 2006 it only allowed the mission to be renewed for two months.[65]

Within the Security Council Russia was seen as supportive of Abkhazia, drawing equivalence between Abkhazia as an unrecognized secessionist entity and Georgia as a UN member state. Russia also invited ministers from Abkhazia to address the Security Council, while the US denied them visas.[66] At the same time, Russia insisted on closed-door meetings of the Council to exclude Georgia.[67] It also sought to weaken the language of Security Council resolutions, which have consistently upheld Georgia's territorial integrity. The standard formula used by resolutions was a commitment to 'the sovereignty, independence and territorial integrity of Georgia, within its internationally recognized borders', and 'the necessity to define the status of Abkhazia within the State of Georgia in strict accordance with these

62 Report (n. 30), II, 80, 99, 121–2; Mark (n. 50), 154.

63 See UNSC Res. 937 (21 July 1994), UN Doc. S/RES/937: 'recognizing that the deployment of a CIS peace-keeping force to the area is predicated upon the request and consent of the parties to the conflict'.

64 UNSC Res. 858 (n. 48).

65 UNSC Res. 1656 (31 January 2006), UN Doc. S/RES/1656.

66 Ministry of Foreign Affairs of the Russian Federation, Press Release: 'Adoption by UN Security Council of a Resolution Extending the UN Observer Mission in Georgia, 13 April 2007' (at: www.ru/brp_4.nsf/e78a48070f128a7b43256999005bcbb3/7b2a2c9cd1097176c32572bf005e9551?OpenDocument; accessed 29 December 2009); UNSC Verbatim Record (15 June 2009), UN Doc. S/PV.6143, 10; V. Socor, 'Moscow Fails to Bring Abkhazia to UNSC, but will Try Again' *Eurasia Daily Monitor* (17 April 2007), 4:75.

67 V. Socor, 'UN Security Council's Handling of Abkhazia: A Disquieting Prelude to Bush–Putin Summit' *Eurasia Daily Monitor* (31 January 2005), 2:21.

principles'.[68] However, Russia was able to modify the language in later resolutions changing the phrase 'Abkhazia, Georgia', which implied that the Abkhaz were a rebel movement within Georgia, to 'the Georgia–Abkhaz conflict', suggesting two equal parties.[69]

Diplomatic activity over the conflict in Abkhazia centred on three strands. First, Russia's general role as facilitator to the peace process. From 1993 to 1997 Russia proposed a series of initiatives for a settlement. Second, from 1997 the two parties established a Bilateral Georgia–Abkhazia Coordination Commission for Practical Issues. Third, there was the UN process, which became known as the Geneva Process. Integral to this was a diplomatic grouping, the Group of Friends of the Secretary-General on Georgia, which included France, Germany, Russia, the UK, the US and the OSCE.[70] The UN process involved a series of conferences, involving the two parties, with Russia as facilitator, and the Group of Friends.[71]

The most substantial proposal for autonomy endorsed by the Group was the so-called 'Boden Paper' of 2002, formulated by the UN Secretary-General's Special Representative for Georgia, Dieter Boden.[72] The paper was repeatedly endorsed by the Council as the model for a political solution to Abkhazia,[73] based on a flexible negotiated model for the broadest autonomy and the return of internally displaced persons (IDPs). However, this formula proved contradictory for Abkhaz authorities. Because of their demographic position, a dominant role for ethnic Abkhaz in Abkhazia's self-government was incompatible with the return of IDPs, which would consign them to a minority. Abkhazia refused to receive the plan and it also attracted only limited support from Russia. On 26 January 2006 Russia officially withdrew its support for the paper.[74] Nonetheless, on 31 March 2006 the Security Council reaffirmed its support for the Boden Paper and continued to refer to it as the basis for a settlement until the conflict in August 2008.[75]

In South Ossetia, unlike Abkhazia, the United Nations was not involved in peacekeeping or negotiations for a political settlement. The 1992 Sochi Agreement provided for a Joint Peacekeeping Force (JPKF) consisting of Georgian, Russian and Ossetian battalions. This was under the control of a

68 E.g. UNSC Res. 1615 (29 July 2005), UN Doc. S/RES/1615.

69 See UNSC Res. 1666 (31 March 2006), UN Doc. S/RES/1666; UNSC Res. 1716 (13 October 2006), UN Doc. S/RES/1716; UNSC Res. 1752 (13 April 2007), UN Doc. S/RES/1752.

70 UNSC 'Report of the Secretary-General Concerning the Situation in Abkhazia, Georgia' (20 January 1997), UN Doc. S/1997/47 para. 6.

71 Report (n. 30), II, 80–3.

72 'Basic Principles for the Distribution of Competences between Tbilisi and Sukhumi.' UNSC 'Report of the Secretary-General Concerning the Situation in Abkhazia, Georgia' (18 January 2002), UN Doc. S/2002/88, 1.

73 UNSC Res. 1393 (31 January 2002), UN Doc. S/RES/1393 onwards.

74 V. Socor, 'Moscow Kills Boden Paper, Threatens to Terminate UNOMIG in Georgia' *Eurasia Daily Monitor* (7 February 2006), 3:26.

75 UNSC Res. 1666 (n. 69); UNSC Res. 1716 (n. 69); UNSC Res. 1752 (n. 69); UNSC Res. 1781 (15 October 2007), UN Doc. S/RES/1781; UNSC Res. 1808 (15 April 2008), UN Doc. S/RES/1808.

Joint Control Commission (JCC) comprising representatives from Georgia, South Ossetia, Russia and North Ossetia.[76] Political negotiations were led by the OSCE, which established a Mission in Georgia in November 1992, though Russia's role as facilitator was also clearly recognized. The EU was also involved, first in post-conflict reconstruction and then as an observer at the JCC. On 16 May 1996, under OSCE auspices, the two sides agreed a Memorandum on Measures of Providing Safety and Strengthening of Mutual Confidence between the Sides in the Georgia–Ossetia Conflict. This document outlined the principles for negotiations on a settlement. However, despite some initial progress, negotiations faltered after 1999.[77]

In addition to policing their de facto borders, Russia assumed many functions of a sovereign state within Abkhazia and South Ossetia, in what has been described as creeping annexation. In both territories key government departments have been largely staffed by Russians or individuals who had previously held equivalent positions within Russia. In South Ossetia this included the ministries for defence, internal affairs, civil defence, state security, border protection and the presidential administration. In Abkhazia, this involved the ministries of security and defence. There have also been very close ties at the leadership level. In elections in South Ossetia in December 2001, Eduard Kokoity, an Ossetian businessman previously based in Moscow, was elected president. However, Abkhazia asserted some independence, by rejecting Moscow's preferred candidate for the Abkhaz presidency, Raul Khadjimba, in favour of Sergei Bagapash in 2004–5.[78]

Russia also exercised state functions within the two territories. From 2002 it began the mass distribution of Russian passports in the territories,[79] a consular function which can only be exercised on the territory of another state with its consent.[80] This policy became known as 'passportification'. This was accompanied by ties of rights and obligations to the Russian state. Russia paid pensions to its passport holders, in the case of elderly Abkhaz, raising their pensions from 100 to 1,600 roubles.[81] The effect was to draw the majority of Abkhaz and South Ossetians into Russian political life, with passport holders participating in Russian presidential and parliamentary elections. They also had obligations to the Russian state to pay taxes[82] and perform military service,[83] and were directly affected by Russian legislation on pensions and health.[84]

76 Report (n. 30), II, 93.
77 *Ibid.* 95–102.
78 *Ibid.* 102, 132–4
79 *Ibid.* 182.
80 Arts. 3 and 4, Vienna Convention on Consular Relations 1963.
81 Report (n. 30), 168.
82 Article 57, Russian Constitution (n. 3).
83 Article 59, Russian Constitution (n. 3).
84 Report (n. 30), 132–3.

Although there were allegations of coercion, the policy was largely voluntary, especially after the 2008 conflict. The policy offered significant benefits in pensions, health care and education as well as the ability to travel abroad, which was impossible on unrecognized Abkhazian and South Ossetian passports. This was also in the context of a visa regime introduced by Russia for Georgian passport holders on 5 December 2000 (after denouncing a 1992 agreement for visa free travel in the CIS), which pointedly excluded residents of Abkhazia and South Ossetia.[85] The Russian policy of naturalization was individual and voluntary, but it was aimed at the mass change of nationality in specific secessionist areas of Georgia with the intention of depriving that country of elements of its statehood.[86]

5.6 The Russia–Georgia Conflict 2008

In 2003 Eduard Shevardnadze was replaced in the Rose Revolution by the election of Mikhail Saakashvili, a US-educated lawyer. This was followed by the Orange Revolution in Ukraine in 2004, which Russia saw as part of a process of encroachment of Western influence on its borders. Saakashvili sought a close relationship with the West and actively sought membership of NATO and the EU. In response, Russia's relations with Georgia became increasingly antagonistic.

A new tension developed after Kosovo's unilateral declaration of independence. The former Serbian province had lain in UN-administered limbo since 1999, when NATO had intervened in reaction to Serbian ethnic cleansing. Russia, a historic ally of Serbia, rejected any political solution which involved the territory's independence, while Western states emphasized the impossibility of restoring Serb rule. On 17 February 2008 Kosovo unilaterally declared its independence and received rapid recognition from the US and most European countries. Russia, in contrast, said it 'set a dangerous precedent'[87] which it considered as applicable to Abkhazia and South Ossetia. Russia established direct relations with the regimes in South Ossetia and Abkhazia in April.[88]

Tensions escalated between the two countries over the summer. There were a series of aerial incidents over Abkhazia. In April an unmanned Georgian drone was shot down by a MiG off the coast of Abkhazia.[89] A series of explosions took place and additional Russian troops were sent to strengthen the CIS force, opposed by Georgia. In South Ossetia there were similarly regular incidents over the ceasefire line, including exchanges of fire and bomb

85 *Ibid.* 167–8.

86 *Ibid.* 171.

87 UNSC Verbatim Record (18 February 2008), UN Doc. S/PV.5839, 7.

88 Report (n. 30), I, 31

89 Littlefield (n. 60), 1470.

explosions, the capture of Georgian servicemen and Russian intrusions into Georgian airspace. Both sides conducted military exercises.[90]

During the night of 7–8 August, Georgia began a large-scale assault on South Ossetia. The circumstances in which it did this remain fiercely contested. Georgia claimed that its actions were in self-defence against attacks from South Ossetia.[91] It cited a number of incidents and claimed that Russia was deploying troops into South Ossetia. However, independent investigations have questioned this. The European Council's Independent Fact-Finding Mission considered that Georgian claims were not sufficiently substantiated.[92]

Georgia's use of force was within its internationally recognized borders. It may, however, have contravened Article 2(4), being a use of force in a manner inconsistent with the purposes of the United Nations, since it contradicted Security Council resolutions on a peaceful settlement. Georgia's actions were also in violation of its previous commitments not to use force against South Ossetia under the 1992 Sochi Agreement and the Memorandum on Security and Mutual Trust. Moreover, Georgian military measures, in particular, the shelling of Tskhinvali with heavy artillery and GRAD multiple rocket launchers, were disproportionate and may have constituted a war crime.[93]

Russia counter-attacked and together with local militias drove Georgia out of all of the territory of South Ossetia and Abkhazia. It then established what it termed 'security zones', which occupied strategic parts of Georgian territory. A ceasefire agreement was reached by negotiations with French President Nicolas Sarkozy on 12 August. Russian units, however, did not fully withdraw until 9 October.[94]

Russia advanced three legal justifications for its actions.[95] The first was self-defence of its peacekeeping troops. This was an established interpretation of the right. Troops on peacekeeping missions have a right to defend themselves if attacked. However, a further requirement for self-defence is proportionality. As a defence of peacekeepers, Russia's action can be seen as disproportionate: in its scope, extending to the occupation of substantial parts of Georgian territory and attacks on Georgia in the Kodori Valley in Abkhazia; in its timing, in that attacks continued after a ceasefire agreement had been signed;[96] and in its methods, with Russian troops possibly failing to provide sufficient protection to ethnic Georgian civilians in the face of ethnic cleansing by Ossetian militias.[97]

90 Report (n. 30), II, 200–9.

91 UNSC Verbatim Record (8 August 2008), UN Doc. S/PV.5951, 3.

92 Report (n. 30), I, 19–20.

93 Report (n. 30), I, 22–3.

94 *Ibid.* II, 219.

95 UNSC 'Letter from the Permanent Representative of the Russian Federation to the UN' (11 August 2008), UN Doc. S/2008/545.

96 'Georgia: Refugees flee after Russian Military breaches ceasefire' *The Times* (13 August 2008).

97 Report (n. 30), I, 23.

Their second interpretation of self-defence, however, was more problematic: the self-defence of their nationals, on account of passports supplied to South Ossetians and Abkhaz. This interpretation of self-defence has not been considered part of international law. There are strong arguments against its inclusion, as it provides an easy pretext for powerful states to intervene in other states. Large states often have significant expatriate communities, who can be seen to be in peril in times of crisis, and, thus, provide a readily available pretext for intervention. This doctrine has been associated with attempts by states to assert spheres of influence in their neighbourhoods. The US, in particular, used it to depose unfriendly governments in Grenada[98] and Panama.[99] A further factor is that the nationality was one specifically accorded by Russia en masse to individuals residing outside the Russian Federation, with a possible motive of creating a pretext for intervention.

The third justification for Russian military action was humanitarian intervention. Russia claimed that it was intervening to prevent 'genocide' in South Ossetia by Georgian forces. Such claims mirror the arguments that were raised in support of NATO's Kosovo intervention. Humanitarian intervention as a legal doctrine in itself is unlikely to confer legality on armed intervention. The concept is not generally considered to be established in international law. Instead, humanitarian intervention functions as an alternative justification for the illegal use of force: that military action may be unlawful, but might in a broader sense be legitimate. As Russia put it before the Security Council, 'how were we supposed to respond to those efforts to wipe Tskhinvali off the face of the earth?'.[100]

Behind the general rejection of humanitarian intervention is the concern to prevent the clear and unconditional prohibition on the threat or use of force in Article 2(4) of the UN Charter being weakened by subjective values. A right of intervention could too easily be abused by powerful countries against their weaker neighbours.[101] There are also more specific objections to particular aspects of humanitarian intervention. First, the humanitarian situation to which the intervention is reacting may not be clear. Especially in a conflict situation, who is responsible for casualties may not be readily ascertainable. There is a danger that a humanitarian crisis might be inflated as justification for intervention. Second, there is the recurrent problem that motives for intervention may not be purely humanitarian. States may act for a variety of motives, which can include their national interests. Third, military intervention inevitably causes damage and casualties. The benefits of any action has to be weighed against the means by which it was achieved.

98 See UNSC Verbatim Record (27 October 1983), UN Doc. S/PV.2491, paras. 55, 65–6.

99 UNSC 'Letter from the Permanent Representative of the United States of America to the UN' (20 December 1989), UN Doc. S/21035.

100 UN Doc. S/PV.5969 (n. 2), 17.

101 *Corfu Channel Case* (*UK* v. *Albania*) [1949] ICJ Rep. 35.

On all these grounds, Russian intervention can be seen to undermine humanitarian intervention. First, Russia's claims of Georgian 'genocide' involving 2,000 civilian deaths[102] proved massively inflated. More reliable casualty figures emerged which put total South Ossetian deaths at 162.[103] Second, Russia had a history of intervention in Georgia and of support for the two secessionist regimes.[104] Third, rather than protecting civilians, Russia's advance into Georgia was followed by the ethnic cleansing of Georgian villages by South Ossetian irregulars, which Russia appeared to do nothing to stop.[105] Overall, the intervention appears to back the International Court of Justice's misgivings in *Corfu Channel* that a right of intervention allows the most powerful states to pervert international justice.[106]

Russia's actions have had two impacts in terms of asserting a sphere of influence. The first is the growing marginalization of the Security Council in the dispute. The Council was unable to respond to the 2008 conflict[107] and on 15 June 2009 the UN's principal involvement in the conflict, UNOMIG, was terminated after Russia vetoed its renewal.[108]

Second, outside the Security Council in terms of unilaterally asserting a sphere of influence, Russia's actions can be seen as a relative success. The Russian challenge caused serious divisions within the NATO alliance and the EU. The US, Britain and most Eastern European states favoured a tough response to Russia. On the other hand, Italy and Germany, with substantial oil and gas interests in Russia, took a much softer line.[109] Georgia had received support from NATO for its eventual membership of the organization in the Bucharest Summit on 3 April 2008, without a specific Membership Action Plan.[110] However, the opposition to Georgia's membership among some NATO countries and the lack of will to intervene on its behalf were laid bare. Russia, with control of the strategic territories of South Ossetia and Abkhazia, demonstrated a clear ability to militarily intervene in Georgia.

5.7 Russian recognition of Abkhazia and South Ossetia as independent states

The next development, on 26 August 2008, was Russia's recognition of Abkhazia and South Ossetia as independent states. Russia's support for these

102 UNSC Verbatim Record (10 August 2008), UN Doc. S/PV.5953, 8.

103 Report (n. 30), I, 21, 26.

104 'Russia has important political and other interests of its own in South Ossetia and the region. In such a constellation, a humanitarian intervention is not recognised at all' (*ibid.* 24).

105 *Ibid.* 27.

106 *Corfu Channel* (n. 101).

107 See comments by Indonesia, UN Doc. S/PV.5969 (n. 2), 14.

108 UNSC Verbatim Record (15 June 2009), UN Doc. S/PV.6143, 2–3.

109 'EU stops short of sanctions on Georgia' *The Times* (1 September 2008).

110 Bucharest Summit Declaration (3 April 2008), NATO Press Release (2008), 49, (at: www.nato.int; accessed 10 January 2010).

measures focused primarily on Georgia, but was also clearly linked to the wider geopolitical context. Statements by the Foreign Ministry, President Dmitry Medvedev and Ambassador Churkin in the Security Council explicitly refer to Kosovo's unilateral declaration of independence as a provocation.[111]

The expressed legal basis for recognition was Abkhazian and South Ossetian self-determination accompanied by remedial secession. First, in the Foreign Ministry statement it was argued that Georgia's declaration of independence had violated the right of Abkhazia and South Ossetia to self-determination. This was expanded with a reference to the Soviet law on secession, which specifically sought to divide a union republic which attempted to leave the USSR, and, consequently, was never used in its dissolution.[112]

Second, Russia's statements of recognition were based on perhaps the most assertive statement on remedial secession from any state. Georgia was alleged to have committed 'genocide' against the South Ossetians, both under the administrations of Mikhail Saakashvili in 2008 and Zviad Gamsakhurdia in 1992. Saakashvili, according to the Foreign Ministry, by using force against South Ossetia, 'put paid to the territorial integrity of Georgia'.[113]

Three instruments were cited in support of this: the UN Charter, the Helsinki Final Act and the Declaration on Friendly Relations.[114] The first two are questionable authorities for remedial secession. While the UN Charter and the Helsinki Final Act both contain references to the principle of self-determination, they balance this by invocation of the principles of non-intervention and respect for the territorial integrity of states.[115] In the context of the Charter, limitations on self-determination were specifically concerned with preventing states redrawing neighbours' borders under the principle.[116] In the Final Act restrictions on territorial integrity are explicit. Moreover, states' comments in the drafting of the instruments underline an opposition to secession.[117] Neither can be seen in themselves as providing a legal basis for secession.

111 Statement by the Ministry of Foreign Affairs of the Russian Federation, 26 August 2008; Statement by President of Russia Dmitry Medvedev, 26 August 2008, (at: www.mid.ru; accessed 20 December 2009); UN Doc. S/PV.5969 (n. 2), 8.

112 UN Doc. S/PV.5969 (n. 2), 8.

113 *Ibid.*.

114 UNGA Res. 2625 (XXV), (24 October 1970), UN Doc. A/RES/2625.

115 Rapporteur, Committee I/1, United Nations Conference on International Organization, 1 June, 17; Rapporteur, Committee I/1, United Nations Conference on International Organization, 15 May, 11; and Rapporteur, Committee I/1, United Nations Conference on International Organization, 15 May 1945, 11.

116 Rapporteur, Committee I/1, United Nations Conference on International Organization 15 May, 12; Rapporteur, Committee I/1, United Nations Conference on International Organization, 1 June, 17. See also Representative of Belgium, Committee I/1, United Nations Conference on International Organization, 14 May, 12.

117 France, Doc. WD 410, CO/170, UNCIO, vol. XVII, 142–3; Columbia, Com. I/1, 15 May, 20. H. S. Russell, 'The Helsinki Declaration: Brobdingnag or Lilliput?' (1976), 70 AJIL 269–70.

The Declaration on Friendly Relations, on the other hand, does contain an ambiguous provision which has been interpreted as providing possible support for remedial secession.[118] This provides that:

> Nothing in the foregoing paragraphs shall be construed as authorizing or encouraging any action which would dismember or impair, totally or in part, the territorial integrity or political unity of sovereign and independent states conducting themselves in compliance with the principle of equal rights and self-determination of peoples as described above and thus possessed of a government representing the whole people belonging to the territory without distinction as to race, creed or colour.[119]

The Foreign Ministry statement clearly draws on this provision, but also selectively uses various paragraphs on self-determination in the Declaration in a somewhat misleading fashion:

> It should be noted that in accordance with the Declaration, every State has the duty to refrain from any forcible action which deprives peoples of their right to self-determination and freedom and independence, to adhere in their activities to the principle of equal rights and self-determination of peoples, and to possess a government representing the whole people belonging to the territory.[120]

The same formula was also used by Russia in the Security Council.[121]

Presented in this form, these provisions sound like a substantial basis for the independence of South Ossetia and Abkhazia. However, this is based on different paragraphs taken out of context. The prohibition of forcible action was not intended to relate to secessionist situations, but to peoples in non-self-governing territories and similar overseas colonial situations, or to racist regimes (essentially Southern Rhodesia and South Africa). The, 'right to self-determination and freedom and independence', is in the same context, and if applied to secession would be a radical reinterpretation, indeed the opposite, of the position of states in the Declaration.[122] Lastly, it can be noted that the

118 See R. McCorquodale, 'Self-Determination: A Human Rights Approach' (1994), 43 ICLQ 879–80; F. L. Kirgis, 'The Degrees of Self-Determination in the United Nations Era' (1994), 88 AJIL 305–6; E. Suzuki, 'Self-Determination and World Public Order: Community Response to Territorial Separation' (1975–6), 16 Virginia JIL 847–8; S. R. Ratner, 'Drawing a Better Line: *Uti Possidetis* and the Borders of New States' (1996), AJIL 611; P. H. Kooijmans, 'Tolerance, Sovereignty and Self-Determination' (1996), 43 NILR 212; V. P. Nanda, 'Self-Determination under International Law: Validity of Claims to Secede' (1981), 13 Case *W.Res.J.Int'l L.* 269–70; C. Tomuschat, 'Self-Determination in a Post-Colonial World', in C. Tomuschat (ed.), *Modern Law of Self-Determination* (Dordrecht: Martinus Nijhoff, 1993), 9–10.

119 UNGA Res. 2625 (XXX), (n. 114).

120 Foreign Ministry Statement.

121 UN Doc. S/PV.5969 (n. 2), 9.

122 See Senegal, A/C.6/SR.1002 (1967), para. 33; US, A/AC.125/SR.92 (1968), 132.

formula, 'representing the whole people belonging to the territory' without the qualification of race, creed or colour is closer to the formula in two later instruments, the Vienna Declaration 1993 and the UN Fiftieth Anniversary Declaration 1995.[123]

Nonetheless, the Declaration does make a connection between the territorial integrity of a state and a government representing the people of a territory without distinctions, which has featured in the legal discourse of secession. However, it can also be noted that the emphasis on this provision has been restrictive, with a presumption that states are representative. 'Representative' itself is an ambiguous standard. It says nothing of the quality and nature of representation and arguably does not need to extend to democratic government. The states which drafted the original formula in the Declaration stated that they were not intending to promote secession but to clarify the protection of territorial integrity.[124] The provision was cited by the Canadian Supreme Court in *Re Secession of Quebec* (1997), though it said the legal status of such a standard was unclear.[125] It was also considered by the First and Second Russian Constitutional Courts in the *Tatarstan* (1993) and *Chechnya* (1995) cases. In *Tatarstan*, the Russian Constitutional Court, referring to the Declaration, considered that it emphasized, 'the impermissibility of making reference to the principle of self-determination in order to jeopardize state and national unity'.[126] In the *Chechnya* case the Russian state was assumed to be representative, despite a violent secessionist struggle that was taking place in Chechnya at that time.[127] All this supports a relatively restrictive interpretation of the provision.[128]

Thus, Russia's use of this provision to promote remedial secession in another state represents a radical interpretation. Whereas representative government had previously been treated as a basic threshold that states could confidently satisfy, Russia elevated it to 'high standards', that Georgia, 'in no way complies with'.[129] Russia here, of course, lays itself open to the charge of double standards. Russia's forcible suppression of the Chechen secession within its own borders is believed to have inflicted civilian casualties far in excess of even its grossly inflated figures for Georgian 'genocide'. Official Russian figures for the First Chechen war estimate 30–40,000 civilian deaths,

123 'A Government representing the whole people belonging to the territory without distinction of any kind' (United Nations World Conference on Human Rights, Vienna Declaration and Programme of Action (1993), 32 ILM 1665); Declaration on the Occasion of the Fiftieth Anniversary of the United Nations, UNGA Res. 50/6 (18 October 1995), UN Doc. A/RES/50/6.

124 UK, A/AC.125/SR.69 19; UK, A/AC.125/SR.105 55; US, A/AC.125/SR.92 133; Italy, A/AC.125/SR.114 (1970), 45.

125 *Re Secession of Quebec* [1998]161 DLR 4th Series 441, para. 135.

126 *Tatarstan* (1994), 30 (3), Statutes and Decisions: The Laws of the USSR and its Successor States 40.

127 *Chechnya* (1995), 31 (5), Statutes and Decisions: The Laws of the USSR and its Successor States 48–94. See J. Summers, *Peoples and International Law* (Leiden: Brill, 2007), 277–8.

128 See Report (n. 30), I, 17.

129 UN Doc. S/PV.5969 (n. 2), 9.

while human rights organizations estimate 50,000 and a further 25,000 in the Second Chechen War.[130]

Russia's recognition of South Ossetia and Abkhazia was rejected by a majority of the Security Council, who also questioned its interpretation of the law, especially the UN Charter and Helsinki Final Act.[131] Nonetheless, Russia's recognition has created a potential legal basis, albeit not one that enjoys general international recognition, for the deployment of Russian troops in South Ossetia and Abkhazia. Before the conflict, Russian troops were deployed as CIS peacekeepers, which legally depended on the consent of Georgia. On 18 August 2008 Georgia withdrew from the CIS and removed that consent.[132] Thus, Russia's recognition allowed it to conclude a friendship treaty with South Ossetia and Abkhazia on 17 September,[133] in which South Ossetian and Abkhaz consent provided the basis for the stationing of its troops. On this basis, Russia deployed 7,400 Russian troops in each territory, establishing a permanent Russian presence south of the Caucasus.

5.8 Legality of the independence of South Ossetia and Abkhazia

Russia's recognition of Abkhazia and South Ossetia on 26 August 2008 has so far met with little support from other states. Despite a concerted campaign by Russia to promote recognition, and generous financial aid for those who do, only three other states have recognized the two entities: Nicaragua, Venezuela and Nauru. This compares with 64 states that recognize Kosovo. Significantly for Russia's sphere of influence, no CIS member has recognized the two, despite Russia reportedly applying considerable pressure on its close ally Belarus to do so.[134] Moreover, despite the notion of a Kosovo precedent, so far (with one exception) there has been no overlap between countries' recognition of Kosovo, and of South Ossetia and Abkhazia. Recognition by Nicaragua and Venezuela can be seen as part of competing spheres of influence, and ideological opposition by two left-wing Latin American states to the regional power, the United States, in addition to financial incentives. Nauru has recognized all three. However, the tiny, economically troubled island has acquired a mercenary reputation over recognition. Previously it played the Republic and the People's Republic of China against each other: switching recognition from

130 'Chechen official puts death toll for 2 wars at up to 160,000' *New York Times* (16 August 2005) (at: www.nytimes.com/2005/08/15/world/europe/15iht-chech.html; accessed 10 January 2010).

131 UNSC Verbatim Record (19 August 2008), UN Doc. S/PV.5961.

132 *Ibid.* 5.

133 *Keesing's Record of World Events* (September 2008), 48789.

134 'Russia offers Belarus $500 million for Abkhazia recognition' (at: www.eurasianet.org/departments/news/articles/eav032409.shtml; accessed 10 January 2010); Unrepresented Nations and Peoples Organization, 'Abkhazia: Recognition may not Ostracize Belarus' (at: www.unpo.org/content/view/9321/236; accessed 10 January 2010).

one to the other and then back again according to the financial incentives on offer.[135]

International law is considered to be generally neutral on secession. However, regardless of whether or not groups within states, such as the Abkhaz or Ossetians have a right to self-determination, the right is not considered to extend to a right of secession.[136]

States have also adopted additional principles which are influential in considering secessionist situations. The principle of the inviolability of frontiers, which upholds existing frontiers, was adopted by European and North American states in the Helsinki Final Act, and reaffirmed in Article 3 of the CIS Charter as one of the principles of the organization. The protection of borders was further developed by the Badinter Commission, established to advise on EU recognition policy in relation to the break-up of Yugoslavia. The Commission considered that *uti possidetis*, the principle by which established frontiers are frozen on independence, was a general principle that applied to the Yugoslav republics.[137] On the establishment of the CIS in Minsk, Russia agreed to respect, 'the inviolability of existing borders within the Commonwealth'.[138] The 'recognition of existing frontiers' was subsequently included in Article 3 of its Charter, as well as a provision on territorial integrity which obliged members to: 'refrain from any acts aimed at separation of foreign territory'.[139]

In terms of the principles of territorial integrity, the inviolability of frontiers and *uti possidetis*, there are notable similarities between Kosovo and South Ossetia and Abkhazia. The break-up of Yugoslavia and the USSR were characterized as federal dissolutions, though this was more accurate for the Soviet Union which was actually dissolved by its founding republics. Independence devolved to the federal units, within their existing frontiers, which prohibited the secessionist claims of autonomies within them.

Another objection that can be levelled at all three secessionist entities is the criteria of an independent government as the definition of statehood. The European Council's Fact-Finding Mission considered that South Ossetia

135 'Nauru recognises South Ossetia and Abkhazia' *Daily Telegraph* (15 December 2009).

136 See J. Crawford, 'State Practice and International Law in Relation to Unilateral Secession', in A. F. Bayefsky (ed.), *Self-Determination in International Law: Quebec and Lessons Learned* (The Hague: Kluwer, 2000), 42–3, 57; A. Buchanan, 'Democracy and Secession', in M. Moore (ed.), *National Self-Determination and Secession* (Oxford: Oxford University Press, 1998), 15; D. Philpott, 'Self-Determination in Practice', in M. Moore (ed.), *National Self-Determination and Secession* (Oxford: Oxford University Press, 1998), 86; D. F. Orentlicher, 'International Responses to Separatist Claims: Are Democratic Principles Relevant?', in S. Macedo and A. Buchanan (eds.), *Secession and Self-Determination* (New York, NY: New York University Press, 2003), 19; D. Murswiek, 'The Issue of a Right of Secession – Reconsidered', in C. Tomuschat (ed.), *Modern Law of Self-Determination* (Dordrecht: Martinus Nijhoff, 1993), 23–4, 37; S. J. Anaya, 'The Capacity of International Law to Advance Ethnic or Nationality Rights Claims' (1993), 13 *Hum.Rts.Q.* 404.

137 Opinion No. 3 (1992), 31 ILM 1500. See also Opinion No. 2, 1498, para. 1.

138 Article 5, Agreement Establishing the Commonwealth of Independent States (1992), 31 ILM 144.

139 Charter of the Commonwealth of Independent States 1993 (1995), 34 ILM 1283–4.

lacked this, as Russia's influence on the territory was systematic, widespread and permanent.[140] On the other hand, it concluded that Abkhazia had the ability to act with a sufficient degree of independence, citing as the only example the defeat of Russia's explicitly preferred candidate in Abkhaz elections.[141] If the Mission considered this was enough to establish independence despite finding that Abkhazia's, 'policies and structures, particularly its security and defence institutions, remain to a large extent under the control of Moscow',[142] this might also reflect the EU's own role, through its EULEX mission, in policing and justice in Kosovo. Nonetheless, there may be a different perception of the roles of international organizations exercising some governmental roles within a territory and a sovereign state controlling government organs.

Perhaps the most significant legal difference, however, between Kosovo and South Ossetia and Abkhazia relates to massive human rights violations. The humanitarian situation in which Abkhazia and South Ossetia established themselves as de facto independent from Georgia militates against them. The creation of both was accompanied by the expulsion of IDPs who have not been allowed to return, thus both entities can be seen not to conform to basic standards on human rights and the protection of minorities.[143] This ethnic cleansing, which appears to have been both widespread and systematic in the territories, may constitute, at a minimum, the crime against humanity of deportation. These violations are particularly acute when considering Abkhazia's statehood, as its status as an Abkhaz-dominated self-governing entity is dependent on the continued displacement of the territory's ethnic Georgian population.

However, the fictitious independence of South Ossetia and Abkhazia belies the more significant legal position that both are effectively under Russian sovereignty. Indeed, South Ossetia did not seek independence as its primary goal, rather union with Russia and North Ossetia, for which it petitioned unsuccessfully in 1992 and again after the 2008 conflict. On each occasion it was formally rejected by Russia.[144] The formal annexation of territory from another state following an armed conflict, and international recognition of this would be unprecedented in the UN era. Nonetheless, despite calling them independent, Russia has continued and refined the policy which it has developed for years of appropriating crucial elements of sovereignty over the territories. Whatever their designation, South Ossetia and Abkhazia are united with Russia through a common nationality, economic union and open borders.

140 Report (n. 30), II, 133
141 *Ibid.* 133–4.
142 *Ibid.* 134.
143 *Ibid.* 134–5.
144 'South Ossetia slapped down over Russia unity claim' *The Times* (11 September 2008).

5.9 Conclusion

The case of Georgia illustrates how states can construct spheres of influence in the UN era. Russia effectively established protectorates within the UN system of peacekeeping. Moreover, rather than annexing territory, it deconstructed statehood, removing and appropriating certain elements, such as population and government. This is not to say that this process conforms with international law. Indeed, serious violations have taken place. It remains to be seen what the outcome of the legal proceedings that Georgia is taking against Russia in the International Court of Justice will be.

6 Hegemony, multipolarity and the system of international law

Alexander Orakhelashvili

6.1 Introduction

At various stages of its development, the international legal system has witnessed events and processes that have raised questions as to its continuing feasibility and adaptability to changing historical circumstances. Over the past two decades, events such as the end of the Cold War and demise of the Eastern bloc, entailing predominance of the power position of the United States in the period immediately following and culminating with wars in Afghanistan and Iraq, have led to doctrinal enquiries into whether these events and processes can explain or influence the essence, content and operation of the international legal system. This doctrinal focus is understandable. The major changes brought about by the end of the Cold War, most importantly the transformation of world politics from the confrontation between the two superpowers into what many in the 1990s saw as a system run by the sole remaining superpower, the United States, and what today is increasingly regarded as a revival of traditional power politics based on multipolarity, could not have taken place without having an impact on both international legal and international political sciences. The principal question to be engaged with is whether these changes in political position can affect the essence and development of the international legal system; whether the nature of international law has been influenced by political factors of hegemony and trends towards unipolarity.

This requires having an adequate focus both in terms of international legal analysis and of historical and political sciences. In order to obtain an outcome that could be defended against systemic and evidentiary considerations, two methodological requirements should be observed. First, it is necessary to locate the political developments over the past two decades in the broader historical context. It is necessary to understand that over many centuries international political and legal systems have been witnessing major transformations alleged to have the potential to affect the essence of the international legal system – what some today would, modishly, denote as international constitutional moments. This broad historical perspective can adequately explain how exceptional the events or processes over the past two decades have been.

The second methodological requirement relates to understanding the nature of international law as a body of rules agreed between, and binding upon, states. Changes within the international legal system are always effected by agreement between states. There have always been doctrinal arguments that, the consensual imperative notwithstanding, international law is not as much about agreement between states, as about some other – deeper, more intricate and subtle – factors that enable writers better to grasp the essence and implications of the international legal system.[1] It is difficult to find any evidence that the international legal system accepts these approaches. It is, after all, states that create international law. In the lawmaking process states can be motivated by multiple considerations of political, economic or strategic character, but the existence of international legal rules depends not on those considerations and motives, but on states giving their consent. This factor is crucial in clarifying the merit of doctrinal positions which argue that changes of power positions on the international plane can affect the essence and content of international legal regulation.

6.2 Unipolarity, multipolarity and hegemony: the policy debate

Following the end of the Cold War, policy debate and related journalism in the 1990s testified to the popularity of the thesis of the unipolar world and hegemony. With Eastern bloc power and influence in different parts of the world curtailed, China still in the nascent state of its 'superpower' status, and Europe far from having a uniform foreign and security policy, the economic and military might of the United States was at that time a significant factor that caused both analysts and scholars to assume that international relations were conducted in a unipolar system, and that the will and power of the United States was essentially what directed that system.

Even as scientific discontents of the American hegemony and unipolar world thesis have never been satisfactorily articulated, this thesis has become a background, sometimes unspoken, assumption to multiple attempts at explaining and understanding both international relations and international law. Zbignew Brzezinski articulated the thesis of the United States as the sole remaining superpower and the indispensable power because of its military, political and economic power. As there was no other state that could contest American leadership, the only alternative to that leadership would be international anarchy.[2] Consciously or not, Brzezinski in fact illustrated the argument that hegemony is in fact antithetical to the anarchical nature of the international society. This is clear from Brzezinski's qualification that the incontestability of American leadership would last 'for more than a generation'.

Another doctrinal policy perspective was developed by Samuel Huntington. His analysis was premised on the existence of core states in each part of the

1 See section 6.5.

2 Z. Brzezinski, 'A Geostrategy for Eurasia' (1997) 75 *Foreign Affairs* 51–2.

world which reinforced multipolarity that would eventually lead to a clash of civilizations. Huntington emphasized that the US leadership in forcing Iraq to withdraw from Kuwait, which it had occupied in August 1990, was a unipolar moment in a world that was bound to remain multipolar. While the unipolar leadership of a superpower presupposed the leadership of the single superpower in setting and enforcing the global agenda, Huntington specified that in the twenty-first century the world would remain multipolar and would witness the clash or compromise between the diverse national interests of major powers. In the same spirit, Huntington specified that major powers would be responsible for maintaining order in the particular regions which they dominate and there would be no need for the US to intervene to perform this task in those regions.[3] Huntington's thesis thus went against that of Brzezinski who called for the establishment of a new security architecture for Eurasia to reflect the change of political positions after the end of the Cold War. Huntington's approach has also been voiced by Kenneth Waltz who argued in 1993 that in a unipolar world, states should want to balance the hegemon's unchecked power and that states would be 'edging away' from the US in order to balance it.[4]

Acceptance of the unipolarity and hegemony thesis is significantly due to the lack of multidisciplinary research in this area to ascertain how far hegemony and unipolarity is feasible in international relations and how far the international legal system can accommodate this phenomenon. If hegemony implies setting and enforcing the global agenda, the international legal system is the most proper place to verify how these attempts work because it is precisely this legal system where, most importantly, albeit not exclusively, attempts are made to consolidate hegemonic positions and reactions to those attempts are expressed.

The unipolarist approach to international politics can easily accommodate the thesis of hegemony, while multipolarity implies the absence of a single hegemon in the world – of one single centre of political power in the international society which would adopt principal international policy decisions – and the adoption of those policy decisions by agreement between various political power centres, whether or not those power centres are ideologically similar to each other. The approach of multipolarity does not rule out the concept of hegemony as such: it opposes the notion of global hegemony but is not inimical to regional hegemonies that give rise to regional spheres of influence. Multipolarity thus implies the distribution of political, economic and military power as between power centres in ways precluding the domination of one power centre over others. One traditional way of

3 S. Huntington, 'The Erosion of American National Interest' (1997) 75 *Foreign Affairs* 28; more specifically, S. Huntington, 'The Lonely Superpower' (1999) 78 *Foreign Affairs* 35. See more generally S. Huntington, *The Clash of Civilizations and the Remaking of World Order* (New York, NY: Simon & Schuster, 1996).

4 Cf. C. Gegout, 'Causes and Consequences of the EU's Military Intervention in the Democratic Republic of Congo: A Realist Explanation' (2005) 10 *European Foreign Affairs* Review 437.

achieving this has been the system of the balance of power in Europe from the sixteenth to the nineteenth centuries under which no state was to become so strong and powerful as to dominate others. The balance of power is sometimes seen as a law of nature.[5]

Multipolarity for the purposes of the international legal system refers to the adoption of legal norms and instruments through a decentralized consensual process under which no power centre is able to bind others unilaterally. It is therefore not surprising that the existence of a balance of power as a political institution has been seen as necessary for international law to exist, operate and survive. According to Oppenheim, the:

> Law of Nations can exist only if there is an equilibrium, a balance of power, between the members of the Family of Nations. If the powers cannot keep one another in check, no rules of law will have any force, since an over-powerful State will naturally try to act according to discretion and disobey the law.[6]

As Waltz explains, a balance of power can impose restraints on the power aspirations of states who may aspire to domination under the guise of survival. In effect this balance prevents a world hegemony.[7] As Hedley Bull states, balance of powers has served to prevent the international system from being transformed by conquest into a universal empire.[8] This factor alone signifies the crucial importance of the balance of power, and is also premised on diversity in international society as a necessary precondition for the survival of international law. Political realism that regards power as a paramount consideration emphasizes the equally vital role of a balance of power. According to Waltz, in international politics an unbalanced power constitutes a danger 'even if it is American power that is out of balance'. Unipolar systems are very precarious.[9] Unipolar hegemony is thus not easily sustainable over the long-term period.

Unipolarism involves risks of hegemonic domination and hence of eroding the international legal system: multipolarity can be based on a balance of power and hence supports the functioning of international law. However, multipolarity can result in core states' domination in what can become their spheres of influence and then potentially cause a reciprocal erosion of pertinent principles of international law, at least of the practical viability of those principles. Whatever the conceptual and ethical concerns this option raises, it still remains the case that in political terms the agreements between 'core'

5 K. N. Waltz, 'Anarchic Orders and Balances of Power', in R. O. Keohane (ed.), *Neorealism and its Critics* (New York, NY: Columbia University Press, 1986), 116.

6 L. Oppenheim, *International Law*, vol. 1 (2nd edn, London: Longmans, Green & Co., 1912), 73.

7 Waltz (n. 5), 119, 127.

8 H. Bull, *The Anarchical Society: A Study of Order in World Politics* (London: Macmillan, 1977), 102.

9 Quoted in S. Burchill, 'Realism and Neo-Realism', in S. Burchill *et al.*, *Theories of International Relations* (2nd edn, Basingstoke: Palgrave, 2001), 97–8.

states to respect each other's spheres of influence is much more likely than general political, still less legal, agreements between power centres to accept a single global hegemon and a unipolar world.[10] Multipolarity can be problematic but, in the first place at least, it essentially accords with the nature of international law. A unipolar world has never existed and is conceptually impossible, as far as international law is concerned.

The United Nations system necessarily implies both multilateral and multipolar foundations for both international political and legal systems. The UN Charter as a constitutional instrument confirms this in several respects. The enhanced role of the UN General Assembly in adopting major policy directions on the international plane is accompanied by the solid representation in this body of the voices and positions from all political and ideological groupings within international society. This influences the process of adoption of all major international policies. The composition of the principal organ of the UN which can adopt binding operative decisions, including economic and military sanctions against the entities that cause threats to international peace and security – the Security Council – ensures that this organ can only act on the basis of the unanimity of the five permanent members. These include three members which are Western and liberal – the United States, Britain and France – and two members – China and Russia – which are non-Western and essentially illiberal. In this framework, important policy decisions can only be adopted on the basis of a multipolar and multilateral approach.

These structural factors notwithstanding, it can still be contended that whatever the procedures and institutions for international lawmaking and law enforcement, it is still power that determines international relations. Consequently the unipolarist hegemon can run the system by wielding its power. This reasoning originally featured in the Schmittian approach to law, whether national or international. Schmitt considered that constitution in formal terms did not matter; it mattered instead who could call the police.[11] Classical realism has also been sceptical about international law, as appears

10 The thesis of multipolarity and non-interference as between centres of powers and spheres of their influence, coupled with a hegemonic dominance, intervention and use of force within the particular region has been articulated at different stages of history. Carl Schmitt's development of the *Grossraum* theory was one of the earlier manifestations. At the San Francisco conference in 1945 when the UN Charter was to be adopted, the idea of incorporation of regional spheres of influence was upheld by Winston Churchill but this view was rejected in favour of the approach propounded by the UN Secretary of State Cordell Hull, who advocated the idea of global responsibility of the UN. The aftermath of the Cold War has, as seen above, witnessed yet another version of this debate, with Brzezinski propagating the idea of global American hegemony and Huntington supporting the idea of core areas run by core states. Whatever the design behind these individual theories, the conceptual essence of approving regional domination through regional centres of power is essentially the same in all pertinent instances. For analysis on the development of the notion of 'spheres of influence', see A. Orakhelashvili, 'International Law and Geopolitics: One Object, Conflicting Legitimacies?' (2008) 39 NYIL 155–204.

11 M. Koskenniemi, 'Carl Schmitt, Hans Morgenthau, and the Image of Law in International Relations', in M. Byers (ed.), *The Role of Law in International Politics* (Oxford: Oxford University Press, 1999), 17.

from the writings of E. H. Carr and Hans Morgenthau. 'Legalism' is understood as 'utopian' thinking. Instead, classical realism sought to provide a conceptual ground for US foreign policy in terms of rationalizing the accumulation of power.[12] To Dean Acheson, 'power is that combination of population, resources, technology, and will which makes a national society dominant among other national societies'.[13] The realist implications of power are presented in two ways. Stronger states can get away with violations of the law as a matter of fact; states will do what they think is in their interest and if they are powerful, international law cannot provide remedies against this.[14] If the argument is taken further, their violations can bring about change in the pertinent legal position: stronger states determine the content of international law.

Neo-realists have criticized Morgenthau's 'murky' concept of power as having little focus on its discontents: this made his theory inconsistent.[15] In addition, power alone is not enough to resolve international problems. As Hurrell explains:

> states need international law and institutions both to share the material and political costs of protecting their interests and to gain the authority and legitimacy that the possession of crude power can never secure on its own. All major powers face the imperative of trying to turn a capacity for crude coercion into legitimate authority...Power is not self-justifying; it must be justified by reference to some source outside or beyond itself, and thus be transformed into 'authority'. For this reason, it is a mistake to view 'law' as something that is, or can be, wholly separated from some separate other thing called 'political interest'.[16]

In an even more complex way, Keohane articulates the notion of fungibility of power, which means that across a variety of fields great powers would necessarily prevail over smaller powers. Still, the failures of great powers to control weaker states in some issue areas can be explained because 'the States that are weaker on an overall basis have more power resources than their stronger partners, and that the use of power derived from one area of activity to affect outcomes in other areas (through "linkages") is difficult'.[17]

12 R. O. Keohane, 'Neorealism in World Politics', in R. O. Keohane (ed.), *Neorealism and Its Critics* (New York, NY: Columbia University Press, 1986), 9.

13 D. Acheson, 'Foreign Policy of the United States' (1964–5), 18 *Ark.L.Rev.* 226–7.

14 E. H. Carr, *The Twenty Years' Crisis, 1919–1939: An Introduction to the Study of International Relations* (2nd edn, Basingstoke: Palgrave, 2001), 297.

15 Keohane (n. 12), 11, 13.

16 A. Hurrell, *On Global Order: Power, Values and the Constitution of International Society* (Oxford: Oxford University Press, 2008), 39, 78.

17 R. O. Keohane, 'Theory in World Politics: Structural Realism and Beyond', in R. O. Keohane (ed.), *Neorealism and Its Critics* (New York, NY: Columbia University Press, 1986), 184, 187. 'No matter how carefully power resources are defined, no power model will be able accurately to predict outcomes.' Non-power factors are also important. *Ibid.* 195–6.

As historical experience indeed shows, power wielders do not always get their way, as was the case with the war in Vietnam or with the US intervention in Somalia. The outcomes of US-led wars in Iraq and Afghanistan are also far from clear. The US/UK power engagement with Libya in the 1990s over the Libyan refusal to extradite two terrorist suspects that were its nationals to those countries did not, despite the prevailing power of the US and the UK, make their policies succeed. Although Security Council sanctions were imposed on Libya, they were not effective and the final outcome of the dispute reflected the original preference of Libya. The normalization of US/UK–Libyan relations took place on the basis of mutual compromise and through the means of international law.[18] In other cases, states in disadvantaged power positions can rely on an alternative power, as the examples of Cuba and more recently of Zimbabwe demonstrate. Power indisputably matters, but it is often spread in such a way that puts limits on either the power wielder's ability to project power, or the effect of the projected power, or causes the power wielder to pay a higher political price than it foresaw.

6.3 'Hegemony' and international law

The current ethos of 'hegemonic international law' follows from a perceived need to explain in legal terms the leading position of the United States in shaping and reshaping international law.[19] The putative implications of the status of a 'hegemon' can relate to its influence in lawmaking, in the application of law to facts, and in the actual enforcement of legal rules. All these can be determined by reference to the ideological and political preferences of the 'hegemon'. The idea of hegemony as related to international law has both a long history and interdisciplinary origins. The division of the history of international law into Spanish, French, British and American periods mirrors the division of history in political science into eras such as the *Pax Britannica* and the *Pax Americana*, which denote the periods dominated by the hegemony of the particular power.[20]

This approach is not always accurate. The British hegemony (*Pax Britannica*) was based on Britain's sea power and liberal economic policies. Under this view, liberal economic values were universal rules and British sea power a potential enforcer. This image of British hegemony survived far longer than its actual hegemony. *Pax Americana* after the Second World War has also been understood as a form of hegemony. But even during the Cold War, there was a doctrinal argument that the United States could no longer act as the

18 J. Schwartz, 'Dealing with a "Rogue State": The Libya Precedent' (2007) 101 AJIL 553. See also section 6.4.

19 D. Vagts, 'Hegemonic International Law' (2001) 95 AJIL 843, referring among others to the view of Charles Krauthammer in *Time*.

20 See P. Taylor and C. Flint, *Political Geography* (4th edn, Harlow: Pearson/Prentice Hall, 2007), referring to Modelski's cycles of hegemony. For attempts to locate this phenomenon in the history of international law, see W. Grewe, *Epochen der Völkerrechtsgeschichte* (Baden-Baden: Nomos Verlagsgesellschaft, 1988).

guarantor of the world order.[21] According to Detlev Vagts, the United States does not have the 'political and psychological infrastructure hegemony calls for'.[22] Thomas Franck seconded the proposition, arguing that America had neither stomach nor purse for a perpetual role as the policeman of the world.[23] Still, policy perceptions in favour of the hegemony approach are widely held in political writings and more generally by political elites.

A major problem with the hegemony approach is the assumption that if, in a particular period of international legal history, the relevant state has exercised political hegemony and the consequent influence on lawmaking, other periods of that history should be seen in the same perspective. But the patterns of hegemony have been diverse. *Pax Romana* was the domination by empire, in one part of the world only; *Pax Britannica* did not, at least in Europe, involve as much domination by Britain as its influence implied the ability to tip the balance in the conflicts between other powers. This was displayed in the context where there was a generally accepted principle of the balance of power which had a semi-constitutional significance and in the maintenance of which Britain had both a vital interest and a unique role. Such coincidence of position and interest ensured that the British hegemonic – or semi-hegemonic – position was relatively uncontested and, on occasion, was actually deemed useful by other powers. These factors furthermore promoted the understanding both by Britain and by other powers that the British hegemonic position was not without limits. This distinguishes this case from other instances where a putative or aspiring hegemon is either uninterested in principles or attempts to revise them.

While the British pattern of 'hegemony' emphasized its global role and function, the portrayal of the American hegemony is presumably the first one that implies a global domination of politics in the international system, which underlines its unreality. As for *Pax Americana*, it was never an incontrovertible reality before 1992, that is at the end of the bipolar world, and then only for a few years. All in all, it is unclear whether historical and political science has ever consistently defined the meaning of hegemony.

Hegemony can imply a degree of unilateralism through which the hegemon shapes and influences the legal framework. The hegemon arguably provides the ideas and composes the agenda both for international political and international legal processes. In political terms, the hegemon often formulates the potential outcomes of international controversies. But can the hegemon impose law on those who do not consent? If so, the hegemonic approach is premised on the denial of the character of international law as the body of

21 R. Cox, 'Social Forces, States and World Orders', in R. O. Keohane (ed.), *Neorealism and Its Critics* (New York, NY: Columbia University Press, 1986), 223–5, 229.

22 Vagts (n. 19), 845.

23 T. M. Franck, 'The United Nations as Guarantor of International Peace and Security: Past, Present and Future', in C. Tomuschat (ed.), *The United Nations at Age Fifty: A Legal Perspective* (The Hague: Kluwer Law International, 1995), 35.

consensually agreed rules. To compose international law, it is not enough to have power; it is also necessary to obtain the consent of others. In socio-political terms, Kingsbury emphasizes 'an unavoidable tension between British advocacy of balance of power and hegemonic arguments for the *Pax Britannica*'.[24] Hegemony also contradicts the fundamental principle of the sovereign equality of states. Oppenheim rejects the thesis that 'political hegemony exercised by the great powers rests on a legal basis'. States may be politically unequal but their legal equality 'must remain valid as long as the family of nations remains in existence'.[25]

Dominance by a powerful state can be a necessary but not a sufficient condition for hegemony.[26] The fact that the state has accumulated power within the international system confirms that the system is organized in such a way as to support this power position. The accumulation of economic and military power by the US in the aftermath of the Second World War, whether economic influence abroad, especially through international financial institutions or with the establishment of military bases, took place consistently with international law. Thus the power-wielding state, if judging rationally, has to be interested in preserving the system and acknowledging the limits it may envisage for its power position. Power accumulation takes place under the conditions prescribed by the system. Attempts to change the system may undermine the very power position of power-wielding states. This, among other reasons, is why at subsequent stages of Cold War enterprises such as the Vietnam War and the 'war on terror' have not attracted legal approval. The main reason for this is that fundamental principles of international law – non-use of force, non-intervention, territorial integrity, and so on – do not exist as doctrinal inventions or ideological precepts, but as principles of timeless value that have been approved and found useful, indeed indispensable, by a great number of states over a very long period of time. Viewing hegemony as having the potential of succeeding even in defiance of these principles is as short-sighted as it is unhistorical.

Images of a particular hegemony certainly outlive its actuality. The reality of hegemony depends on the hegemon's interaction with the system where, as E. H. Carr observed, the status quo justifies the privileged position of dominant entities. Just as the domestic political class prays for domestic peace, so will internationally dominant entities seek to maintain peace in international affairs.[27] Thus the 'hegemon' is supposed to want peace and continuity. The attitude of the United States towards a number of international legal questions aimed at changing international law certifies that, to use

24 B. Kingsbury, 'Legal Positivism as Normative Politics: International Society, Balance of Power and Lassa Oppenheim's Positive International Law' (2002) 13 EJIL 419.

25 L. Oppenheim, 'The Science of International Law: Its Task and Method' (1908) 2 AJIL 347.

26 Cox (n. 21), 223.

27 Carr (n. 14), 102–4.

Henry Kissinger's classification,[28] the US is a revolutionary power, attempting to change significant aspects of international law. Obviously there may be an argument that the hegemon actually uses force to manage the system. But this does not correspond to the attitude of international society towards the actions of the 'hegemon'. It is the system that makes a hegemon and not vice versa. Hegemony can survive only if the aspirations of a hegemon overlap with the basic requirements of the system. This is, among other reasons, why there can be no hegemonic international law: an entity, however major and powerful, cannot direct the system. There is no government on the international plane and 'hegemons' cannot imitate it.

6.4 Theories of domination

The thesis of hegemony is based on an approach of exceptionality. It is opportune to examine those doctrinal approaches that have over the past two centuries tried to justify the exceptional treatment of certain states in terms of their rights and obligations.

Presumably, the oldest theory of exceptionality and domination is that of 'European international law', which was professed over the entire nineteenth century and in the early twentieth century by European legal scholars as the mainline tradition of European thought in this area. The principal thesis of this theory was that international law is part of the European tradition which entails placing European states in a privileged position in relation to non-European uncivilized countries and excludes the latter from the ambit of international law, consequently justifying European freedom of action in relation to those countries through a variety of means ranging from the use of force to colonial domination. The proponents of 'European international law' advanced hardly any evidence to demonstrate how this doctrine could be viewed as part of positive international law, and chose to ignore the evidence pointing to the fact that at no stage of its existence has international law been a truly or exclusively European system. This doctrine was, then, a profound example of putting ideology over evidence to justify policies of appropriation and domination.[29]

The establishment of the Third Reich in Germany in the 1930s gave a fresh impetus to reappraising the basic categories of international law, such as territoriality and the inviolability of borders, to suit the policy aims of the Reich. In its treatment of Czechoslovakia, the Reich played the self-determination card in defiance of the principle of territorial integrity. As early as 1934, a number of German lawyers worked to introduce the concept of *Lebensraum* into international legal reasoning. This would be the new German international law and replace traditional legal institutes laid down in

28 H. Kissinger, *A World Restored: Metternich, Castlereagh and the Problems of Peace 1812–1822* (London: Phoenix Press, 1957), 1.

29 For detail, see A. Orakhelashvili, 'The Idea of European International Law' (2006) 17 EJIL 315–45.

pursuance of British and French policies. New German principles were derived from 'the right to space and soil', and focused on the notion of Greater Areas (*Grossraum*). This approach was supported by Carl Schmitt who opposed applying 'empty legalism', which had no relation to the live issues of world policy, to international relations. Schmitt criticized political institutions, such as the balance of power and natural frontiers, which, in his opinion, were received categories of international law. The Monroe Doctrine, in contrast, was the most revolutionary departure from international law, and was seen as suitable for justifying the principle of German *Grossraum* in international law. Schmitt accepted the principle of non-intervention but only in relation to greater areas as opposed to states. The will of the German Reich, based on the power of its people, would be the basis of this 'new' international law.[30]

The New Haven policy-oriented theory, which contends that international law is a process of policy decisions and not a body of rules,[31] reveals similar methodological traits in the approach against legalism, and attempts to provide the policy reasons for justifying breaches of international law by reference to a particular power or ideological position of the pertinent state. By attempting to substitute for the criteria of legality its 'major purposes' and 'human dignity' approach, which in essence refers to ideological preferences, the New Haven school contains the doctrinal potential for justifying almost every action, whether or not 'technically' and 'formally' lawful, if perpetrated by those who stand for freedom. The reasons advanced to justify the US hydrogen test practices despite the problems with compliance with the law of the sea illustrate this position.[32] The same applies to the New Haven school's reaction to events such as the Vietnam War, the Cuban quarantine and several others.

The liberal theory of international law developed in the 1990s tries to understand international law redesigned according to ideological premises. It is asserted that 'Liberals distinguish among states on the basis of their regime type',[33] and that liberal market democracy is an internationally sanctioned legitimate model of domestic governance.[34] The most distinctive aspect of the liberal theory is that 'it permits, indeed mandates, a distinction among different types of States based on their domestic political structure and ideology'.[35] But in order for this to be so, the agreement of states to this effect ought to be demonstrated. Linking liberal ideology to the content of

30 R. Strausz-Hupé, *Geopolitics: The Struggle for Space and Power* (New York, NY: G.P. Putnam's Sons, 1942), 88–90.

31 M. McDougal, 'International Law, Power and Policy: A Contemporary Conception' (I–1953) 82 *Recueil des Cours*. McDougal's Hague Lectures acknowledge that his policy-oriented approach went against the mainline international law theory, see 143–4.

32 M. McDougal, 'The Hydrogen Bomb Tests and the International Law of the Sea' (1955) 49 AJIL 356.

33 A.-M. Slaughter, A. Tulumello and S. Wood, 'International Law and International Relations Theory: A New Generation of Inter-Disciplinary Scholarship' (1998) 92 AJIL 373.

34 I. Clark, *Legitimacy in International Society* (Oxford: Oxford University Press, 2007), 180.

35 A.-M. Slaughter, 'International Law in a World of Liberal States' (1995) 6 EJIL 504.

international law contradicts the nature of international law as the body of rules established through the agreement of states not subject to any overarching sovereign – states who subscribe to diverse ideologies.

Liberal theory is effectively an attempt to redefine international law and discover its broader concept,[36] which goes hand in hand with the refusal of liberals to acknowledge the dividing line between law and politics. This further emphasizes the similarities between liberal theory and the New Haven school. Slaughter's emphasis on behavioural difference between states in terms of their legal position is generically similar to McDougal's reference to 'major purposes' and 'human dignity' as factors that can justify a 'technically' illegal action. The opposition of liberalism to the basic structure of international law also reveals its methodological similarity with the Schmittian theory – as Slaughter claims, 'territorial boundaries become increasingly meaningless, so that situs analysis cedes its place to interest analysis'.[37] Last but not least, the insistence on the behavioural difference thesis confirms that the liberal theory is a repetition of the European international law approach.

As Koskenniemi aptly demonstrated, the liberal theory and its interdisciplinary focus essentially on the application of Schmitt's ideas to international law and a search for 'a neo-liberal *Grossraum*'.[38] Schmitt was keen to see formality and territoriality as basic precepts of international law displaced by the dynamism and flexibility that would enable various national power interests get their way, whether or not this was compatible with the 'formal' law. The New Haven School, too, has attempted to do away with the formal requirements of international law to justify and excuse wrongful conduct whenever it is seen as suitable from particular ideological and political standpoints. So liberal theory attempts to justify differential treatment for states in terms of their political and economic systems. All these approaches express dismay at the focus of legal science on the formal and normative character of law, and strive to have the legal reasoning complemented by, or fused with, political or ideological reasoning. These doctrinal attacks notwithstanding, international law has to maintain its formality to keep its independent standing in the international system alive. If it becomes so flexible and dynamic as to adapt to the relevant political and factual trends, it will become assimilated with and indistinguishable from them, and it would then be difficult to speak of international law as law.[39]

According to the liberal view of international politics, relations between democracies form a sort of 'security community' in which states do not fight

36 As conceded by liberal authors, Slaughter, Tulumello and Wood (n. 33), 378.

37 A.-M. Slaughter, 'International Law and International Relations Theory: A Dual Agenda' (1993) 87 AJIL 236.

38 Koskenniemi (n. 11), 34.

39 On this substantial, as opposed to structural aspect of the legal character of international law, see A. Orakhelashvili, *Interpretation of Acts and Rules in Public International Law* (Oxford: Oxford University Press, 2008), chs. 1 and 2.

or expect to fight each other.[40] If this were taken as a principle as opposed to an empirical description, then it would involve a differentiation as to how a fundamental principle of international law – that of prohibition of the use of force – applies to relations between liberal and non-liberal states. In a way reflecting the preferences of liberal theory, the US administration in the 1990s considered it right for NATO to use force without UN Security Council authorization when the US thought it was useful. The Clinton administration would presumably not have envisaged organizations such as the Arab League or the CIS being equally free in this field. Yet, distinguishing NATO from those other organizations could not be accomplished without an accepted legal principle.[41] Along similar lines, Brunée criticizes as problematic Slaughter's view that a permanent coalition of liberal states might be the decision-making body to authorize the use of force when the Security Council is paralysed. This idea is unacceptable to developing states as contradicting the pluralist background of international law, and such 'a banding together of a coalition of democratic States would only further poison international relations'.[42]

Recent developments also demonstrate that the liberal behavioural distinction does not work in practice. Cuba has been readmitted to the Organization of American States and the 1962 Resolution which excluded the government of Cuba from its participation in the Inter-American system has ceased to have effect.[43] But the liberal approach to international law was not asserted even in the Cold War period of confrontation of such gravity as the placement of Soviet nuclear missiles on Cuba produced. In the Security Council, protesting against the deployment of Soviet missiles, the US Representative spoke in defence of political pluralism under the UN Charter:

> The vision of San Francisco was the vision of a world community of independent nations, each freely developing according to its own traditions and its own genius, bound together by a common respect for the rights of other nations and by a common loyalty to the larger international order. This vision assumes that this earth is quite large enough to shelter a great variety of economic systems, political creeds, philosophical beliefs, and religious convictions. The faith of the Charter is in a pluralistic world, a world of free choice, respecting the infinite diversity of mankind and dedicated to nations living together as good neighbours in peace.

40 Cf. E. Adler and M. Barnett (eds.), *Security Communities* (Cambridge: Cambridge University Press, 1998), 12.

41 M. E. O'Connell, 'The United Nations Security Council and the Authorisation of Force', in N. Blokker and N. Schrijver, *The Security Council and the Use of Force* (Leiden: Nijhoff, 2005), 53.

42 J. Brunée, 'The Security Council and Self-Defence: Which Way to Global Security?', in N. Blokker and N. Schrijver, *The Security Council and the Use of Force* (Leiden: Nijhoff, 2005), 114.

43 OAS assembly resolution on Cuba (XXXIX-O/09) (9 June 2009) UN Doc. AG/RES/2438, para. 1

The US Representative pressed this point further by asking, 'Has the Soviet Union ever really joined the United Nations? Or does its philosophy of history and its conception of the future run counter to the pluralistic concept of the Charter?'.[44]

If this approach was correct during the Cold War when confrontation between states representing different political systems was more intense than ever, it should be even more compelling in the post-Cold War period. A cynical 'realistic' view could be that stating one's allegiance to pluralism and diversity could be due to one having been driven into a defensive position. But such a view would even more vividly discredit any inherent value that liberalism could claim to have in international relations.

Myres McDougal was presumably aware of the above official US position. Yet, writing on the quarantine introduced by the US government against Cuba, McDougal proceeded not to justify it by legal evidence but by the 'general community expectation' of 'free peoples'. 'Free Peoples', McDougal asserted, 'do not, as some have insisted, have to choose between the historic restraints of international law and their own survival'.[45] This mirrors, at one time, the Schmittian reference to survival and necessity as an excuse to bypass the antiquated 'historic' law; and is also reflected in Thomas Franck's attempts to reinterpret the prohibition of the use of force so as to enable the emergency action to secure survival,[46] and in the liberal attempts to justify discrimination with regard to the rights and duties of states on the basis of whether a particular ideology considers them to be free.

6.5 'Hegemons' versus 'rogue', 'pariah' or 'outlaw' states

One of the implications of the hegemonic perception is a policy which attempts to degrade the political or legal standing of certain states by denoting them as rogues, pariahs or outlaws. The policy of the 'outlawing' of states refers to such issues as poor human rights records, their involvement in terrorism or in producing weapons of mass destruction, but it goes considerably beyond what would be needed to reverse these shortcomings in the political and legal approach of 'outlawed' states, for instance in terms of the law of state responsibility. It aims systemically to enshrine and perpetuate the isolation and diminution in status of those states. It is an ironic implication that in practice this 'outlawing' process has no consequences of its own and that it is over and above the consequences of consensual decisions, such as collective security decisions to impose sanctions. The conceptual problems entailed by the liberal theory are likewise present in this context.

44 A. E. Stevenson, 'Statement' (23 October 1962) 47 Dept. of St. Bull. 723, 724, 726.

45 M. McDougal, 'The Soviet–Cuban Quarantine and Self-Defense' (1963) 57 AJIL 603–4.

46 See, for detail, T. M. Franck, *Recourse to Force: State Action against Threats and Armed Attacks* (Cambridge: Cambridge University Press, 2002), ch. 10.

There are various ways of stating or enforcing such policies. The efforts by US and UK succeeded, years after the Lockerbie terrorist bombing of a civilian plane, in having sanctions imposed on Libya under Security Council Resolutions 748 (1992) and 883 (1993). The aim was to induce Libya to extradite the alleged perpetrators of the Lockerbie attack to one of the sponsoring states. When the matter was pending before the Security Council, Libya reacted to the US accusations that Libya was complicit to terrorism by submitting that 'The United States is exploiting the current international situation to set itself up as a world government and an international policeman determining what is true and what is false and defining ethics and good conduct'.[47]

Even if the intention of proponents of the 'hegemonic' approach does not go as far as the Libyan statement goes, it certainly has the potential to be viewed by much of the rest of the world along the lines similar to those uttered in the Libyan statement. Even though the Security Council imposed the sanctions on Libya, compliance by states with those sanctions was not perfect, and regional organizations such as the Arab League, the Organization of African Unity and the Organization of Islamic Conference opposed this sanctions regime. In the end, the sanctions did not prove effective, regional opposition increased and prospects of the successful prosecution of the alleged perpetrators faded away.[48] The US and the UK eventually had to reverse their original position and withdraw their original demands. The settlement of the issue of trying terrorist bombing suspects went in accordance with Libya's original approach, that is, on the territory of a third state.[49]

The Libyan sanctions case witnessed how the hegemonic approach has pervaded the official policy line of the United States. This is clear from a US statement made in 2003 when the Security Council decided to lift sanctions from Libya in return for a settlement that would allow compensation arrangements for the families of the Lockerbie bombing victims to go through:

> Our decision, however, must not be misconstrued by Libya or by the world community as tacit United States acceptance that the Government of Libya has rehabilitated itself. The United States continues to have serious concerns about other aspects of Libyan behaviour, including its poor human rights record, its rejection of democratic norms and standards, its irresponsible behaviour in Africa, its history of involvement in terrorism, and – most important – its pursuit of weapons of mass destruction and their means of delivery.[50]

47 UNSC, 'Letter from the Secretary of the People's Committee for Foreign Liaison and International Cooperation of the Libyan Arab Jamahiriya, addressed to the Secretary-General' (13 January 1992) UN Doc. A/46/884, S/23416, 3.

48 Schwartz (n. 18), 565–6.

49 A. Aust, 'Lockerbie: The Other Case' (2000) 49 ICLQ 283.

50 UNSC 'Libyan Arab Jamahiriya' (12 September 2003) UN Doc. S/PV.4820 (Part II), 3.

This policy had earlier been institutionalized in the 2002 National Security Strategy of the United States, which stated that 'In the 1990s we witnessed the emergence of a small number of rogue states that, while different in important ways, share a number of attributes'. These are states that brutalize their citizens, strive to obtain WMDs, support terrorism, do not respect human rights, and, importantly, have strained relations with the US.[51] The underlying spirit of the strategy document was to provide conceptual justifications for treating such states in ways which bypass international law, and even to use pre-emptive force against them. US policy denoted North Korea, Libya, Cuba, Iran and Syria as rogue states. The 'Axis of evil' and the 'outposts of tyranny' have also become part of the accepted vernacular, reflecting the doctrinal precepts of the New Haven School and liberal theory, which also advocate the differentiated application of international law to states based on their political organization and orientation.

A more subtle and seemingly moderate approach on this subject has been adopted by the EU. In its security strategy document, the EU pointed out that:

> A number of countries have placed themselves outside the bounds of international society. Some have sought isolation; others persistently violate international norms. It is desirable that such countries should rejoin the international community, and the EU should be ready to provide assistance. Those who are unwilling to do so should understand that there is a price to be paid, including in their relationship with the European Union.[52]

There are some differences between European and American approaches to the criteria for qualifying states in an exclusionary manner. The EU emphasizes that the notion of a 'failed state' refers to the inner workings of a state and not to its foreign policy outlook. This is specified in the ESS as bad governance – corruption, abuse of power, weak institutions and lack of accountability.[53]

The categorization of states as rogue, failed or outlaw essentially represents a modern version of those older doctrines that divided the world into civilized and uncivilized parts, and thus into those who can act free of legal and moral constraints and those who are merely objects of domination and acquisition. For if some states are rogue, failed and outlaw, the next logical step in the policy reasoning is to aspire to establish some sort of tutelage over them that would prevent those entities from having harmful effects, or at least to enforce a regime change to bring to power administrations that would be more beneficial to those who allocate such. Even if, as in some cases, concerns about

51 *US National Security Strategy* (Washington, DC: USGPO, 2002), 13–14.

52 *A Secure Europe in a Better World* (12 December 2003) (European Security Strategy, Brussels 2003), 10.

53 A. Toje, 'The 2003 European Union Security Strategy: A Critical Appraisal' (2005) 10 *European Foreign Affairs* Review 125.

terrorist threats are genuine, the underlying economic interest relating to states denoted as failed, rogue or outlaw is difficult to underestimate.

6.6 'Hegemony' and international lawmaking: the case of *jus ad bellum*

In the post-Cold War period, the relative frequency of US-led unilateral uses of force, notably against Yugoslavia, Afghanistan and Iraq, has led to the development of doctrinal opinion that the single remaining superpower is essentially in charge of how the law of the use of force develops, when the use of force has to be seen as lawful or unlawful, and whether the conduct of the hegemonic superpower has to be seen in terms of criteria of exceptional legality that would not be applicable to the uses of force by other states.[54] More recently, another author articulated a hegemonic effect on *jus ad bellum* thus:

> a significant number of States now believe that their vital national security interests require them to act in a manner that is in breach of the laws governing international uses of force laid down in the UN Charter. This is not a temporary policy shift, nor are actions taken in pursuance of counter proliferation policies isolated or extraordinary events. Policies of counter proliferation-oriented pre-emptive use of force are a part of a systematic rethinking within a significant number of States about the security environment in which States find themselves, and the policy options those States feel they must maintain in order to defend themselves against modern threats, and to pursue their national security interests internationally.

Even if small in number, such states could effectively evade any possible law enforcement if the majority of states consider their action illegal. This can bring the international law on the use of force into crisis, as the Iraq War demonstrated.[55]

The question arising is that, if in this area there is more than a temporary policy shift, or even a shift at all, and if states feel so strongly about it, why do they not agree to reflect it in the legal framework? On the contrary, there is no evidence that international society as a whole accepts this interpretation of the legal framework of the use of force. This position of changes to the existing legal position under the *jus ad bellum* towards admitting pre-emptive and preventive use of force has been argued by the coalition states in relation to

54 For an overview of the arguments, see M Byers, 'Preemptive Self-Defense: Hegemony, Equality and Strategies of Legal Change' (2003) 11 *Journal of Political Philosophy* 176.

55 D. H. Joyner, *International Law and the Proliferation of Weapons of Mass Destruction* (Oxford: Oxford University Press, 2009), 339, 331.

the war in Iraq and by a number of scholars.[56] It seems that the international community has not subscribed to such modifications of the law or of the admission of exceptions.[57] A reinterpretation of the *jus ad bellum* was likewise opposed by the UN Secretary-General's High Level Panel, which justified its approach by considerations directly opposite to those underlying a theory of superpower hegemony, namely that allowing one state to use force in a particular manner would mean allowing all to do so.[58]

The same approach towards the *jus ad bellum*, favouring legal stability over normative change, has been repeatedly upheld by the International Court of Justice (ICJ) in several cases decided in the period when the US-led wars against Afghanistan and Iraq were undertaken. In cases of *Oil Platforms*, *Wall in Palestine* and *DRC* v. *Uganda*, the ICJ subscribed to the strict traditional understanding of the *jus ad bellum*, manifested in its consistent adherence to principles that the consent of states inviting foreign armed presences has to be clearly and convincingly demonstrated; that force in self-defence can be used only if one state suffers armed attack from another state, to the exclusion of attacks perpetrated by non-state actors; and that the use of force in self-defence is not warranted unless the attack triggering it is clearly and transparently proved.[59] The ICJ's approach, expressed precisely in the period when policy shifts were asserted in this field, is premised on the regular applicability of the *jus ad bellum*. It is conceptually unsustainable to judge the (crisis of) law by reference to how it is implemented in practice. As soon as law is resilient enough to withstand pressures of power and politics, its validity does not depend on its enforcement.

56 Byers (n. 54). See also T. J. Farer, 'The Prospect for International Law and Order in the Wake of Iraq' (2003) 97 AJIL 626, 627.

57 See, for instance, NAM, 'Declaration of the Meeting of Ministers of Foreign Affairs of the Non-Aligned Movement' (New York, 18 September 2002) which emphasized, in paras. 11 and 12, 'the urgent need for a peaceful solution of the issue of Iraq in a way that preserves the authority and credibility of the Charter of the United Nations and international law as well as peace and stability in the region'. The Non-Aligned Movement reiterated 'its firm rejection of any type of unilateral action against any Member State of the United Nations'. See also Non-Aligned Movement, 'Statement of the XIII Non-Aligned Movement Summit Concerning Iraq' (Kuala Lumpur, 25 February 2003) which likewise opposed any unilateral action. On state practice regarding the anticipatory or pre-emptive self-defence claims, see also C. Gray, *International Law and the Use of Force* (2nd edn, Oxford: Oxford University Press, 2004), 174–9.

58 *A More Secure World: Our Shared Responsibility, Report of the Secretary-General's High-level Panel on Threats, Challenges and Change* (UN Department of Public Information, 2004) (at: www.un.org/secureworld/report2.pdf).

59 *Oil Platforms* (*Islamic Republic of Iran* v. *United States of America*) General List No. 90 [2003] ICJ; *Legal Consequences of the Construction of the Wall in the Occupied Palestinian Territory* (Advisory Opinion) General List No. 131 [2004] ICJ; *Case Concerning the Armed Activities on the Territory of the Congo* (*Democratic Republic of the Congo* v. *Uganda*) General List No. 116 [2005] ICJ. For analysis, see A. Orakhelashvili, 'Legal Stability and Claims of Change: the International Court's Treatment of *Jus ad Bellum* and *Jus in Bello*' (2006) *Nordic Journal of International Law* 371–407.

6.7 Competing drives for hegemony: the United States versus the European Union

The process of European integration triggered doctrinal speculation about whether the European Union could compete for hegemony with the United States and what would be the implications of such competition for international law. The divisions between US and Europe have been witnessed even in the Cold War period in relation to the assertion by the United States of extra-territorial jurisdiction in the area of international economic relations:

> In 1982 a new low in transatlantic legal relations was reached when, in the context of the US export controls associated with the Soviet Gas Pipeline project, there arose the bizarre spectacle of one NATO State, the United Kingdom, making it a criminal offence for certain of its nationals to comply with orders issued by another NATO State, the United States, in relation to their dealings with the two States' supposed common antagonist, the Soviet Union.[60]

Having failed to secure voluntary cooperation, in June 1982 President Reagan extended the embargo not only to American companies but also to their subsidiaries in France, Germany, England and Italy. This generated increased European resistance, as witnessed by the statement of the EEC foreign ministers, as well as by those of the French and Italian governments, who professed to honour the relevant contracts despite the US actions. In August of the same year the US administration began to realize that continuing this confrontation was counter-productive and sanctions were eventually lifted in November 1982.[61]

Divergences between European and American positions in the post-Cold War period became most vivid in the process of the adoption of the ICC Statute in 1998 where the US ended up isolated; the European opposition to exempting US personnel from the ICC jurisdiction, which led to the consequent refusal to extend that exemption as was provided for in Security Council resolutions 1422(2003) and 1487(2004); broader policy disagreements about the death penalty; the invasion of Iraq in 2003; and, last but not least, the EU's effort to establish an independent capacity for conflict prevention and crisis management which will eventually lead to the establishment of a European Army.

An important issue on which Europe and America seem to substantially disagree, at least in principle, is whether states are justified to use force unilaterally in the face of international crises if multilateral institutions such

60 A. V. Lowe, 'US Extraterritorial Jurisdiction: The Helms–Burton and D'Amato Acts' (1997) 47 ICLQ 378.

61 P. J. Desouza, 'The Soviet Gas Pipeline Incident: Extension of Collective Security Responsibilities to Peacetime Commercial Trade', in W. M. Reisman and A. R. Willard (eds.), *International Incidents: The Law that Counts in World Politics* (Princeton, NJ: Princeton University Press, 1988), 96–7.

as the UN fail to respond to those crises adequately. The doctrinal argument has for a long time been that the prohibition of the use of force operates only to the extent that the principal organs of the UN effectively respond to the relevant crisis. If it does not, the argument goes that the UN Charter is not a suicide pact and states can then use force to protect their security as well as to perform so-called humanitarian interventions.[62] This approach has underlined the position stated towards the *jus ad bellum* in US national security strategies of 2002 and 2006. The 2002 National Security Strategy points out that:

> While the United States will constantly strive to enlist the support of the international community, we will not hesitate to act alone, if necessary, to exercise our right of self-defense by acting pre-emptively against such terrorists, to prevent them from doing harm against our people and our country.

Furthermore:

> The United States has long maintained the option of pre-emptive actions to counter a sufficient threat to our national security. The greater the threat, the greater is the risk of inaction – and the more compelling the case for taking anticipatory action to defend ourselves, even if uncertainty remains as to the time and place of the enemy's attack. To forestall or prevent such hostile acts by our adversaries, the United States will, if necessary, act preemptively.[63]

The claim to the pre-emptive use of force as articulated by the US encompasses action even in the absence of a clear threat and is essentially based on the auto-interpretation by the US of the applicable law as well as the factual circumstances that justify acting in self-defence. The 2006 National Security Strategy reiterates the identical approach on pre-emptive use of force, stating that 'When the consequences of an attack with WMD are potentially so devastating, we cannot afford to stand idly by as grave dangers materialize. This is the principle and logic of preemption'.[64]

However, unilateralism in this field goes back further than the Bush administration in the 2000s, and was practised by the administrations of Presidents Bush Senr. and Clinton, in the contexts of protecting US nationals (Panama 1989), combating terrorism (Sudan 1998), counter-proliferation (Iraq 1998) and 'humanitarian' intervention (Yugoslavia 1999). A well-known justification for such unilateralism in using force has been linked to the perception of the US hegemony, as is clear from the statement made by

62 T. M. Franck, 'Who Killed Article 2(4)? Or: Changing Norms Governing the Use of Force by States' (1970) 64 AJIL 809.

63 *US National Security Strategy* (n. 51), 6.

64 *US National Security Strategy* (2006): 18, 23.

Secretary of State Albright that 'if we have to use force, it is because we are America. We are the indispensable nation. We stand tall, and we see further than other countries in the future'.[65] This reflects Brzezinski's notion of the 'indispensable nation'.

In policy terms, the US approach in the early 1990s was 'assertive multilateralism', which then 'was replaced in the USA by a reassertion of national interest-derived policy captured in the phrase "multilateral when we can, unilateral when we must"'. Later on, the focus of the US government shifted even more strongly towards unilateralism. Secretary of State Condoleezza Rice has on occasions criticized the multilateral approach of the Clinton administration, and the statement was made during the US President's visit to London in November 2003 that the guiding approach would be 'effective multilateralism, and neither unilateralism nor international paralysis will guide our approach'.[66] What matters more than the abstract terminology is the statement that multilateral approaches are not going to deter unilateral action if the US government considers that the alternative is an 'international paralysis'. Effective multilateralism is, under this approach, a commitment to the concept of multilateralism with the condition that in practice unilateral actions remain permissible if that suits the interests of the relevant power-wielding state.

The European approach to this question is interesting. The 2003 document on European Security Strategy specifies that:

> In a world of global threats, global markets and global media, our security and prosperity increasingly depend on an effective multilateral system. The development of a stronger international society, well functioning international institutions and a rule-based international order is our objective.[67]

But the actual problem relates not so much to the existence of institutions and rule-based order but to how far one is committed to observing obligations assumed in relation to these multilateral frameworks. A number of obligations of a fundamental character, such as the prohibition of the use of force, the principle of non-intervention in internal affairs of a state and the principle of self-determination of peoples, operate and bind states independently of those institutional frameworks and decisions adopted within them. Despite that, unlike the US policies during the Bush administration, the EU approach has been to emphasize the importance of multilateralism; it still does not explain the position of the EU as to what policy it would adopt if it cannot secure such multilateral decisions as would be acceptable to its interests and perceptions.

65 Quoted in B. S. Brown, 'US Objections to the Statute of the International Criminal Court: A Brief Response' (1999) 31 *NYUJ Int'l Law & Pol.* 876.

66 Toje (n. 53), 130–1.

67 *Secure Europe* (n. 52), 9.

Would the EU policy be to refrain from unilateral action, or to act unilaterally, blaming the lack of effectiveness of multilateral mechanisms?

The expansion of the EU security profile was manifested by its approach to establishing fully operational armed units that could be used for the purposes of crisis management in various parts of the world, and the EU Rapid Reaction Force was declared operational in 2001. However, the adoption of the 2003 EU Security Strategy was accompanied by comparably little discussion among the member states as to the directions of a firmer foreign policy platform. Instead, the 2003 Strategy was essentially a reaction to the US decision in the same year to go to war with Iraq. The Strategy document is thus less a purpose-directed policy statement and more an inspirational sketch.[68] There has thus been no consistent EU understanding as to its role in the global security system and this obviously matters for potential EU aspirations for the role of a global hegemon.

The EU Security Strategy has not clearly expressed what action it considers legitimate as part of its early crisis prevention approach, which in essence is similar to the US approach, in that it aims at defusing crises before they arise.[69] However, the EU High Representative Javier Solana has somehow clarified the implications of such ambiguity by stating that 'preventive engagement implies a "mainstreaming of conflict prevention without implying any obligation to undertake pre-emptive military strikes either by the EU or by individual member states"'.[70] It is noteworthy that Solana has spoken of the absence of an obligation to undertake pre-emptive strikes, which leaves it open to speculation whether the EU is contemplating a policy where it would assert a policy favouring the right to use force pre-emptively or otherwise in a unilateral manner whenever its interests would so require. Given that the EU has not demonstrated its opposition to this approach, coupled with its current lack of concerted will and capacity to act as a global hegemon, it might be indicative of the kind of policies that would be adopted should such hegemony materialize.

It is also possible that the EU preference towards multilateralism and its limited emphasis on the use of force is a strategy of opportunity, concerned in the first place with effecting and consolidating European emancipation from American influence in security affairs. This drive for emancipation can be seen as overlapping with European hegemonic aspirations, if not categorically then at least empirically. A useful insight into this approach is provided by the *Kadi* decision of the European Court of Justice which asserts that the EU organs are not bound by mandatory sanctions imposed by resolutions of the UN Security Council, even if EU member states are so bound. The judgment justifies this approach by subscribing to the thesis of autonomy of the EU

68 Toje (n. 53), 118–19.
69 *Secure Europe* (n. 52), 6–7, 11.
70 Quoted in Toje (n. 53), 128.

legal regime from the rest of international law.[71] If this approach is applied across the board, then the EU is essentially asserting its freedom of action over a broad range of matters, and essentially asserting its own hegemonic aspiration – an aspiration that is currently manifested through the emancipation drive in multiple fields. It is probably not right to read too much about a hegemonic policy from a single judicial decision whose motivations are open to different interpretations. However, it is plainly obvious that if the need for legal justification of the political aspirations of the EU despite the primacy of the UN Charter ever arose, doing it the *Kadi* judgment way would represent at least one available route.

Nor does the EU Security Strategy per se express hegemonic aspiration: it speaks of rule-based multilateralism as the basis of the international system. Yet, this still fits with the possible European aspiration to act as a hegemon, if different from the American way. European multilateralism would be an alternative to American unilateralism and exceptionality, yet could represent a hegemonic model just as the British reliance on the multilateral political institution of balance of power did. Even in such context if, in the future, the EU were to be endowed with political will and crisis management and enforcement machinery, it could aspire to projecting power and policies so as to use decisions adopted within multilateral frameworks in its own foreign policy interests. The difference between exceptionality and multilateralism would then become rather minor and mostly form related. It is not immediately apparent whether this hegemony would know any effective limits. If, on the other hand, the *Kadi* approach were to pervade the mainstream of the EU foreign policy thinking, the multilateral approach would begin to ring hollow, giving way instead to a subtle unilateralism.

6.8 Conclusion

If there is going to be a hegemon, whatever it is, an inevitable condition is that it has to be happy with the contemporary arrangement of the international system and rules that govern it. The US unilateralist hegemonic drive after the Cold War has encountered cardinal opposition from several parts of the world and promoted, in a counter-productive manner, the development of multipolar international politics. It might be thought that the EU approach in favour of multilateralism would, conceptually at least, enable it to make a better prima facie case for claiming hegemonic status, just as the British adherence to the principle of the balance of power promoted and enhanced its power position. At the same time, conceptual likelihood does not always translate into practical feasibility. Actual EU hegemonic potential will depend on the development of its independent security potential, its relative power

71 Joined Cases C-402P and C-415/05P, *Yassin Abdullah Kadi and Al Barakaat International Foundation* v. *Council of the European Union and the Commission of the European Communities* [2008] ECR I-6351.

status in relation to other power centres in the world, and also how it actually proposes to affect international politics.

The only sustainable version of a hegemon is one that not only has exceptional power, but is also the only one that has this power and is prepared to put its power position at the service of the system and its policies the way the system defines them, as opposed to the way they are to be defined by the hegemon. This would secure for the hegemon the acceptance of its position in international society, possibly in the longer term, which in its turn would guarantee its increased political, economic and security benefits.

Making an across-the-board argument about the primacy of power in international relations, or arguing that power determines the nature and content of international legal relations, would be unsound and counter-factual. For hegemony to succeed, a hegemon's logic needs to be not just 'realistic' the way it would itself perceive, but also oriented to what is acceptable to the system with its multiple constituents. But as both distant and recent historical experiences demonstrate, there are cases when national elites reassured by national power are neither willing to think of systemic considerations nor to be guided by considerations of longer-term sustainability of their ambitions. In such circumstances, hegemonic projects have turned into adventures with adverse repercussions for the aspiring hegemon, and in some cases a heavy price has been paid by national societies. In the age of rising multipolarity, where hegemonic aspirations are as a rule unwelcome, any rising power planning to become a hegemon will have to consider both systemic considerations and the experience accumulated so far before ascertaining whether such an aspiration is worth pursuing.

7 Orthodox generalists and political activists in international legal scholarship

Jörg Kammerhofer[*]

7.1 Introduction

This is a difficult argument. Criticizing one's colleagues is fraught with the danger of being misunderstood as wanting to appear cleverer than they, which is emphatically not the case here. Yet the state of international legal scholarship today prompts the writing of this chapter, for while in general the academic climate in our field is exceptionally open and tolerant and while this tolerance extends to radical theories which have but the most tenuous connection to international law itself, the notion that legal scholars ought to focus on the law is not as easily accepted. It seems that scholars working on international law are tempted too much by factors beyond the sum total of the positive law to be able to restrict themselves to it. At crucial junctures non-legal factors, considerations and methods enter the argument of many writers on international law, so much so that international legal scholarship has retained a distinctive literary quality,[1] rather than applying a more 'scientific' and 'strict' methodology.

At this point it is very important to stress, however, that the present analysis attaches no moral opprobrium to these tactics. The writers cited are all above reproach and the following should not be read as *ad personam* argument. The point of the following pages is merely to argue that the adoption of these tactics has a specific result, namely that the likelihood of correctly cognizing the law is reduced by this methodical syncretism.

This chapter will highlight and explain one particular aspect of this phenomenon in more depth. Today, international legal scholars can largely be classified as either 'orthodox generalists' or 'political activists' according to their approach to theoretically complex or politically sensitive questions. Scholars subconsciously adopt tactics in dealing with, for example, the influence of political pressure on their work. Scholarship does not happen in a vacuum and academics face external influence in forming their views. They may, for example, have grown up in an environment where certain states are invariably viewed as 'rogue nations'. In some states political traditions or

* The author would like to thank Grietje Baars, Jason Beckett and André de Hoogh for their help.

1 P. Allott, 'Language, Method and the Nature of International Law' (1973) 45 BYIL 1971 79–135.

factual imperatives noticeably shape international legal doctrines. Scholars may also be personally appalled by developments with respect to, say, human rights or indigenous cultures. Thus, consciously or subconsciously, they react to these influences by adapting their perception and analysis of international law. This is not a peripheral matter: tactics such as these are decisive for the way international law is 'handled' on a day-to-day level.

Yet such a classification can only serve as a polemical–didactical tool. Reality is considerably less clear-cut and the dichotomy of orthodoxy and activism may not reflect the complexity of motivations and methods scholars adopt. In a certain sense, the two approaches are two sides of the same coin (section 7.4). But they are subtly different even where the results are the same; the protagonists usually do not belong to both groups at the same time and on the same issue. Also, the distinction serves to demonstrate the middle ground held by those seeking to discover the law only – thus the categorization is valuable to establish a dialectic argument. In the following, we will first look at the generalist position, with a case study on the new orthodox reading of the law on the use of force under the UN Charter (section 7.2), and follow this by analysing the political activist reading of human rights (section 7.3), whereupon the 'third way' – focusing on the law only – will be presented as synthesis or alternative (section 7.4).[2]

7.2 The scholar as diplomat: the law on the use of force

Of the two archetypes for the twenty-first century international legal scholar, the orthodox generalist still holds more influence with decision makers. Generalists form the *ancien regime*, are well represented in scholarly organizations and make up the core membership of international organs such as the International Law Commission and the International Court of Justice. This does not mean, however, that they necessarily stick to a strict conception of law or to traditional interpretations of it. They may be quite flexible: if it serves their purpose they may stick only to certain parts of tradition, such as the role of subsequent practice, but abandon other elements. A good example for this tactic is the post-2001 change in the orthodox doctrine on self-defence law under the UN Charter. Here, it is submitted, a strictly legal analysis of the positive law and orthodox scholarship diverge.

Since 11 September 2001, the perception of the law on the use of force among scholars has changed perceptibly while the law on which it is based (Article 51 UN Charter) has not. Not as paradoxically as it may seem, orthodoxy in this case means movement. The '*Nicaragua* consensus', i.e. the view that the judgment on the merits in *Nicaragua*[3] accurately reflects the

2 Only a very limited cross-section of literature has been used in this article in order to demonstrate the point made herein.

3 *Military and Paramilitary Activities in and Against Nicaragua* (*Nicaragua* v. *United States of America*) (Merits, Judgment of 27 June 1986) ICJ Rep. 14.

position of the orthodoxy – as tenuous as it may have been – may no longer be orthodox. 'Sceptics upholding the restrictive view may still draw support from the text of the Charter rules (as traditionally interpreted), but by and large seem to be on the defensive.'[4] In other words: those who have *not* changed their conception of self-defence since 2001 are now considered unorthodox. A narrative of progressivism has replaced the pre-2001 conservativism. The apologist strain in the orthodox lawyer now requires him/her to react to state practice by re-reading the law in the light of new behaviour. A current phenomenon will be analysed below: the use of Security Council Resolutions 1368 and 1373 (2001)[5] by scholars to sever the connection between armed attacks and state behaviour. As this is primarily a theoretical chapter, we will not linger on the minutiae of Charter interpretation, but focus on analysing and criticizing the tactics employed by the 'new orthodoxy'.[6] This is a case study and the law on the use of force is used exemplarily to show a general trend.

These two resolutions, adopted on 12 and 28 September, respectively, were the Council's first response to the 11 September 2001 terrorist attacks on New York and Washington. In the preambles of both resolutions, the Council recognizes or reaffirms 'the inherent right of individual or collective self-defence'. A number of scholars have taken this general reaffirmation to have 'noted that the attacks of 9/11 had triggered a right of self-defence'.[7] This is an important starting point for the new orthodoxy. By arguing that the Council had 'affirm[ed] the inherent right of individual and collective self-defence in the specific context of those attacks',[8] they have used the two resolutions to support the contention that self-defence against armed attacks by non-state actors is in some sense covered by Article 51 of the UN Charter.[9]

4 C. Tams, 'The Use of Force against Terrorists' (2009) 20 EJIL 359, 374.

5 UNSC Res. 1368 (12 September 2001) UN Doc. S/RES/1368 (2001); UNSC Res. 1373 (28 September 2001) UN Doc. S/RES/1373 (2001).

6 The present author has had the opportunity to publish on both issues before: J. Kammerhofer, 'Uncertainties of the Law on Self-defence in the United Nations Charter' (2005) 35 *Netherlands Yearbook of International Law 2004* 143–204; J. Kammerhofer, 'The *Armed Activities* Case and Non-state Actors in Self-defence Law' (2007) 20 LJIL 89–113.

7 Tams (n. 4), 377.

8 D. Bethlehem, 'International law and the Use of Force: The Law as it is and as it should be', in UK House of Commons Select Committee on Foreign Affairs, *Foreign Policy Aspects of the War against Terrorism*, Seventh Report of Session 2003–4 (2004), written evidence (Ev. 100), para. 17 (at: www.publications.parliament.uk/pa/cm200304/cmselect/cmfaff/441/4060808.htm).

9 *Legal Consequences of the Construction of a Wall in the Occupied Palestinian Territory* (Advisory Opinion of 9 June 2004) ICJ Rep. 136, separate opinion Kooijmans at 229–30 (para. 35), declaration Buergenthal at 244 (para. 6); *Armed Activities on the Territory of the Congo* (*Democratic Republic of the Congo* v. *Uganda*) (Merits, Judgment of 19 December 2005) ICJ Reports 168, separate opinion Simma at 337 (para. 11); separate opinion Kooijmans at 313 (para. 26); Bethlehem (n. 8), para. 17; E. Wilmshurst, 'The Chatham House Principles of International Law on the Use of Force in Self-defence' (2006) 55 ICLQ 963, 970; A. Randelzhofer, 'Article 51', in Bruno Simma *et al.* (eds.), *The Charter of the United Nations: A Commentary* (2nd edn, Oxford: Oxford University Press, 2002), 788, 802 (RN 35); Y. Dinstein, *War, Aggression and Self-defence* (4th edn, Cambridge: Cambridge University Press, 2005), 207; T. M. Franck,

The contention here is that this has been a pragmatic move with an uncertain basis in law and hiding a tendency for methodological 'fudging' in order to reach an outcome that is judged as beneficial, even if the law would not support it. By using the two resolutions orthodoxy is employing a borderline method. However, this argument develops its full force for the archetypical orthodox scholar only, who, as archetype, does not exist. The real arguments are far more nuanced, less clear-cut and sometimes less fully argued than the archetype. Hence we will try to merge the actual supporting arguments with the theoretical possibilities while keeping our focus on the methodology, rather than the doctrinal detail. Three avenues to justify the movement in the orthodox position through the two resolutions are possible:

1 The resolutions constitute a formal Council authorization to use force in self-defence. Since the right of self-defence in Article 51 UN Charter is not subject to Council authorization – only to a suspension once the Council 'has taken measures necessary' – a resolution to that effect would clearly be *ultra vires* and void. However, it seems that not even non-orthodox scholars have interpreted the two preambular paragraphs as encompassing such an authorization or have argued that the Council may authorize self-defence. The late Thomas Franck, not known for holding ultra-orthodox views, dismissed Security Council mandated self-defence in the middle of a vigorous defence of the initial Coalition action against Afghanistan: '[t]he resolution ... does not authorise its exercise since that right is "inherent"'.[10] This approach is too extreme to form the basis of an orthodox argument and will not be discussed further.

2 The resolutions constitute 'practice' that is somehow relevant to our understanding of the law. This argument, in turn, can be developed in two branches, for 'practice' is used to further (a) an interpretation of the Charter or (b) to allege a tacit change in the Charter. The latter variant itself consists of various approaches, where change is allegedly effected (i) by the force of facts (practice) alone (ii) by practice constituting evidence of the objective and subjective elements for customary lawmaking and (iii) by it evidencing a tacit amendment treaty between the parties to the Charter. While this is an interesting argument and worthy of more theoretical critique,[11] it may also be too radical and too much of a break

'Terrorism and the Right of Self-defense' (2001) 95 AJIL 839, 839–40; P. H. Kooijmans, 'The Legality of the Use of Force in the Recent Case Law of the International Court of Justice', in S. Yee and J.-Y. Morin (eds.), *Multiculturalism and International Law: Essays in honour of Edward McWhinney* (Leiden: Martinus Nijhoff, 2009), 455, 465; Tams (n. 4), 377; K. N. Trapp, 'Back to Basics: Necessity, Proportionality, and the Right of Self-defence against Non-state Terrorist Actors' (2007) 56 ICLQ 141, 143, 151.

10 Franck (n. 9), 840.

11 On the possibility of subsequent practice changing treaties, see W. Karl, *Vertrag und spätere Praxis im Völkerrecht* (Berlin: Springer, 1983); J. Kammerhofer, *Uncertainty in International Law: A Kelsenian Perspective* (London: Routledge, 2010), 125–38.

with the received notions of Charter interpretation to really form the core of the 'new orthodoxy' on self-defence law. Because the majority of recent writings have formulated a 'reinterpretation thesis', we will focus on the usefulness of this practice for interpretation and on what interpretation can do in the following paragraphs.

3 The third possibility is to argue that the resolutions are in some sense an 'authoritative' interpretation of self-defence law. Some of Judge Kooijmans' academic and judicial writings can be read to support this thesis[12] and, since he is one of the most prominent advocates of the 'new orthodoxy' and since this is a variant of the reinterpretation thesis it will be discussed there.

The thrust of the reinterpretation thesis is twofold and to an extent paradoxical. On the one hand, nearly all of those in the new orthodoxy claim that the wording of Article 51 'does not make its exercise dependent upon an armed attack by another State',[13] i.e. that the law always has allowed self-defence against non-state attackers.[14] This is curiously combined with the notion of a fundamental change in our common understanding of the Charter rules, of a reinterpretation to meet the new challenges of terrorism in a post-September 11 world.[15] When the law has always allowed this, why would we now need 'change' in any sense of the word? What are the merits of using Resolutions 1368 and 1373 in this connection? For the purpose of this discussion, we will omit the textual problems that two very unspecific references in the preambles to the right of self-defence pose, for they are hardly an explicit affirmation of the applicability of self-defence to the specific response to the 11 September attacks.

The new orthodoxy uses the two resolutions (and other factual developments) as practice to evidence a new interpretation of self-defence law by the majority of states and international organs. (The International Court of Justice's *jurisprudence constante* that seems to contradict this reinterpretation[16] is downplayed or lamented.)[17] But is interpretation that powerful? Can it do what these scholars promise? Is the law – in any sense of the word – 'changed' by a 're-'interpretation? In a nutshell, interpretation is a hermeneutic process for the cognition of legal norms. Legal norms need to be cognized in order to be understood by humans. Humans start a process of interpretation as soon as they look at a text. However, interpretation is also no more than that, for as hermeneutic process it is anterior to and removed from the norms. Interpretation primarily as scholarly cognition of the law is categorically different from the application of the law by organs. Norms may have multiple

12 E.g. Kooijmans (n. 9), 465.

13 Wall (n. 9), declaration Buergenthal, 242 (para. 6).

14 Wall (n. 9), separate opinion Kooijmans at 229–30 (para. 35); *Armed Activities* (n. 9), separate opinion Simma at 337 (para. 11); Wilmshurst (n. 9), 970; Kooijmans (n. 9), 465; Tams (n. 4), 390.

15 Kooijmans (n. 9), 455, 466; Tams (n. 4), 390.

16 *Nicaragua* (n. 3); *Wall* (n. 9); *Armed Activities* (n. 9).

17 Kooijmans (n. 9), 465; Tams (n. 4), 384.

meanings and are therefore merely a frame of possible meanings.[18] Interpretation as cognition of the norm can only identify the frame[19] and not decide between them. That is the role of application within the dynamic operation of the hierarchy of legal norms.[20] Application determines and decides – reduces, for the concrete case, multiple meanings to one – but as such it is not interpretation.

In our case it is quite clear that the text of Article 51 does not say 'armed attack *by a state*';[21] the text seems to support including action by non-state actors as armed attack. Yet even if this is the case, the state requirement is another possible meaning of Article 51 and not excluded by it, and we are left with at least two meanings. Practice cannot reduce multiple meanings – that would mean changing the norm and the Charter cannot be changed by practice alone.

In addition, there are arguments from the decades-long debate on this issue that the new orthodoxy tends to treat perhaps a bit too lightly. A systematic interpretation of whole Charter regime on the use of force may, for example, result in a different emphasis.[22] As the Chatham House principles rightly state:

> What is questioned is the right to take action against the State that is the presumed source of such attacks, since it must be conceded that an attack against a non-state actor within a State will inevitably constitute the use of force on the territorial State.[23]

Military action *against* private individuals or groups is by definition not a use of force in the sense of Article 2(4) UN Charter, since they are not protected by that rule. Hence – whatever other rules of international law the state may be prima facie breaching – in this respect the defending state does not need to and cannot justify its military actions under Article 51 UN Charter. However, unless the individuals are outside state territory, the defender's military actions will be a use of force against the state on which the individuals are staying. Only vis-à-vis the territorial state is Article 2(4) violated and only against it must the defender's actions be justified. Hence, the condition which justifies the defender's actions must also be fulfilled by the state against which the defender has acted – the armed attack must have been committed by the same state against which a prima facie unlawful use of force is now exercised. The interstate nature of the Charter and the Charter's purpose in primarily averting large-scale interstate wars also support this contention.

18 H. Kelsen, *Reine Rechtslehre* (2nd edn, Wien: F. Deuticke, 1960), 348–9.

19 *Ibid.* 353.

20 *Ibid.* 350–2; R. Walter, 'Das Auslegungsproblem im Lichte der Reinen Rechtslehre', in G. Kohlmann (ed.), *Festschrift für Ulrich Klug zum 70. Geburtstag* (Köln: Deubner, 1983), 187, 188.

21 Dinstein (n. 9), 244–5; Franck (n. 9), 840.

22 For a more detailed discussion, see Kammerhofer (n. 6), 179–87.

23 Wilmshurst (n. 9), 670.

But, as so often in legal scholarship, this matter is contentious and it is not so much the result as the method with which it is achieved that is problematic and shows the divergence here-and-there of orthodoxy from a strictly legal approach. On a legal–theoretical point of view, state and institutional practice cannot be determinative of the content of a treaty, despite Article 31(3)(b) Vienna Convention on the Law of Treaties 1969 (VCLT). No legal scholar working in domestic criminal law would interpret a rise in murders as having changed the statutory prohibition of murders.

Arguing with Judge Kooijmans that in the two resolutions the Council is 'authorized to' reinterpret 'the existing law'[24] unfortunately does not eliminate the methodological problems. The term 'authoritative interpretation' is used where an organ is authorized by the law to 'interpret' norms. The Charter, however, does not authorize the Council to interpret Article 51, for the operation of the right of self-defence (largely, see above) does not fall within the Council's powers. This would ring even more true if indeed – as Kooijmans argues – the right of self-defence were inherent or merely recognized by the Charter.[25] Leaving aside the problems of the 'inherent right theory',[26] to argue that the Council is authorized to reinterpret what is, on this approach, an 'inherent right' of states is in danger of being perceived as contradictory. Perhaps this is also a purely instrumentalist view of the Council's power – the Council is authorized to interpret the rights of states to defend themselves widely, but not to curtail it? On a more theoretical note, interpretation understood as hermeneutic tool is independent of authorization but is limited in power. An interpretation properly speaking by the Security Council cannot be more 'authentic' than that by scholars. In *Jaworzina*, the Permanent Court of International Justice held, 'the right of giving an authoritative interpretation of a legal rule belongs solely to the person or body who has power to modify or suppress it'.[27] Only by fulfilling all conditions for lawmaking or change is the 'interpretation' truly authentic. If it is truly authentic, however, the 'interpretation' ceases to be an interpretation.

In no case can the meaning chosen to be integrated in an individual norm (e.g. a Council resolution) go beyond the individual decision. Even if the Council had pronounced on the scope of the right of self-defence, all possible meanings of the norm remain open. Security Council pronouncements may be the very best indication of what the state parties think is the scope of self-defence, but 'the current beliefs of the state parties' is categorically different

24 Kooijmans (n. 9), 465.

25 *Ibid.* 464.

26 A right 'recognized' is by definition incorporated into the receiving norm and is part of that norm, not of its original normative context. Incorporation is law-making by shorthand, not linking one norm to another. See J. Kammerhofer, 'Systemic Integration, Legal Theory and the ILC' (2010) 19 FYBIL 2008, 343, 357–60; for more detailed arguments on the so-called 'black hole theory' of Article 51, see Kammerhofer (n. 6), 149–53.

27 *Delimitation of the Czechoslowak–Polish Frontier* (*Question of Jaworzina*) (Advisory Opinion of 6 December 1923) PCIJ Series B No. 8, 6, 37.

from 'the objective content of a norm'. Also, a 'very good indication' is categorically different from 'authentic'.

But what is behind this trend? How do our 'generalists' respond to political influence even if that response is subconscious? It is argued here that their main goal is to find amicable, practicable or desirable solutions to disputes in accordance with their personal cosmopolitanism or internationalism. They have developed a 'toolbox' of methods for coping with the increasing fragmentation, specialization, politicization and moralization of international legal practice and scholarship. In their work we can clearly see a response to pressure, a desire to be pragmatic and to make the law conform to their view of what is a desirable outcome.

Whenever the going gets tough – whenever the strict application of law would not lead to the desired outcome – the positive law gets fudged. In this case, continuing the old orthodox reading of the law on self-defence (the *Nicaragua* consensus) would, it is argued, either restrict states' freedom of action to protect themselves and to wage the war on terror or it needs to be brought in line with the new realities of international life.[28] Because the law 'needs' to change it is perceived as having changed.

The particular example presented does not exhibit the full spectrum of orthodox tactics, but some typical elements are present. (a) The fundamental reinterpretation of Article 51 (as against the old orthodoxy) is an attempt at balancing; interpretation is instrumentalized for political purposes. The law is re-read in light of the behaviour of the subjects of law; the law has allegedly changed with state practice, not (as would have been common pre-2001) that the instances of unlawful use of force have increased. As such, legal scholarship becomes an apology for state behaviour – law gets fudged if what is (state practice) alone in some sense determines what ought to be (the law). (b) Next to the deference to authorities – state practice or international organs: the 'international community' – a defining characteristic of orthodoxy is its unquestioned acceptance of generally accepted doctrines of law. The role of practice in the interpretation of treaties – expressed in Article 31(3) (b) VCLT – is, as has briefly been discussed above, not as straightforward as its unquestioned acceptance by the new orthodoxy would have it. To stick with a problematic notion just because it is generally accepted may be considered methodologically unsound. Legal epistemology is difficult. Our ability to cognize law as counter-factual thought-objects in the ideal realm is limited, hence prime importance attaches to method. Common sense indicates that if we want to cognize the law, then we should choose *legal* methodology, because by incorporating non-legal elements (politics, morals), we will probably not be able to find out exactly what is the positive law in force.

28 Kooijmans (n. 9).

7.3 The scholar as activist: human rights law

The second type of scholar tends to incorporate a strain of political activism. The views expressed will be far less flexibly argued than that of generalists. Whatever cause such scholars hold as important – and they tend to be leftist causes: human rights, the environment, poverty, minorities – will be defended with great zeal; there is also a tendency to hold certain values as immutably absolute. Since it is usually only the 'right causes' that are defended, this second type of scholar could (polemically speaking) be called the 'do-gooders' (*Gutmenschen*) of the international law world. Again, an example of divergence of scholarship as it is practised and a strict scholarly ethos of the analysis of the law may clarify the methods of this group. In this case, we will focus on human rights and humanitarian law. The basic argument employed can be summarized thus: 'Because human rights are absolute values, they are inherent in the very nature of man. Because they are inherent, they also have a fixed content. Since human rights – existing in the cosmos of values – ought not to be constrained by the wording of treaties, we should be guided rather by the objective and eternal nature of human rights'.

It must be admitted, though, that the most political forms of activism are difficult to find in scholarly literature; there are two levels of activism. On the one hand, there is the 'coffee-break' activism of a more anecdotal nature. This is where these scholars pronounce their faith in the cause, rather than the law, but it is difficult to find in their writings. What the 'human rightists'[29] will say in conference breaks is different from what they will write in books and articles. One or two examples can be provided, however. When Julie Mertus says: 'I want the "kitchen tablers" to matter'[30] ('kitchen tablers' being individuals), she has articulated a political preference before starting her legal analysis; when Louis Sohn submits that 'international law on the subject of human rights is made by *the people that care*',[31] legal scholarship admits to having a role that transcends its proper role and doing the politicians' job.[32]

On the other hand, there are strains of argument running throughout human rights scholarship that admit of a moralist-political instrumentalization of the role of legal scholars, even if they are advocated in a far more cautious manner. Human rights somehow need to be protected to avoid 'an international legal order containing ominous silences';[33] if we adopted a strict approach looking at the positive law only:

29 A. Pellet, 'Droits-de-l'Hommisme et Droit International' (2001) 1 *Droits Fondamentaux* 167, 167.

30 J. Mertus, 'Considering Nonstate Actors in the New Millennium: Toward Expanded Participation in Norm Generation and Norm Application' (2000) 32 *N.Y.U.J.Int'l Law & Pol.* 537, 546.

31 L. B. Sohn, 'Sources of International Law' (1995) 25 *Ga.J.Int'l.& Comp.L.* 399, 399 (emphasis added).

32 See also B. Stevens, 'Litigating Customary International Human Rights Norms' (1995) 25 *Ga.J.Int'l.& Comp.L.* (1995) 191, 200; R. B. Lillich, 'The Growing Importance of Customary International Human Rights Law' (1995) 25 *Ga.J.Int'l.& Comp.L.* 1, 28–30.

33 F. L. Kirgis, 'Custom on a Sliding Scale' (1987) 81 AJIL 146, 148.

> many important political values would seem to lack adequate protection… Some norms seem so basic, so important, that it is more than slightly artificial to argue that states are legally bound to comply with them simply because there exists an agreement between them to that effect.[34]

In this manner human rights activist scholars are led to a methodological decision against the law as strictly or traditionally conceived and against all forms of positivism to an approach that they believe will further the cause of human rights.

> Clearly, doctrinal rigour is not of the utmost importance for modern positivists [i.e. the authors' modification of positivism]; treaty practice, custom and general principles are liberally combined so as to achieve the desired result: increased promotion and protection of human rights.[35]

This mindset has been applied to customary international lawmaking and in the following we will analyse the human rights approach to customary law.[36] For Jason Beckett, this is a dangerous trend.

> Personal preferences are being passed off as legal rules…Not that anyone actually admitted to offering no more than a personal preference. All hid behind a veneer of legal formality, and yet their answers nonetheless held that unmistakeable air of unreality.[37]

Because of the perceived incommensurability of what is regarded as traditional or orthodox methods of customary international lawmaking with the humanist goals espoused by the activist scholars,[38] an influential part of human rights and humanitarian legal scholarship has developed a new approach to customary international law for these areas of international law over the past decades. In its most cautious form, this theory – which is supported by a multitude of arguments – is expressed by the Restatement (Third): 'Therefore, the practice of states that is accepted as building customary international law of human rights includes some forms of conduct different from those that build customary international law generally'.[39] Three main approaches to explain the change vis-à-vis human rights and humanitarian law have been used:

34 M. Koskenniemi, 'Human Rights and Humanitarian Norms as Customary Law' (1990) 88 *Mich.L.Rev.* 1946, 1946–7.

35 J. Wouters and C. Ryngaert, 'Impact on the Process of the Formation of Customary International Law', in M. T. Kamminga and M. Scheinin (eds.), *The Impact of Human Rights Law on General International Law* (Oxford: Oxford University Press, 2009), 127.

36 For a more detailed discussion of the rules on lawmaking in international law, see Kammerhofer (n. 11), 59–86, 195–240.

37 J. Beckett, *The End of Customary International Law?: A Purposive Analysis of Structural Indeterminacy* (Saarbrücken: VDM Verlag Dr Müller, 2008), 1–2.

38 Pellet (n. 29), 168.

39 American Law Institute, *Restatement of the Law, Third. The Foreign Relations Law of the United States* (St Paul, MN: American Law Institute Publishers, 1987), Volume 1, 154.

1 In customary international human rights and humanitarian law, lawmaking is nominally not different, but different evidences for state practice may be used vis-à-vis other customary international law. Verbal practice – utterances of what states see as the law, such as General Assembly resolutions – is double-counted as state practice and *opinio iuris*.[40]
2 In this area, customary law-making is changed vis-à-vis 'ordinary' customary international law-making. (a) More or exclusive emphasis is placed on *opinio juris* as against traditional state practice. (b) Practice as traditionally conceived (e.g. as 'battlefield practice') cannot be used but is supplanted by diplomatic or aspirational – verbal – practice. (c) State practice contrary to the emerging *opinio juris* or violations of a rule thus established count less than in regular customary lawmaking.[41]
3 Customary international law cannot itself sustain a large proportion of non-treaty human rights and humanitarian law, hence new forms of law or lawmaking apply in this area.[42]

In line with the instrumentalist mindset of this group of scholars (on this, further below), the writings are mostly based on more than one approach and the three approaches tend to be commingled. From a legal (theoretical) perspective they are all to some degree problematic.

7.3.1 New evidence?

The most widespread variant of the 'customary human rights law' doctrine, 'weigh[s] statements both as evidence of practice and as articulation of *opinio juris*, which in the formation of humanitarian and human rights law is cardinal'.[43] Because 'one can find scarce State practice accompanied by *opinio juris*', 'arguments advanced in support of a finding that rights are a part of customary law rely on different kinds of evidence' – such as provisions in municipal constitutions, United Nations resolutions or ICJ judgments – none of which 'conform to the traditional criteria'[44] for the two elements.

40 Lillich (n. 32), 12–14, 18; T. Meron, 'The Continuing Role of Custom in the Formation of International Humanitarian Law' (1996) 90 AJIL 238, 239–40; T. Meron, 'International Law in the Age of Human Rights: General Course on Public International Law' (2004) 301 *Recueil des Cours 2003* 9, 383, 388; O. Schachter, 'International Law in Theory and Practice: General Course on Public International Law' (1985) 178 *Recueil des Cours 1982* V 9, 334–5, 338; Wouters (n. 35), 125.

41 Mertus (n. 30), 560–1; Schachter (n. 40), 334–5, 338; Wouters (n. 35), 112, 115.

42 L. Henkin, 'Sibley Lecture March 1994: Human Rights and State "Sovereignty"' (1995) 25 *Ga.J.Int'l.& Comp.L.* 31, 37; Koskenniemi (n. 34), 1959; B. Simma and P. Alston, 'The Sources of Human Rights Law: Custom, *Jus Cogens* and General Principles' (1992) 12 *Aust. YBIL* 82, 96, 102–6; Wouters (n. 35), 124.

43 Meron (n. 40), 386.

44 Schachter (n. 40), 334–5.

Human rights scholars have rightly been among the first to point out that the orthodox view on customary international lawmaking does not distinguish between the objective and subjective elements for lawmaking (*opinio juris* and state practice) on the one hand, and the evidences used to prove the two elements, on the other hand.[45] In other words, we must distinguish between the conditions for law creation (meta-law) and our epistemological tools; this is reminiscent of the notions of formal and material sources of law. 'There is an unlimited multiplicity of material sources both regarding the existence of the practice relevant for the creation of customary law and regarding the connected legal conviction.'[46] The subjective element, for example, as the sense of an act of will (the norm-making component of customary law) is not immediately perceptible, but perceived through its manifestations in reality only. We have stopped taking scholars at their words when they claim that 'state practice' is evidence of *opinio juris*, because the term 'state practice' does not refer to the objective element, but to a superstructure of proofs. If we need to take the use of the term 'state practice' with a pinch of salt in order to reconcile it with the 'element versus evidence' distinction, the danger of mistakes and of confounding the two elements[47] is apparent. However, the problems that arise now are anterior to positive law, a problem of cognition. How do we know which fact is legitimate evidence of an element? What evidentiary value do the various manifestations have, in particular when we expect practice and *opinio* to diverge significantly?[48] Is there a free appraisal of evidence in the sense that as long as some manifestation has value it can be used? Would that not presuppose knowing the object to be proven beforehand and thus make evidence irrelevant? Are there 'rules of evidence' and where can they be found?

Moreover, while a divorce of element and evidence is legitimate, a more indirect argument against trusting too much on statements and verbal evidence for information on practice can be brought to bear from the very nature of customary law as based on *customs* or usage. Customary norm creation is a primitive form of regulation and cannot be used to achieve a specific regulatory aim, because it is based on usage (customs). This is repetitive factual behaviour, a series of more or less similar events in reality,[49] a behavioural regularity, which makes customary law customary in the first

45 See H. Thirlway, *International Customary Law and Codification: An Examination of the Continuing Role of Custom in the Present Period of Codification of International Law* (Leiden: AW Sijthoff, 1972), 57; K. Wolfke, *Custom in Present International Law* (2nd edn, Dordrecht: Martinus Nijhoff, 1993), 42.

46 'Es gibt eine offene, nicht abgeschlossene Vielzahl unterschiedlicher Erkenntnisquellen sowohl für das Bestehen einer für die Bildung von Gewohnheitsrecht relevanten Praxis als auch für die damit verbundene Rechtsüberzeugung' (R. Bernhardt, 'Ungeschriebenes Völkerrecht', (1976) 36 *Zeitschrift für ausländisches öffentliches Recht und Völkerrecht*, 50, 65). All translations are the present author's.

47 B. Simma and A. Paulus, 'The Responsibility of Individuals for Human Rights Abuses in Internal Conflicts: A Positivist View' (1999) 93 AJIL 302, 306–7.

48 Simma (n. 42), 97.

49 U. Fastenrath, *Lücken im Völkerrecht: Zu Rechtscharakter, Quellen, Systemzusammenhang, Methodenlehre und Funktionen des Völkerrechts* (Berlin: Duncker & Humblot, 1991), 157.

place. Customary norms receive their content from the repetition of similar behaviour – state practice. The practice of using white paper can give rise only to a norm prescribing the use of white paper, e.g. 'white paper ought to be used' or 'white paper may be used'. State practice forms the content of the customary norm,[50] whereas *opinio juris* delivers its normativity.

Hence, because the content of customary law is forged from a pattern of behaviour, customary norms are not a series of words and sentences – customary law's content is a behavioural pattern. Customary norms can only have content which can potentially form a pattern in reality; a most important limit of customary regulation. The *opinio juris*, however, does not have the power to verbalize or change the content, as it is merely the normative *imprimatur* upon a behavioural regularity to which the *opinio* corresponds. On this view, the evidentiary function of statements is reduced, because verbal practice is the verbal act itself and a reference to its content. Practice can encompass only the factual regularity of making statements, not a regularity of the content of statements.

7.3.2 New customary law?

Another approach – not easily distinguishable from the 'evidence' argument – is that the process of customary international law formation itself is qualitatively different for human rights or humanitarian norms.[51]

> It is often argued, especially by human rights-oriented lawyers, that the method of customary law formation in the field of human rights and international humanitarian law is structurally different from the traditional method of customary law formation in public international law... Classical methods of law formation based on state consent and extensive and uniform state practice may be relaxed somewhat if 'the stakes are high'... Put differently, state practice is selectively used to justify a customary norm that is not morally neutral.[52]

While explanations as to why this is seen as necessary abound – '[t]he classical positivist approach may...pose serious difficulties for the legal protection and promotion of human rights'[53] – little guidance is given by the proponents as to what the *legal* basis for such a move is. Bruno Simma and Philip Alston are right to interject that 'it is surely open to doubt whether the concept of custom should be so fundamentally reshaped in a manner which disregards [customary law's] intrinsic limitations...in order to accommodate a desired...policy

50 H. Kelsen, *Hauptprobleme der Staatsrechtslehre entwickelt aus der Lehre vom Rechtssatze* (Tübingen: JCB Mohr, 1911), 236–7; Kelsen (n. 18), 9.

51 Meron (n. 40), 387.

52 Wouters (n. 35), 111, 129, 130.

53 *Ibid.* 119.

outcome'.[54] Indeed, how do our activist scholars propose this change of the meta-law level (the rules on customary international lawmaking) comes about? How do the rules on custom creation change? Can they change at all? While these theoretical questions of the 'structural constitution' of international law are highly uncertain and cannot be the focus of this short chapter, proposing legal change at the level of the sources of international law and not adequately discussing how that change is supposed to come about is not likely to increase the chances that these scholars' views corresponds with the law in force.

7.3.3 *Proving change?*

When change in evidences or rules on lawmaking is justified by this group of scholars, the methods used tend to beg a question. When Theodor Meron, for example, takes deviations by international tribunals – such as (arguably) the ICJ's *Nicaragua* judgment 1986[55] and the ICTY's Appeals Chamber 1995 decision on jurisdiction in *Tadić*[56] – as proof of change in lawmaking or of the proofs,[57] he is begging a question, since it is merely assumed that the tribunals are correct when they allegedly tell us whether that lawmaking has changed. Deviations by courts are counted as change, not as violation of the law on customary lawmaking. When Anthea Roberts, in analysing the human rights doctrines on customary lawmaking, accepts the challenge posed by 'modern custom' (rather than 'recent scholarly doctrines on customary law-making')[58] as such, the assumption is all too easily made that new law has created a crisis[59] in justifying it as belonging to the source, rather than questioning whether these claims by scholars are indeed law. The well-known words of Robert Jennings can also be given as an example, because they are perhaps not commonly understood in their full significance.

> Certainly practice over a more or less long period is an essential ingredient of customary law. But most of what we perversely persist in calling customary international law is not only *not* customary law: it does not even faintly resemble a customary law. Accordingly, an attempt to test it by examining practice merely introduces an element of confusion.[60]

54 Simma (n. 42), 96.

55 *Nicaragua* (n. 3).

56 ICTY Appeals Chamber, *Duško Tadić a/k/a 'Dule'* (Decision on the Defence Motion for Interlocutory Appeal on Jurisdiction) IT-94-1-AR72 (2 October 1995), para. 99.

57 Meron (n. 40), 386.

58 A. E. Roberts, 'Traditional and Modern Approaches to Customary International Law' (2001) 95 AJIL 757, 759–60.

59 Simma (n. 42), 88, 96.

60 R. Y. Jennings, 'The Identification of International Law', in B. Cheng (ed.), *International Law: Teaching and Practice* (London: Stevens, 1982), 3, 5.

He does not criticize the development of new rules on lawmaking, as this passage is usually read, but that we have a different source on our hands while insisting on calling that new source 'customary law'. 'Now that such [new] procedures [for making and changing law] are actually developing before our eyes, we persist in refusing to see, and still babble about international customary law.'[61] Again, the process of 'it is actually there' that he employs to prove it is not adequate, for it begs a question. If we propose that all procedures that usually succeed in creating international law do create law, how can we find out what process usually creates customary international law if we do not know when law has validly been created? Knowing when law is usually created requires knowing the meta-norm of international law creation – and finding this is the object of the exercise.

7.3.4 *Why human rights and humanitarian law?*

Perhaps the most salient point – one that may tell us more about the motivation and tactics of this group of scholars – that can be brought to bear against these arguments is that if any of these changes in evidences or rules of lawmaking have taken place, they cannot be confined to these two areas. Human rights lawmaking cannot be different from lawmaking in other areas just because of the subject matter covered. It is submitted that activist scholars differentiate only because of their politico-moralist activism. Meron argues that '[t]here is direct relationship between the importance attributed by the international community to particular norms and the readiness to lower the burden of proof required to establish custom'.[62] Yet who would ever think of arguing in a municipal setting that if an amendment of the constitution adds a new civil right, rather than a morally neutral provision, the number of parliamentarians required to pass the amendment is lower? Who would argue that somehow the provisions for changing the constitution are different just because more human rights protection is seen as politically beneficial or required by morality? If the notion of law is taken seriously, why would the situation be different in international law? The answer is that activist scholars fudge the law to further goals which are not expressed as positive international law. On a legal view, this is the imposition of personal politico-moral values upon the positive law. It is just as ineffective to try to change the law on lawmaking by scholarly designs as it is to try to change the substantive provisions themselves.

The propensity of political activists is to put their own politico-moral views above a strictly legal reading of the positive law in force. They identify themselves so strongly with the perceived political goals that they see the law and its means of enforcement as responding to the political goals. The result is that they supplant scholarly analysis by their special interest where the

61 *Ibid.* 6.

62 Meron (n. 40), 388.

outcome of the former could hurt the latter. Martti Koskenniemi asks provocatively:

> What could be sillier – or more dangerous – than to argue, for instance, that the validity of the prohibition of torture outside specific conventional frameworks is dependent on the presence of the formal conditions of customary international law?[63]

For legal scholars, only one thing could be sillier: to assume the validity of the prohibition of torture in international law without serious legal analysis just because they personally happen to agree with the idea that torture should be prohibited. What is required is precisely the absence of political ideals which – as can be seen above – do influence and motivate scholars to change the law, propose new law and incorporate external elements into their legal analysis. It is utopian 'à tenir pour vérités juridiques des tendances encore balbutiantes ou, pire, qui n'existent que dans leurs espoirs'.[64]

7.4 A stark choice for international legal scholarship?

The counter-positing of these two views can to some extent be brought within the framework of Martti Koskenniemi's duality of apologetic and utopian arguments. The 'descending' and 'ascending' patterns of justification[65] identified in Koskenniemi's 1989 book to an extent correspond to the two methods used by the 'diplomats' and 'activists'. While the new orthodoxy on the law on the use of force in effect provides a non-law-based apology for changes in state behaviour since 2001 (section 7.2), the 'human rightist'[66] seeks to impose a set of non-law-based utopian absolute values upon the body of customary international law (section 7.3). This dichotomy is, of course, not an invention of either Koskenniemi or the present author; the two modes of argument or theoretical approaches have long been part of legal scholarship. They used to be known as positivism or realism and natural law, but these badges may have become so overused as to be positively unhelpful. Both have long been appealing because of the need for scholarship to explain two aspects of 'law' at the same time: its positivity (a connection to 'reality') as well as its normativity (a counter-factual 'oughtness').

Before we continue with this train of thought, it may be worth pointing out that the two groups are not as far apart as they seem on first glance and that there may be instances where the same scholar's arguments may, at times, fit in both categories. Also, sometimes changes in the legal basis occur to fit

63 M. Koskenniemi, 'Letter to the Editors of the Symposium' (1999) 93 AJIL 351, 359–60.

64 Pellet (n. 29), 170.

65 M. Koskenniemi, *From Apology to Utopia: The Structure of International Legal Argument* (1989; Cambridge: Cambridge University Press, 2005, repr.).

66 Pellet (n. 29), 167.

in with the needs of the moment. While in the 1990s the orthodox view of the law on the use of force argued for downgrading state practice,[67] the new orthodoxy requires using it.[68] Humanitarian activism, on the other hand, still requires downgrading the role of practice in order to negate the tendency of states to behave in less than perfect accordance with activist views on human rights values.[69] Instrumentalization tactics have led Martti Koskenniemi and others to argue that for 'international lawyers' (practitioners and scholars alike) the choice between approaches is tactical and depends only on the likelihood of success or that it is a matter of etiquette where one would use which sort of language to support one's claims.

> What works as a professional argument depends on the circumstances. I like to think of the choice lawyers are faced with as being not one of method...but of language or, perhaps better, of style. The various styles – including the styles of 'academic theory' and 'professional practice' – are neither derived from nor stand in determinate hierarchical relationships to each other.[70]

However, the second part of Koskenniemi's argument – namely that the choice is, should be, or cannot but be, free or open for each new setting or argument rather than one of conviction and that it is a matter of tactical choice – must be disputed most emphatically if scholarship is to remain an academic enterprise rather than a quest for the pursuance of individual interests. If we were to transpose this idea to the natural sciences (and such a transposition is legitimate if there is to be such a thing as legal scholarship), it would be unlikely to find much support. Imagine a zoologist who claims that a neon-pink butterfly exists because the existence of such butterflies accords with his personal idea of aesthetics. Scholarship cannot be a tool to fulfil one's personal wishes – even in non-empirical disciplines.[71]

7.5 The scholar as scholar: common legal sense as the third way

But why are international lawyers, in particular, so responsive to not talking about the law and focusing on other factors, such as morals, politics and

67 E.g. by switching the legal basis of the prohibition of the use of force (outside the purview of Article 2(4) of the UN Charter) from customary law to general principles of law: Simma (n. 42), 102–4.

68 In the post-2001 world, practice is accorded much more weight in defining the prohibition on the use of force and its exceptions, whether as customary norm or within the Charter, see e.g. *Armed Activities* (n. 9), separate opinion Simma at 337 (para. 11).

69 Again: Simma (n. 42), 104.

70 Koskenniemi (n. 63), 356.

71 See O. Pfersman, 'Hans Kelsens Rolle in der gegenwärtigen Rechtswissenschaft', in Robert Walter, Werner Ogris and Thomas Olechowski (eds.), *Hans Kelsen: Leben–Werk–Wirksamkeit. Ergebnisse einer Internationalen Tagung, veranstaltet von der Kommission für Rechtsgeschichte Österreichs und dem Hans Kelsen-Institut* (*19–21 April 2009*) (2009), 375–9.

reality? An important aspect of the *problématique* was highlighted by Hans Kelsen in 1911.

> No other discipline is as in danger of acting *ultra vires* as is jurisprudence. This is so because it is very difficult to limit one's gaze to the realm of the Ought. It is difficult, because this means a painful limitation of one's mental manoeuvrability in the face of the eternal temptation to escape to the real world, the realm of the Is, and to explain what actually happens.[72]

There is a third way to international legal scholarship beyond the stark choice of apology and utopia. Why not focus exclusively on the analysis of the positive international law in force? Why not restrict ourselves to what is our business and leave external elements aside? Why not use a 'legal common sense approach' in international legal scholarship? This is the 'third way' beyond the dichotomy of apology and utopia, the dialectical completion to Koskenniemi's problem which ends the 'constant movement from emphasizing concreteness to emphasizing normativity and vice-versa'.[73] It is submitted here that such an approach – taking the notion of law seriously and combining the reality of law's positivity with the 'oughtness' of law's normativity – can be found in the writings of the Pure Theory of Law. The notion of 'purity' in this tradition of legal scholarship does not concern the content of the law, but the use of the right methodology in perceiving the law. 'It calls itself a "pure" theory of law, because it only describes the law and attempts to eliminate from this object of cognition everything that is not strictly law.'[74] Thus it directly connects to the point made above about scholars using a mixture of methods in order to come to a predetermined 'solution'. Such syncretism of method (*Methodensynkretismus*)[75] has direct results for the accuracy of the scholarly analysis: if unsuitable methods are used, scholars will have their chances of being correct vastly reduced.

In this connection, the Pure Theory of Law adopts two core tenets. First, it believes that the categories of Is and Ought must be kept apart in order to be able to perceive law in its proper form. Second, it demands scientific rigour for legal scholarship. These two tenets are connected and cannot be separated without leaving the Pure Theory's project. This may sound stark and restrictive

72 'Kaum eine andere Disziplin ist so sehr der Gefahr ausgesetzt, ihre Kompetenz zu überschreiten, als gerade die Jurisprudenz. Denn es ist nicht leicht und bedeutet eine empfindliche Beengung der geistigen Bewegungsfreiheit, seinen Blick immer nur auf die Welt des Sollens gerichtet zu halten, wo doch immer wieder die Versuchung an einen herantritt, in die Welt des wirklichen Lebens, des Seins zu entweichen und das tatsächliche Geschehen zu erklären' (Kelsen (n. 50), vii).

73 Koskenniemi (n. 65), 46.

74 'Wenn sie sich as eine "Reine" Lehre vom Recht bezeichnet, so darum, weil sie nur eine auf das Recht gerichtete Erkenntnis sicherstellen und weil sie aus dieser Erkenntnis alles ausscheiden möchte, was nicht zu dem exakt als Recht bestimmten Gegenstande gehört' (Kelsen (n. 18), 1).

75 Hans Kelsen, *Reine Rechtslehre. Einleitung in die rechtswissenschaftliche Problematik* (Wien: F Deuticke, 1934), 2.

but it is no more than a form of 'legal common sense'. Why? Because it is a matter of common sense to seek to know the law on a given subject without falsifying the outcome by indulging in wishful thinking. That this reduction sounds somewhat stark may be partially a function of the specific tradition of international legal scholarship, for in which domestic tradition can legal scholars proclaim openly that a legal analysis should not be the primary method for analysing the law in force? The Pure Theory of Law combines positivist faithfulness to the law in force with the restriction of legal reasoning to legal arguments, excluding non-legal arguments. It is only commonsensical to expect to talk about the law when one sets out to talk about the law.

Only by distinguishing Is and Ought can humans perceive 'norms' (Ought); hence the dichotomy is the basis of the Pure Theory of Law.[76] Without the possibility of Ought no ideals could be perceived or could exist, for 'you ought to do something' is a categorically different sentence from 'you are doing something'. Mixing Is and Ought reduces ideals to reality and the possibility of ideals placing a non-real requirement vanishes.

In contradistinction, to many it seems callous to ignore law's environment and to focus on the law only. They argue that this means ignoring that the 'real world', that politics, psychological (and even ethnological) factors, morality and personal value preferences do actually influence the law. We should be knowledgeable about these factors; this is not a plea against interdisciplinarity or, rather, pluridisciplinarity.[77] It does not mean that we need to ignore the results of other scholarly enterprises such as political sciences, sociology or psychology. Contrary to the recent cry for interdisciplinarity as an active intermixture of methodologies, Otto Pfersman has recently pointed out that Kelsen has a different, and, it is submitted, more productive, understanding of the relationship of various scholarly enterprises.

> Kelsen argues for a concept of pluridisciplinarity, i.e. the strict distinction between disciplines while at using multiple disciplines contemporaneously (each according to its own object of cognition and within its own canon of method)...It is this strict distinction of method which leads to reciprocally beneficial enrichment of knowledge.[78]

Take, for example, an international lawyer's knowledge about geopolitics. No one describing the law that governs the Security Council's votes should be

76 H. Kelsen, 'Was ist die Reine Rechtslehre?', in *Demokratie und Rechtsstaat. Festschrift für Zaccharia Giacometti* (1953), 143–161, repr. in H. Klecatsky, R. Marcić and H. Schambeck (eds.), *Die Wiener rechtstheoretische Schule. Ausgewählte Schriften von Hans Kelsen, Adolf Julius Merkl, Alfred Verdross* (Wien: Europa-Verlag, 1968), 614.

77 Pfersman (n. 71), 378.

78 'Kelsen [vertritt] ein Konzept der Pluridisziplinarität, das heißt der strikten Unterscheidung und gleichzeitigen Übung mehrerer Disziplinen nach deren jeweils eigener Objektbestimmung und Methodenkanon...[Es ist] eben diese strenge Verfahrenstrennung...die zu wechselseitger Erkenntnisbereicherung führt' (*ibid.*).

ignorant of the power constellations and political interests that govern the Permanent Members' voting. But if the various findings are admixed willy-nilly, our knowledge of the world (either of ideas or of reality) will not be increased, because syncretism of method can justify any solution that suits the scholar. Legal scholars should not give up their trade and defer to other disciplines. Continuing with our example, to argue that a Security Council veto[79] is legally invalid because it seems politically or morally illegitimate is to admix what needs to be kept apart. Factual influences upon lawmaking are – on a legal view – mediated through the rules on lawmaking. Permanent Members were granted veto power in the Charter as an expression of their position in 1945. The Charter mediates the power position through law; a change in the power structure also needs to be reflected in the Charter, in law, in order to be legally relevant.

7.6 Conclusion

This plea may seem simplistic, but it is not. It is not, because international legal scholarship as practised in the current climate tends to 'give in' to external pressure in a way which falsifies our view of positive international law by importing external elements. In modern international legal scholarship one seems to need to apologize for sticking to the law. What is needed from international lawyers is responsibility for their own actions in the application of law and objectivity in the perception of law with a realization that the role of scholars is limited.

On a realistic view, the approach presented here is not likely to succeed. It is simply too tempting to give in to the tactics presented above. Sometimes it seems heartless to abstain from wanting to change the world for the better when we international lawyers are just discovering the power our words can have on those in power. The Pure Theory of Law is also too culturally removed from the very central Anglo-Saxon cultural influences on modern international legal scholarship and practice. But that does not mean that the arguments for this approach are without merit. To paraphrase Martti Koskenniemi:[80] what could be sillier than to say that the specifically legal point of view does not have the most important role in the analysis of international law? If we are to catch up with the rest of legal scholarship and no longer to be regarded as apologists for foreign ministries or serve as propagators for our personal values writ large, we will have to find that self-discipline and restraint to do what we are here for – analyse the law in force – and leave the rest for others.

79 Article 27(3) UN Charter.

80 Koskenniemi (n. 63), 359–60.

8 Basic rights and global justice

The problem of international coercion

Silviya Lechner

Charles Beitz articulated the problem of global justice three decades ago by asking 'Do citizens of relatively affluent countries have obligations founded on justice to share their wealth with poorer people elsewhere?'.[1] This chapter employs the philosophical literature on socio-economic justice (henceforth 'global justice') to explore this problem through the concept of *basic rights*.[2] It asks which basic rights ought to be coercively imposed across state borders in the name of global justice.[3] In taking up this question, part of the task will be to sketch out the contours of the relevant political structures that can sustain rights of this elementary sort globally in a world which is still dominated by states. Because international law is a 'law of nations' or law between states, my

1 C. R. Beitz, 'Justice and International Relations' (1975) 4(4) *Philosophy and Public Affairs* 360, 360.

2 The literature on global justice is burgeoning. Key contributions have been collected in an edited volume: T. Pogge and D. Moellendorf (eds.), *Global Justice: Seminal Essays* (St Paul, MN: Paragon House, 2008). Central sources for my argument are: B. Barry, *The Liberal Theory of Justice: A Critical Examination of the Principal Doctrines in A Theory of Justice by John Rawls* (Oxford: Clarendon Press, 1973); B. Barry, 'Humanity and Justice in Global Perspective', in T. Pogge and D. Moellendorf (eds.), *Global Justice: Seminal Essays* (St Paul, MN: Paragon House, 2008), 179–209; C. R. Beitz, *Political Theory and International Relations* (Princeton, NJ: Princeton University Press, 1979); C. R. Beitz, 'International Liberalism and Distributive Justice: A Survey of Recent Thought' (1999) 51(2) *World Politics* 269; T. Nagel, 'The Problem of Global Justice', (2005) 33(2) *Philosophy and Public Affairs* 113; H. Shue, *Basic Rights: Subsistence, Affluence, and US Foreign Policy* (2nd edn, Princeton, NJ: Princeton University Press, 1996); T. Pogge, *World Poverty and Human Rights: Cosmopolitan Responsibilities and Reforms* (2nd edn, Cambridge: Polity Press, 2008); J. Rawls, *A Theory of Justice* (Cambridge, MA: Harvard University Press, 1971); J. Rawls, *The Law of Peoples* (Cambridge, MA: Harvard University Press, 1999).

3 I define rights as claim-rights familiar from H. L. A. Hart's and W. N. Hohfeld's juridical analysis of rights. But my discussion draws on deontological or Kantian moral theory which supposes that rights are *moral* claims and specifically morally validated claims, as theorized by Joel Feinberg. See J. Feinberg, 'The Nature and Value of Rights', *Journal of Value Inquiry* (1970) 4(4) 243; J. Feinberg, *Social Philosophy* (Englewood Cliffs, NJ: Prentice Hall, 1973); J. Feinberg, 'The Social Importance of Moral Rights' (1992), 6 *Philosophical Perspective {Ethics}* 175, 180; J. Feinberg, 'In Defence of Moral Rights' (1992) 12(2) *Oxford Journal of Legal Studies* 149; W. N. Hohfeld, *Fundamental Legal Conceptions: As Applied in Juridical Reasoning*, ed. Walter Wheeler Cook (New Haven, CT: Yale University Press, 1919); C. Fried, *Right and Wrong* (Cambridge, MA: Harvard University Press, 1978); H. L. A. Hart, 'Are There Any Natural Rights?', *Philosophical Review* (1955) 64(2) 175 repr. in J. Waldron (ed.), *Theories of Rights* (Oxford: Oxford University Press, 1984), 77–90; H. L. A. Hart, 'Legal and Moral Obligation', in A. I. Melden (ed.), *Essays in Moral Philosophy* (Seattle, WA: University of Washington Press, 1958).

argument has implications for the normative standing of the international human rights regime, as reflected in three key international legal documents – the Universal Declaration of Human Rights (UDHR), the International Covenant on Civil and Political Rights (ICCPR) and the International Covenant on Economic, Social and Cultural Rights (ICESCR).[4]

I begin with the premise of justice as juridical coercion,[5] to develop a Hobbesian argument that links justice to authorization and freedom.[6] An analysis of basic rights from the standpoint of global justice together with the prospect of coercively imposing such rights by means of international legal institutions can be carried out at three levels: individual, international (state-to-state relations) and global (individual-to-individual relations). In what follows the aim is to show that the international level is an analytical element that affects the global level. The discussion proceeds in three sections. Section 8.1 grounds justice in rights as opposed to welfare.[7] And since the focus is on global socio-economic justice rather than on the morality of war, the concept of basic rights is not restricted to political rights but includes economic rights.[8] Section 8.2 asks whether prosperous states have strict obligations of justice as opposed to obligations of humanitarianism towards poor states and their citizens. While my argument favours a minimum standard of global redistribution and identifies transnational structures of authority sensitive to the demands of justice, it offers no blueprint for global institutional reform. To what extent the present international legal system can be said to cohere with the ideal of global redistribution is the theme of section 8.3.

8.1 Basic rights and justice

My strategy is to anchor global justice in the concept of basic rights. What sort of rights fit this category? The concept of 'inalienable' or 'absolute' rights is a bad candidate for a number of reasons. To begin with, it would be hard to defend the view of rights as inalienable 'property' that the agent retains regardless of external conditions of emergency (famine or war) or wrongful actions (crime). When Bentham scornfully dismissed the concept of rights as

4 The texts of key international legal conventions and the UDHR have been collected in P. R. Ghandhi (ed.), *Blackstone's International Human Rights Documents* (5th edn, Oxford: Oxford University Press, 2006), hereafter *Blackstone's*.

5 T. Nardin, 'Justice and Coercion', in A. J. Bellamy (ed.), *International Society and Its Critics* (Oxford: Oxford University Press, 2005), 247–64.

6 T. Hobbes, *Leviathan*, ed. C. B. MacPherson (London: Penguin, 1968). On rights and juridical justice see chs. 14 and 26 (esp. Hobbes's notion of laws as 'rules of just and unjust', ch. 26, 312), and on authorization and freedom ch. 16 and ch. 21, 268–9.

7 I depart from utilitarian account of rights such as Peter Singer's or Amartya Sen's welfarist 'goal-rights system'. See P. Singer, 'Famine, Affluence, and Morality' (1972) 1(3) *Philosophy and Public Affairs* 229 and A. Sen, 'Rights and Agency' (1982) 11(1) *Philosophy and Public Affairs* 3, 15.

8 Shue (n. 2), 7.

nonsense upon stilts,[9] he was referring not to the genus, rights, but to this problematic species, inalienable rights. So 'basic' for the purposes of the incipient discussion cannot plausibly mean 'inalienable'. Second, my argument is contractarian as opposed to utilitarian or welfarist and the talk of inalienable rights has little purchase for contractarians. A contract, Hobbes writes, is a mutual transfer of right.[10] If Hobbes is correct, the social contract cannot take place unless it is assumed that rights can be alienated from the right-holder. Rights are peculiar powers enabling agents to achieve wished-for goals.

Rights constitute such potent powers because the right of one person typically creates a corresponding obligation or duty in another. In this familiar Hohfeldian model of rights as duty correlates, the right-holder has a claim that must be honoured by another person whom we say is duty-bound (or is under an obligation) to the right-holder.[11] Rights are instruments of 'social' relations. That a right can spring into being on the condition that agents maintain a degree of contact, be it a transaction or a more stable relation, marks a crucial distinction between rights and duties. We can imagine a purely duty-based code of morality such as the Decalogue where a group of individuals have duties but no rights.[12] They stand in a moral relation to God, or 'under the moral law' in more secular Kantian terms, but in no direct moral relation to each other.[13] No member of the group is in a position to press claims, or hold rights, against any other group member.

The proposition 'A holds a right to do *x against* B' can be taken to imply antagonism between A and B over external objects or actions (*x*). It also suggests that agents hold or possess rights as if they were some kind of resources. But I wish to recommend an identity-centred view of rights where a right is a symbol of moral status or personhood. It is instructive to contrast Kant's idea of persons with Feinberg's idea of persons with rights. For this purpose, we must invoke the Kantian idiom of duty with its duo of regulative ideals: impartiality and non-interference. 'Person' for Kant is a rational agent governed by the supreme principle of duty (the moral law), and it is imperative that duty-bound agents respect each other's moral autonomy.[14] Autonomy as freedom obligates each agent to choose ends in a manner that prevents interference with the free choice of like agents. Moreover, no agent can use another as a means for one's ends ('respect for persons'). For theorists such as Feinberg persons are not merely autonomous agents, but autonomous right-holders who can demand respect from others in fulfilling their freely chosen projects or ends. As Feinberg argues, Kant's concept of respect for persons is

9 J. Bentham, 'Anarchical Fallacies', in A. I. Melden (ed.), *Human Rights* (Belmont, CA: Wadsworth, 1970), 32.

10 Hobbes (n. 6), 192.

11 Hohfeld (n. 3), 38–9.

12 Hart 1955 (n. 3), 78.

13 Feinberg 1970 (n. 3), 244.

14 J. W. Ellington (tr.), I. Kant, *Grounding for the Metaphysics of Morals* (Indianapolis, IN: Hackett, 1993), paras. 432–3, 447–8.

equivalent to respect for persons' rights.[15] Right-holding, then, is an emblem of moral status because it puts agents 'into a position' where they can claim the object of their rights as their *due* (and not as mere gratuity).[16] Right-holders owe each other mutual consideration and possibly assistance beyond the austere Kantian requirement of non-interference. Rights and not duties constitute the morally basic idiom in this case.

Rights and duties can be correlated in two senses: logical and moral. In Hohfeld's account, a right is a duty upside down – so logically neither concept is more basic than the other: 'A's right' is another way of speaking of 'B's duty towards A'. But it is possible to think of rights as having a moral priority over duties – (this is what we may term a right-priority theory). Thus on Feinberg's model, A's right constitutes a moral ground for B's corresponding duty towards A.[17] A's right is the reason why B is duty-bound to A. A right-priority theory reflects the premise that agents are linked by a morally significant relation. Justice is one such relation.

But the place of rights in an argument for justice is ambiguous. Justice here means social justice: a standard of moral evaluation that it would be justifiable to coercively impose on a group of individuals who partake in a shared activity. On certain philosophical accounts such as James Griffin's, rights and justice are antithetical notions. Rights, the argument goes, enable the individual person to be a free, thinking and choosing being – a Kantian autonomous self – whereas justice is a public standard of distributing goods in an equitable manner. Justice defined in this way is a right to equality (equal distribution of material goods), but all we can hope for is to have equal rights (even though the outcome might be an unequal distribution of material goods).[18] 'If you free-ride on the bus because you know that no harm will come as the rest of us are paying our fares', Griffin writes, 'you do not violate my rights, even though you clearly act unfairly'.[19] The free-rider violates the condition of fairness by cheating, but not the rights of the complying agents (the passengers), because the act of cheating does not diminish their capacity to exercise free choice (no harm has been done).

In *A Theory of Justice* John Rawls offers an alternative view of rights as compatible with justice. As in Griffin's account, justice is a public standard for allocating resources among a group of associates engaged in a cooperative activity, hence the criterion of justice is fairness. A distribution is fair whenever agents who have received benefits from the cooperative game also discharge its burdens.[20] However unlike Griffin, Rawls regards rights as resources that can be distributed in the allocation process.[21] Rawls's conception of justice is

15 Feinberg 1970 (n. 3), 252 and Feinberg, 'The Social Importance of Moral Rights' 1992 (n. 3), 180.

16 Feinberg 1970 (n. 3), 245 and Feinberg 1973 (n. 3), 63.

17 Feinberg 1970 (n. 3), 250 and J. Raz, 'On the Nature of Rights' (1984) 93(370) *Mind,* 199.

18 J. Griffin, 'First Steps in an Account of Human Rights' (2001) 9 *European Journal of Philosophy* 317.

19 Griffin (n. 18), 306, 317.

20 Rawls 1971 (n. 2), 112.

21 *Ibid.* 7, 58.

institutional – it concerns the 'basic structure' of the liberal state,[22] and the principles that rational agents in the 'original position' would select in justifying this structure.[23] There are two cardinal principles – according to the equal liberty principle 'each person is to have an equal right to the most extensive total system of equal basic liberties compatible with a similar system of liberty for all'; and the difference principle in turn announces that 'social and economic inequalities are to be arranged so that they are both: (a) to the greatest benefit of the least advantaged, consistent with the just savings principle, and (b) attached to offices and positions open to all under conditions of fair equality of opportunity'.[24] The central unit of analysis for Rawls is not the individual agent but the share of *basic goods* – things that 'every rational man is presumed to want' such as opportunities, liberties, wealth and income – which can be purchased in the political market place subject to the limiting condition of fairness.[25] This is disclosed by Rawls's reference to 'a total *system* of basic liberties' (societal notion) as opposed to the classical liberal idea of 'freedom of choice' (individualist notion). Analogously, the difference principle maximizes the overall distribution of life prospects of a given class of individuals inside society, the least advantaged (it is a maximin principle).

Rawls offers us a liberal theory of justice, not a theory of rights.[26] Rights matter to the extent that they can be transformed into resources for the purposes of social allocation. Of relevance are institutional rights that belong to agents as members of political or legal structures – a right to free speech, a right to assembly, a right to property[27] – in contrast to individual rights that are held by uniquely designated persons (John's right to enter Bruno's house). The latter category of rights can be termed transactional since they are incurred by means of promises or contracts (John is entitled to enter the house because of a contract signed with Bruno). Second, despite its normative aura, Rawls's liberalism is a theory of politics, not of morality. It gravitates around a quartet of premises: (a) social cooperation generates benefits; (b) benefits concern desirable 'goods', rights being such goods or instruments for the distribution of goods; (c) benefits ought to be distributed fairly, in accordance with principles of justice; (d) the producers of benefits, or those who stand in a relation of justice, are members of a single political association: the state. In the remainder of this chapter my task will be to question premises (b) and (d)

22 *Ibid.* On the definition of a basic structure, see 7–11, 55; on the institutional focus of justice, 54–6, 64.

23 On rationality in the original position see Rawls 1971 (n. 2), 142–3. That the original position is not a contract is a view developed by T. Heyd, 'Justice and Solidarity: The Contractualist Case against Global Justice' (2007) 38(1) *Journal of Social Philosophy* 112, 114.

24 Rawls 1971 (n. 2), 302; see also 60–5. My argument focuses on the difference principle, bracketing the principle of equal opportunity, and the just savings aspect of the difference principle dealing with intergenerational justice.

25 For the concept of basic goods, see Rawls 1971 (n. 2), esp. 62, 396, and for fair shares of basic goods, 112.

26 A. I. Melden, *Rights and Persons* (Berkeley, CA: University of California Press, 1977), ch. 4.

27 Rawls 1971 (n. 2), 61.

and adduce support for the position that relations of justice cannot be arrested at the border of the state. Before examining the question of global justice in section 8.2, it is requisite to scrutinize the nature of rights that can affect relations of justice inside domestic political society.

Liberalism is a domestic theory of the good because the state is seen as a central locus of value. Rights, on this Hobbesian view, exist inside the state; there are no rights in the state of nature. But what kind of rights can these be? Contemporary theorists conventionally assign rights into two categories: civil (negative) and economic (positive),[28] negative rights calling for non-interference with their positive counterpart presupposing effort or care. Civil rights are held against the state whereas economic rights are to be actively provided by the state. But as Henry Shue has shown, neither category of rights is purely positive or purely negative.[29] My analysis of basic rights in sections 8.2–8.3 builds upon Shue's argument which can be summarized as follows. From the standpoint of the duty-bound agent, rights are instruments of coercion – the object of a right is something due, a pending obligation that cannot be put back on the shelf; from the right-holder's standpoint rights represent securities designed to protect the agent against standard harms or threats (hunger and physical violence). Protection is a paradigmatic notion. Protecting the supposedly negative right to physical security demands non-interference, but it also requires the active creation of institutions (police, prisons, courts).[30] So a simple dichotomy between negative and positive rights will not do. The dichotomy characterizes *duties*,[31] where negative duties reveal a higher degree of responsibility compared to positive duties.

While consistent with Shue's approach, my argument digs all the way down into Hobbesian moral theory and its fundamental relationship between coercion and freedom.[32] This Hobbesian perspective permits us to overcome the orthodox division between civil and economic rights. Hobbes portrays civil rights as coeval with the liberal state. The state is a guardian of liberty or the condition of individual freedom of choice. It is not a managerial enterprise promoting a common conception of the good for all of its citizens.[33] But to ensure that the principle of freedom of each individual is compatible with equal freedom for all, binding rules of non-interference must be enforced across the entire domain of state authority. As a system of coercion, the state works to prevent or punish illegitimate, because private, modes of coercion. It

28 M. Haas, *International Human Rights: A Comprehensive Introduction* (London: Routledge, 2008), 112–13.

29 Shue (n. 2), ch. 2, esp. 35–40. But see Fried (n. 3), 110–114.

30 Shue (n. 2), 33, 37.

31 Shue (n. 2), 53.

32 This relationship between coercion and freedom has been associated with Robert Nozick's libertarian approach. See R. Nozick, *Anarchy, State, and Utopia* (New York, NY: Basic Books, 1974), ix, 28–35, 166. Unlike Nozick, I do not see coercion as infringing on the domain of freedom when the question concerns rights. Nozick's notion of rights as 'entitlements' is more demanding than my Feinberg-derived notion of rights as 'justified claims'.

33 M. Oakeshott, *On Human Conduct* (Oxford: Clarendon Press, 1975), esp. 112–13, 119.

is a system of legitimate coercion: 'legitimate' in the sense that its ultimate preoccupation is the protection of freedom rather than the provision of public order. A civil right – such as the right of freedom of expression – is a title that each citizen holds against any other citizen but also, and this is crucial, against the state. What makes this right and the freedoms it guarantees a valid title is the background of coercion.

When it comes to economic rights, the liberal state is still committed to the ideal of freedom, but does economic freedom have the same ground as civil freedom? If not, a theory of political conduct that combines economic and civil rights in a coherent whole would be hard to devise. It may appear that political freedom is an altogether different creature from the freedom of the market, which assumes unbridled competition between advantage-seeking agents. But when attended to carefully, the concept of competition proves to be a mixture of conflict and cooperation: a race against an opponent within the bounds of a higher-level cooperation over the rules of the game. Rules of the game include laws regulating property and money exchange, as well as prohibitions against unlawful interference: illegitimate coercion, blackmail, threats. It follows that civil rights oblige us to consider the state in its totality, as a system of law, while economic rights pertain to one of its subsystems – the economy. But the market is 'free' because it is embedded within the general system of law or within the state as a coercive apparatus. Freedom both in its civil and economic dimension is contingent on (state-based) coercion.

The idea that something is due or coercively enforceable is part of the definition of a right – and it applies to both economic and civil rights. But it is also part of the definition of justice because justice is an idiom of relations that can be enforced by law. If this position bears scrutiny, distributive justice as a standard of allocating resources within a community implies a substantive degree of coercive back-up. My point is not that retributive justice (punishment) is a precondition for distributive justice, but that the idea of justice, in all its denominations, implies juridical coercion. This explains why we are wary of undertaking obligations of justice (which require strict compliance) as opposed to obligations of humanity (which are discretionary). Obligations of justice accord a corresponding right to the party to whom we are obligated, whereas obligations of humanity do not accord such a right.

8.2 Can justice be globalized?

The state, be it a cooperative game (Rawls) or a system of legitimate coercion (Hobbes), is a precondition for the emergence of rights and relations of justice. Let us suspend this corollary for a moment and return to Beitz's formulation of the question of global justice: do affluent states have obligations of justice towards economically burdened societies and individuals living inside such societies? Or paraphrased in the language of rights, can burdened societies claim the assistance of the advanced world as a right? This section will make a case for global justice adopting Shue's notion of basic rights, defined as 'everyone's minimum reasonable demands upon the rest of humanity'.[34] Shue outlines three basic kinds of rights – subsistence rights, rights to security and rights to liberty – as guarantees against standard threats: physical violence; malnutrition and hunger; obstacles to exercising one's free choice.[35] My approach posits two basic rights: (a) a 'right to life' (Hobbes's notion comprising a basket of rights),[36] compressing Shue's triad into a single analytical component; and (b) a 'right to leave' (a political right to leave the territory of one's own state).[37]

8.2.1 *Globalizing domestic justice: Rawls and critics*

The global justice debate has had its formative voices – Brian Barry, Charles Beitz, Thomas Pogge and more recently Thomas Nagel. Almost all have criticized Rawls for neglecting socio-economic justice as a global problem so it is pertinent to re-examine the elusive master's views from this particular standpoint. Recall that, in Rawls's political conception of justice, domestic society represents a cooperative enterprise of shared burdens and benefits. According to the difference principle, well-off members of society agree to participate in social institutions that maximize the advantages of the worst-off, with Rawls assuming that the primary moral unit when it comes to relations of justice is a 'self-contained national community'.[38] In *A Theory of Justice* Rawls examines in passing the unlikely scenario of international justice between states by postulating a second original position whose participants are not individuals but representatives of states or 'peoples' (agreeing on principles of justice behind a 'veil of ignorance': a heuristic device that withholds information contractors may have about their identity or conceptions of the good life).[39] Rawls finalizes this argument for interstate relations in *The Law of Peoples* by refining the idea of a second original position to include two types of states: liberal democracies and 'decent hierarchical' peoples (political communities which deserve to be tolerated by liberal regimes). He concludes that the difference principle has no global application because decent peoples may find it unappealing. That is, affluent nations have obligations of humanity towards societies in economic distress – the affluent may aid the poor at little

34 Shue (n. 2), 19; fn. omitted.

35 *Ibid.* 9, 27, 32–3.

36 Hobbes (n 6), ch. 21, 269.

37 Shue's *right to liberty*, which my argument brackets, has been incorporated into the right to life as a limiting condition, to show that the freedom to hold rights is a basic premise in a rights-priority theory. *The right to leave* reflects the value of freedom as well. But unlike a right to free speech or freedom of assembly characteristic of liberalism, the right to leave measures the degree of legitimacy of both liberal *and* non-liberal societies. Both must be part of a coherent theory of global justice but this point cannot be pursued here.

38 Rawls 1971 (n. 2), 457.

39 *Ibid.* 378.

cost to themselves (logic of humanitarianism) but are not required to do so (the logic of justice).[40] Yet, as Barry has suggested, if parties to the original position are peoples, then they will be more willing rather than less willing to agree on a global difference principle because it is an empirical fact that the number of poorer states (relative to richer states) in the world is overwhelmingly large. The risk that upon lifting the veil of ignorance one might turn out to be an economically burdened country is too high for any reasonable agent to ignore.[41]

Suppose that the argument for obligations of global justice is valid. What is the thing that affluent nations owe to the less fortunate ones as a matter of justice? Some of Rawls's critics have assumed that because the problem is global socio-economic justice, the solution must be economic too: global redistribution must be about resources in the economist's sense of the term. Beitz thus has argued that the resource endowment of nations is arbitrary from a moral point of view, using as a parallel Rawls's argument that talents are morally arbitrary with respect to the individual person.[42] Talents are unobjectionable natural facts but when institutions begin to coercively perpetuate patterns of social relations based on such facts, the result is injustice. (The concept of coercion is crucial and I will return to it shortly.) While talents determine who the person is – and here Beitz is attacking Rawls's argument – resources are something that the person has. Since resources do not affect the identity of the self, stripping somebody from their resources is not morally objectionable the way stripping them from their talents would be.[43] Beitz proposes a global redistribution plan, operating to the benefit of resource-poor countries, on the basis of an index comparing a given country's food production to its arable land.[44] But the moral ground that motivates redistribution is global rather than international: the scheme should benefit the least advantaged individuals (instead of states) in the present system of worldwide inequality.[45] Reasoning along similar lines Pogge has put forward a project for a Global Resources Dividend fund that would tax resource-abundant states for the purposes of alleviating global poverty.[46]

Rawls has responded to critics by arguing that resource endowments cannot be a key worry in an argument for distributive justice because how resources would be used or misused, and whether they would generate wealth, depends on the political culture of a society: its civic virtues, birth control policies, degree of industriousness.[47] But part of the confusion on this point stems from

40 Rawls 1999 (n. 2), 106.
41 Barry 1973 (n. 2), 129.
42 Beitz 1975 (n. 1), 367 and Beitz 1979 (n. 2), 138.
43 Beitz 1975 (n. 1), 368 and Beitz 1979 (n. 2), 139.
44 Beitz 1975 (n. 1), 372.
45 *Ibid.* 371 and Beitz 1979 (n. 2), 152.
46 See Pogge (n. 2), ch. 8.
47 Rawls 1999 (n. 2), 108, 117.

Rawls's failure to clarify the status of resources or basic goods in his theory. Is 'liberty' for example a resource (which can be traded off) or a right (which cannot be so traded off)? The idea that I wish to emphasize is that rights are not resources *simpliciter*. We cannot 'distribute' rights the way we distribute money. Rights determine our identity (for example, as right-holders in a court of law) by imposing limits on other agents (or soliciting their assistance) in terms of what they are permitted to do in relation to *our* basic interests, needs or plans. Although we speak of 'holding rights', a right is a characteristic of the person: it is not an object or a state of affairs in the external world that exists apart from the agent. The analogy to capture the notion of rights is power, not money. Contrast 'John is powerful' with 'John has money'. So a theory of justice which articulates principles for allocating basic goods (such as Rawls's) is diametrically opposed in its concerns to a theory of justice which prioritizes rights (which I favour).

What is a right-priority theory of justice? Such a theory would elevate rights into a theoretically primitive concept, so rights normally associated with distinct spheres of human activity would be treated as representatives of the same genus. Economics and politics are different spheres governed by different principles – cost efficiency vs. principled decision-making or 'deliberation' – but economic rights and political rights are rights. Shue's is a right-priority theory because it subsumes economic rights (right to subsistence) and political rights (right to security, right to liberty) under the common umbrella of basic rights. Armed with the concept of basic rights, we can embark on an argument for domestic justice, but also – and significantly – for global justice. Rawls's theory of justice is about principles regulating the distribution of resources within a single political association or state; rights are derivative. The cooperative game that creates benefits (which ought to be distributed justly) is a game of politics, with the political principle of equal liberty having a lexical priority over the economically-orientated difference principle.[48] Since politics always comes first and economics, second, Rawls seems to think that political and economic rights must end up on different sides of the fence too. But general principles are neutral in respect to rights. Rawls's assumption that economic issues of redistribution arise *after* we have settled the political rules of the game explains why it is hard to globalize economic justice on Rawls's premises – the snag is that doing so would require a world state.

The rigid dichotomy between economic and political rights also permeates Rawls's *Law of Peoples*. Rawls asks what principles of conduct a well-ordered state (liberal democracy or a non-liberal 'decent' society) would choose to govern its external relations with other states.[49] To qualify as decent, a state (or a 'peoples') must recognize a set of basic rights, but basic rights in Rawls's conceptualization are rights of the person conceived politically: a right to participation in representative public institutions, a right to due process and fair

48 Rawls 1971 (n. 2), 42–3.

49 Rawls 1999 (n. 2), 83, 86.

trial. This set does not incorporate classical liberal rights associated with the notion of free and equal citizens (a right to vote in free elections, a right to run for public office, freedom of conscience).[50] In the second original position, liberal and decent peoples are expected to agree on principles of international peaceful coexistence: *pacta sunt servanda*, non-aggression, non-intervention and the peaceful resolution of disputes. These are political principles enshrined in international law.[51] Economic rights are excluded from consideration of international justice. Although Rawls acknowledges that a country which starves its citizens to death when the disaster could have been prevented does not meet the criterion of decency because it violates basic human rights,[52] he does not specify what kinds of rights have been infringed or what course of action is open to other states who may wish to intervene and aid the victims.

Rawls cannot be specific because his *Laws of Peoples* articulates principles of foreign policy as opposed to international relations. The book has its pedigree in Kant's *Perpetual Peace* but the similarity between the two should not be overstated.[53] While Rawls grapples with the question of how each state, looking inwards at its domestic constitution, ought to conduct itself on the international scene, Kant conjures up a *sui generis* realm of 'international right' which generates independent normative demands, including demands of justice, on its members – sovereign states.[54] Peace among states for Kant is not a consequence of good behaviour domestically, as it is for Rawls, but an independent condition of membership that each state ought to satisfy to join the pacific federation of states. *The Law of Peoples* is not a genuine theory of international relations or international right in Kantian language. But even if it were, Kant theorizes justice in retributive rather than distributive terms.[55] To defend socio-economic justice we must search further than the articles of *Perpetual Peace*.

8.2.2 Global justice: coercion and harm

A recent contribution to the global justice debate that takes the idea of economic rights seriously is Pogge's *Word Poverty and Human Rights*. All human beings have a basic right to be protected from serious harms, especially harms brought about by severe life-threatening poverty. By participating in the coercive imposition of a global economic order, through institutions such as the World

50 *Ibid.* 70–2.

51 *Ibid.* 37.

52 *Ibid.* 109.

53 I. Kant, 'Perpetual Peace: A Philosophical Sketch', in H. Reiss (ed.), *Kant: Political Writings* (Cambridge: Cambridge University Press, 1991), 93–130.

54 *Ibid.* 102–5.

55 As Kant writes in the *Metaphysics of Morals*, ed. Mary Gregor (Cambridge: Cambridge University Press, 1996), 'one can locate the concept of right directly in the possibility of connecting universal reciprocal coercion with the freedom of everyone' [6:232]. Thus, the principle of international right which postulates coercion as a condition of freedom regulates the external relations of states as free agents and permits wars of self-defence but not wars of acquisition or punitive wars [6:347]. Self-defence is a just retribution for a wrong suffered unjustly.

Trade Organization (WTO),[56] affluent countries and their citizens are harming the global poor. As Pogge warns us, 'inflicting seriously unjust rules upon others [the global poor] is harming them'.[57] Coercion is manifested in the fact that the poor individuals around the globe cannot opt out of these institutions. Causal and moral responsibility befalls the governments and citizens of the developed world.[58] Harm ought to be prevented or, when it has been caused, its victims ought to be compensated by means of reforming unjust global institutions. It follows that we, in the affluent Western countries, have obligations of justice to protect poor states and individuals living inside their borders from harms for which we are causally responsible. The reforms that are called for include WTO restructuring – providing more equitable terms of trade to poor countries, reduction of agricultural subsidies, and abolition of patents that prohibit the production of life-saving generic medicines in third world counties – and possibly a Global Resources Dividend.[59]

Besides, the opportunity cost of bringing the poorest in the world up to the desirable threshold of tolerable poverty is not too high.[60] Pogge regards with suspicion Kantian arguments asserting that we merely fail to act in preventing harm (such as world hunger and severe poverty) instead of actively causing harm.[61] Feinberg writes in a similar spirit that 'to be effectively deprived of all food is clearly to be harmed as much as to be given poisoned food'.[62] Pogge and Feinberg are alluding to the distinction between acts and omissions found in Kantian and deontological theories of action. This distinction is a dangerous one when pressed to the extreme, but have we reached the extreme?

Pogge concludes that certain rights rooted in basic human needs – physical integrity, subsistence supplies (of food, clothing and drink), freedom of movement, basic education and economic participation – ought to be guaranteed globally.[63] And indeed the proposition that there ought to be such rights, specifically a right to subsistence that guards individuals against the harm of severe poverty, is morally appealing. But fulfilling this right to subsistence is a second step in the argument which depends on limiting conditions such as scarcity. It is a non sequitur to insist that because A desperately needs *x*, A has a right to *x*, and, that furthermore B has a correlative obligation to provide A with *x*. This is so even if *x* is something essential to A's life. Considerations of distance may be involved (is B A's parent or friend?); can somebody else (C, D, ...) provide *x*?; can *x* be supplied at a reasonable cost (should B kill himself or herself to protect A's life?)? Aside from this extreme life-sacrificing scenario, the last condition is a condition of scarcity – it is a

56 Pogge (n 2), 5, 30.

57 *Ibid.* 16.

58 *Ibid.* 28–9, 55, 115, 205, 207.

59 On the necessity for a WTO reform, see *ibid.* 22 and on the Global Resources Dividend, ch. 8, 210–14.

60 Pogge's estimate is $300 billion annually (2005 baseline), *ibid.* 211.

61 *Ibid.* 14–15.

62 Feinberg 1973 (n. 3), 30.

63 Pogge (n. 2), 55.

restrictive criterion because it envisages a situation where B de facto does not have x (the opportunity cost of giving x to A is too high). This argument can be conveyed in less abstract language – why protect the global poor when we have poor individuals inside our own societies? Would the measuring rod for global redistribution be resources, income, or wealth? If we, citizens of the first world, accept the argument that destitute individuals abroad have a right to be protected from hunger and dire poverty and that the obligation towards such individuals is a strict obligation of justice, we may need to protect them on an ongoing basis, institutionally and not simply transactionally. But who is to manage global institutions of this scope and how much will it cost?

Much like Rawls's, Pogge's argument for global justice entails a recommendation for a world state because it assumes that the global poor ought to be guaranteed a minimum standard of living.[64] Maintaining a standard of living is a daunting task of a continuous and coordinated intervention by a public authority acting to ensure that the affected individuals (the poor in this case) are lifted up to the requisite floor. Traditionally the state has been burdened with this role. But would anything that resembles a super-state be a feasible structure of authority for battling global poverty in the world as we know it? It seems advisable to abandon the idea of a standard of living in favour of a less demanding premise – a right to life – because this would eliminate the necessity of a world state. The right to life, as a basket of rights, includes Shue's basic right to subsistence. In addition to it, I discuss the right to leave one's own political association. The latter is of major importance because as Beitz contends, regardless of talents or education, a person born into a less developed state has severely limited life prospects.[65] And it is relatively harder for a poor individual to exit an economically burdened state than to exit a local community (including one's family) inside an affluent state.

8.2.3 *Global justice: coercion and freedom*

Nagel has recently argued in an important article that the idea of global justice is premature – it requires something that does not yet exist: a world state. While the international realm has normative texture, it would be erroneous to think that states can stand in a relation of justice. Citizens (inside the individual state) alone are bound by this relation: justice is an 'associative obligation'.[66] Nagel in effect arrives at Rawls's conclusion – membership inside the state is a precondition for entering obligations of justice, hence the international realm can only accommodate obligations of humanity (the obligation to protect the innocent from attack, or obligations of mutual aid). But the logic of argumentation is distinct, since for Nagel the state is a

64 Pogge (n. 2), 45.
65 Beitz 1975 (n. 1), 379–80 and Beitz 1979 (n. 2), 163.
66 Nagel (n. 2), 121.

Hobbesian structure of legitimate coercion to be distinguished from the Rawlsian cooperative enterprise.[67]

Hobbes's conception of the state combines coercion and authorization. To authorize something is to trace it back to an author's decision; or as Hobbes expresses the idea, 'no man is obliged by a Covenant, whereof he is not Author'.[68] In the state of nature, no relation of justice constrains the agents. But once they decide to delegate authority to the state via the social contract – each by transferring his or her 'right of nature' (or absolute liberty) – the relation of justice emerges. Justice embodies a juridical or coercively enforceable public standard.[69] It also has a second meaning – justification or supplying moral reasons for decisions or actions. The possibility of justice as justification arises, Nagel argues, because each citizen is subject and author of the state as a system of law. Hobbesian authorization means that justice cannot be naked coercion: it must be legitimate or justified coercion.

Notice that membership inside political society is non-voluntary or coercive: we are born into a state as subjects. Justice (as coercion) paradoxically entails moral vulnerability or demands for justice (as justification) of which the citizens are authors. The state is vulnerable because the citizens as a group may demand that it justifies its policies, and similarly, each individual citizen, aside from being a source, constitutes a target for the justificatory demands of other citizens.[70] Extending the boundaries of domestic society to encompass the globe would give rise to demands for justice and economic redistribution targeting the most advanced countries. Understandably, these countries would be reluctant to align behind any global justice programme.

Three aspects of Nagel's conception of justice are noteworthy. First, Nagel portrays citizens as right-holders and not as Rawlsian cooperators, indicating that his theory favours rights over resources. Nagel's reasoning mirrors Feinberg's argument for rights – allowing outsiders to enter our domestic society puts them into a position to have rights against us. Society is a web of rights and corresponding obligations, whereas justice is the glue that holds the web together. As Nagel is quick to point out –'everyone may have the right to live in a just society, but we do not have an obligation to live in a just society with everyone'.[71] Second, because Nagel's starting premise is justice as legitimate coercion, the rights that citizens enjoy inside their political community are not bifurcated into economic and civil. Obligations of justice can be, and often are, about economic redistribution. Third, justifiable claims for redistribution from rich to poor sectors of the global economy can be grounded in coercive, authoritatively enacted, institutions – ideally, a world state. However, transnational trade and financial regimes, even when their

67 *Ibid.* 114–15.

68 Hobbes (n. 6), ch. 16, 218.

69 Hobbes's argument is complex since Hobbes speaks of injustice as a contract violation, *ibid.* ch. 14, 191. 'Injustice' (or 'injury'), however is not the simple opposite of 'justice'.

70 Nagel (n. 2), 128–30.

71 *Ibid.* 132.

operation bestows considerable benefits on the majority of the actors concerned, do not qualify as such a ground. Regimes of this sort are transactional in nature even though they function through highly complex organizations such as the World Bank, the International Monetary Fund or the WTO: their ethos is interest, voluntary agreement (contract) and bargaining.[72] Justice by contrast is institutional – it presupposes non-voluntary relations (coercive institutions) and moral authority that transcends short-lived interests. Nagel's argument effectively rebuts Pogge's contention that citizens of prosperous states should be held responsible for WTO-generated harms. The WTO is an organization, not a coercive institution; moreover, individuals in the West have not authorized it (at least not collectively) in the moral sense of Hobbesian authorization.

8.3 Global justice through international law

Theorists in the global justice literature for the most part have treated the international (state-to-state) and the global (individual-to-individual) as mutually exclusive normative domains.[73] But a conception of the global can include international relations. This section will defend the view that international law may be pivotal in realizing the ideal of global justice.

Why choose international law? Would not global law suit better the aspirations of global justice? Global law is equivalent to a world state. That a state of this formidable size would tend to be tyrannical has worried Kantians and balance-of-power theorists since the eighteenth century.[74] Since its authoritative sway would cover the entire globe, its subjects would have no alternative route to escape: there will be no other political association to emigrate to. The right of the person to leave one's domestic society articulated in section 8.2 responds to this fear of global empire. It replaces empire with an image of international plurality, a society of states whose key organizing principle is international law.

How can international law promote global justice? If, as I have been arguing, global justice is about basic rights – a right to life and a right to leave – and about their coercive enforcement, multiple avenues are left open for bringing about the desired result. The notion of basic rights is already global in spirit because it underwrites the concept of moral personhood. Any step in

72 *Ibid.* 137–8, 140. Critics have underestimated Nagel's point that only stable, coercive, and authoritatively established and reproducible institutions can be loci of claims for justice. A. J. Julius, 'Nagel's Atlas' (2006) 34(2) *Philosophy and Public Affairs* 176, 178, 187, 189; and J. Cohen and C. Sabel, 'Extra Rempublicam Nulla Justitia?' (2006) 34(2) *Philosophy and Public Affairs* 147, 169.

73 Beitz's 'International Liberalism and Distributive Justice' is an exception but even there Beitz focuses on the differentia in the *moral grounds* for global redistribution and not on differentia in the *political structures* of authority that such redistribution might implicate.

74 A. H. L. Heeren, *Manual of the History of the Political System of Europe and its Colonies, from its Formation at the Close of the Fifteenth Century, to its Re-establishment upon the Fall of Napoleon*, 2 vols. (tr. from 5th German edn; Oxford: Talboys, 1834).

the direction of securing basic rights would bring us closer to the ideal of global justice. International agencies and structures can be tools for global change. Yet international law is particularly apt for the task of securing basic rights globally for a special reason. Relevant here is Hobbes's injunction that both freedom and coercion constitute indispensible conditions of justice. If the state conceived as an individual unit is a coercive framework, then a system of multiple coercive units (a society of states) would enable freedom. Freedom here refers to freedom of disassociation or (in my terminology) a right to leave. According this right to individuals is a way to measure political legitimacy because people vote with their hands and feet.[75] Masses of emigrants at the border are a symptom that things are going badly inside the country and that it may suffer from a legitimacy deficit. Any decent society should allow its members to emigrate, if they are unhappy with its political structures.

We must not lose sight of the point that basic rights are not given in the nature of things: if we claim that a certain right ought to count as basic, the claim must be buttressed by argument. The right to leave one's own state, for example, implies the presence of political institutions; its meaning cannot be exhausted by abstract discussions of moral agency. So provided we posit this kind of right as basic, we would have to say something about the actual political structure of international relations. This structure, it has been assumed here, comprises a society of states: a game whose constitutive rules reveal a commitment to international law and international morality. This premise entails the question about borders: should the right to leave one's own state be accompanied by a corresponding right to enter another state (a right of citizenship)? Probably not, because preventing states from setting restrictions on entry would put the idea of statehood as a bounded community of members under strain.[76] Whether a state ought not to deny entry to nationals, who might not be citizens, or a 'right to return' is a further question whose answer hinges on a full-blown political theory (communitarianism or liberalism). Here my goal is limited to a brief overview of the status of basic rights in canonical texts of international human rights law, the 1966 Covenants on civil and economic rights and the UDHR.

What obstructs the protection of the right to leave and the associated right to enter a state in international practice is their conceptual tension. Granting solely the first right would be tantamount to the grim prospect of an expanding pool of stateless people, granting both rights unconditionally would dissolve the very idea of state borders, and thus of states as agents of international law dedicated to the cause of basic rights. In light of this tension, it is not surprising that both have received a relatively weak support in the ICCPR and the UDHR. ICCPR's Article 12(2) reads: 'Everyone shall be free to leave any

75 A. O. Hirschman, *Exit, Voice and Loyalty: Responses to Decline in Firms, Organizations and States* (new edn, Cambridge, MA: Harvard University Press, 1990).

76 M. Walzer, 'The Distribution of Membership', in T. Pogge and D. Moellenrorf (eds.), *Global Justice* (St Paul's, MN: Paragon House, 2008), 153.

country, including his own' and Article 12(4): 'No one shall be arbitrarily deprived of the right to enter his own country'.[77] (Both rights derive from the earlier text of a single UDHR's Article 13.)[78] But Article 12(2) (together with Article 12(1) according individuals freedom of intranational movement) are qualified by Article 12(3) stating that 'the above-mentioned rights shall not be subject to any restrictions except those which are provided by law, are necessary to protect national security, public order (*ordre public*), public health or morals or the rights and freedoms of others, and are consistent with other rights recognized in the present Covenant'.[79] This disturbingly restrictive qualification does not apply to Article 12(4) granting a right to enter one's own country. While the right to leave is secured symbolically, at least the right to enter one's own country appears to be strongly protected by the ICCPR. But even the latter's protection is circumscribed since the expression 'one's own country' equivocates between nationality and citizenship. Both rights as a result are modestly guaranteed in current international human rights law.

But if the ICCPR, whose remit is politics, falters as a guarantor of basic rights (of entry and exit) what about the ICESCR and economic rights? Another corollary of the discussion so far is that the normative ideal of basic rights ought to supersede the conventional dichotomy between economic and civil rights. The dichotomy lacks a moral foundation in so far as human life can be endangered by malnutrition as much as by physical threat. Yet it has been perpetuated by the division between the 'political arm' of the ICCPR and the 'economic arm' of the ICESCR.

Analogously to the right to leave from the ICCPR, the right to subsistence expounded in the ICESCR is not firmly secured. ICESCR's Article 11(1) announces that 'the States Parties to the present Covenant recognize the right of everyone to an *adequate standard of living* for himself and his family, including adequate food, clothing and housing, and to the continuous improvement of living conditions. The States Parties will take appropriate steps *to ensure the realization* of this right, recognizing to this effect the essential importance of international co-operation based on *free consent*'.[80] Article 11(2) further acknowledges the 'fundamental right of everyone to be free from hunger', advising states to undertake initiatives individually or within fora of international cooperation, while taking into account the 'problems of both food-importing and food-exporting countries, to ensure an equitable distribution of world food supplies in relation to need'.[81] The ICESCR's subsistence right – comprising a bundle of rights to guarantee an adequate standard of living, food, clothing, and housing – constitutes a modest baseline

77 ICCPR, Article 12(2), and Article 12(4) (n. 4), 65–6.

78 UDHR, Article 13(2): 'Everyone has the right to leave any country, including his own, and to return to his country' (n. 4), 23.

79 ICCPR, Article 12(3), (n. 4), 65–6.

80 ICESCR, Article 11(1) (n. 4), 82 emphasis added.

81 *Ibid.*

because 'adequate' standard of living is a less exacting condition than 'sufficient' standard of living. One possible interpretation of Article 11(1) is that each individual state should provide an adequate standard of living for its citizens by participating in voluntary ('free consent') initiatives of international cooperation with other states. And while the ICESCR state parties ought to promote the realization of the right to subsistence, this idiom of gradual realization discloses an aspirational orientation rather than a firmer ground for action. The UDHR's Preamble is aspirational as well, describing the Declaration's mission as a 'common standard of achievement'.[82] Article 3 of the UDHR sums up this mission in the idiom of rights: 'everyone has the right to life, liberty and the security of person'.[83] The pivotal role of the UDHR, the ICCPR and the ICESCR, then, is to set standards of civilized conduct, urging respect for basic rights in the global public realm. But we cannot expect such documents to accomplish the task of realizing basic rights in the absence of functioning international institutions, strategizing and political will to act.

Some have argued that the rights these documents classify as basic or elementary with respect of the dignity of the person cannot properly be guaranteed because international law cannot enforce such rights against non-complying states.[84] But the difficulty has little to do with the enforceability of international legal instruments. It derives from the fact that the individual state – and not the society of states or its organizational arm, the UN – is the primary agency responsible for procuring economic redistribution and some standard of living for the body of citizens inside its territory. What this suggests is that third parties, or the society of states, ought to have obligations of justice towards poor states only when there is evidence that the burdened state under consideration cannot guarantee a minimum level of subsistence to its citizens: a situation where the citizens' right to life, and not simply standard of living, is under severe threat. The idiom at work is third-party protection (by the society of states), not direct responsibility incurred by a wrongdoer or a second party.

International law can manage to protect basic rights globally primarily by means of establishing standards of civilized conduct for states and less so by the direct enforcement of international agreements. Indeed, it can have little direct impact in securing the subsistence rights of the global poor because it is weak law when compared to municipal law. Its provisions are enforceable through the national courts of individual states – a practice traceable to the doctrine of auto-limitation of sovereignty. Unlike the domestic legal system, the international legal system does not implicate a straightforward mode of coercion. There is an unavoidable element of voluntarism – this is why

82 UDHR (n. 4), 21.

83 *Ibid.* 22.

84 E. A. Heinze, *Waging Humanitarian War: The Ethics, Law, and Politics of Humanitarian Intervention* (Albany, NY: SUNY Press, 2009), 69.

international coercion is a standing problem. Affluent states would be unwilling to voluntarily commit themselves to global redistribution since they would be donors as opposed to beneficiaries of global redistributive arrangements. Besides, to be effective, redistributive agreements may require transborder management mechanisms generating additional costs for the affluent. But, to mine Shue's argument one more time, it may not be necessary to redistribute resources from rich to poor or to set up global economic institutions. One way to enable poor individuals in foreign states to make a living is to shield them from harms (physical threats) in their local environment.[85] When, for example, their government has failed or is unwilling to protect them against hazards such as famine, or itself perpetrates atrocities (mass deportation or genocide), the society of states may have a right or even a duty to intervene to protect the victims. International law has achieved a good deal in this sphere, as evident from the Convention on the Prevention and Punishment of the Crime of Genocide,[86] and the creation of the International Criminal Court.

It may be objected at this juncture that voluntarism casts a long shadow over the coercive force of international law. After all, the ICCPR and the ICESCR are treaties or voluntary arrangements which fail to meet Nagel's criterion of non-voluntary or coercive institutions that alone put agents into a relation of justice. International treaty law can institutionalize obligations of humanitarianism and aid, but not obligations of justice. Even if obligations of justice were somehow introduced in the relations of states and rendered legally binding, their imposition would be illegitimate. One way out of this conundrum is to show that an argument for humanitarianism could, under certain conditions, produce the same conclusion as an argument for justice.

My strategy is to begin with the standpoint of natural justice (obligations of humanitarianism) and to arrive at a conclusion consistent with social justice (obligations of justice). Natural justice operates under state-of-nature conditions where no special ties connect us to distant others. Consider a paradigmatic pre-political right, the right of the innocent to be free from attack, which does not arise from membership in a political association. Defending this right against aggressors is a matter of natural justice. But the agent who intervenes to protect the victims (their right to life) against an aggressor is a third party, an outsider to the relationship between wrongdoer and the agent who has been wronged. The practice of humanitarian intervention resonates with natural justice considerations because it does not suppose that the intervening agents are parties to a special relation (say, shared citizenship) with the victims. Unlike natural justice, social justice assumes a background of social relations. Agents maintain special ties within institutions – this membership (inside common institutions) makes them vulnerable to coercive principles of justice. Distributive justice is a form of social justice.

85 Shue (n. 2), 40.

86 Convention on the Prevention and Punishment of the Crime of Genocide (n. 4), 19–21.

However, the principles of justice must themselves be justified, for otherwise it might be possible to treat all societal members equally (or 'justly') by treating them in the same undignified manner: like dogs.[87] As we saw, Rawls justified the principles of justice by a standard of fairness – it would be unfair to be a free-rider in a cooperative activity from which one benefits. Natural justice too has its justification – it would be wrong (rather than unfair) to stand idly by and to abandon the victims of aggression to their own devices. Social justice and natural justice overlap to a degree because each depends on justificatory moral premises.

Because of this overlap, obligations of beneficence can be approached as if they were strict obligations of justice. Severe global poverty imposes demands on our moral conscience ('us' being citizens of affluent states) parallel to the situation where genocide inside a foreign state sends a signal for the society of states to intervene and protect the innocent. If both cases embody an obligation of humanitarianism (that extends beyond the state), why insist that it is, at bottom, an obligation of justice? The response I deem coherent is that obligations should not be sharply differentiated into positive and negative – and here my argument parts with Shue's.[88] A distinction is in order which focuses our attention on circumstantial evidence, for 'a prohibition may be categorical, but the boundaries of that concept may be susceptible to judgements of degree'.[89] That is, we should not be asking whether a given obligation is more stringent than another but what specific circumstances warrant the verdict that an obligation binds us here and now (on the proposed view all obligations are equally stringent). This idea invokes Hume's 'circumstances of justice' or contextual characteristics telling us when a relation of justice can emerge.[90] Under conditions of extreme scarcity, a fair distribution of resources (distributive justice) may become impossible but we may not need it at all in a society of benevolent altruists. This indicates that obligations of justice, whose object is the prevention of crippling poverty abroad, would in all likelihood require more circumstantial evidence than obligations of justice whose object is to halt an ongoing massacre.[91] But once the evidence has been collected (assuming that we are in position to act, not facing intolerable scarcity ourselves), we would not be morally justified in pretending that we have no obligations of justice towards the global poor.

87 This is a paraphrase of Henry Jordan's remark as quoted in Feinberg 1973 (n. 3), 98 fn.

88 Shue (n. 31)

89 Fried (n. 3), 31.

90 Hume's circumstances of justice and their place in Rawls's theory of justice are discussed in D. Clayton Hubin, 'The Scope of Justice' (1979) 9(1) *Philosophy and Public Affairs* 3.

91 Nagel has argued that affluent states must provide protection against dire starvation, when such starvation is the outcome of coercive institutions of global inequality (originating in the global property system), as a matter of strict obligations of justice. T. Nagel, 'Poverty and Food: Why Charity is Not Enough', repr. in T. Pogge and D. Moellendorf (eds.), *Global Justice* (St Paul's, MN: Paragon House, 2008), 49–59.

So far I have abstained from speculative ideas for a global institutional reform. If the aim is global socio-economic justice, historians and economists would have to join philosophers and jurists in crafting an institutional blueprint, and much would depend on empirical considerations that cannot be talked about *in abstracto*. In concluding this discussion I wish to flag three points to support my contention that the ideal of global justice and basic rights may be better served by a system of international law, relying on the agency of states, rather than by global law. First, global law is still an ideal, while international law is an ideal actualized into a political structure: the society of states. Second, building a unified global structure to discharge obligations of justice towards the global poor may be counterproductive. The risk is that it would ignore the 'circumstances of justice', since global poverty is not a single problem but a string of multiple problems – what might work in Latin America might not work in Sub-Saharan Africa. Whereas Article 11(2) of the ICESCR, for example, mentions the fundamental right of everyone to be free from hunger, in certain areas of the world the lack of clean water may pose the greatest threat to life. Some of the institutional arrangements necessary to create conditions for protecting basic rights on a global scale would have to be regional. The decentralized nature of international law may be an advantage in this respect. Third, a single global institutional structure may prove logistically unworkable due to problems linked to efficiency, cost or speed of response on the ground (aside from the moral apprehension of global tyranny). For this reason alone, obligations of humanitarianism which depend on the self-initiative of donors would have to continue. In this category falls aid supplied by governments but also non-governmental organizations and even individuals who are willing and capable to assist victims of dire poverty living outside their political association through monetary transfers or voluntary work. But humanitarianism alone is not going to solve the problem of global socio-economic justice – we need the concerted effort of the society of states and a cultivated moral understanding that obligations of justice do not end at the doorstep of our own state.

9 The duality of the legitimacy of global actors in the international legal order

Jean d'Aspremont and Eric de Brabandere

Global governance rests on the exercise of power by a myriad of actors. In the international order, the more powers and influence these authorities acquire, the more their legitimacy proves to be a matter of controversy. The legitimacy of international, regional and domestic actors that partake in global governance – those that we consider here as global actors – must be appraised from a twofold standpoint. Their legitimacy can first be gauged through the lens of the origin of their powers ('the legitimacy of origin'). The origin of the power may often prove an insufficient indicator of an actor's legitimacy. For this reason, legitimacy can also be evaluated in the light of the way in which it exercises its power ('the legitimacy of exercise'). This chapter argues that failing to recognize this dual character of legitimacy of actors involved in global and regional governance undermines any endeavour to grasp the contemporary complexity of the latter.

After sketching some of the contemporary features of legitimacy in international law (section 9.1), this chapter considers the extent to which the so-called principle of democratic legitimacy has impinged on how the legitimacy of global actors is nowadays conceived (section 9.2). The chapter then turns to assessing how, against that backdrop, the legitimacy of global actors is evaluated in contemporary practice (section 9.3). The chapter focuses on two public global actors in particular, namely governments and international organizations, with a view to demonstrating that the appraisal of the legitimacy of governments differs from that of the legitimacy of international organizations. While the legitimacy of origin has constituted the classical yardstick to evaluate the legitimacy of governments, recent practice shows a shift of paradigms towards the legitimacy of exercise. However, at the same time we are witnessing the exact opposite change of paradigms in the context of appraising the legitimacy of international organizations, for the legitimacy of international organizations is increasingly reviewed from the vantage point of the legitimacy of origin, despite having classically been based on the legitimacy of exercise.

9.1 Legitimacy in global governance

As has been indicated, this chapter draws on a distinction between the legitimacy of exercise and the legitimacy of origin. This dichotomy points to a distinction between legitimacy pertaining to the source of power and legitimacy related to the exercise of power.[1] The division between these two dimensions of legitimacy has been part of the legal and political discourse for a number of years.[2] The terminology has varied. Some have used the terms 'original legitimacy' and 'legitimacy of conduct',[3] while others have preferred 'instant legitimacy' and 'continual legitimacy',[4] or have used the similar notions of 'representative democracy' and 'participatory democracy'.[5] We will here use the terms 'legitimacy of origin' and 'legitimacy of exercise'.[6]

The distinction between the legitimacy of origin and the legitimacy of exercise has traditionally been explored in relation to the legitimacy of governments. In this particular context, the legitimacy of origin is a tool to assess the manner in which a government comes to power, while the legitimacy of exercise permits evaluation of the way in which the government exerts its power. It is also the intention of this chapter to examine how this dichotomy applies to actors other than governments, in particular international organizations.

In the context of the legitimacy of governments, the distinction between legitimacy of origin and legitimacy of exercise only concerns the external legitimacy of a government and does not address its internal legitimacy. The legitimacy of a government can be measured from two different standpoints. One can assess its internal legitimacy – that is, how it is perceived by the people subject to it – and its external legitimacy – that is, how it is perceived by other international authorities. The internal legitimacy of an authority is usually related to the achievement of social and distributive justice[7] and thus revolves around the existence of a government for the people.[8]

1 Though not addressing the issue of legitimacy, F. A. Hayek offers a good explanation for the distinction between the exercise of power and the source of power. See F. A. Hayek, *The Road to Serfdom* (new edn, London: Routledge, 1976), 71.

2 See General Secretariat of the Organization of American States, 'Meeting the Political Priorities of the Organization of American States', OEA Ser. G CP/doc.4071/05 (14 December 2005), 3.

3 See also T. Cottier and M. Hertig, 'The Prospects of 21st Century Constitutionalism' (2003) 7 *Max Planck Yearbook of United Nations Law* 261–328.

4 See e.g. V. Pusic, 'Democracy Versus Nation: Dictatorships with Democratic Legitimacy' (1994) 5 *Helsinki Monitor* 69.

5 See J. Chopra and T. Hohe, 'Participatory Intervention' (2004) 10 *Global Governance* 289.

6 This distinction has been used by J. d'Aspremont, 'Legitimacy of Governments in the Age of Democracy' (2006) 38 *NYUJ Int'l L. & Pol.* 877.

7 On the relationship between justice and democracy, see I. Shapiro, *Democratic Justice* (New Haven, CT: Yale University Press, 1999).

8 This has been called the 'output legitimacy' as opposed to the 'input legitimacy' (i.e., a government *by* the people): see F. W. Scharpf, 'Legitimacy and the Multi-actor Polity' in M. Egeberg and Plægreid (eds.), *Organizing Political Institutions: Essays for Johan P Olsen* 268 (Oslo: Scandinavian University Press, 1999).

Internal legitimacy is, however, of little relevance to the appraisal of government from the standpoint of international law. International law is only concerned with the way in which a government's legitimacy is perceived by other international authorities. In that sense, the application of international law is not directly contingent upon the perception of the people, although it cannot be excluded that the internal legitimacy of a given authority affects the way other actors assess the external legitimacy of that authority.[9]

The distinction between internal legitimacy and external legitimacy has traditionally been less relevant in the context of international organizations. Strictly speaking, people are not subject to international organizations, for such organizations do not exercise sovereign powers. However, recently some international organizations have embarked on missions that include the administration of territories, in the framework of which they subject individuals to their powers.[10] Other international organizations such as the European Union (EU) are endowed with sweeping powers that directly affect the lives of people. This means that there are more and more instances where the legitimacy of international organization can be construed from an internal perspective as well.

A remark must also be made about when and how the legitimacy of global actors is generally tested. Governmental legitimacy is not constantly under scrutiny in the international legal order. Legitimacy is only intermittently put to test. This is well illustrated by the question of the legitimacy of governments. Even if much attention is often paid to the form of governments in the international arena, the assessment of their legitimacy is not systematic. The mere measurement of the democratic character of government does not necessarily involve an evaluation – which is very common in international relations – of its legitimacy. The question of legitimacy only arises when there is a need to determine the authority entrusted with the power to act and speak on behalf of the state. Such a determination is only required in limited, but significant, situations. The authority that can speak and act on behalf of the state in the international legal order must be determined ahead of any recognition of its government, when accreditation within international organizations is sought by two warring governments, and, finally, when a state invites another state to carry out a military operation on its own territory.[11]

In the case of international organizations, occasions where the legitimacy of an international organization is tested have, until recently, been rather uncommon. However, in recent years, the greater involvement of international organizations in the reconstruction and administration of states in the

9 See S. Talmon, 'Who is a Legitimate Government in Exile?: Towards Normative Criteria for Governmental Legitimacy in International Law', in G. S. Goodwin and S. Talmon (eds.), *The Reality of International Law: Essays in Honour of Ian Brownlie* (Oxford: Clarendon Press, 1999), 509–17.

10 See E. de Brabandere, *Post-conflict Administrations in International Law: International Territorial Administration, Transitional Authority and Foreign Occupation in Theory and Practice* (Leiden: Martinus Nijhoff, 2009).

11 See J. d'Aspremont (n. 6), 877.

aftermath of conflicts has offered new instances where the legitimacy of international organizations has been tested.[12] Because on these occasions the international organizations concerned have been endowed with wide-ranging powers bearing inevitable resemblance to sovereign powers over individuals, the question of their legitimacy has been raised. The last part of this chapter is specifically devoted to the question of legitimacy of international organizations in the context of post-conflict administrations.

9.2 Legitimacy in the age of democracy

The end of the Cold War and the sweeping fallout of that event on the international plane impinged significantly on international law and the manner in which legitimacy is perceived in the international legal order. The demise of communist regimes put an end to an ideological division that had gripped the world for nearly fifty years, causing remarkable changes in international society. In particular, the idea that democracy is the only acceptable type of regime has gained broad support, even monopolizing the political discourse[13] (despite a lingering disagreement about its accurate meaning).[14] It is accordingly no surprise that international law and its rules pertaining to the legitimacy of governments have been deeply affected by the rise of democracy as the only acceptable model of governance at the domestic level. However, before spelling out the precise consequences of the emergence of a consensus about democracy on the legitimacy of global actors itself (9.2.2), it is necessary to briefly take stock of the state of international law pertaining to democratic governance (9.2.1).

9.2.1 Democracy in international law

International legal scholars promptly recognized that the post-Cold War international legal order had become more amenable to the prominent role of democracy. American liberal scholars, in particular, enthusiastically supported the idea that democracy today plays a crucial role in the international legal order and swiftly provided various optimistic accounts of the extent of the legal changes brought about by democracy.[15] French positivist lawyers,

12 See de Brabandere (n. 10).

13 See generally, S. Marks, *The Riddle of all Constitutions* (Oxford: Oxford University Press, 2003), 30–49. See also G. H. Fox and B. R. Roth, 'Introduction: The Spread of Liberal Democracy and its Implications for International Law', in G. H. Fox and B. R. Roth (eds.), *Democratic Governance and International Law* (Cambridge: Cambridge University Press, 2000), 1–4.

14 G. Sartori, *The Theory of Democracy Revisited* (Chatham, NJ: Chatham House Publishers, 1987), 6.

15 The most radical liberal view on this question is probably offered by F. R. Tesón, 'The Kantian Theory of International Law' (1992) 92 *Colum.L.Rev.* 53, 54–5. For milder forms of the democratic entitlement theory, see T. M. Franck, 'The Emerging Right to Democratic Governance' (1992) 86 AJIL 46; C. M. Cerna, 'Universal Democracy: An International Legal Right or the Pipe Dream of the West?' (1994–5) 27 *NYUJ Int'l Law & Pol.* 289, 329. For an overview of how participatory rights emerged in international law, see generally G. H. Fox, 'The Right to Political Participation in

although they usually voiced greater scepticism and refrained from embracing the whole array of consequences that liberals attached to a lack of democracy, also recognized that democracy can play a role in the international legal order.[16] Even if one does not agree with all the legal consequences that American liberals have associated with the emergence of democracy in the international legal order,[17] it is not unreasonable to contend that living up to some democratic standards corresponds to an international customary obligation. Indeed, contemporary practice shows that, to a large degree, states consider the adoption of the main characteristics of a democratic regime to amount to an international obligation and act accordingly toward non-democratic states.[18] Indeed, many non-democratic states do not oppose the principle of democracy, and even claim that they are themselves in the midst of progress towards the establishment of democracy. Non-democratic states, with a view of strengthening the legitimacy of their governments, often try to portray their political regimes in a democratic light rather than choosing to dispute the role that democracy plays in the international order.

Nonetheless, this customary legal obligation to adopt a democratic regime must not be exaggerated – such an overreaching is where the aforementioned liberal theories about democracy prove unconvincing.[19] First, the scope *ratione materiae* of the principle of democracy in international law is limited, as the obligation rests on an electoral and procedural understanding of democracy.[20] States are customarily obliged to abide by democracy to the extent only that their effective leaders (or the parliamentary body that oversees their executive mandate) are chosen through free and fair elections.[21] Likewise, this customary obligation, while being *erga omnes*,[22] is certainly not of a *jus cogens* character, as it

International Law' (1992) 17 *Yale J.Int'l L.* 539. For a basic account of the arguments for and against the democratic entitlement theory, see generally G. H. Fox and B. R. Roth, 'Introduction: The Spread of Liberal Democracy and Its Implications for International Law', in G. H. Fox and B. R. Roth (eds.), *Democratic Governance and International Law* (Cambridge: Cambridge University Press, 2000) 1, 11.

16 See J. d'Aspremont, *L'Etat Non Démocratique en Droit International. Etude Critique du Droit Positif et de la Pratique Contemporaine* (Paris: Pédone, 2008).

17 For one criticism of the liberal theories of democracy, see *ibid.*

18 *Ibid.* For a more recent re-appraisal, see J. d'Aspremont 'The Rise and Fall of Democratic Governance in International Law' 22 *EJIL*, 549.

19 See the criticism raised by d'Aspremont (n. 16).

20 G. H. Fox, 'The Right to Political Participation in International Law', in Fox and Roth (n. 15), 48–9. For criticism of this 'minimalistic' understanding of democracy, see B. Gills, J. Rocamora and R. Wilson, 'Low Intensity Democracy', in B. Gills, J. Rocamora and R. Wilson (eds.), *Low Intensity Democracy: Political Power in the New World Order* (London: Pluto, 1993) 3, 21; J. R. Pennock, *Democratic Political Theory* (Princeton, NJ: Princeton University Press, 1979), 3–15; R. Burchill, 'The Developing International Law of Democracy' (2001) 64 MLR 123, 128 (review of Fox and Roth (n. 15)); R. A. Miller, 'Self-Determination in International Law and the Demise of Democracy' (2003) 41 *Colum.J.Transnat'l L.* 601, 603–5.

21 d'Aspremont (n. 16), 15.

22 *Ibid.* 291.

is underscored by the existence of numerous persistent objectors to that customary rule.[23]

It would also be a mistake to consider the obligation to be democratic utterly groundbreaking. Indeed, international law has long regulated some aspects of states' political regimes. Through human rights law, the international community has regulated the way in which power is exercised and has prohibited some types of political regimes – for example, apartheid[24] and, to a lesser extent, fascism.[25] Moreover, the obligation to organize free and fair elections is not entirely new in the international legal order, as a similar obligation is already embedded in the International Covenant on Civil and Political Rights (ICCPR),[26] which has been ratified by 165 states.[27] In addition, even if the international legal order enshrines a principle of procedural democracy applicable to states, there is no corresponding requirement of democracy applicable to the structure and the functioning of the international legal system as a whole. This is not surprising, given the inapplicability of the classical domestic blueprints of governance to the international system.[28]

9.2.2 Democratic legitimacy

Because rules pertaining to democracy in international law are restricted to domestic governance, their impact is unsurprisingly almost exclusively limited to the legitimacy of governments. Their application to the legitimacy of international organizations is also less evident given that rules pertaining to domestic governance cannot always easily be transposed as such to the level of international organizations. International organizations are not subject to international obligations to abide by some procedural form of democracy in organizing free and fair elections. However, this does not mean that democratic legitimacy is of no relevance in the case of international organizations. As will be argued in section 9.2, the legitimacy of international organizations is no longer entirely alien to criteria of democracy. For the time being, however, this chapter only deals with the democratic legitimacy of governments.

23 The People's Republic of China and several states in the Middle East can probably be considered persistent objectors to the rule.

24 See International Convention on the Suppression and Punishment of the Crime of Apartheid (30 November 1973) 1015 UNTS 243; International Convention on the Elimination of All Forms of Racial Discrimination (21 December 1965) 660 UNTS 195 Art. 3.

25 In particular, see UNGA Res. 36/162 (16 December 1981) UN Doc. A/RES/36/162.

26 International Covenant on Civil and Political Rights, UNGA Res. 2200A (XXI) (16 December 1966) UN Doc. A/6316 (ICCPR).

27 See Status of Ratification of the Principal International Human Rights Treaties (6 May 2010), (at: http://treaties.un.org/Pages/ViewDetails.aspx?src=TREATY&mtdsg_no=IV-4&chapter=4&lang=en).

28 See generally J. H. H. Weiler, 'The Geology of International Law: Governance, Democracy and Legitimacy' (2004) 64 *Heidelberg Journal of International Law* 547.

In the case of the legitimacy of governments, it is important to realize that, while probably constituting a customary international legal obligation the breach of which triggers the legal consequences described above, democracy has simultaneously become a fundamental criterion for the legitimization of governments in the sense that, nowadays, a new government hardly qualifies as the legitimate representative of a state if it has not been democratically elected.[29] This formidable development is not a consequence of the abovementioned obligation to have democratic institutions, but rests on the discretion of states to choose whether to recognize a new government. There is no obligation not to recognize non-democratic governments. As mentioned above, the obligation to be democratic does not constitute a *jus cogens* norm. Even if it were a *jus cogens* norm, it is not certain that a state, in recognizing a non-democratic government, would also recognize as legal the violation of the obligation to be democratic.[30]

However, even though this does not correspond to any legal obligation, it seems uncontested that, since the end of the Cold War, the (external) legitimacy of an authority has come to depend almost entirely upon its democratic character.[31] The idea of a government based on the will of the people 'expressed in periodic and genuine elections which shall be by universal and equal suffrage and shall be held by secret vote or by equivalent free voting procedures'[32] – which during the Cold War had been loosely interpreted by states to legitimize any sort of government – is now understood to require a democratic political regime. Thus, there is little doubt today that democracy has become a prominent yardstick with which to assess the legitimacy of governments.[33] This is not to say that a non-democratic government will never be deemed legitimate, especially if that government has been in power for a long time.[34] The non-democratic character of a government is sometimes disregarded because of overriding geopolitical and strategic motives.[35] But, leaving these exceptional situations aside, it can reasonably be argued that, since the end of the Cold War, democracy has become 'the touchstone of legitimacy'[36] for any new government.

29 See d'Aspremont (n. 6).

30 d'Aspremont (n. 16), 151.

31 See for instance the 1990 Charter of Paris which provides that: 'Democratic government is based on the will of the people, expressed regularly through free and fair elections'.

32 See Universal Declaration of Human Rights, UNGA Res. 217A (10 December 1948) GAOR, 3rd Session, 183 Plen. Meeting, UN Doc. A/810, 75.

33 E. Stein, 'International Integration and Democracy: No Love at First Sight' (2001) 95 AJIL 489, 494; Franck (n. 15), 46.

34 This has led some authors to contend that 'double standards' exist in that regard. See M. G. Kohen, 'La création d'états en droit international contemporain' *Cursos Euromediterráneos Bancaja de Derecho Internacional* 6 (Centro Internacional Bancaja para la Paz y el Desarrollo, Castellón 2002), 619.

35 The most obvious example is the government of the People's Republic of China which is seen as legitimate by almost all countries in the world although it does not rest on any free and fair electoral process.

36 D. Bodansky, 'The Legitimacy of International Governance: A Coming Challenge for International Environmental Law?' (1999) 93 AJIL 596, 599.

Because democracy has turned into one of the central yardsticks to appraise the legitimacy of governments, it is important to clarify how democratic legitimacy applies against the backdrop of the abovementioned distinction between the legitimacy of origin and the legitimacy of exercise. In the context of democracy, the legitimacy of origin addresses the procedural elements of democracy that ensure that the authority originates in popular sovereignty through free and fair elections. A democratic legitimacy of exercise, on the contrary, bears upon some substantive elements of democracy. The application of the distinction between legitimacy of exercise and legitimacy of origin in the context of democracy thus presupposes the existence of a substantive understanding of democracy. Although the idea remains controversial, this chapter argues that besides procedural features democracy also embodies substantive elements.

The question of whether democracy includes only procedural elements or also embodies substantive features has gripped theory[37] and practice[38] for a long time. Given the complex character of the concept of democracy[39] and its bent for relentless re-contextualization,[40] an accurate meaning of democracy will probably never be agreed.[41] But this should not prevent us from discussing its main components. It does not seem unreasonable to defend the concept of democracy as including some substantive requirements, namely some basic political freedoms and civil rights and some traces of the rule of law. The reason why we include some political and civil human rights in the concept of democracy goes back to the democratic procedural requirements themselves. There can hardly be a free democratic process if basic political rights are infringed. The 'freedom' of elections must take place in a 'free market of ideas'[42] where free political competition is assured.[43] To ensure free competition in this market of ideas, a respect for basic political freedoms must be ensured. The organization of a 'free' electoral process thus requires respect for freedom of expression, freedom of assembly, freedom of thought, freedom of press,

37 Many authors have criticized what they saw as an electoral, or 'cosmetic' (Gills, Rocamora and Wilson (n. 20)) conception of democracy because of its 'low intensity'. These authors have put forward a substance-oriented conception of democracy embodying compliance with Human Rights. See B. R. Roth, 'Evaluating Democratic Progress', in Fox and Roth (n. 15), 493–5; T. Carothers, 'Empirical Perspectives on the Emerging Norm of Democracy in International Law' (1992) 86 ASIL PROC. 261, 264.

38 This debate between procedural democracy and substantive democracy has also been echoed in the interpretation of the major human rights conventions, which although they often enshrine a right to political participation through regular elections, are hardly explicit on whether an electoral process is the core element of a democratic regime.

39 M. Koskenniemi, 'Intolerant Democracies: A Reaction' (1996) 37 *Harv. Int'l LJ* 231, 234. This is a response to G. H. Fox and G. Nolte, 'Intolerant Democracies' (1995) 36 *Harv. Int'l LJ* 1.

40 See Marks (n. 13), 151.

41 For a different opinion, see Fox (n. 20), 90.

42 Franck (n. 15), 90.

43 Molly Beutz, 'Functional Democracy: Responding to Failures of Accountability', 44 *Harv. Int'l LJ* 387 (2003) at 418.

etc.[44] These freedoms are 'democratic rights'[45] or, as stated by the UN Commission on Human Rights, 'rights pertaining to democratic governance'.[46] In that sense, one can contend that the requirement of free elections already encompasses a substantive component, that is, compliance with the political freedoms that ensure pluralism. Nor does it seem unreasonable to contend that the concept of democracy also includes respect for the rule of law. As the Human Rights Committee has emphasized, there can hardly be a free and fair election if the rules regulating the electoral process have not been established prior to the holding of the elections and are not complied with by the authorities.[47]

The inclusion of substantive elements in the concept of democracy seems underpinned by contemporary international relations, for states often voice their support for 'democratic values'[48] and note that 'elections are only a step towards the establishment of a democratic regime'.[49] Likewise, in cases of massive and gross violations of human rights, states tend to deny the democratic character of the states responsible.[50] The mere fact that an infringement of the rule of law and human rights, whatever its extent, prompts systematic disapproval in the name of democracy demonstrates that, in practice, democracy is construed as including certain substantive elements.

If, as is argued here, democracy embraces some substantive elements, then the distinction between origin and exercise proves of fundamental relevance

44 UNGA Res. 55/96 (28 February 2001) UN Doc. A/RES/55/96, para. i (on the promotion and consolidation of democracy); UNHCR Res. 1999/57 (27 April 1999) para. 1(a); UNHCR Res. 2002/46, para. 1; General Comment of the Human Rights Committee No. 25, CCPR/C21/Rev.1/Add.7, para. 25ff. See also the case law of the Inter-American Court of Human Rights, Compulsory Membership in an Association. Prescribed by Law for the Practice of Journalism (Advisory Opinion) OC-5/85 para. 69 or that of the European Court of Human Rights, e.g. *Lingens* v. *Austria* (App. no. 9815/82) (1986) 8 EHRR 407; *Open Door and Dublin Well Woman* v. *Ireland* (App. no. 14234.88) (1992) 15 EHRR 244; *United Communist Party of Turkey and Others* v. *Turkey* (App. no. 19392/92) (1998) 26 EHRR 121; *Handyside* v. *The United Kingdom* (App. no. 5493/72) (1972) 1 EHRR 737; Inter-American Democratic Charter (11 September 2001) OAS Doc. OEA/Ser.P/AG/RES.1 (XXVIII-E/01) (at: www.oas.org/charter/docs/resolution1_en_p4.htm).

45 R. J. Arneson, 'Democratic Rights at the National Level', in T. Christiano (ed.), *Philosophy and Democracy: An Anthology* (Oxford: Oxford University Press, 2003) 95.

46 UNCHR Rights Res. 1997/64 (16 April 1997) (on Myanmar). See also UNCHR General Comment 25 (7 December 1996) CCPR/C/21/Rev.1/Add.7.

47 UNCHR General Comment 25 (n. 44), para. 10.

48 The Heads of Government of the Commonwealth of Nations, *Coolum Declaration* (5 March 2002) (at: www.thecommonwealth.org/document/34293/35468/35799/coolum.htm).

49 See Secretary of State Condoleezza Rice, *Joint Remarks of the Secretary of State*, 27 April 2005; excerpted in M. Delcas and P. A. Paranagua, 'Les Etats-Unis comptent sur le Brésil pour modérer le Venezuela' *Le Monde* (29 April 2005), 2.

50 See e.g. UNGA Res. 46/7 (1 October 1991) UN Doc. A/RES/46/7 (on Haiti); UNCHR Res. 55/18 (23 April 1999) UN Doc. E/CN.4/RES/1999/18 (on the Federal Republic of Yugoslavia, Croatia and Bosnia-Herzegovina); Organization of American States, *Declaration on Democracy in Venezuela,* UNGA Res. 32/28 (4 June 2002) OAS Doc. AG/DEC. 28 (XXXII-O/02); Third Conference of the New or Restored Democracies on Democracy and Development, Bucharest, Romania (11 September 1997) UN Doc. A/52/334.

and any monolithic conception of legitimacy reveals itself insufficient to explain how the legitimacy of global actors is appraised in the post-Cold War world. From the standpoint of the democratic legitimacy of origin, a government is legitimate if it rests on the 'will of the people' expressed through a free and fair electoral process. From the vantage point of the democratic legitimacy of exercise, a government is legitimate if it exerts its power in a manner consistent with basic political freedoms and the rule of law. Drawing on this distinction between the democratic legitimacy of origin and the democratic legitimacy of exercise, the next section seeks to shed light on how the legitimacy of global actors is evaluated.

9.3 Contemporary oscillations between exercise and origin

The legitimacy of governments and the legitimacy of international organizations are subject to contradictory dynamics. On the one hand, in modern practice the legitimacy of governments – classically judged form the standpoint of the origin of its powers – is incrementally tested on the basis of its legitimacy of exercise (9.3.1).[51] On the other, the practice of international organizations shows the exact opposite move when the legitimacy of international organizations is at stake, for their legitimacy is increasingly evaluated from the vantage point of their origin rather than the legitimacy of exercise, which had been, until recently, the traditional yardstick to gauge their legitimacy (9.3.2).

9.3.1 Legitimacy of governments: from origin to exercise

The question of governmental legitimacy has always been controversial. This can be traced back to a basic reality of the international order, namely that states act through their government. The international order is consequently an order where its main actors act via proxies. These surrogates are not, however, immutable entities. Governments are short-lived bodies whose existence is contingent upon the form of the political regime of the state concerned or the internal stability of the latter, and, ultimately, the life span of the human beings at their helm. This means that the representatives of the states in the international order are frequently replaced. This recurrent and inescapable change of governments has prompted a need for criteria to determine who is entitled to speak and act on behalf of each state. This need constantly to identify each state's representative in the international arena lies at the heart of the question of the legitimacy of governments in international relations.

The highly controversial character of governments' legitimacy mostly stems from the subjectivity of its evaluation. Indeed, there are no objective criteria to determine governments' legitimacy. This means that each state

51 This section is a condensed version of d'Aspremont (n. 6).

enjoys a comfortable leeway when asked to recognize the power of an entity that claims to be another state's representative in their bilateral intercourse. International relations are therefore replete with situations where a government is deemed legitimate by some states and illegitimate by others.

However, despite the prominent role played by elections in legitimizing governments in contemporary practice, the 'monopoly' of the legitimacy of origin to gauge the legitimacy of governments has recently been curtailed by the growing importance of the legitimacy of exercise. This means that for a government to be seen as legitimate, it must not only be '*by* the people' but also '*for* the people'.

This practice has been analysed elsewhere[52] and, although contemporary developments have confirmed it, we will not reiterate our conclusions here. It is sufficient to recall that, as the practices pertaining to recognition, accreditation and intervention demonstrate, both the origin and the exercise of power have played roles in evaluating the legitimacy of governments. Legitimacy of origin has remained the decisive factor. However, recent practice shows that more emphasis has been put on the legitimacy of exercise. To understand the different roles played by the two types of legitimacy, and hence the shift of paradigm, one must draw a distinction between the qualifications and disqualifications of governments. If it secures international recognition or its delegates are accredited, a new government qualifies as the legitimate representative entitled to speak and act on behalf of the state. But legitimacy can also have a disqualificatory function when a government, previously recognized as the legitimate representative entitled to act and speak on behalf of a state, loses this recognition. In other words, it is disqualified from being the representative of that state. In the situation of intervention by invitation, disqualification occurs when the state's requests for intervention are refused. In the situation of the accreditation of delegates by international organizations, disqualification occurs when the state's delegates are refused accreditation. This chapter argues that the effect of the legitimacy of origin test has been confined to a qualificatory role, whereas the legitimacy of exercise has been confined to a disqualificatory function.

The question of determining who qualifies as the legitimate government of a state has almost always been resolved through the legitimacy of origin test. States must determine the legitimate authority entitled to act and speak on behalf of a state in instances of recognition and accreditation. A new government will typically be recognized so long as its power originates in a free and fair electoral process and such democratic origins can usually overcome a government's ineffectiveness. In the case of credential controversies within international organizations, only the democratic (or constitutional) origin of a government generally matters. The way that government exercises (or plans to exercise) its power is discounted so long as it has been democratically (and constitutionally) elected.

52 d'Aspremont (n. 6), 877 and d'Aspremont (n. 16).

The exercise of power has, however, been the basis for the disqualification of a government previously considered the legitimate representative of a state. A legitimately elected government can lose its legitimacy and be barred from speaking and acting on behalf of the state because its exercise of power conflicts with substantive elements of democracy. This is well illustrated by the aforementioned practice in regard to invitations for intervention. Likewise, the UN General Assembly disqualified the government of South Africa because of the way in which the government exercised its power, namely through its racist apartheid policy.

This distribution of roles between the legitimacy of exercise and the legitimacy of origin is unsurprising. No one will dispute the necessity in contemporary international relations for a swift assessment of governments' legitimacy to determine quickly who can act and speak on behalf of a state. No state or international organization can afford to leave the determination of the legitimacy of a foreign government – upon which any conclusion as to who can act on behalf of the foreign state depends – pending for long. An appraisal of the legitimacy of a government's exercise of power necessarily requires that the government exercises power over a period of time. In cases of an unconstitutional change of government or credentials controversies, there has usually yet to be any 'exercise' of power. As such, the legitimacy of exercise test does not comport with the necessity for swift determination of a state's legitimate representatives. In this context, the origin of power has been seen as a more appropriate test of legitimacy. Legitimate origins entail a free and fair electoral process, so foreign states can typically rely just on the accounts of elections monitoring missions sent by international organizations to make their decisions quickly.[53] To put it differently, free and fair elections are 'easier to capture' than the substantive elements of democracy.[54] This is the reason why the legitimacy of exercise has not played a role in the qualification of governments and has been confined to a disqualificatory function.

However, owing to the persistence of illiberal democracies, the disqualificatory role of the legitimacy of exercise is due to increase dramatically with respect to the recognition of governments and the accreditation of their delegates within international organizations. By 'illiberal democracy' we mean a democratically elected government exercising its power in violation of the substantive elements of democracy which we have referred to above.[55] The persistence of illiberal democracies has already prompted some Western states

53 See e.g. the electoral missions set up by the OSCE Office for Democratic Institutions and Human Rights (at: www.osce.org/odihr). Regarding UN electoral missions, see UNGA Res. 46/137 (17 December 1991) UN Doc. A/RES/46/137, para. 3 (on enhancing the effectiveness of the principle of periodic and genuine elections); and 'Report of the Secretary General on Enhancing the Effectiveness of the Principle of Periodic and Genuine Elections' (19 December 1991) UN Doc. A/46/609, para. 13 (discussing the close relationship between UN electoral missions and election processes).

54 F. Zakaria, 'The Rise of Illiberal Democracies' (1997) 76 *Foreign Affairs* 22, 40.

55 *Ibid*. 22.

to reconsider their policy in matters of democratization.[56] These policies have, so far, largely relied on the assumption that free and fair elections necessarily go hand in hand with respect for human rights.[57] This chapter argues that among the changes that will be brought about by the persistence of illiberal democracies in the international arena will be a revamping of the way that governmental legitimacy is assessed. More specifically, the legitimacy of exercise will play a greater disqualificatory role in the accreditations processes within international organizations. Indeed, in the situation of the accreditation of delegates of a democratically elected government, the legitimacy of exercise could be a factor prompting the refusal of credentials. An international organization could refuse to recognize delegates of a government whose exercise of power is significantly at odds with the substantive elements of democracy. Denying accreditation to delegates of illiberal democracies would undoubtedly increase the disqualificatiory role of the legitimacy of exercise, as a government would be judged according to the manner in which it exercises power.

Likewise, illiberal democracies will drive states to reconsider their policy of recognition. The legitimacy of exercise could affect recognition in two ways. First, it could induce states to not recognize a government whose expected policies are likely to be contrary to the substantive elements of democracy. Second, if the expected exercise of power does not deter states from granting recognition, a subsequent exercise of power inconsistent with human rights could lead to a withdrawal of a previous recognition.

It must be acknowledged that the withdrawal of recognition is extremely rare in practice. The withdrawal of recognition of the government in Taiwan as the government of China after the recognition of the communist government in Beijing is one of very few examples.[58] The growing importance of the legitimacy of exercise could spawn a sweeping change in this respect, thereby making the withdrawal of recognition of governments more common. Contemporary practice already contains some hints of this leaning, as is

56 This phenomenon has, for example, triggered an important debate about the United States foreign policy's priorities. See S. R. Weisman, 'Democracy Push by Bush Attracts Doubters in Party' *New York Times* (17 March 2006), A1; H. M. Fattah, 'Arab democracy, a US goal, falters' *New York Times* (10 April 2006), A1.

57 See e.g. the European Convention for the Protection of Human Rights and Fundamental Freedoms (4 November 1950) Europe TS 5 (at: http://conventions.coe.int/treaty/en/Treaties/html/005.htm). See also *United Communist Party of Turkey and Others* v. *Turkey* (n. 44); Inter-American Democratic Charter (n. 44), Art. 7.

58 See H. Chiu, 'The International Law of Recognition and the Status of the Republic of China' (1989) 3 *J.Chinese L.* 193; V. H. Li, 'The Law of Non-Recognition: The Case of Taiwan' (1979) 1 *Northwest.J.Int'l L. & Bus.* 134. See generally J. Crawford, *The Creation of States in International Law* (Oxford: Oxford University Press, 1979), 198–220.

illustrated by the partial withdrawal of recognition of the branch of the Palestinian Authority controlled by Hamas.[59]

If the legitimacy of governments is assessed in a few specific situations, states have only a limited number of tools to deal with the difficulties caused by illiberal democracies. Recognition and accreditation are two of these instruments, and it would be surprising if they were not used to fight the persistence of illiberal democracies. These changes could also underpin the disqualificatory role already played by the legitimacy of exercise in situations of intervention by invitation.

9.3.2 *Legitimacy of international organizations: from exercise to origin*

Interestingly, the practice pertaining to international organization weathers the exact opposite phenomenon. International organizations derive their legitimacy from the powers that have been conferred to them by the member states of that organization. The source of their powers is thus only very briefly tested through the consent of states when signing the constitutional treaty of the organization. In this sense, the legitimacy of origin of international organizations is not a challenging issue. But more importantly, as a consequence of the legitimacy of origin derived from the consent of the member states which have endowed the organization with a specific function, international organizations need to ensure that they exercise their powers in conformity with the functions assigned to them by the states. Therefore, international organizations traditionally legitimate the exercise of their functions by ensuring that decision making in respect of the exercise of their specific functions is in conformity with the institutional law of the organization and international law in general: this is what is described in the previous sections as the legitimacy of exercise.

It is submitted here that the question of how authority is exercised by international organizations, classically viewed as the criterion to measure the legitimacy of these institutions is increasingly supplanted by the question of how authority to exercise a certain activity is granted to international organizations. Recent developments in the roles and functions of international organizations, such as the increasing involvement of international organizations in the exercise of governmental functions, have caused a cross-fertilization of both forms of legitimacy, with a clear move from the legitimacy of exercise to various forms of legitimacy of origin. The question of how power is bestowed upon international organizations, especially for those activities which have potential far-reaching influences on the daily lives of citizens, has become an

59 In addition to suspending aid to the government, several countries completely severed their relations. See S. R. Weisman, 'US Digs in on Withholding Aid to Hamas Government' *New York Times* (17 February 2006), A12; S. R. Weisman and C. S. Smith, 'US and Europe halt aid to Palestinian government' *New York Times* (8 April 2006), A6. But see J. Brinkley, 'France backs Putin on speaking to Hamas' *New York Times* (11 February 2006), A7.

essential question in international law and international relations. This section starts by depicting the traditional conception of institutional legitimacy based on the exercise of powers (9.3.2.1) before turning to the reasons underlying the move towards the legitimacy of origin of international organizations (9.3.2.2).

9.3.2.1 *International organizations and the legitimate exercise of powers*

International organizations, although created by states, cannot be seen as equivalent to them, especially in terms of democratic legitimacy. Decision making at the international level by international organizations lacks any direct electoral foundation, since intergovernmental organizations have no direct popular legitimacy of origin. The functioning of international organizations and global governance in general is thus often considered as naturally illegitimate[60] or 'undemocratic'.[61]

However, since an international organization is created by states, the source of and the legitimacy for the exercise of powers by international organizations is derived from the consent validly expressed by the different states party to the constitutional treaty of the organization. Since states and their governments are to be considered as the legitimate representatives of the populations in their territories, under the conditions described and discussed in the sections above, the delegation of certain powers to international organizations by these representatives is indirectly based on a form of popular consent. Consequently, the exercise of powers by international organizations cannot be considered as illegitimate by definition, although its legitimacy will often not be 'democratic' as is traditionally understood.[62]

In view of this lack of direct legitimacy of origin, and the absence of a periodical legitimacy or accountability test through direct elections or any other mechanism, the legitimacy of international organizations has traditionally been addressed through the way in which their functions were exercised, i.e. through the legitimacy of exercise. The exercise of powers by international organizations is then subjected to a legitimacy assessment principally through the procedures followed,[63] often referred to as input legitimacy.[64] From a legal perspective, the most obvious method to ensure the legitimate exercise of powers by an international organization through a focus

60 D. C. Esty, 'Good Governance at the Supranational Scale: Globalizing Administrative Law' (2005–6) 115 *Yale LJ* 1490, 1515.

61 J. Rubenfeld, 'Unilateralism and Constitutionalism' (2004) 79 *NYUL Rev.* 1971, 2020ff.

62 See P. L. Lindseth, 'Democratic Legitimacy and the Administrative Character of Supranationalism: The Example of the European Community' (1999) 99 *Colum.L.Rev.* 646.

63 See Franck (n. 15), 204–7.

64 See generally, M. Krajewski, 'International Organizations of Institutions, Democratic Legitimacy', in R Wolfrum (ed.), *Max Planck Encyclopedia of Public International Law* (Oxford: Oxford University Press, 2008). The substantive outcome of the decisions of international organizations is then referred to as output legitimacy.

on the procedural aspects of decision making is to ensure that decisions taken are in conformity with the legal obligations of the organization,[65] in particular in terms of the legal restraints stemming from the application of general international law and the organization's constitution. Especially when international organizations take action which has potential impact on human rights, such as in the case of the Security Council, there is a tendency to subject this exercise of power to some form of *ex post facto* legitimacy or legality check.[66] A decision which is taken within the limits of the constitutional treaty will be seen as a legitimate decision.[67]

Against this backdrop, and taking into account the legitimacy of international organizations derived from the consent expressed by member states, the debate on the legitimacy of origin of international organizations is, in theory, relatively unequivocal. International organizations habitually and as a matter of principle have no ambition to exercise governmental functions, and the need to establish their legitimacy of origin therefore appears to be a theoretical issue only. Two developments nevertheless confirm that international organizations are increasingly seeking to establish forms of legitimacy of origin beyond the mere consent of the member states, and beyond the legitimacy in the exercise of their functions. These developments show that the question of the legitimacy of origin of international organizations has particular relevance for those organizations which have activities that go beyond technical interstate cooperation.[68]

The first development towards the establishment of a form of legitimacy of origin relates to the European Union (EU). The functioning and legitimacy of the EU lies at the intersection between states and international organizations in terms of democratic legitimacy. An evidence of this is the direct election by the citizens of the Members of the European Parliament. As such, the legitimacy of the EU in the exercise of its functions is very well established, since the decisions of the various institutions of the Union are, under certain conditions, subjected to direct judicial scrutiny by the General Court and/or the European Court of Justice. But the direct election of the Members of the European Parliament also is instrumental in sustaining the legitimacy of the EU, for it endows it – or at least the decision-making processes in which the Parliament plays a significant role – with some legitimacy of origin. This has particular relevance taking into consideration the undeniable strong(er) impact of the EU's decisions on the daily lives of the European citizens. It is for the same reason that several member states have decided to organize

65 See in respect of Security Council action, E. de Wet, *The Chapter VII powers of the United Nations Security Council* (Oxford: Hart, 2004).

66 J. Klabbers, *An Introduction to International Institutional Law* (Cambridge: Cambridge University Press, 2005), 250.

67 See also T. M. Franck, *Fairness in International Law and Institutions* (Oxford: Oxford University Press, 1995), 219–21.

68 Krajewski (n. 64), para. 11.

referendums in order to give a certain popular legitimacy to proposed institutional changes.[69]

A second example providing evidence of an apparent shift from the legitimacy of exercise to the legitimacy of origin in assessing institutional legitimacy is the discussions on the reform of the Security Council and the need to expand (permanent) membership of the Security Council. The question of whether a decision is taken in conformity with the UN Charter and other principles of general international law, i.e. whether a decision is legitimate from the perspective of the exercise of functions, is incrementally being complemented by the question whether the Security Council as an institution has the necessary legitimacy to take certain decisions.[70] The recommendations of the High-Level Panel on Threats, Challenges and Change, besides suggesting a set of guidelines to be used by the Security Council in its decision-making process (legitimacy of exercise), also proposed a reform of the Council in order to 'increase the democratic and accountable nature of the body' (legitimacy of origin).[71]

This position was also adopted by the then Secretary-General Kofi Annan, in his report *In Larger Freedom*.[72] The Secretary-General suggested making the Security Council 'more broadly representative of the international community as a whole'.[73] The justification of the Security Council's authority is thus no longer seen as a consequence of state consent to the constitutional treaty of the organization, which grants certain functions and powers to the Security Council, but rather as the 'universal' acceptance of certain decisions. The guarantee that the Security Council exercises its functions within the framework and limits set by the UN Charter and general international law thus is increasingly complemented by a tendency to ensure that the origin of the functions exercised by that organ is 'democratic'. Of course, and as noted, these developments towards the legitimacy of origin are both a consequence of, and proportional to, the impact of the activity of the organization on the population. The debate on the legitimacy of origin of international organizations has no or little relevance for those organizations of which the direct impact on individuals is limited.

Recently, this dual character of the legitimacy of international organizations has been at the forefront of legal and political discourse through the greater

69 See J. H. H. Weiler, 'A Constitution for Europe? Some Hard Choices' (2002) 40 *Journal of Common Market Studies* 563; J. Zemánek, 'Consent of Parliament or People's Referendum?', in I. Pernice and J. Zemánek (eds.), *A Constitution for Europe: The IGC, the Ratification Process and Beyond* (Baden-Baden: Nomos, 2005), 141–8.

70 See J. Taubman, 'Towards a Theory of Democratic Compliance: Security Council Legitimacy and Effectiveness after Iraq' (2004) 37 *NYUJ Int'l Law & Pol.* 161, 192ff.

71 UNGA, Report of the High-level Panel on Threats, Challenges and Change, 'A more secure world: our shared responsibility' (2 December 2004) UN Doc. A/59/565, para. 73.

72 UNGA, Report of the Secretary-General, *In Larger Freedom: Towards Development, Security and Human Rights for All* (21 March 2005) UN Doc. A/59/2005, para. 165.

73 *Ibid.*

involvement of organizations in the reconstruction and administration of states in post-conflict situations.[74] On these occasions, international organizations have been endowed with wide-ranging powers over individuals, of the sort which were usually only exercised by states. The question of legitimacy then becomes central since such activities will traditionally be seen as legitimate from an institutional perspective, but the exercise of powers by UN subsidiary organs often lack the legitimacy of origin of national governments. In these cases, the dual character of legitimacy has played a prominent role and that practice has weathered a shift from one type of legitimacy to the other.

9.3.2.2 Institutional legitimacy and post-conflict international administrations

Traditionally, the UN's task in conflict or post-conflict situations was limited to the deployment of military personnel and a limited number of civilian staff to assist or advise the existing governmental structures. Recent peace-building or post-conflict reconstruction missions are the latest manifestation of an evolution in the approach towards situations presenting a (potential) threat to international peace and security. Within this evolution, international administrations take a special place. The cases of Kosovo and East Timor are to a certain extent a culmination of this evolution since the UN has, in post-conflict scenarios, taken over the entire administration of territories.

Following NATO's armed intervention in Kosovo in March 1999, the Security Council adopted Resolution 1244 establishing the United Nations Interim Administration Mission in Kosovo (UNMIK).[75] Resolution 1244 called upon UNMIK to promote the establishment of substantial autonomy and self-government in Kosovo, perform basic civilian administrative functions, support the reconstruction of key infrastructure, maintain civil law and order, promote human rights, and assure the safe return of all refugees and displaced persons.[76] UNMIK's competences included full legislative and executive power in the areas of responsibility laid down by Resolution 1244. A few months later, the Security Council authorized the establishment of the United Nations Transitional Authority in East Timor (UNTAET).[77] An earlier 'popular consultation' conducted among the East Timorese had resulted in them expressing their clear wish to begin a process of transition towards independence. For the transitional process, UNTAET was endowed with overall responsibility for the administration of East Timor and empowered to exercise all legislative and executive authority, including the administration of justice.[78]

74 See de Brabandere (n. 10).

75 UNSC Res. 1244 (10 June 1999) UN Doc. S/RES/1244.

76 *Ibid.* Para. 11 (a)–(k).

77 UNSC Res. 1272 (25 October 1999) UN Doc. S/RES/1272.

78 *Ibid.* Art. 1.

Essentially, the dual character of legitimacy under international administrations is the consequence of the 'functional duality' of the exercise of public authority by an international organization. On the one hand, an international administration is a subsidiary organ of an international organization; on the other hand, it functions as the government of a territorial entity. The acts of the international administration are thus both international acts of the international organizations and internal acts of the state. When such missions are seen in their first capacity, such missions will be tested through the legitimacy of exercise; when international administrations are essentially seen as national surrogate governments there is a tendency to concentrate on the legitimacy of origin as the appropriate method to assess the legitimacy of the exercise of such functions.

9.3.2.2.1 LEGITIMACY OF EXERCISE: THE LEGAL AUTHORITY OF POST-CONFLICT ADMINISTRATIONS

Even if there has been some reluctance in the past to accept the UN's capacity to take over the administration of a territory, this controversy is now at an end.[79] Despite some contentions to the contrary in the literature,[80] there are clear bases for the legal authority to exercise administrative functions in post-conflict situations. Several articles can be considered to authorize peace-building missions and international administrations, according to whether or not the consent of the host state has been obtained. Article 39 of the UN Charter gives the Security Council the power to make recommendations to the parties concerned. Operations authorized under that article are therefore based not only on the Security Council's recommendatory power, but also on the consent of the state concerned. Article 41 of the UN Charter gives the Security Council the power to impose measures not involving the use of armed force. In theory, when the consent of the host state cannot be obtained for any reason whatsoever, and if a situation presents a threat to the peace or a breach of the peace, or in the event of an act of aggression, this article can be considered an adequate legal basis to authorize such a mission. One might of course consider that in view of the expansion in the interpretation of what constitutes a 'threat to international peace and security,' the Security Council has a particular duty to act in good faith when making determinations in this respect.[81]

Taking a traditional approach to the legitimacy of international organizations and their exercise of powers, the establishment of such missions in

79 See also E. de Wet, 'The Direct Administration of Territories by the United Nations and Its Member States in the Post Cold War Era: Legal Basis and Implications for National Law' (2004) 8 *Max Planck Yearbook of United Nations Law* 291, 306ff.

80 See H. K. Dickerson, 'Assumptions of Legitimacy and the Foundations of International Territorial Administration' (2006) 100 ASIL PROC. 144.

81 F. L. Kirgis, 'Security Council Governance of Postconflict Societies: A Plea for Good Faith and Informed Decision Making' (2001) 3 AJIL 579, 581.

conformity with the UN Charter would be sufficient to label international administrations as legitimate. The legitimacy of the setting up of international post-conflict administrations is then principally derived from the procedural and legal validity of the action taken, i.e. its conformity with the UN Charter and other rules of international law. Such activity is however also legitimate as a consequence of the general consent of member states to the power of the Security Council to deal with situations which can be categorized as threats to international peace and security, since the delegation[82] by states of certain competences to international organizations, is accomplished through being a party to the UN Charter which grants the UN Security Council the power to establish this type of mission. Despite some reluctance in the legal literature to accept the expanding role of the Security Council and the expanding range of measures the Security Council adopts under Chapter VII,[83] recent comprehensive peace-building mandates have not been objected to by UN member states.[84] However, despite these relatively undisputed legal bases, the question has been raised as to whether, in view of the impact of such decisions, the consent of either the host state or the host population should not form the legitimate basis for the exercise of such functions, since these requirements would be placed onto a national government exercising these functions.[85]

9.3.2.2.2 SHIFTING TO THE LEGITIMACY OF ORIGIN: CONSENT, CONSULTATION AND POST-CONFLICT ADMINISTRATIONS

The consent of the host state is not absolutely necessary when the Security Council acts under Chapter VII. However, when it is possible, the consent of the host state is often sought and obtained for intrusive reconstruction activities.[86] One reason for this is that from a practical perspective international administrations cannot adequately operate without the consent of the sovereign state. However, more importantly, the specific case-based consent of

82 See C. A. Bradley and J. G. Kelley, 'The Concept of International Delegation' (2008) 71 LCP 1.

83 See B. Conforti, *The Law and Practice of the United Nations* (Leiden: Martinus Nijhoff, 2005), 205–6.

84 As noted by Erika de Wet, the international community has accepted such mandates, either through explicit support in the General Assembly, or indirectly by the acceptance of the expenses for such missions as expense of the organization. E. de Wet, 'Beginning and End of Occupation: UN Security Council's Impact on the Laws of Occupation' (2006) 34 *Collegium* (special edn) 37.

85 See H. K. Dickerson, 'Assumptions of Legitimacy and the Foundations of International Territorial Administration' (2006) 34 *Denv. J. Int'l L. & Pol'y* 161.

86 In the case of Kosovo, the plan presented by Martti Ahtisaari and Victor Chernomyrdin, which contained the general principles of an agreement on the Kosovo crisis, was accepted by the Federal Republic of Yugoslavia (Agreement on the principles (peace plan) to move towards a resolution of the Kosovo crisis) presented to the leadership of the Federal Republic of Yugoslavia by the President of Finland, Martti Ahtisaari, representing the European Union, and Viktor Chernomyrdin, Special Representative of the President of the Russian Federation. UNSC 'Letter from the Permanent Representative of Germany to the UN' (7 June 1999) UN Doc. S/1999/649. See also UNSC Res. S/RES/1244 (n. 75), preamble. See generally, J. d'Aspremont, 'Regulating Statehood: The Kosovo Status Settlement' (2007) 20 *Leiden Journal of International Law* 649.

the host state plays an important function from the perspective of the legitimacy of international administrative missions. Next to the legal basis for the creation of comprehensive peace-building missions by the Security Council, the consent of the host state is sought to enhance the legitimacy of origin, from an institutional perspective, for the exercise of such intrusive powers on a state's territory. The consent of the host state, in general, to the authority of the Security Council then is complemented by the specific consent of the state for a particular type of activity; the legitimacy of exercise is complemented by the legitimacy of origin.

In the case of Kosovo, the Federal Republic of Yugoslavia explicitly consented to the deployment of both the civil and military presences.[87] Consent here was not absolutely necessary as UNMIK was established under a Chapter VII resolution. In this particular case, a purely legal argument could explain why the consent of Yugoslavia was sought. The consent of the Federal Republic of Yugoslavia was crucial in view of the ambiguities concerning the Federal Republic of Yugoslavia's membership of the UN, as both the Security Council[88] and the General Assembly[89] had clearly indicated that it could not automatically be seen as the successor of the Socialist Federal Republic of Yugoslavia. The Federal Republic nevertheless was considered the de facto successor of the Socialist Federal Republic by the Secretariat.[90] But the consent of Yugoslavia not only legalized the deployment of the mission on its territory, it also added the necessary legitimacy to the authorization by the Security Council for this international administrative mission.

The case of UNTAET also is rather unusual in this respect, since Indonesia's consent also was sought in spite of the very doubtful character of Indonesian sovereignty over East Timor.[91] East Timor was still formally a non-self-governing territory at the date of the 1999 popular consultation which led to the establishment of an international administration. According to the principles applicable to non-self-governing territories,[92] Portugal retained formal sovereignty over East Timor. However, an agreement was concluded between Portugal and Indonesia to organize the referendum and the international administration in the event of a vote in favour of independence.[93] The consent of Indonesia in this case could by no means legitimate the creation

87 See UNSC Res. S/RES/1244 (n. 75), preamble.

88 See e.g. UNSC Res. 757 (30 May 1992) UN Doc. S/RES/757 and UNSC Res. 777 (19 September 1992) UN Doc. S/RES/777.

89 See e.g. UNGA Res. 47/1 (22 September 1992) UN Doc. A/RES/47/1.

90 See *Application of the Convention on the Prevention and Punishment of the Crime of Genocide* (*Bosnia and Herzegovina* v. *Serbia and Montenegro*) (Judgment of 26 February 2007) 2007 ICJ 91 (at: www.icj-cij.org).

91 *Case concerning East Timor* (*Portugal* v. *Australia*) 1995 ICJ Rep. 90, para. 37. See also S. R. Ratner, 'Foreign Occupation and International Territorial Administration: The Challenges of Convergence' (2005) 16 EJIL 697.

92 Crawford (n. 58), 614.

93 Agreement between the Republic of Indonesia and the Portuguese Republic on the Question of East Timor (5 May 1999) 2062 UNTS 7.

of an international administration on the territory of East Timor, and can perhaps be explained by pragmatism. On the other hand, the consent of Portugal, which formally still had sovereignty over the territory, had also been obtained through the conclusion of a treaty.

However, when the consent of the state is problematic, such as in East Timor, the lack of consent from the host population is often advanced as the reason why such intrusive operations lack legitimacy.[94] The focus here thus shifts from international administrations as subsidiary organs of international organizations, to international administrations as substitute national governments. Clearly, the legitimacy of these missions from an international organization perspective is established, but international administrations will typically lack the necessary democratic legitimacy usually required for national governments. Popular consent indeed has never been the basis for the establishment of the latest post-conflict administrations or peace-building missions. Even in East Timor, when prior to the establishment of UNTAET a referendum had been organized, the only questions put to the citizens was whether they agreed or not to independence. There was no attempt explicitly to seek the consent of the East Timorese for the exercise of administrative powers by the UN, although the choice for an independent East Timor implied the exercise of such powers by the organization.

In the absence of popular legitimacy of origin, post-conflict international administrations have been 'forced' to enhance the legitimacy of their exercise of legislative, executive and even judicial powers through consultation with national authorities. This type of legitimacy, although incomplete when viewed using the standards set out above in respect of national governments, in fact combines elements relating to the source of authority (legitimacy of origin) and elements relating to the legality and thus legitimacy of the decision-making process on the national level by international administrations in their function as national governments (legitimacy of exercise).[95] At the same time, the former transitional administrator also questioned the appropriateness of such an approach.[96]

In practice, consultation with local actors has been paramount to enhance the legitimacy of such missions, and local institutions often have been created for this purpose. The Special Representative in Kosovo, upon his arrival established a 'Kosovo Transitional Council', as a consultative, legislator-like organ.[97] A few months later it was expanded and integrated into the first Kosovar multi-ethnic governmental structure: the 'Joint

94 See e.g. Dickerson (n. 80), 144–5.

95 This has been well explained by the former UNTAET transitional administrator S. Vieira de Mello. S. Vieira de Mello, 'How Not to Run a Country: Lessons for the UN from Kosovo and East Timor' (June 2000) (at: www.jsmp.minihub.org/Resources/2000/INTERFET%20DETAINEE%20MANAGEMENT%20UNIT%20(e).pdf).

96 *Ibid.*

97 UNMIK press release, 'UNMIK convenes first meeting of Kosovo Transitional Council' (16 July 1999) UN Doc. UNMIK/PR/12.

Interim Administrative Structure'.[98] Soon after UNTAET's arrival, the Transitional Administrator for East Timor equally established the National Consultative Council, a political body consisting of 11 East Timorese and four UNTAET members, to oversee the decision-making process.[99] The Council's primary responsibility was to make policy recommendations on significant executive and legislative matters, and to consult with the Timorese on all aspects of UNTAET's involvement. All UNTAET regulations adopted during the National Consultative Council's tenure were endorsed by the Council.[100]

In consequence, although the legitimacy of international organizations has been traditionally tested only from the perspective of the legitimacy of exercise, recent developments show a tendency towards assessing decision-making power within international organizations through the lens of the legitimacy of origin as well. The dual character of legitimacy is of course most visible when international organizations take over administrative functions within a state, therefore effectively combining the two forms of legitimacy. In those cases, the decision-making process at the institutional level tends to be supported both by the legal validity of the decisions taken and by the consent of the host state. During the performance of their missions, international administrations, although legitimate from an institutional perspective, typically will lack popular legitimacy of origin. In those circumstances, international post-conflict administrations have sought to legitimize their activity by consulting with local ad hoc authorities, therefore offering some form of legitimacy of origin in their decision-making power at the national level.

9.4 Concluding remarks

This chapter has argued that the complexity of global governance can hardly be disentangled if one fails to understand the dual nature of legitimacy of its main actors, i.e. governments and international organizations. Legitimacy should, for each of them, be gauged from the standpoint of both their origin and the way in which they exercise their powers. Such a distinction has been insufficiently taken into account both in practice and by scholars. Moreover, the significance of both the legitimacy of origin and the legitimacy of exercise has changed. With respect to the legitimacy of governments, the emphasis traditionally put on origins is no longer exclusive and more attention is paid to the legitimacy of their exercise of power, whereas, as regards international organizations, recent practice and contemporary literature show that the question of legitimacy is no longer solely about the way in which these

98 UNMIK Regulation 2000/1 on the approval Kosovo Joint Interim Administrative Structure (14 January 2000) UN Doc. UNMIK/REG/2000/1.

99 UNTAET Regulation 1999/2 on the establishment of a National Consultative Council (2 December 1999) UN Doc. UNTAET/REG/1999/2.

100 Report of the Secretary-General, *Financing of the United Nations Transitional Administration in East Timor* (7 March 2000) UN Doc. A/54/769, para. 14.

organizations exercise their powers but also about their origin. This chapter ultimately formulates the wish that the conceptual clarifications that have been put forward here will be instrumental in stimulating more systematized research about the legitimacy of global actors in the context of global governance.

10 Democracy as a global norm

Has it finally emerged?*

Christian Pippan

10.1 Introduction

Twenty years after the fall of the Berlin Wall and the opening of the Iron Curtain, the legacy of the 'year of the truth' is mostly approached from general political, historical and/or socio-cultural perspectives.[1] From an international legal perspective, however, it is also worthwhile to recall the inspirational impact of 1989 on normative theories of democracy and its role in the international system. Their basis was a decidedly liberal reading of the revolutions of 1989, which were widely regarded as a confirmation of the superiority of Western-style multiparty democracy (with its typical emphasis on political pluralism, individual rights and the rule of law) over other political regimes and forms of government. In both Europe and the United States, influential political thinkers interpreted the dramatic changes in Central and Eastern Europe as a belated 'catching-up' of the region with the achievements of Enlightenment and the French Revolution and the expression of a liberal revolutionary tradition deeply rooted in American and modern European notions of democratic constitutionalism.[2] International institutions, in Europe and elsewhere, quickly reacted to the events of the epoch and the new era of democracy that they promised to evoke. Only a year after the advent of what in German is referred to as 'die Wende' (the turning point), the

* This chapter is dedicated to the memory of Thomas M. Franck (1931–2009), who – both as teacher and scholar – has had such a profound impact on so many of us.

1 T. Garton Ash, 'The Year of the Truth', in Vladimir Tismăneanu (ed.), *The Revolutions of 1989* (London: Routledge, 1999), 105.

2 See Paul Blokker, 'The Impact of 1989 on Theoretical Perceptions of Democracy' (2008) Research Network 1989, Working Paper No. 21/2008 (at: www.cee-socialscience.net/1989/papers/papers.html; accessed 1 December 2009). Blokker cites J. Habermas, *Die nachholende Revolution*, 3rd edn (Frankfurt aM: Suhrkamp, 1999) and B. Ackerman, *The Future of Liberal Revolution* (New Haven, CT: Yale University Press, 1992) as archetypical representatives of the predominant view in social and political science that reads 1989 as an affirmation of the irresistible appeal of liberal democracy. More radical was Francis Fukuyama who took the demise of Eastern European communism as the last step in the ideological evolution of humankind which would pave the way for the universalization of liberal democracy as the 'final form of human government', F. Fukuyama, *The End of History and the Last Man* (New York, NY: Free Press, 1992).

Conference on Security and Cooperation in Europe (CSCE), which included among its members the main rivals of the waning East–West conflict, solemnly professed to 'build, consolidate and strengthen democracy as the only system of government of our nations'.[3] In mid-1991, the Organization of American States (OAS) likewise affirmed that 'representative democracy is the form of government of the region'.[4] Another six months later, eleven former Soviet Republics adopted the Alma Ata Declaration, which confirmed the formation of the Commonwealth of Independent States (CIS) and the intention of its members 'to build democratic states under the rule of law'.[5]

Against the backdrops of political transition and reform in many parts of the world and a growing interest in democracy on the part of a number of international organizations, Thomas Franck proclaimed the emergence of an internationally constituted 'right to democratic governance'. In a seminal article published in 1992, he asserted that, 'both textually and in practice, the international system is moving toward a clearly designated democratic entitlement, with national governance validated by international standards and systematic monitoring of compliance'.[6] Franck's thesis had a significant resonance in international legal scholarship and ushered in what came to be labelled as the 'democratic entitlement school'. Although the debate over the sweeping claim that, in the post-Cold War era, democracy was gradually becoming a universal norm probably saw its heyday in the 1990s, it has neither lost attraction nor relevance.[7] The claim's provocative nature in light of international law's traditional indifference towards domestic constitutional orders, its assumptions about the kind of democracy advanced by the international system and its potential consequences for states deemed to be in violation of the purported norm continue to inspire scholars of international law and fuel controversial discussions.[8]

3 Charter of Paris for a New Europe (21 November 1990) (1991) 30 ILM 190, 193.

4 Santiago Commitment to Democracy and the Renewal of the Inter-American System, OAS General Assembly, 21st Session (4 June 1991) OAE/Ser.P/AG Doc. 2734/91; Representative Democracy, OAS General Assembly Res. 1080 (5 June 1991) OAE/Ser.P/AG Doc. 2739/91.

5 Alma Ata Declaration and Protocol (21 December 1991) (1992) 31 ILM 147. On the basis of the Alma Ata documents, eight newly independent states joined the so-called 'Minsk Agreement' initially concluded by the CIS founding states Belarus, Russia and Ukraine: Minsk Agreement Establishing the Commonwealth of Independent States (8 December 1991) (1992) 31 ILM 138.

6 T. M. Franck, 'The Emerging Right to Democratic Governance' (1992) 86 AJIL 46, 91. See by the same author: 'The Democratic Entitlement' (1994) 29 *U.Rich.L.Rev.*1; 'Democracy as a Human Right', in L. Henkin and J. L. Hargrove (eds.), *Human Rights: An Agenda for the Next Century* (Washington, DC: ASIL, 1994), 73; *Fairness in International Law and Institutions* (Oxford: Clarendon Press, 1995), 83–139.

7 See G. H. Fox and B. R. Roth (eds.), *Democratic Governance and International Law* (Cambridge: Cambridge University Press, 2000) and R. Burchill (ed.), *Democracy and International Law* (Aldershot: Ashgate, 2006).

8 Among the more recent literature, see E. Macdonald, 'International Law, Democratic Governance and September the 11th' (2002) 3 *German LJ* (at: www.germanlawjournal.com; accessed 1 December 2009); S. Wheatley, 'Democracy and International Law: A European Perspective' (2002) 51 ICLQ 225; J. I. Ibegbu, *Right to Democracy in International Law* (Lewiston, ID: Mellen Press, 2003); J. N.

A central feature of Franck's thesis is its distinctly normative character, with the right advocated by him 'always falling short of the law of the moment, always "emerging", not quite yet there, though well under way'.[9] Interestingly, in a speech reprinted in the very same issue of the American Journal of International Law that included Franck's first elaboration of his thesis, Sir Robert Jennings stated that 'a right – even human rights – does not amount to much in practice unless it is established and seen to be established as an integral part of the whole system of international law which alone can create effective corresponding obligations in the international community'.[10] Although Sir Robert's remark was not directly related to Franck's article, the question suggests itself: is the democratic entitlement today, nearly two decades after Franck predicted its global expansion, 'established as an integral part of the whole system of international law' – as, for instance, Theodor Meron seemed to imply recently?[11]

The present chapter aims to revisit the democracy and international law puzzle in light of recent international developments, particularly within the United Nations. Section 10.2 briefly recapitulates the major strands of the democratic norm thesis and some of the more fundamental critique it has received. Section 10.3 then approaches the principal problématique associated with the thesis by addressing three interrelated, yet eventually distinct, legal issues: (10.3.1) Does the international legal order display any preference for democracy over other political regimes? (10.3.2) Does the international system embrace a normative minimum standard of democracy? (10.3.3) Are any of the elements of a presumed international minimum standard of democracy of a universal legal character? The chapter concludes by arguing that, unless one (inappropriately) equates democracy with free and fair

Maogoto, 'Democratic Governance: An Emerging Customary Norm?' (2003) 5 *U. Notre Dame Austl L. Rev.* 55; J. Wouters, B. de Meester and C. Ryngaert, 'Democracy and International Law' (2003) 34 NYIL 139; T. J. Farer, 'The Promotion of Democracy: International Law and Norms', in E. Newman and R. Rich (eds.), *The UN Role in Promoting Democracy: Between Ideals and Reality* (Tokyo: UNU Press, 2004) 32; J. Kokott, 'Souveräne Gleichheit und Demokratie im Völkerrecht' (2004) 64 *ZaöRV* 517; N. Kofele-Kale, 'The Global Community's Role in Promoting the Right to Democratic Governance and Free Choice in the Third World' (2005) 11 *Law and Business Review Americas* 205; S. Varayudej, 'A Right to Democracy in International Law: Its Implications for Asia' (2006) 12 *Annual Survey of International and Comparative Law* 17; V. Huet, 'Vers l'Emergence d'un Principe de Légitimité Démocratique en Droit International?' (2006) 67 RTDH 573; C. Pippan, 'Gibt es ein Recht auf Demokratie im Völkerrecht?', in E. Riefler (ed.), *Sir Karl Popper und die Menschenrechte* (Frankfurt aM: Lang, 2007), 119; J. d'Aspremont, *L'Etat Non Démocratique en Droit International* (Paris: Pedone, 2008); N. Petersen, *Demokratie als teleologisches Prinzip. Zur Legitimität von Staatsgewalt im Völkerrecht* (Berlin: Springer, 2009).

9 M. Koskenniemi, 'Legal Cosmopolitanism: Tom Franck's Messianic World' (2003) 35 *NYUJ Int'l Law & Pol.* 471, 484. See also D. Kennedy, 'Tom Franck and the Manhattan School' (2003) 35 *NYUJ Int'l Law & Pol.* 397, 432.

10 R. Jennings, 'Speech on the Report of the International Court of Justice' (1992) 86 AJIL 249, 254.

11 See T. Meron, *The Humanization of International Law* (Leiden: Martinus Nijhoff, 2006), 497 (positing that, 'it is undeniable that democracy has become both an expectation of peoples and a universal norm').

elections, no general rule of international law can be identified requiring states to design their constitutional orders along liberal–democratic lines. Increasingly, however, an international regime on democratic governance is taking shape; a regime that comprises principles, rules and standards with varying degrees of normativity and around which the expectations of international actors regarding domestic efforts 'to implement the principles and practices of democracy'[12] converge.

10.2 The democratic norm thesis and its discontents

10.2.1 From aspiration to entitlement: a beginner's guide to the democratic norm thesis

The basic ingredients of the Franckian conception of democracy as a global legal entitlement are well known. At its heart lies the idea of democracy as a sine qua non for the validation of governance. This idea is no longer limited to states that, by their own choice, have subscribed to it as a matter of domestic constitutional law. Rather, it is also seen as a requirement of international law, 'applicable to all and implemented through global standards'.[13] According to this view, the democratic entitlement is the synthesis of three functionally interrelated 'sub-entitlements', which are grounded in part in customary law and in part in a new interpretation of international treaties. The peoples' right to self-determination is seen as the oldest and most basic element of the democratic entitlement.[14] It was later supplemented by discursive and associational entitlements in the form of internationally guaranteed individual rights such as freedom of speech, freedom of the press and freedom of assembly.[15] The latest and most significant addition to this catalogue is the 'right to (electoral) democracy' which is considered 'to extend the ambit of other protected rights to ensure meaningful participation by the governed in the formal political decisions by which the quality of their lives and societies are shaped'.[16] Ultimately, this latter aspect would become the fulcrum of the democratic norm thesis.

It is evident that Franck's argument about the place of electoral democracy in international law was inspired by the widespread optimism prevailing at the time regarding the advent of a new world order based on generally accepted 'community values'. In constructing his thesis, Franck pointed to the growing number of states which, following the end of the Cold War, had joined the

12 See United Nations Millennium Declaration, UNGA Res. 55/2 (8 September 2000) UN Doc. A/RES/55/2, para. 25.

13 Franck 1992 (n. 6), 47.

14 Self-determination, as understood by Franck, postulates 'the right of a people organized in an established territory to determine its collective political destiny in a democratic fashion' (*ibid.* 52).

15 *Ibid.* 61–3.

16 T. M. Franck, 'Legitimacy and the Democratic Entitlement', in G. H. Fox and B. R. Roth (eds.), *Democratic Governance and International Law* (Cambridge: Cambridge University Press, 2000), 25, 26.

older democracies in committing themselves to the principle of periodic and free elections.[17] He also referred to the firm support for electoral democracy by the UN and many regional organizations, which is generally based on the understanding that the will of the people shall be expressed in 'free and fair' elections.[18] For Franck, these developments were clear confirmations by international practice of both the principle of popular sovereignty and the right of citizens to vote and to be elected, as enshrined in Article 21 of the 1948 Universal Declaration of Human Rights (UDHR).[19] Accordingly he also ascribed great significance to the fact that, by the early 1990s, the International Covenant on Civil and Political Rights (ICCPR) and the Covenant on Economic, Social and Cultural Rights (ICESCR) had been ratified by more than two-thirds of all states.[20] Franck added an observation that the balance within the community of states was increasingly tilting toward a 'substantial new majority…actually practicing a reasonably credible version of electoral democracy'. He concluded that Article 25 of the ICCPR (on the right to political participation) 'also begins to approximate prevailing practice and thus may be said to be stating what is becoming a customary legal norm applicable to all'.[21]

Once its universal character is deduced from its articulation in the UDHR and subsequent UN resolutions,[22] international treaties[23] and the corresponding practice of a vast majority of states, the focus shifts to the actual meaning and scope of the democratic entitlement; that is, the normative determinacy of a 'right to democratic governance'. Adherents to the democratic norm thesis usually turn to the jurisprudence of bodies charged with the interpretation of human rights treaties and to the standards used by various international actors in the field of electoral assistance and election monitoring (particularly the UN, the OSCE, the OAS, the EU, the African Union and the Commonwealth).

17 Franck 1992 (n. 6), 47–9.

18 *Ibid.* 63–9.

19 UNGA Res. 217 (III) (10 December 1948), UN Doc. A/810. It is important to note here that Franck considered the UDHR (which was originally adopted as a legally non-binding instrument by the UN General Assembly) as reflecting, in its entirety, 'a customary rule of state obligation' (*ibid.* 61). For a similar argument, see C. M. Cerna, 'Universal Democracy: An International Legal Right or the Pipe Dream of the West? (1995) 27 *NYUJ Int'l Law & Pol.* 289, 294–7; R. Ezetah, 'The Right to Democracy: A Qualitative Inquiry' (1997) 22 *Brook JIL* 495, 507.

20 As of December 2009, the number of states party to the ICCPR has risen to 164; see United Nations, Multilateral Treaties Deposited with the Secretary-General (at: http://treaties.un.org/Pages/ParticipationStatus.aspx; accessed 1 December 2009).

21 Franck 1992 (n. 6), 64.

22 The General Assembly periodically adopts (since 1988) specific resolutions entitled 'Strengthening the role of the United Nations in enhancing the effectiveness of the principle of periodic and genuine elections', which regularly reaffirm the central message embodied in art. 21 UDHR; see below (n. 74).

23 In addition to the ICCPR, see at the regional level: Protocol to the European Convention on Human Rights and Fundamental Freedoms (20 March 1952) (1952) ETS No. 9 (art. 3); American Convention on Human Rights (22 November 1969) (1969) 9 ILM 99 (art. 23); African Charter of Human and Peoples' Rights (27 June 1981) (1982) ILM 21 58 (art. 13).

The latter is regarded as particularly relevant for the emergence of democracy as a global norm. For one, the large number of requests for electoral assistance from practically all regions of the world is seen as further proof that elections are seen as the most reliable way of ascertaining popular will.[24] Moreover, it is argued that international election monitoring, which indeed has evolved into a routine exercise in recent years, particularly in countries striving for a transition to or consolidation of democracy,[25] has produced a coherent set of international standards that clearly indicate what free and fair elections are. As a result, the ordinary meaning of provisions in international treaties affirming the right to take part in genuine periodic elections is said to have acquired a 'universal understanding'.[26]

The idea that domestic governments are under an emerging international obligation to comply with global standards of democracy clearly forms the core of the democratic norm thesis. Even among its proponents, however, opinions differ as to the potential legal consequences of the purported norm for non-democratic states. In the view of some, its gradual recognition by the international community necessarily calls for a new approach to the concept of 'governmental legitimacy' in international law. This should look beyond the traditional criteria of effective territorial control and the habitual obedience of the bulk of the population concerned. Franck indicated that a regime's non-compliance with an internationally guaranteed 'right to democracy' would inevitably cast doubt on its legitimacy and would ultimately put the international legal standing of the state it purports to represent at risk.[27] In a similar vein, Gregory Fox has opined that, if faced with a systematic violation of democratic rights, 'the international community...would seem obliged to avoid treating the illegitimate regime as the proper agent of its state'.[28] To be sure, Fox himself has called this a 'rather black and white conception of governmental legitimacy' and has conceded that – the occasional non-recognition of regimes resulting from coups against freely elected leaders

24 From 1989 to 2007, the UN alone has received more than 400 official requests for electoral assistance: Report of the Secretary-General, 'Strengthening the Role of the United Nations in Enhancing the Effectiveness of the Principle of Periodic and Genuine Elections and the Promotion of Democratization' (2007) UN Doc. A/62/293, para. 3.

25 See C. Binder and C. Pippan, 'Election Monitoring, International', in R. Wolfrum (ed.), *The Max Planck Encyclopedia of Public International Law* (online edn) (Oxford: Oxford University Press, 2008) (at: www.mpepil.com; accessed 1 December 2009).

26 G. H. Fox, 'The Right to Political Participation in International Law', in G. H. Fox and B. R. Roth (eds.), *Democratic Governance and International Law* (Cambridge: Cambridge University Press, 2000), 48, 85. See also Y. Beigbeder, *International Monitoring of Plebiscites, Referenda and National Elections. Self-Determination and Transitions to Democracy* (Dordrecht: Martinus Nijhoff, 1994), 148; E. Theuermann, 'Legitimizing Governments through International Verification: The Role of the United Nations' (1995) 49 AJPIL 129, 146.

27 In the forward-looking, idealistic tone that is typical of his writings at the time, Franck posited that 'we stand on the cusp of a remarkable new idea: that each state owes an obligation of democratic governance to all other states as a price of its membership in the community of nations' (Franck 1994 (n. 6), 7).

28 G. H. Fox, 'Election Monitoring: The International Legal Setting' (2001) 19 *Wis.Int'l LJ* 295, 312.

notwithstanding – there is virtually no international practice indicating that the capacity of long-standing authoritarian regimes to act on behalf of the state they claim to represent would generally be called into question simply because of the absence of free and fair electoral processes.[29]

10.2.2 Going too far, or not going far enough? Two major concerns about the democratic norm thesis

A major critique of the democratic entitlement rests on a more conservative reading of the relevant sources and practices cited by its advocates as evidence for the emergence of a right to democracy in international law.[30] As a general matter, it is not disputed that the ICCPR or most regional human rights conventions require state parties to ensure some form of competitive electoral processes within their domestic jurisdictions.[31] However, in light of the absence of genuine elections in a number of states, including powerful states such as China and Saudi Arabia, it is questioned whether a global legal standard of democratic governance has truly emerged. Scholars sceptical of the democratic entitlement do not deny that the world community has come to regard the holding of 'free and fair' elections as the preferred method for the selection of national leaders. They do, however, take issue with the view that states were now obliged, as a matter of general international law, to apply a particular procedure in order to ascertain the will of the people. Brad Roth, for example, emphasizes that election monitoring by international observers is carried out only upon request by the country concerned.[32] UN resolutions that proclaimed support for the principle of periodic and genuine elections were usually accompanied by counterpart resolutions affirming 'respect for the principles of national sovereignty and diversity of democratic systems in electoral processes'.[33] While he agrees that, based on a modern understanding of self-determination, sovereignty ultimately belongs to peoples and not to governments, Roth insists that international law does not reduce popular will to the outcome of elections, let alone any specific electoral processes. Rather, a government's effective control, coupled with the habitual obedience of the population, is taken by international law as presumptive evidence that the existing regime constitutes a legitimate expression of self-determination by the people concerned.[34] According to Roth, this presumption is rebutted only

29 *Ibid.* 314.

30 For a concise account of this critique, see G. H. Fox and B. R. Roth, 'Democracy and International Law' (2001) 27 *Rev. Int'l Stud.* 327, 343.

31 See A. Conte, 'Democratic and Civil Rights', in A. Conte, S. Davidson and R. Burchill, *Defining Civil and Political Rights* (Aldershot: Ashgate, 2004), 43, 73; S. Wheatley, *Democracy, Minorities and International Law* (Cambridge: Cambridge University Press, 2005), 136.

32 B. R. Roth, *Governmental Illegitimacy in International Law* (Oxford: Oxford University Press, 1999), 338–43.

33 See below (n. 75).

34 Roth (n. 32), 343.

if 'well-nigh incontrovertible evidence exists to the contrary', e.g. when a regime's claim to power results from a coup against a freely elected predecessor government or if a regime has 'itself conceded a crises of legitimacy by agreeing to predicate its authority on processes certified by the international community'.[35]

A second key concern about the democratic norm thesis pertains to the limited conception of democracy ('low intensity democracy' in Susan Marks' term) that it involves. The focus on periodic elections – which, pursuant to Franck, is currently all a positivistic approach to the identification of an international norm of democracy can support – is deemed by many as insufficient to attain the beneficial substantive ends that almost all democratic theories ultimately aspire to.[36] Specifically, it is questioned whether the exclusive reliance on political participation and materially related rights and freedoms is adequate to achieve what David Beetham has identified as the common core objectives of virtually all concepts of democracy: popular control and political equality.[37] Most notably, a universal norm subjecting political leaders to regular control by citizens may be of little value to those lacking the capacities necessary to exercise that control effectively. In other words, if control of public decision making is to be exercised by all on a basis of equality, then 'all must be not just entitled, but also enabled to undertake it, and that calls for access to the requisite social, economic and cultural resources'.[38] For advocates of an 'inclusionary' vision of democracy, therefore, the realization of social and economic rights is at least as relevant as the guarantee of participatory (and other political) rights. A related misgiving about the democratic entitlement is that by focusing on procedural democracy as the decisive determinant for governmental legitimacy, international responses to failures of democracy may become vulnerable to manipulation. Ruling elites may thus secure international validation by adhering to certain procedures (such as elections), while they in fact remain unaccountable to large parts of the populace by keeping existing inequalities and established structures of social and economic power untouched.[39]

To be sure, practically all international actors engaged in the promotion of democracy within states firmly subscribe today to the idea that democratic

35 *Ibid.* 419.

36 See S. Marks, *The Riddle of all Constitutions: International Law, Democracy and the Critique of Ideology* (Oxford: Oxford University Press, 2000), 52–3; M. Koskenniemi, 'Whose Intolerance, Which Democracy?', in G. H. Fox and B. R. Roth (eds.), *Democratic Governance and International Law* (Cambridge: Cambridge University Press, 2000), 436, 438; B. R. Roth, 'Evaluating Democratic Progress: A Normative Theoretical Approach', in G. H. Fox and B. R. Roth (eds.), *Democratic Governance and International Law* (Cambridge: Cambridge University Press, 2000), 493, 498.

37 D. Beetham, *Democracy and Human Rights* (Cambridge: Polity Press, 1999), 5.

38 S. Marks and A. Clapham, *International Human Rights Lexicon* (Oxford: Oxford University Press, 2005), 64–5.

39 See M. Beutz, 'Functional Democracy: Responding to Failures of Accountability' (2003) 44 *Harv. Int'l LJ* 387, 399.

governance entails more than the holding of periodic and free elections.[40] In the case of the most prominent actor on the global stage, the United Nations, a particularly illustrative example is provided by Resolution 55/96 of the General Assembly, adopted in December 2000, on 'Promoting and consolidating democracy'.[41] The Assembly called on states to take action in a range of areas (including human rights, electoral systems, the rule of law, civil society participation, good governance, sustainable development and social cohesion) to signal its support for a broad approach to democracy which comprises both procedural and substantive elements. The 2005 World Summit also provided evidence of the international community's general favour for a non-exclusive and dynamic understanding of democracy. In the resolution that resulted from the event, the participating heads of state and government explicitly recognized democracy as a 'universal value' but also added that, 'while democracies share common features, there is no single model of democracy'.[42]

Overall, the notion originally developed by political theorists that democracy constitutes an 'essentially contested concept' appears to be well reflected in both international legal scholarship and practice.[43] It should be recalled, however, that the international legal system frequently operates with under-defined terms and concepts, which may nevertheless provide the basis for generally accepted norms. The right of peoples to self-determination – according to Franck one of the building blocks of the democratic entitlement – is a case in point. That right's recognition as a fundamental principle of international law is beyond any doubt.[44] So far, however, the international system has not clarified its exact meaning beyond the context of decolonization or conclusively answered questions about how 'peoples' are to be distinguished from 'minorities' that are endowed with specific individual rights but not, according to prevailing doctrine, a collective right to self-determination. The proclamation that self-determination entails a right of peoples 'to freely determine their political status and freely pursue their economic, social and cultural development'[45] does not seem to offer more determinacy than, say, the UN World Conference on Human Rights' proposition that 'democracy is based on the freely expressed will of the people to determine their own political, economic, social and cultural systems and their full participation in

40 See E. R. McMahon and S. H. Baker, *Piecing a Democratic Quilt? Regional Organizations and Universal Norms* (Bloomfield: Kumarian Press, 2006), 17–34.

41 UNGA Res. 55/96 (4 December 2000) UN Doc. A/RES/55/96.

42 World Summit Outcome, UNGA Res. 60/1 (16 December 2005) UN Doc. A/RES/60/1, para. 135.

43 On Walter B. Gallie's analysis of 'essentially contested concepts' and its application to the principle of democracy, see D. Collier, F. D. Hidalgo and A. O. Maciuceanu, 'Essentially Contested Concepts: Debates and Applications' (2006) 11 *J. Pol. Ideologies* 211, 222.

44 See *East Timor Case (Portugal* v. *Australia)* (Judgement) [1995] ICJ Rep. 102, para. 29.

45 This standard definition of self-determination first appeared in the UN General Assembly's 'Declaration on the Granting of Independence to Colonial Countries and Peoples', UNGA Res. 15/1514 (14 December 1960) UN Doc. A/RES/15/1514, para. 2. It was later prominently included in common art. 1 of the ICCPR and ICESCR.

all aspects of their lives'.[46] Arguably, this latter account of democracy, which combines the basic idea of self-determination (popular sovereignty) with a vague notion of popular participation, will hardly be rejected today by any state. And yet, this still leaves unanswered whether international law embraces this – or, for that matter, any other – understanding of democracy as the basis of a global norm, the respect of which each state would now owe to 'the international community as a whole'.

10.3 Democracy and the international legal order: a rapprochement in three steps

10.3.1 Does the international legal order display any preference for a particular political (and concurrent constitutional) regime?

Given the international community's recent advocacy for democracy (along with human rights and the rule of law), the question above almost seems superfluous.[47] At least at the global level, however, clear-cut commitments to democracy can only be found in legally non-binding instruments. Hence, further evidence is needed to sustain the argument that the modern international legal order has accommodated a preference for democracy over other political regimes. Arguably, one area to turn to is international human rights law, where – at least formally – the relevance of democratic internal structures has long been recognized. Both of the 1966 Covenants, as well as key regional human rights instruments, explicitly employ the vision of a 'democratic society' as a normative standard to control the reasons under which certain rights may be restricted.[48] While it had hardly any practical significance under the adverse conditions of pre-1989 world politics, the criterion's inclusion in major human rights treaties can still be understood as a value judgement. In view of the spirit and purpose of the treaties, the reference point for lawful limitations of individual rights is not any society; it is a democratic society. International standards providing guidance on its interpretation were until recently scarce, but the 'democratic society clause' appears to have been an early affirmation in international treaty law of the more general and now widely supported principle that 'human rights, the rule of law and democracy are interlinked and mutually reinforcing'.[49]

46 World Conference on Human Rights, Vienna Declaration and Programme of Action (25 June 1993) UN Doc. A/CONF.157/23 (12 July 1993), para. 8.

47 See World Conference on Human Rights (n. 46); United Nations Millennium Declaration (n. 12), para. 24; World Summit Outcome (n. 42), para. 119.

48 See arts. 14(1), 21, 22(2) ICCPR; arts. 4, 8(1) ICESCR; arts. 15, 16, 22, 32 of the American Convention of Human Rights; arts. 6(1), 8(2), 9(2), 10(2), 11(2) of the European Convention of Human Rights and Fundamental Freedoms.

49 See UNCHR, Interdependence between Democracy and Human Rights, Res. 2003/36 (23 April 2003) UN Doc. E/CN.4/RES/2003/36; World Summit Outcome (n. 42), para. 119; 'Support by the United Nations system of the efforts of Governments to promote and consolidate new or restored democracies', UNGA Res. 62/7 (8 November 2007) UN Doc. A/RES/62/7 preamble, paras. 4 and 5.

The belief that human rights are generally better protected in a democratic than an authoritarian, or otherwise non-democratic, constitutional setting is today also deeply entrenched in the normative fabric of the United Nations. The UN's engagement with democracy can no longer be understood in instrumental terms or as a means of achieving other primary UN objectives, such as the maintenance of international peace and security and universal respect for human rights and fundamental freedoms.[50] Though these aspects remain important, democracy is today viewed as a general good; or, in UN parlance, a 'universal core value and principle of the United Nations'.[51] It is true that UN activities in this area (electoral assistance, UNDP governance assistance, project support by the recently established Democracy Fund) usually require a request of the state concerned. Only if a situation gives rise to a threat or breach of international peace and security may the Security Council use its powers under Chapter VII of the Charter to authorize action in support of democracy, even if local consent is unavailable or unclear.[52] These rules, however, only apply to UN activities on the ground and to enforcement measures. Beyond that, UN bodies, including the General Assembly, are in no way barred from passing judgement on political and constitutional issues arising in a member state, from addressing the responsible government, or even from calling on other states to act in a particular manner vis-à-vis the state concerned. The Assembly's unrelenting calls for democratic transition in Myanmar,[53] or its recent condemnation of the disruption of the democratic and constitutional order in Honduras,[54] are just two of many examples confirming this point.

Admittedly, the UN's espousal of democratic principles is not entirely new. Even prior to 1989, it has been the driving force behind the international denunciation of fascist, colonial and racist regimes and thus, arguably, of some

50 See Charter of the United Nations arts. 1(1) (3) and 55 (c).

51 See UNGA Res. 62/7 (n. 49), para. 4. The resolution, which was adopted without a vote, was sponsored by states as diverse as Albania, Germany, Japan, Kuwait, Libya, Mali, Saudi Arabia and Thailand; UN Doc. 62/PV.46 (8 November 2007), 1.

52 The adoption by the Council of enforcement measures against regimes having seized power by way of a *coup d'état* against a democratically elected government (the Haiti scenario) is a case in point; the integration of a democracy component into the mandate of UNSC-authorized governance and state-building operations is another. On UN-backed 'pro-democratic interventions', see M. Byers and S. Chesterman, '"You, the People": Pro-Democratic Intervention in International Law', in G. H. Fox and B. R. Roth (eds.), *Democratic Governance and International Law* (Cambridge: Cambridge University Press, 2000), 259, 281; on the role of democracy in UN-led post-conflict reconstruction and state-building, see G. H. Fox, *Humanitarian Occupation* (Cambridge: Cambridge University Press, 2008), 52;

J. d'Aspremont, 'Post-Conflict Administrations as Democracy-Building Instruments' (2008/09) 9 *Chicago JIL* 1.

53 See UNGA Res. 59/263 (23 December 2004) UN Doc. A/RES/59/263, para. 3 lit (c) (m); UNGA Res. 61/232 (22 December 2006) UN Doc. A/RES/61/232, para. 4(a). These calls were made regardless of the fact that Myanmar is neither a party to the ICCPR nor to any other international convention containing an explicit right of citizens to political participation.

54 See UNGA Res. 63/301 (1 July 2009) UN Doc. A/RES/63/301, paras. 1 and 2.

of the most extreme negations of democratic governance.[55] The organization's latest emphasis on democracy, however, is of a different quality. This is no longer the selective outlawing of some particularly repulsive regimes (typically characterized by the systematic oppression and disfranchisement of large parts of the population) by an institution that otherwise remains strictly committed to the principle of political and ideological neutrality. Rather, two decades into the post-Cold War era, democracy has ascended to a core principle of the UN and is now advocated vis-à-vis all member states. Given the near-universal membership of the UN, these developments cannot remain without effect for the international legal order as a whole. At a minimum, they support the view that domestic constitutional issues, including the origin and structure of government, are increasingly becoming 'internationalized' and have thus ceased to be dogmatically regarded by the international community as 'matters which are essentially within the domestic jurisdiction of any state'.[56]

10.3.2 Provided democracy is the preferred political regime, does the international legal order embrace a normative minimum standard of democracy?

As already indicated, no generally agreed definition of democracy can be identified at the global level of international cooperation and lawmaking.[57] Indeed, the mantra that, 'while all democracies share common features, there is no one universal model of democracy' runs through almost all UN documents on democracy and its promotion since the adoption of UNGA Resolution 55/96 (2000).[58] At the same time, an international normative framework for democratic governance has clearly taken shape in recent years. Rooted to a large extent in the existing international human rights canon, it sets out some of the basic components regarded by the international community as indispensable for any democratic constitutional order. According to a formula used both by the UNGA and the UN Commission on Human Rights (in resolutions which in neither case provoked any explicit protest):

55 See C. C. Joyner, 'The United Nations: Strengthening an International Norm', in P. J. Schraeder (ed.), *Exporting Democracy: Rhetoric vs. Reality* (London: Lynne Rienner, 2002), 147; Farer (n. 8), 35.

56 This does not answer the question about how far, in terms of international law, foreign actors may go in promoting democratic structures of government. See C. J. Tams, *Enforcing Obligations Erga Omnes in International Law* (Cambridge: Cambridge University Press, 2005), 220; d'Aspremont (n. 8), 294; Petersen (n. 8), 177.

57 See (n. 43). See also G. H. Fox, 'Democracy, Right to', in R. Wolfrum (ed.), *The Max Planck Encyclopedia of Public International Law* (online edn) (Oxford: Oxford University Press, 2008) (at: www.mpepil.com; accessed 1 December 2009, para. 12); P. R. Baehr, 'Democracy and the Right to Political Participation', in D. P. Forsythe (ed.), *Encyclopedia of Human Rights*, vol. I (Oxford: Oxford University Press, 2009), 487.

58 UNGA Res. 55/96 (n. 41), preamble, para. 8.

> the essential elements of democracy include respect for human rights and fundamental freedoms, inter alia, freedom of association and peaceful assembly and of expression and opinion, and the right to take part in the conduct of public affairs, directly or through freely chosen representatives, to vote and to be elected at genuine periodic free elections by universal and equal suffrage and by secret ballot guaranteeing the free expression of the will of the people, as well as a pluralistic system of political parties and organization, respect for the rule of law, the separation of powers, the independence of the judiciary, transparency and accountability in public administration, and free, independent and pluralistic media.[59]

Differences in detail notwithstanding, there is a striking degree of convergence between the 'essential elements of democracy', as defined by the UN, and the democracy-related criteria elaborated by other intergovernmental institutions.[60] Obviously, this does not end debates over the precise form of democracy in diverse social and cultural settings. In light of recent standard-setting processes within the UN and other fora, however, it is also evident that the meaning of references in various international instruments to 'global standards of democracy',[61] 'universally recognized democratic principles'[62] or 'international democratic standards'[63] is no longer obscure. Though most UN and regional documents dealing with democracy and democratization are formally non-binding, they nonetheless reflect a broad international consensus on some of the procedural and institutional building blocks of democratic governance. The result is not a comprehensive blueprint for democracy. Rather it is a normative minimum standard that provides guidance for

59 UNGA Res. 59/201 (20 December 2004) UN Doc. A/RES/59/201, para. 1 (adopted by 172 votes to none, with 15 abstentions); UNCHR Res. 2005/32 (19 April 2005) UN Doc. E/CN.4/2005/L.10/Add.11, para. 1 (adopted by 46 votes to none, with 7 abstentions).

60 See CSCE, Document of Copenhagen of the Meeting on the Human Dimension of the Conference for Security and Co-operation in Europe (29 June 1990) (1990) 29 ILM 1305; *Charter of Paris for a New Europe* (n. 3); The Commonwealth, Harare Commonwealth Declaration (20 October 1991) (at: www.thecommonwealth.org; accessed 1 December 2009); Inter-Parliamentary Union, Universal Declaration on Democracy (16 September 1997) (at: www.ipu.org/cnl-e/161-dem.htm; accessed 1 December 2009); Council for a Community of Democracies, Warsaw Declaration: Toward a Community of Democracies (27 June 2000) (2000) 39 ILM 1306; Organisation Internationale de la Francophonie, Bamako Declaration (3 November 2000) (at: www.francophonie.org/doc/txt-reference/decl_bamako_2000.pdf; accessed 1 December 2009); OAS, Inter-American Democratic Charter (11 September 2001) (2001) 40 ILM 1289; African Union, African Charter on Democracy, Elections and Governance (30 January 2007) (at: www.africa-union.org/root/au/Documents/Treaties/treaties.htm; accessed 1 December 2009).

61 The New Partnership for Africa's Development (NEPAD) (October 2001), para. 79 (at: www.nepad.org/home/lang/en; accessed 1 December 2009).

62 Agreement amending the Partnership Agreement between the members of the African, Caribbean and Pacific Group of States, of the one part, and the European Community and its Member States, of the other part, signed in Cotonou on 23 June 2000 (25 July 2005) EU Doc. [2005] OJ L 209/27, art. 9(2).

63 UNSC Presidential Statement 50 (2005) UN Doc. S/PRST/2005/50.

international actors in those instances in which they are called upon to support a country's democratic transition. Moreover, it can be used to judge adherence by states to general commitments accepted by them regarding the promotion and protection of democratic governance.

10.3.3 Provided an international minimum standard of democracy exists, do any of its components have a universal legal character?

Asserting the existence of an increasingly coherent international framework for democracy does not imply the argument that it is, in its entirety, of a universal legal character. In fact, while the international system has recently generated a fairly clear picture of at least the core elements of democratic government, this cannot be taken as evidence that (all) these elements are now also binding on states as a matter of international law. Even if the content of the relevant international framework is restricted to the 'essential elements of democracy' listed in UNGA Resolution 59/201 (2004)[64] the question remains as to which of the criteria included in the Assembly's list can be considered as reflecting universal legal obligations rather than merely being programmatic or 'soft' legal standards and principles.

In 1999, in a remarkable resolution entitled 'Promotion of the right to democracy', the UN Commission on Human Rights (UNCHR) pointed to 'the large body of international law and instruments…which confirm the right to full participation and the other fundamental democratic rights and freedoms inherent in any democratic society'.[65] Ten years later, the UN Secretary-General similarly explained that the organization's position on democracy was based on 'universal principles, norms and standards' derived, in particular, from 'references to essential democratic underpinnings' in the preamble and Article 1 of the UN Charter ('life in larger freedom', 'self-determination', 'human rights, 'fundamental freedoms') as well as provisions on political rights contained in the UDHR and subsequent UN treaties and instruments.[66] If these statements of the UNCHR and the Secretary-General are accepted, the question of whether segments of an overall larger international framework for democracy are legally binding on states is ultimately a question about the universality of human rights; or at least of those rights which, taken

64 See (n. 59).

65 See UNCHR Res. 1999/57 (27 April 1999) UN Doc. E/CN.4/RES/1999/57 preamble, para. 5 (adopted by 51 votes to none with 2 abstentions). A Cuban initiative against the title of the resolution was subject to a separate vote but eventually defeated by 28 votes to 12, with 13 abstentions; UNCHR, 55th Session, Summary Record of the 57th Meeting (27 April 1999) UN Doc. E/CN.4/1999/SR.57.

66 See 'Guidance Note of the Secretary-General on Democracy' (September 2009) 1–2 (at: www.un.org/democracyfund/Docs/UNSG Guidance Note on Democracy.pdf; accessed 1 December 2009). The Secretary-General also recalled that the commitment to support democracy was accepted by 'all the world's governments' at the 2005 World Summit (*ibid.* 2).

together, form the political part of the often quoted 'International Bill of Rights'.[67]

Arguably, among the 'fundamental democratic rights' in question, the right of citizens to take part in the government of their country – particularly (though not exclusively) through periodic and free elections – takes the most prominent place.[68] Has the right, the normative roots of which go back to Article 21 UDHR, evolved into a rule of customary international law? Admittedly, addressing this question is a somewhat daunting task, not only because it has caused such a formidable rift in international legal scholarship but also because, in a way, it threatens to reopen the Pandora's box of the entire international human rights discourse. Are all human rights truly universal, not only in a moral and political, but also in a legal sense? If this is rejected, have at least some of the rights contained in the International Bill of Rights been transformed, through subsequent practice and opinio juris, into customary legal entitlements (as the prevailing doctrine seems to hold)? If so, is the right to vote and to be elected at genuine elections among those entitlements?

It could be argued that these questions have lost much of their provocative nature since, as of late 2009, more than 80 per cent of all states had become parties to the ICCPR.[69] It is generally accepted that multilateral treaties may be considered elements of state practice relevant for determining the existence of a rule of customary international law.[70] Of course, for such a rule to be actually established, additional evidence of relevant practice and opinio juris is needed.[71] As the International Court of Justice has confirmed, such evidence may, under certain circumstances, be deduced from the attitude of states towards certain UN General Assembly resolutions. Their content, as well as 'the conditions of [their] adoption', are viewed by the Court as particularly relevant in determining the significance of such resolutions for the

67 The 'International Bill of Rights' is commonly understood to consist of the human rights-related provisions of the UN Charter, the UDHR, and the two UN Human Rights Covenants (ICCPR, ICESCR).

68 According to the Human Rights Committee (the monitoring body established within the framework of the ICCPR), the right to political participation 'lies at the core of democratic government based on the consent of the people'; Human Rights Committee, CCPR General Comment No. 25 (12 July 1996), para. 1 (at: www.unhchr.ch/tbs/doc.nsf; accessed 1 December 2009).

69 See (n. 20). The Covenant expressly affirms the right to political participation in art. 25, a provision widely seen as the spiritual child of art. 21 UDHR; see H. Steiner, 'Political Participation as a Human Right' (1988) 1 *Harvard Human Rights Yearbook* 77, 79; Farer (n. 8), 37; M. Nowak, *UN Covenant on Civil and Political Rights – CCPR Commentary* (2nd edn, Kehl: Engel, 2005), 567.

70 See T. Treves, 'Customary International Law', in R. Wolfrum (ed.), *Max Planck Encyclopedia of Public International Law* (online edn) (Oxford: Oxford University Press, 2008), para. 47 (at: www.mpepil.com; accessed 1 December 2009). According to the ICJ, 'multilateral conventions may have an important role to play in recording and defining rules deriving from custom, or indeed in developing them' (*Continental Shelf* (*Libyan Arab Jamahiriya* v. *Malta*) (Judgement) [1985] ICJ Rep. 20, para. 27).

71 See Continental Shelf (n. 70); specifically regarding democratic rights: Wheatley (n. 8), 232–3; Varayudej (n. 8), 17; N. Petersen, 'The Principle of Democratic Teleology in International Law' (2008) 34 *Brook JIL* 33, 56.

establishment of the existence of a general rule of international law.[72] In considering the customary legal potential of the right to political participation, due account must be accorded to the fact that the General Assembly has consistently recalled, in a 'series of resolutions',[73] both 'the principle that the will of the people, as expressed through periodic and genuine elections, shall be the basis of government authority' and 'the right freely to choose representatives through periodic and genuine elections'. Open rejections of these explicit affirmations of Article 21 UDHR have recently not only dwindled in numbers – they have practically disappeared.[74] In contrast, the notorious so-called 'Respecting Resolutions', which typically reiterate 'the richness and diversity of democratic political systems and models of free and fair electoral processes in the world', have never received similarly strong support among UN members.[75] Perhaps tellingly, the practice of adopting these resolutions in tandem with the UNGA's biennial 'Enhancing Resolutions' recently appears to have come to a general halt.[76]

It could of course be argued that, when assessing the relevance of state conduct for the creation of customary international law, a distinction must be drawn between the (voting) behaviour of states in international organizations and their actual practice 'at home'. While broad support for affirmations by UN bodies of the right to vote and be elected at genuine elections may be indicative of the existence of relevant opinio juris, some states are still loath to hold truly free and fair elections. This could be taken as evidence that a respective customary rule has not yet emerged, or that it applies only to states which in practice have indicated acceptance of the rule by actually allowing

72 See *Legality of the Threat or Use of Nuclear Weapons* (Advisory Opinion) [1996] ICJ Rep. 226, para. 70.

73 As the ICJ noted 'a serious of resolutions may show the gradual evolution of the *opinio juris* required for the establishment of a new rule' (*ibid.*).

74 UNGA Res. 64/155 (18 December 2009) UN Doc. A/RES/64/155 (without a vote); UNGA Res. 62/150 (18 December 2007) UN Doc. A/RES/62/150 (adopted by 182 votes to none, with 2 abstentions); and UNGA Res. 60/162 (16 December 2005) UN Doc. A/RES/60/162 (adopted by 182 votes to none, with 1 abstention) are the three most recent examples. The fact that these so-called 'Enhancing Resolutions' (on the role of the UN in enhancing the effectiveness of the principle of periodic and genuine elections) consistently confirm that electoral assistance is only provided at the request of the state concerned does not affect the significance of the UNGA's affirmation of the gist of art. 21 UDHR. Nothing in these resolutions indicates that the principle's validity is limited to states that request UN electoral assistance. The Assembly only clarified that, in light of the sovereignty and territorial integrity of states, no assistance is provided by the UN without explicit domestic consent.

75 See, for instance, UNGA Res. 60/164 (16 December 2005) UN Doc. A/RES/60/164 (adopted by 110 votes to 6, with 61 abstentions); UNGA Res. 58/189 (22 December 2003) UN Doc. A/RES/58/189 (adopted by 111 votes to 10, with 55 abstentions); UNGA Res. 56/154 (19 December 2001) UN Doc. A/RES/56/154 (adopted by 99 votes to 10, with 59 abstentions).

76 In a deviation from earlier practice, no 'Respecting Resolution' has accompanied the 2007 and 2009 'Enhancing Resolutions' of the UNGA. In their latest available versions, however, even the 'Respecting Resolutions' have explicitly reaffirmed art. 21 UDHR, the wording of which was literally repeated in the resolution' operative part. See UNGA Res. 60/164 (n. 75), para. 7 and UNGA Res. 58/189 (n. 75), para. 7.

for genuine periodic elections; whereas states that do not and that also have not accepted any treaty obligations in this respect, would have a valid claim to be regarded as 'persistent objectors'.[77] Upon closer inspection, however, these approaches are not compelling. First, it must be recalled that the practice relevant for the formation of customary international law has to be 'general' (and not universal) and must therefore neither necessarily include all states nor be entirely homogeneous.[78] Second, it is widely recognized that a state can be considered a persistent objector only if it has consistently and clearly expressed its opposition to the rule in question during the process of its formation.[79] Given these strict requirements for the application of the doctrine, it seems highly problematic to regard as persistent objectors to the right to political participation states that have repeatedly acquiesced in international documents affirming the universal nature of all human rights in the clearest conceivable terms.[80] The truism that these documents are as such not legally binding is irrelevant; what counts is that they express a collective interest of the international community against which no state has explicitly 'objected'.

Even if one is willing to accept the customary law character of the principle of periodic and genuine elections, the question arises whether there also exists a generally shared understanding as to how exactly this norm is to be interpreted. After all, while genuine elections must certainly be 'by universal and equal suffrage', 'held by secret ballot' and 'free' from any form of coercion, neither Article 21 UDHR nor Article 25 ICCPR, explicitly require a pluralistic electoral process. In fact, it was precisely the provisions' indeterminacy upon which the former Soviet Union and its allies (later joined by a number of African and Asian states) had based their claim that single-party elections were fully compatible with the UDHR and their obligations under the ICCPR.[81] Clearly, this anti-liberal reading of the respective provisions has lost most of its former supporters and, as far as the Covenant is concerned, is now also firmly rejected by the Human Rights

77 See d'Aspremont (n. 8), 290–1 who argues that, while the holding of free and fair elections can be seen today as a customary international law obligation, China and certain states in the Middle East and South-East Asia are, based on the persistent objector rule, effectively exempted from it.

78 Art. 38, para. 1(b) of the Statute of the ICJ defines international custom as 'evidence of a *general practice* accepted as law' (emphasis added).

79 See *Fisheries Case* (*United Kingdom* v. *Norway*) ICJ Rep. 1951, 131; I. Brownlie, *Principles of Public International Law*, 6th edn (Oxford: Oxford University Press, 2003), 11. The persistent objector thesis is viewed with a heavy dose of scepticism by a number of scholars. See Treves (n. 70), para. 39; J. I. Charney, 'Universal International Law' (1993) 87 AJIL 529, 538. According to Shaw, 'constant protest on the part of a particular state when reinforced by the acquiescence of other states might create a recognized exception to the rule, *but it will depend on a great extent on the facts of the situation and views of the international community*' (M. N. Shaw, *International Law* (6th edn, Cambridge: Cambridge University Press, 2008), 91 (emphasis added)).

80 See World Conference on Human Rights (n. 46), para. 5; UNGA Res. 63/116 (10 December 2008), UN Doc. A/RES/63/116, para. 6.

81 See Steiner (n. 69), 91; Roth (n. 32), 329–32.

Committee.[82] Moreover, political pluralism is a fundamental criterion used by virtually all organizations in the area of international election monitoring in order to assess whether a given electoral process was 'free and fair'.[83] In referring to the ideological contestation at the time of the Covenant's adoption and the ambiguity of the right to political participation resulting from it, Roth however argued that it is difficult to justify an interpretation of 'genuine' elections that 'simply excludes the openly espoused understandings of non-liberal-democratic signatories'.[84] The evaluation standards used by election observers were not formally developed within any human rights treaty system and neither global nor regional treaties would provide for election monitoring to enforce their norms. Roth therefore denies that their application by organizations engaged in international election monitoring qualifies as 'subsequent practice'[85] relevant to the interpretation of Article 25 ICCPR.[86]

If the focus is on a historic interpretation of the norm and if the relevance of the standard-setting practice of election monitoring missions for treaty-based participatory rights is looked at in isolation from other developments in this area, Roth may have a point. Eventually, however, the persuasiveness of his arguments is weakened when one considers the broader international picture. Because of its universal membership, the UN is once again the preferred forum to turn to if the aim is to look for new or modified positions held by the community of states in respect of unspecified international principles and rules, provided relevant practice exists. With regard to the principle of genuine elections, such practice indeed exists – and it is no longer limited to the application of electoral standards vis-à-vis states that have explicitly consented to UN observer missions. For its part, the General Assembly made it clear in Resolution 55/96 (against which no direct protest was recorded) that the 'genuineness' of elections requires, inter alia, enabling the political opposition to participate in the electoral process on a basis of equality and non-discrimination.[87] The UNCHR clearly shared this position.[88] More recently, even the UN Security Council upheld this approach; for

82 See Fox (n. 26), 55–9; Nowak (n. 69), 575, 584.

83 See for an in-depth account, G. S. Goodwin-Gill, *Free and Fair Elections* (2nd edn, Geneva: Inter-Parliamentary Union, 2006).

84 Roth (n. 32), 332.

85 See Vienna Convention on the Law of Treaties (23 May 1969) (1969) 8 ILM 679, art. 31(3)(b).

86 Roth (n. 32), 342.

87 See UNGA Res. 55/96 (n. 41), para. 1(d)(iv).

88 See UNCHR Res. 2005/32 (n. 59), para. 2.

instance regarding Haiti in 2005[89] or Zimbabwe in 2008.[90] In sum, it seems clear that the international community simply no longer recognizes elections as 'genuine' if political groups peacefully opposing the incumbent regime are unduly inhibited from participating on equal terms in the electoral process.

10.4 Concluding remarks

In his account of democracy as an emerging global norm, Thomas Franck did not concern himself with the intricacies involved in the identification of customary international law in any detail. For him, the growing number of states that are committed by their own constitutional systems to the holding of periodic multiparty elections, combined with the solid entrenchment of participatory rights in global and regional human rights instruments and an increasingly coherent international practice regarding their interpretation, provided sufficient evidence to bolster the argument that democracy, 'while not yet fully word made law, is rapidly becoming in our time a normative rule of the international system'.[91] If one sticks to the Franckian conception of the democratic entitlement, it may well be concluded that its ascendance into 'fully word made law' is now almost complete. According to Franck, the right to democracy does not involve a 'Lockian or Montesquieuian ideal', but rather the fairly modest claim that 'international law protects the right of people, anywhere, to a legitimate political process, which is one in which the people are given an opportunity to participate in their national process of value-formation and decision-making'.[92]

If it is indeed understood in these narrow terms, democracy's status as a customary norm is now well grounded in a modern, 'post-colonial' interpretation of the right to (internal) self-determination and the ever-increasing normative strength of the principle that the will of the people, as expressed through genuine periodic elections, shall be the basis of government authority. Eventually, the problem with this approach is less one of content but rather one of terminology. On a normative basis, states and international institutions have come to understand democracy not in the purely electoral terms suggested by Franck but rather in the 'Lockian or Montesquieuian'

89 In June 2005, on the occasion of the extension of the mandate of the UN Stabilization Mission in Haiti (MINUSTAH), the Council stressed that 'free and fair elections, open to all political parties that have renounced violence and with the broadest possible participation of the Haitian people, must take place in 2005'; UNSC Res. 1608 (22 June 2005), UN Doc. S/RES/1608 (2005), preamble, para. 3.

90 Following Zimbabwe's June 2008 presidential elections, the UNSC declared that 'violence and the restrictions on the political opposition have made it impossible for a free and fair election to take place on 27 June'. The Council also called on Harare to cooperate fully with all efforts 'aimed at finding a peaceful way forward … that allows a legitimate government to be formed that reflects the will of the Zimbabwean people' (UNSC Presidential Statement 23 (2008) UN Doc. S/PRST/2008/23, paras. 3–4).

91 Franck 1992 (n. 6), 46.

92 Franck 1994 (n. 6), 82.

terms he excluded as possible determinants of the democratic entitlement. To verify this, one only needs to look, among numerous other examples, at the General Assembly's inventory of 'essential elements of democracy', cited above;[93] or, in more practical terms, to the democracy-related activities of the UN in the field of post-conflict reconstruction and state-building.[94] This is not to say that a global consensus on any specific interpretation of democracy has emerged; rather that international practice has coalesced into a widely shared understanding that democracy entails more than the holding of elections at regular intervals.[95] Grand assertions regarding the emergence of democracy as a global norm thus seem to be beside the point, when all that the norm is said to entail is one (albeit highly important) element of a broader, yet so far mostly programmatic international vision of democracy.

It is true, however, that international law speaks the 'language of democracy' in a number of areas, from the protection of human rights to membership in international organizations, international development assistance, international territorial administration, and the recognition of states and governments.[96] Although states are not legally required to organize themselves along liberal–democratic lines (understood in the 'Lockian or Montesquieuian' terms generally promoted today by the international community), these developments contribute to democracy's ongoing normative consolidation as a major principle of the contemporary international order. Perhaps the best way to describe this process is by using the political science notion of 'international regimes'. According to a standard definition developed by Stephan Krasner, an international regime can be defined as a set of implicit or explicit principles, rules and procedures around which actors' expectations converge in a given area of international relations.[97] Given the recent wide-ranging efforts of various international actors at defining, promoting and (under certain circumstances) safeguarding a normative minimum standard of democracy, it does not seem far-fetched to interpret this as the gradual emergence of an international regime on domestic democratic governance.[98]

93 UNGA Res. 59/201 (n. 59). See also the regional documents on democracy cited above (n. 60).

94 See Fox (n. 52), 52, 154; C. Stahn, *The Law and Practice of International Territorial Administration* (Cambridge: Cambridge University Press, 2008), 266, 751.

95 This is also confirmed by more than twenty inter-governmental and international non-governmental organizations concerned with the monitoring of elections in the 'Declaration of Principles for International Election Observation' (adopted 27 October 2005) (at: http://ec.europa.eu/europeaid/observer/declaration_of_principles_code_of_conduct_en.pdf; accessed 1 December 2009, paras. 1 and 2).

96 See R. Burchill, 'Introduction', in R. Burchill (ed.), *Democracy and International Law* (Aldershot: Ashgate, 2006), xi, xxiii.

97 See S. D. Krasner, 'Structural Causes and Regime Consequences: Regimes as Intervening Variables', in S. D. Krasner (ed.), *International Regimes* (Ithaca, NY: Cornell University Press, 1983), 2.

98 For a similar argument, see UNCHR, 'Promotion and Consolidation of Democracy', Expanded working paper by Mr Manuel Rodríguez Cuadros on the measures provided in the various international human rights instruments for the promotion and consolidation of democracy; UN Doc. E/CN.4/Sub.2/2002/36 (10 June 2002), para. 91.

The contours of this unfinished and evolving regime are not yet settled. As is typical for international regimes, it consists of principles, rules and standards with varying degrees of 'normativity'. Situated at its core is the principle of genuine periodic elections, which – based on a growing amount of circumstantial evidence – may be said to have evolved into a customary international law rule. Also endowed with a comparatively high degree of normativity are the political freedoms functionally associated with genuine elections; e.g. the freedoms of assembly, association, expression and opinion. This group of rather specific entitlements is followed by some of the more general principles of democracy; e.g. the rule of law, the separation of powers and media pluralism. While to some extent rooted in international human rights law, they do not constitute clearly defined rules of conduct and are therefore characterized by a considerably lesser degree of normativity. Finally, an international regime on democratic governance would also seem to embrace criteria generally associated with the notion of 'good governance'; e.g. transparency, accountability, civil society participation, civil control of the military, etc. However, since these standards are still largely undefined and only incoherently applied by international actors,[99] they are – contrary to other components of the emerging regime – effectively useless as global normative benchmarks for a meaningful evaluation of state behaviour.

99 See J. N. Maogoto, 'The "Good Governance" Crusade in the Third World' (2007) 9 ICLR 375.

11 International law and East Asia's regional order

The strengthening of a fundamental institution

Pablo Pareja-Alcaraz

Over the last two decades, the rise of the People's Republic of China and East Asia has given rise to an intense debate on its consequences for United States' hegemony, the distribution of global power and the dynamics of an international system leaning towards multipolarity.[1] Some authors have gone farther, pointing out that this 'global power shift'[2] also represents an unprecedented challenge to the role of international law as the key institution of the current international order. According to these analysts, this transformation will eventually relegate international law to a secondary position, similar to that which it held during the balance of power system of the nineteenth century or the bipolar system of the Cold War.[3] This chapter argues against such interpretations, positing that the rise of Beijing and other East Asian capitals over the twenty-first century will not necessarily lead to the marginalization of international law. Indeed, since the early 1950s, international law has been one of the fundamental institutions of East Asia's regional order.[4]

1 For further reading on this debate, see R. K. Betts, 'Wealth, Power and Instability: East Asia and the United States after the Cold War' (1993/94) 18(3) *International Security* 34–77; A. L. Friedberg, 'Ripe for Rivalry' (1993/94) 18(3) *International Security* 5–33; G. Segal, 'East Asia and the Constrainment of China' (1996) 20(4) *International Security* 107–35; R. Bernstein and R. H. Munro, *The Coming Conflict with China* (New York, NY: Knopf, 1997); T. J. Christensen, 'Posing Problems without Catching Up: China's Rise and Challenges for US Security Policy' (2001) 25(4) *International Security* 5–40; I. J. Alastair, 'Is China a Status Quo Power' (2003) 27(4) *International Security* 5–56; B. Zheng, 'China's Peaceful Rise to Great-Power Status' (2005) 84(5) *Foreign Affairs* 18–24; S. Shirk, *China: Fragile Superpower* (New York, NY: Oxford University Press, 2007); G. J. Ikenberry, 'The Rise of China and the Future of the West: Can the Liberal System Survive?' (2008) 87(1) *Foreign Affairs* 23–37; C. F. Bergsten and others, *China's Rise: Challenges and Opportunities* (Washington, DC: Peterson Institute for International Economics, 2008).

2 J. Hoge, 'A Global Power Shift in the Making' (2004) 83(4) *Foreign Affairs* 2–7.

3 E. Posner and J. Yoo, 'International Law and the Rise of China' (2006) 7 *Chicago JIL* 1–15.

4 Using the work of Hedley Bull and the recent work by Joseph M. Parent and Emily Erikson as a base, in this chapter regional order is interpreted as a *pattern of activity which limits the frequency and magnitude of violent interactions between the members of a particular region*. This definition contains three constitutive parts: (a) the prior existence of a system, that is, a set of two or more politically organized units which are relatively independent from each other but which interact with a certain degree of frequency and which influence each other and act as parts of a whole; (b) the regular repetition of a certain pattern of international activity which reduces unpredictability amongst members of the system; and (c) a quantitative and qualitative limitation of violence in relations. H Bull, *The Anarchical Society: A Study*

Leading on from these initial reflections, the following section provides a brief review of the process of constructing the regional order over the last seventy years. This brief coverage of how the regional order was established will help to interpret the second section, which analyses the structure and content of the constitutional base of this order, which international law rests on. In general terms, Christian Reus-Smit has defined this base as a coherent set of 'beliefs, principles and intersubjective norms' which help identify the legitimate actors interacting within the order and the parameters limiting their actions.[5] In analysing the main components of this group we contextualise the third and final section, which centres on the study of international law as a key institution within the regional order.

11.1 The process of constructing East Asia's regional order

The process leading to the construction of East Asia's current regional order and the anchoring of international law as a fundamental institution can be split into three different periods that, in spite of some overlap, can be viewed as following a chronological sequence. The formation period of this order started in December 1941 with the United States' entry into the Second World War after the Japanese attack on Pearl Harbor, and terminated in March 1955 with the ratification of its mutual defence agreement with Taiwan. This period witnessed the definition of the basic features of the new order, as well as the design of its most basic structure. The two main actors were the United States and, to a lesser extent, the Soviet Union, both fuelled by their ideological rivalry and their desire to expand the geographical areas under their influence. In parallel to the decolonization process, the confrontation between these two superpowers, their role in the First Indochina War, the occupation of Japan, the Korean War and the Chinese Civil War led to the configuration of the region's geopolitical organization. In addition, the United States' security strategy of hubs and spokes with its East Asian allies promoted bilateralism and international law as the two fundamental institutions of the emerging order. The consolidation period comprises the years between March 1955 and February 1972, when Washington and Beijing agreed on the first Shanghai Communiqué and embarked on the normalization of their bilateral relationship. Throughout this period the United States remained the most influential actor in shaping the regional order, whereas the Soviet Union's room for manoeuvre decreased. By renewing previous agreements and signing new ones with their respective allies, both superpowers reinforced bilateralism and international law as the order's fundamental institutions. In addition, the creation of the Association of Southeast Asian

of Order in World Politics (3rd edn, Basingstoke: Palgrave, 2002) 8, 16; J. M. Parent and E. Erikson, 'Anarchy, Hierarchy and Order' (2009) 22 *Cambridge Review of International Affairs* 129–45.

5 C. H. Reus-Smit, 'The Constitutional Structure of International Society and the Nature of Fundamental Institutions' (1997) 51 *Int'l Org.* 555, 566.

Nations (ASEAN) saw the birth of the order's norm of procedural justice, the so-called 'ASEAN way'.[6] Finally, the current adaptation period began with Nixon's visit to China in 1972. During this period the constitutional structure and fundamental institutions of East Asia's regional order finally took root. The traditional dominance of bilateralism, however, has been partially challenged by the advance of multilateralism.[7] In parallel, the United States has lost its absolute control over the process, and other state and non-state actors have gained prominence. Moreover, economic issues have made significant inroads into the regional agenda, thus contributing to the creation of new organizations and to the transformation of the former hegemonic order into a contractual one.

This contractual order is built on a regional system in which states share at least some minimal values based around the ideals of justice and equality, and within which there are some links of association between the component members. Each state maintains its own identity which differentiates it from other members of the order, but the links between the member states may give rise to a feeling of collective identity, even though this may be weak. The distribution of power within the system, on the other hand, is variable in nature; although states continue to maximize their own interests, at the same time they also seek out common interests through various principles, norms and institutions. The principles in question refer to 'beliefs of facts, causation and rectitude', while norms consist of 'standards of behaviour defined in terms of rights and obligations'.[8] The principles and norms are expressed through specific rules whose content and formulation have been precisely defined and which, when brought together, determine the framework and normative foundation of the system. The institutions are built on this foundation and can be defined as 'constant sets of formal and informal norms which prescribe patterns of behaviour, constrain actions and create expectations'.[9] The set of principles, norms and institutions determine the legitimacy or otherwise of possible courses of action and work as a limiting factor against the concentration

6 A. Acharya, 'Ideas, Identity, and Institution Building: From the "ASEAN Way" to the "Asia-Pacific Way"?' (1997) 10(3) *Pacific Review* 3–46.

7 J. Ravenhill, 'The New Bilateralism in the Asia-Pacific' (2003) 24 *Third World Quarterly* 299–317.

8 S. D. Krasner, 'Structural Causes and Regime Consequences: Regimes as Intervening Variables', in S. D. Krasner (ed.), *International Regimes* (Ithaca, NY: Cornell University Press, 1983), 2. In accordance with the ideas of M. Alagappa, the set of norms that guide the relations between states can be classified according to their nature (constitutive or regulative norms) or the purpose they serve in relation to the international order (norms of coexistence, coordination or collaboration). M. Alagappa (ed.), *Asian Security Order: Institutional and Normative Features* (Stanford, CA: Stanford University Press, 2003), 40.

9 R. O. Keohane, *International Institutions and State Power* (Boulder, CO: Westview Press, 1989), 3. Christian Reus-Smit posits that these institutions work to deal with two key problems which, according to Arthur Stein, hinder the construction and maintenance of the international order: the problems related to collaboration are associated with states seeking out common interests, and the coordination problems surround those situations in which collective action is essential in order to avoid certain consequences. C. H. Reus-Smit (n. 5), 557; A. Stein, *Why Nations Cooperate: Circumstance and Choice in International Relations* (Ithaca, NY: Cornell University Press, 1990), 39–44.

of power. In the short term, any concentration of power is made difficult as obligations are established for all states within the system and cooperation is fostered. In the medium and long term, a concentration of power is unattractive for actors within the system because there are costs for non-compliance with the laid-down obligations, thus reducing the incentives for states within the system to maximize their power. These principles, norms and institutions affect the interests and identities of all states within the system; furthermore, the fact that these states adhere to and observe the aforementioned principles, norms and institutions creates stability within the order. Finally, the regional order within East Asia differs from the broader international order, but both forms of order are compatible and they tend mutually to reinforce each other.

11.2 The constitutional base of East Asia's regional order

The base – or constitutional structure – of East Asia's regional order comprises three interconnected elements: a hegemonic belief with regard to the moral objective of a centralized and autonomous political organization, the organizational principle of sovereignty, and the norm of procedural justice.

11.2.1 The 'developmental' hegemonic belief with regard to the moral objective of the state

Since the beginning of the 1940s, it has been an accepted fact in East Asia that the autonomous and centralized state is the key and legitimate form of political organization within the regional system. Additionally, during the intervening period a hegemonic belief has taken hold that the moral role of the state is to promote and sustain economic development, so we can thus consider the state as being developmentalist. The main explanation behind the establishment of this belief among the countries which have led the gradual economic growth in the region lies in the central role played by governmental administrations in this process. This central role has traditionally rested on four complementary factors. The first factor relates to the existence of societies which were poorly organized and relatively weak, thus meaning there was no societal element to hold back the concentration of power in the hands of small government elites during the decades following the end of the Second World War. The armed conflicts of the 1940s and 1950s broke up the political and economic communities that had previously existed in East Asia. Furthermore, these conflicts gave rise to a more generalized worry regarding security that favoured the establishment of government administrations that were able coercively to maintain domestic stability and territorial integrity in the face of possible external attacks.[10] The second factor stems from the economic interests of certain groups within the elites; these groups had

10 R. Stubbs, 'What ever happened to the East Asian Developmental State? The Unfolding Debate' (2009) 22 *Pacific Review* 1, 6.

sufficient resources and influence so as to be able to push forward governmental policy and their own economic ideologies. Initially these groups were found around the Ministry of International Trade and Industry (MITI) in Japan in the early 1960s, but similar groups began appearing in the 1970s in Hong Kong, Taiwan, South Korea and Singapore, with others emerging later in Malaysia, the Philippines, Thailand and Indonesia.[11] The third factor is the centralizing impact of the communist threat on the United States' allies in East Asia. In most of these countries the population either did not oppose the concentration of power as a means of holding back the advance of communism or, in cases such as Singapore and Malaysia, was relatively supportive of this policy.[12] In all cases, the demands that came with the military alliances with Washington worked to strengthen state structures.[13] The fourth factor is the United States' aid and trade policy in the region. Between the end of the 1940s and the mid-1970s the United States' administration invested large sums of capital in East Asia, as well as opening up its own market to products from the region and purchasing numerous products and raw materials there in order to sustain its troops in the Korean and Vietnam Wars.[14]

The content of these factors, and their impact on the establishment of the developmental hegemonic belief as regards the moral objective of the state, have been altered by the end of the Cold War and the consequent transformation of the regional security scene. At the domestic level, democratization processes have been activated in the majority of East Asian economies and the communist threat no longer exists as a unifying element for government policies, which has resulted in a loss of support for the concentration of power in the hands of elites. At the regional level, the partial withdrawal of the United States from South-East Asia at the beginning of the 1990s, the gradual closing-off of the US market to Asian products and the reduction in US economic aid have led to the erosion of government elites and the traditional development model. At the global level, changes in the nature of capital flows and the growing power

11 J. Fallows, *Looking for the Sun: The Rise of the New East Asian Economies and Political System* (New York, NY: Pantheon, 1994). See also C. Johnson, *MITI and the Japanese Miracle: The Growth of Industrial Policy, 1925–1975* (Stanford, CA: Stanford University Press, 1982); K. E. Calder, 'Japanese Foreign Economic Policy Formation: Explaining the Reactive State' (1988) 40 *World Politics* 517–48; World Bank, *The East Asian Miracle: Economic Growth and Public Policy* (New York, NY: Oxford University Press, 1993), esp. ch. 2; P. Krugman, 'The Myth of Asia's Miracle' (1994) 73(6) *Foreign Affairs* 62–78; R. Wade, *Governing the Market: Economic Theory and the Role of Government in East Asian Industrialization* (Princeton, NJ: Princeton University Press, 2003); H.-J. Chang, *Globalisation, Economic Development & the Role of the State* (London: Zed Books, 2003).

12 M. J.-E. Woo-Cumings, 'National Security and the Rise of the DS in South Korea and Taiwan', in H. S. Rowen (ed.), *Behind East Asian Growth: The Political and Social Foundations of Prosperity* (London: Routledge, 1998), 319–37; T. Zhu, 'DSs and Threat Perception in Northeast Asia' (2002) 2(1) *Conflict, Security and Development* 5–29.

13 B. Cumings, 'The Origins and Development of the Northeast Asian Political Economy: Industrial Sectors, Product Cycles and Political Consequences' (1984) 38 *Int'l Org.* 1–40; M. Yahuda, *The International Politics of Asia-Pacific, 1945–1995* (London: Routledge, 1996), 9–10.

14 B. Harland, 'Whither East Asia?' (1993) 6 *Pacific Review* 9–16; R. Stubbs, *Rethinking Asia's Economic Miracle: The Political Economy of War, Prosperity and Crisis* (Basingstoke: Palgrave Macmillan, 2005).

of actors and authorities other than states have further accentuated this trend.[15] However, far from disappearing, the developmental hegemonic belief has continued to be relevant in all cases. On the one hand, the adhesion to traditional economic and trading practices on the part of regional economic agents, who benefited from the economic growth model between the mid-1960s and the end of the 1980s, has guaranteed the survival of this belief beyond any formal regulatory changes. On the other hand, the generally positive opinion held by East Asian societies with respect to their states as guarantors of security and providers of welfare over the same period has contributed to states maintaining their central role, albeit in a slightly weakened form. Finally, the survival of a complex network of regional interconnections built on multiple trading agreements and organizations has reinforced the influence of the government and economic elites, favouring the continuation of the status quo.[16]

In parallel to this, the last twenty years have seen the developmental hegemonic belief spread to countries which either did not participate, or only partially participated, in the gradual economic growth model of the Cold War. Vietnam and the People's Republic of China took on this belief in the mid-1980s, but it really started to take hold after the end of the Cold War, as the ideological conflicts that had previously dominated were greatly relaxed and communism was no longer a legitimising force.[17] The societies of Brunei, Laos and Cambodia, with much weaker state structures, have started to go down this route more recently.[18] In contrast, the societies of North Korea and Myanmar have not formed a similar link between the legitimacy of their governments and their capacity to promote and sustain economic development. In fact, the majority consider that the moral objective of the state is still connected to cultural and ideological factors.[19] The impact of these two

15 Stubbs (n. 10), 9–12.

16 *Ibid.* 12–13.

17 F. Chen, 'The Dilemma of Eudaemonic Legitimacy in Post-Mao China' (1997) 29 *Polity* 421–39; D. Phong and M. Beresford, *Authority Relations and Economic Decision-Making in Vietnam: An Historical Perspective* (Copenhagen: Nordic Institute for Asian Studies Publications, 1998); Y. Zheng, *Discovering Chinese Nationalism in China: Modernization, Identity and International Relations* (Cambridge: Cambridge University Press, 1999), esp. ch. 2; S. Zhao, 'China's Pragmatic Nationalism: Is It Manageable?' (2005) 29(1) *Washington Quarterly* 131–44; C. A. Thayer, 'Challenges to the Legitimacy of the Vietnamese One-Party State', presented at the conference 'The Search for Legitimacy: Managing the Consequences of Asian Development', Singapore, 27–8 July 2009.

18 M. Alagappa (ed.), *Political Legitimacy in Southeast Asia: The Quest for Moral Authority* (Stanford, CA: Stanford University Press, 1995); S. Narine, 'State Sovereignty, Political Legitimacy and Regional Institutionalism in the Asia-Pacific' (2005) 17 *Pacific Review* 423–50.

19 D. I. Steinberg, 'On Patterns of Political Legitimacy in North Korea', in S. S. Kim (ed.), *The North Korean System in the Post-Cold War Era* (New York, NY: Palgrave Macmillan, 2001), 87–113; A. Cheng, 'Political Legitimacy in Myanmar: The Ethnic Minority Dimension' (1997) 3 *Asian Security* 121–40; T. Maung Maung Than, *State Dominance in Myanmar: The Political Economy of Industrialization* (Singapore: Institute of Southeast Asian Studies, 2007), esp. ch. 9; D. I. Steinberg, '"Legitimacy" in Burma/Myanmar: Concepts and Implications', in N. Ganesan and K. Yin Hlaing (eds.), *Myanmar: State, Society and Ethnicity* (Singapore: Institute of Southeast Asian Studies, 2007), 109–42.

exceptions on the establishment of the developmental hegemonic belief in the regional order should not, however, be overestimated. In order to be legitimate, this belief must be accepted by the majority and must not be significantly questioned by the most powerful actors within the order, but it does not necessarily have to be shared by each and every one of the actors within the system.[20] In other words, for the belief in the moral objective of the state to be hegemonic does not imply that it must be universally and wholly accepted, nor that it be exclusive, as there is room for a certain degree of dissent.

11.2.2 The organizational principle of Westphalian-style sovereignty

Underlying the developmental hegemonic belief, the constitutional structure of East Asia's regional order includes the organizational principle of sovereignty, which is strongly influenced by Westphalian ideals. This sovereignty, as in all forms of contractual order, serves to 'differentiate political units on the basis of particularity and exclusivity, creating a system of territorially demarcated, autonomous centres of political authority'.[21] Compared with liberal and anti-utopian concepts,[22] the Westphalian idea of sovereignty is based around state authority and autonomy. The concept of authority refers to the right of the state to govern the population within a demarcated territorial area, and the state provides a guarantee to defend both its people and its land.[23] Autonomy, on the other hand, claims independence and equality for this state within the system.[24] In East Asia, both concepts are viewed as inseparable to such an extent that, as Christopher Clapham and Shaun Narine have pointed out, for most countries in the region 'authority without autonomy is an empty sovereignty'.[25] Both concepts are also fiercely defended by government elites in the region, which has traditionally been

20 Reus-Smit (n. 5), 566–7.

21 *Ibid*. 567.

22 Following the classification set out by Takashi Inoguchi, the liberal or 'Philadelphian' concept of sovereignty is constructed around the popular nature of sovereignty and the dilemma surrounding whether or not this should be promoted and exported to all the states within the system, while the anti-utopian concept is based on the idea of incomplete sovereignty or of loss of sovereignty and is expressed in the resistance of some states and cultures to yield to Western attempts to impose liberal values and the logic of globalization on them. T. Inoguchi, 'Peering into the Future by Looping Back: The Westphalian, Philadelphian and Anti-utopian Paradigms' (1999) 1 *International Studies Review* 173–91; T. Inoguchi and P. Bacon, 'Sovereignties: Westphalian, Liberal and Anti-utopian' (2001) 1 *International Relations of the Asia-Pacific* 285–304.

23 R. Jackson, 'Sovereignty in World Politics: A Glance at the Conceptual and Historical Landscape', in R. Jackson (ed.), *Sovereignty at the Millennium* (Malden: Blackwell, 1999), 9–34.

24 S. D. Krasner, 'Problematic Sovereignty', in S. D. Krasner (ed.), *Problematic Sovereignty* (New York, NY: Columbia University Press, 2001), 1–23.

25 C. H. Clapham, 'Sovereignty in the Third World State', in R. Jackson (ed.), *Sovereignty at the Millennium* (Malden: Blackwell, 1999), 100–15; S. Narine (n. 18), 429.

evidenced in a strong belief in non-interference in the domestic affairs of other states.[26]

This concept began to take hold in the region in the mid-nineteenth century, because of intervention by Western powers in North-East Asia and because Japan, China and Korea became sovereign states.[27] These three countries took the principle of sovereignty on board more for reasons of pragmatism than conviction, though the process took on its own characteristics in each case. In Japan, the government elites clung onto the Westphalian concept of sovereignty because of their fear of a confrontation with Western powers, as well as seeing sovereignty as a way of guaranteeing their hold over any future territorial expansions. In China, the widely held conception of the governing elite as a political and moral entity that was hierarchically superior to all others, coupled with certain deeply rooted principles and institutions from the previous order, meant that the elites were less predisposed to the idea. However, the elites were able to meet their needs through the formal acceptance of sovereignty alongside the informal continuance of some more traditional practices, mostly based in Confucianism. In Korea, it was impossible to abandon these practices, either formally or informally, because of their strong links to government legitimacy; this heavily limited the elites' scope of action. In the medium term, this limitation led to absorption into the Japanese Empire and, conversely, to a gradual acceptance of the Westphalian concept of sovereignty.[28]

The spread of the principle of sovereignty to South-East Asia came about later, during the first half of the twentieth century. The dependence on colonial hierarchies and the development of state structures by colonial metropolises during this period incited the rise of nationalist feeling.[29] Meanwhile, the experience of their neighbours to the north further encouraged the development of nationalism, as well as fostering a growing regional hostility towards the West. This brought about a growing belief in sovereignty as a means for achieving independence through a process that Hendrik Spruyt

26 Having borne witness to the deeply rooted nature of this phenomenon throughout East Asia, D. Dickens and G. Wilson-Roberts have shown that it is more strongly emphasized in the countries of South-East Asia than in those of North-East Asia and they have suggested that this divergence could be explained by the distinct colonial traditions of these countries, the differing degree of consolidation of the state structures in each sub-region and the variable geopolitical weight of each of these within contemporary international society. D. Dickens and G. Wilson-Roberts (eds.), *Non-Intervention and State Sovereignty in the Asia-Pacific* (New Zealand: Centre for Strategic Studies/China Centre for International Studies/Institute of Strategic and International Studies, 2000); J. Funston, 'ASEAN and the Principle of Non-intervention: Practice and Prospects', in D. Dickens and G. Wilson-Roberts (eds.), *Non-Intervention and State Sovereignty in the Asia-Pacific* (New Zealand: Centre for Strategic Studies/China Centre for International Studies/Institute of Strategic and International Studies, 2000), 9–22.

27 S. D. Krasner, 'Organized Hypocrisy in 19th Century East Asia' (2001) 1 *International Relations of Asia Pacific* 173–97.

28 *Ibid.*

29 Alagappa (n. 18).

has labelled as 'ironic'.[30] The irony comes from the fact that it was the refusal on the part of the European metropolizes to grant their colonies sovereignty that led the latter to rebel, which saw them adopting the principle of sovereignty within their discourse in order to demand independence. The concept of sovereignty thus became universalized, as did the European organizational basis of Westphalian sovereignty.

Once it had spread throughout East Asia, the establishment of Westphalian sovereignty as part of the constitutional structure of the regional order took place during the second half of the twentieth century. Three factors contributed to this process. First, memories of the Second World War and the wars of independence lived on within societies of the region. In a context shaped by instability and ideological rivalry between communism and capitalism, these memories led to an attachment to sovereignty as a means of guaranteeing security. The second factor was the deeply-rooted belief in nationalism and anti-colonialism within these societies, which was occasionally instrumentalized by leaders of the newly independent states in order to consolidate their authority.[31] The third factor relates to the impact of the cultural, ethnic and religious diversity of the majority of East Asian states on the political legitimacy of their governments: right from the start, this political legitimacy was conditional on governments' capacity to maintain national unity. Looking to guarantee their permanence in power, the governments of the region resorted to the strengthening of state structures and, just as in other regions of the Third World, made the concept of Westphalian sovereignty the central theme of their discourse.[32]

In the post-Cold War period, the arrival of growing communal and transnational pressures, driven forward by globalization, has weakened the hegemonic position of the concept of sovereignty in East Asia. The communal pressures are linked to the claims of groups which operate within states. As has been witnessed in the cases of the province of Aceh in Indonesia and the regions of Tibet and Xinjiang in China, these question the capacity and legitimacy of central governments to exercise their authority over the entirety of their territory. The transnational pressures derive from the emergence of actors and authorities other than the state and the rise of

30 H. Spruyt, 'The End of Empire and the Extension of the Westphalian System: The Normative Basis of the Modern State Order' (2000) 2(2) *International Studies Review* 65–92.

31 C.-I. Moon and C. H. Chun, 'Sovereignty: Dominance of the Westphalian Concept and Implications for Regional Security', in M. Alagappa (ed.), *Asian Security Order: Institutional and Normative Features* (Stanford, CA: Stanford University Press, 2003), 106–37.

32 M. Alagappa (n. 18); M. Ayoob, *The Third World Security Predicament* (Boulder, CO: Lynne Rienner, 1995), 'Subaltern Realism: International Relations Theory Meets the Third World', in S. G. Neuman (ed.), *International Relations Theory and the Third World* (Houndsmills: Macmillan, 1998), 31–54; M. Ayoob, 'Inequality and Theorizing in International Relations: The Case for Subaltern Realism' (2002) 4(3) *International Studies Review* 27–48; H. Kraft, 'The Principle of Non-Intervention: Evolution and Challenges for the Asia-Pacific Region', in D. Dickens and G. Wilson-Roberts (eds.), *Non-Intervention and State Sovereignty in the Asia-Pacific* (New Zealand: Centre for Strategic Studies/China Centre for International Studies/Institute of Strategic and International Studies, 2000), 23–41; Narine (n. 18).

regional challenges of a transnational nature, such as terrorism, organized crime or pollution, with the implications for governments being the same as in the case of communal pressures.[33] However, the continued presence of the previously mentioned factors, which have strengthened the concept of Westphalian sovereignty over the last two decades, has acted as a counterpoint to these pressures.[34] This is not to say that the principle of Westphalian sovereignty has always been respected or that all the actors within the region defend it with the same passion.[35] However, even authors who question its primacy accept that 'Westphalian sovereignty…is still deeply entrenched' and it has assured itself a prominent position in the bases of East Asia's regional order. [36]

11.2.3 *The 'consensual' norm of procedural justice*

The final component of the constitutional structure of this order is the norm of procedural justice for the adoption of decisions; this stresses the value of consensus and its main function consists of specifying 'the correct procedures that "legitimate" or "good" States employ collectively to formulate basic rules of inter-State conduct'.[37] This norm has three main features. The first and most significant is, as noted above, a preference for consensus. In keeping with the Westphalian concept of sovereignty, this is based on the inclusion of all participating actors on equal terms,[38] though consensus should not be confused

33 M. Beeson, 'Sovereignty Under Siege: Globalization and the State in Southeast Asia' (1993) 24 *Third World Quarterly* 357–74; Moon and Chun (n. 31), 126–9.

34 M. Oksenberg, 'The Issue of Sovereignty in the Asian Historical Context', in S. D. Krasner (ed.), *Problematic Sovereignty* (New York, NY: Columbia University Press, 2001), 84, 87; S. Narine (n. 18), 433.

35 Aihwa Ong notes that the region currently embraces a concept of 'graduated' sovereignty which seeks to reconcile Westphalian elements of sovereignty with the pressures of globalization faced by states, though she recognizes the predominant nature of the former. A. Ong, 'Graduated Sovereignty in South-East Asia' (2000) 17(4) *Theory, Culture and Society* 55–75. Going a step further, Chung-In Moon and Chaesung Chun have noted that in recent years 'empirical sovereignty' – more rhetorical than real and with varying content depending on the circumstances – has prevailed over 'Westphalian sovereignty' in East Asia. This notwithstanding, they recognize the almost exclusive use of the latter in official discourses and accept that on most occasions the content of Westphalian sovereignty has predominated over other concepts of sovereignty. Moon and Chun (n. 31), 111–13. For a more detailed investigative study on the evolution of non-interference in South-East Asia, see Funston (n. 26), 13–15. Finally, discussions on non-interference in the context of ASEAN, which have been echoed by various authors, stress the existence of differing degrees of adhesion to the Westphalian concept of sovereignty within the region, see Funston (n. 26), 14–15; M. Alagappa, 'Gestión de la seguridad asiàtica. Competitividad, cooperación y evolución', in S. Golden (ed.), *Multilateralismo* versus *unilateralismo en Asia: el peso internacional de los 'valores asiáticos'* (Barcelona: Fundació CIDOB, 2004), 23, 26; Kraft (n. 32), 34.

36 Moon and Chun (n. 31), 129.

37 Reus-Smit (n. 5), 567.

38 A. Acharya, 'Culture, Secutiry, Multilateralism: The "ASEAN Way" and Regional Order' (1998) 19 *Contemporary Security Policy* 55, 62–3; W. Christopher, *In the Stream of History: Shaping Foreign Policy for a New Era* (Stanford, CA: Stanford University Press, 1998), 28. On the general features of this norm

with unanimity. As far as is possible, the decisions adopted reflect the positions of all actors involved, but in general there is a commitment to those points on which there is majority agreement and which do not raise significant opposition from any of the participants. In this sense, the preference for consensus can be interpreted as a mechanism via which all involved can 'agree on the existence of disagreements without discord'.[39] The second feature of this norm is conflict avoidance, which is expressed as a marked predilection for discretion and a pragmatic and flexible approach to negotiations. The majority of discussions are held in private, far from the media spotlight and public opinion, and generally the only matters dealt with are those on which it is assumed that there will be a minimum level of agreement, with more controversial issues thus avoided.[40] Finally, the third feature of the norm is the informality of the cooperative framework, which highlights the importance of personal relationships within debates and which allows for more flexibility in the organization of meetings, the structuring of the agenda and the creation of an atmosphere which allows all to express opinions.[41] Together, these three features define a norm of procedural justice which, unlike that which prevails in the wider international order of today, does not place a premium on legalistic and confrontational aspects.[42] Furthermore, together with the developmental hegemonic belief on the moral objective of the state and the Westphalian concept of sovereignty, this norm defines a coherent and cohesive normative system.[43]

also see H. Soestastro (ed.), *ASEAN in a Changed Regional and International Political Economy* (Yakarta: Centre for Strategic and International Studies, 1995); Acharya (n. 6); D. Capie and P. Evans, 'The "ASEAN Way"', in S. Siddique and S. Kumar (eds.), *The 2nd ASEAN Reader* (Singapore: Institute of Southeast Asian Studies, 2003), 45–51.

39 S. Nordin, 'ASEAN Towards 2020: Strategic Goals and Critical Pathways', presented at the 'Second ASEAN Congress', 20–3 July 1997, 9. An illustrative example of consensus that is not necessarily unanimous is the 'five-minus-one formula' set out by the Prime Minister of Singapore, Lee Kuan Yew, at the beginning of the 1970s in relation to ASEAN policy on tariff reductions and joint ventures. In accordance with this formula, 'when four agree and one does not, this can still be considered consensus and the five-minus-one scheme can benefit the participating four without damaging the remaining one' (cited in R. Irvine, 'The Formative Years of ASEAN: 1967–1975', in A. Broinowski (ed.), *Understanding ASEAN* (London: MacMillan, 1982), 8–36).

40 This second feature has been criticized by authors who consider that rather than resolving conflicts, this norm is limited to avoiding them. M. Leifer, *ASEAN and the Security of South-East Asia* (London: Routledge, 1989); Narine (n. 18); D. Martin Jones and M. L. R. Smith, 'Making Process, Not Progress: ASEAN and the Evolving East Asian Regional Order' (2007) 32 *International Security* 148–84; Y. Nishikawa, 'The "ASEAN Way" and Asian regional security' (2007) 35 *Politics & Policy* 42–56; A. Jetschke and J. Rüland, 'Decoupling Rhetoric and Practice: The Cultural Limits of ASEAN Cooperation' (2009) 22 *Pacific Review* 179–203. In this respect it should be noted, however, that the pragmatic approach contained within the norm has been useful in guaranteeing regional stability and that, furthermore, it does not imply permanently avoiding conflicts, rather it means postponing them until the appropriate conditions arise in order for them to be included within the negotiation agenda (Acharya (n. 38), 61).

41 Acharya (n. 38), 58–9; Capie and Evans (n. 38).

42 Acharya (n. 6), 329; Reus-Smit (n. 5), 576–85.

43 Reus-Smit (n. 5), 568.

This 'consensual' norm of procedural justice within the regional order has spread to both bilateral and multilateral relations among the various states of East Asia, though it is within the framework of the latter which it has become more established. In addition, it is not only limited to official initiatives, as it has spread to unofficial debate and negotiation forums. There are three main reasons for this widespread projection of the norm. First, as Nikolas Busse has observed, the construction of the post-colonial states in the region was left in the hands of a small group of government elites who, via clientelist practices, promoted a political culture characterized by privacy and informality, especially in South-East Asia.[44] Second, the historically high levels of mistrust among the countries within the region led to the putting into place of a procedural norm that was able to encourage a minimum level of cooperation without requiring high levels of formality or bringing state sovereignty into question. Third, the use of this norm by ASEAN during the Cold War and its positive effect on regional stability served to highlight the advantages of this type of practice, thus promoting its adoption by neighbouring countries in North-East Asia.[45] Additionally, in countries such as Indonesia, Malaysia, the People's Republic of China and both Koreas, these three factors were facilitated by a deeply rooted tradition of personal, informal and non-contractual political relations, shared by both Javanese and Confucian cultures.[46]

From the perspective of the strengthening of East Asia's regional order, on the other hand, this 'consensual' norm of procedural justice has three constituent functions which influence the content and workings of its main institutions. First, this norm defines the cognitive horizons of the actors responsible for the design of these institutions. Second, it constitutes a meta-norm which structures the communication process within which the production and reproduction of these institutions takes place. Finally, once it has become interiorised by the majority of states within the region, this 'consensual' norm limits the actions of those actors which do not feel deeply cognitively or morally connected to the institutions.[47]

11.3 International law as a fundamental institution of the regional order

At the beginning of this chapter institutions were defined as sets of norms which guide the behaviour of actors, limit the range of actions which they can carry out and introduce certainty into their relations. Far from being uniform and permanent, these sets of norms vary in different geographical spaces and evolve over time, either due to external factors such as changes in international power

44 N. Busse, 'Constructivism and Southeast Asian Security' (1999) 12 *Pacific Review* 39, 47.

45 B. Job, 'ASEAN Stalled: Dilemmas and Tensions over Conflicting Norms', presented at the annual meeting of the American Political Science Association, 2–5 September 1999.

46 L. W. Pye, *Asian Power and Politics: The Cultural Dimension of Authority* (Cambridge, MA: Harvard University Press, 1985), esp. ch. 2. Acharya (n. 38), 62.

47 Reus-Smit (n. 5), 569.

structures or as a result of the emergence of new challenges. What is more, in each specific order, these sets of norms maintain a certain hierarchical relationship, meaning that some may be more predominant and more highly developed than others, which can lead to certain tensions.[48] Over the last sixty years, East Asia's regional order has adopted various institutions, such as the balance of power, coordinated control of the great powers and even war,[49] but only international law has become fully consolidated. The idea of international law as an international institution is not new. Several authors from the English School and from within neo-liberal institutionalism have recognized international law as a key institution within the contemporary international order,[50] with some even going as far as to claim that it represents the key institution of this order. Friedrich Kratochwil, for example, has indicated that the existence of legal international order defines the interplays within international relations, while James Mayall has argued that international law constitutes the cornerstone on which international society rests.[51] In more resounding terms, Terry Nardin states that 'international society is not merely regulated by international law but constituted by it'.[52] In the contemporary international order, the institution of international law has been expressed through various international treaties, agreements and commitments with varying levels of legalisation, that is to say, with differing levels of obligation, precision and delegation.[53]

Since the beginning of the 1950s, international law within the East Asian regional order has taken the form of 'soft' law, referring to legal provisions with low legalization. This international law is characterized by three

48 M. Wight, *Power Politics* (London: Penguin, 1979), 111, 143–4; A. Hurrell, 'Norms and Ethics in International Relations', in W. Carlsnaes, T. Risee and B. A. Simmons (eds.), *Handbook of International Relations* (London: Sage Publications, 2002), 146–7; B. Buzan, *From International to World Society? English School Theory and the Social Structure of Globalisation* (Cambridge: Cambridge University Press, 2004), 194–5.

49 On the secondary nature of war or the use of force as an institution of the regional order see, for example, Alagappa (n. 35), 35–7. On the secondary nature of balance of power, see A. Goldstein, 'Balance-of-Power Politics: Consequences for Asian Security Order', in M. Alagappa (ed.), *Security Order: Instrumental and Normative Features* (Stanford, CA: Stanford University Press, 2003), 171–209.

50 Bull (n. 4); Buzan (n. 48); Keohane (n. 9); Reus-Smit (n. 5); Wight (n. 48).

51 F. Kratochwil, *Rules, Norms and Decisions: On the Conditions of Practical and Legal Reasoning in International Relations and Domestic Affairs* (Cambridge: Cambridge University Press, 1989), 251; J. Mayall, *World Politics: Progress and its Limits* (Cambridge: Polity, 2000), 94.

52 T. Nardin, 'Legal Positivism as a Theory of International Society', in D. R. Mapel and T. Nardin (eds.), *International Society: Diverse Ethical Perspectives* (Princeton, NJ: Princeton University Press, 1998), 17, 20.

53 K. W. Abbott *et al.*, 'The Concept of Legalization' (2000) 54 *Int'l Org.* 401–19. These authors define legalization as a particular set of characteristics that institutions may or may not possess in terms of three dimensions: obligation, which refers to the extent to which actors are legally bound by a norm, commitment or set of norms or commitments; precision, which alludes to the clarity with which norms define required, authorized or prohibited forms of conduct; and delegation, which refers to the cession of authority to a third party in order to implement, interpret and apply the agreed-upon norms, resolve disputes and, on occasions, elaborate new norms.

elements.[54] The first of these is that there is a strong tendency towards non-binding legal instruments, that is to say, with low levels of obligation. In East Asia the majority of bilateral or multilateral agreements which have been reached over the last half-century have adopted the form of declarations of principles, political commitments or guidelines. Leaving aside notable exceptions such as the Treaty of Amity and Cooperation in South-East Asia or the Treaty on the South-East Asia Nuclear Free Zone, there are few regional treaties or conventions of a binding nature. The second element is a notable degree of imprecision. The normative instruments developed in the region have a larger degree of variance in this respect, but the majority are characterized by high levels of vagueness, with required and prohibited forms of conduct remaining poorly defined. This results in states having considerable freedom in how they choose to interpret appropriate forms of behaviour. An example of this is the Declaration on the Conduct of Parties in the South China Sea, which includes the commitment on the part of signatory countries to 'exploring ways for building trust and confidence', but which barely alludes to the instruments, timeframes or actors which should participate in this exploration.[55] Another illustrative example is the agreement of 1992 which brought about the creation of the ASEAN Free Trade Area (AFTA), which John Ravenhill ironically dubbed Agree First, Talk After due to its brevity of merely fifteen pages and the lack of specific regulations on the products and sectors to be affected by it, the tariff reductions to be included and the deadlines to be met.[56] The third element refers to the reduced possibilities for delegating legal authority to supranational entities or third parties in order for these to implement, interpret and apply the agreements reached, and to develop new norms or resolve disputes. With respect to the adoption, implementation and interpretation of decisions, the experience of ASEAN – the most highly developed regional integration initiative – is very revealing. All ASEAN decisions are still adopted at intergovernmental meetings or summits; these are then implemented at a national level and there is no supranational body with the power to discuss or amend these decisions. As regards dispute resolution, hardly any of the normative instruments developed in East Asia have considered adjudication mechanisms. Within the framework of bilateral agreements, the few exceptions to this rule are limited to the occasional memorandum on issues of little importance to the involved parties, two of which particularly stand out. The first of these occurred in 1997, when Malaysia and Indonesia signed a memorandum of understanding to take their dispute over the sovereignty of the Sipidan and Ligatan islands to the

54 On the general features of international law which is soft or of low legalization, see K. W. Abbott *et al.* (n. 53), and K. W. Abbott and D. Snidal, 'Hard and Soft Law in International Governance' (2000) 54 *Int'l Org.* 421–56. On the link between international law in East Asian regional order and this type of international law, see M. Kahler, 'Legalization as Strategy: The Asia-Pacific Case' (2000) 54 *Int'l Org.* 549–71.

55 ASEAN, *Declaration on the Conduct of Parties in the South China Sea* (4 November 2002) (at: www.aseansec.org/13163.htm; accessed 12 August 2009).

56 J. Ravenhill, 'Economic Cooperation in Southeast Asia' (1995) 35 *Asian Survey* 850–66.

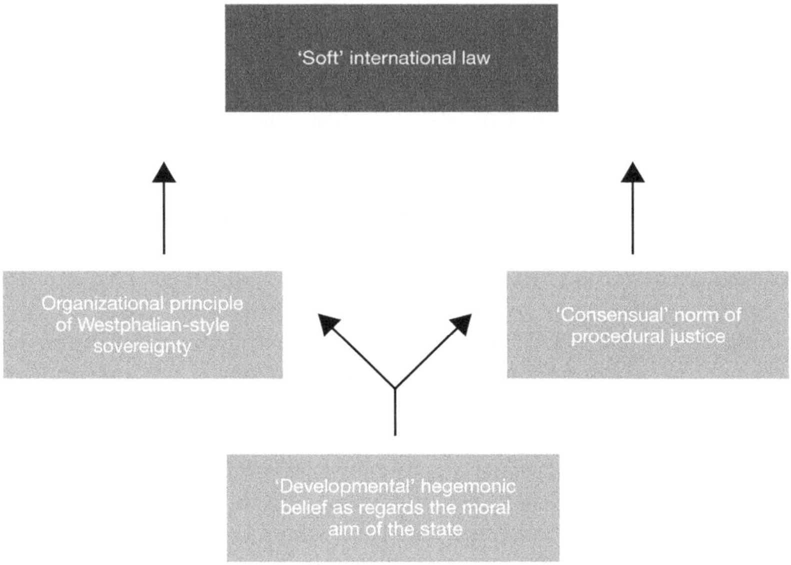

Figure 11.1 International law and the constitutional base of East Asia's regional order

Source: Own elaboration based on C. H. Reus-Smit, 'The Constitutional Structure of International Society and the Nature of Fundamental Institutions' (1997) 51 *Int'l Org.*

International Court of Justice (ICJ), which found in favour of Malaysia on 17 December 2002.[57] The second case took place in 2003 when, after several years of negotiations, Malaysia and Singapore signed a memorandum to refer their dispute over the sovereignty of various islets in the Malacca Straits to the ICJ; in this case the judges granted Pedra Branca to Singapore, Middle Rocks to Malaysia and South Ledge to whichever state in whose territorial waters it lies.[58] In the framework of multilateral agreements, exceptions are even harder to find and are limited to cases such as the aforementioned Treaty of Amity and Cooperation in South-East Asia, which leaves it up to the states directly involved in a dispute to decide whether or not to resort to adjudication mechanisms.[59] Figure 11.1 illustrates the relationship between international law and the constitutional base of East Asia's regional order.

57 *Case Concerning Sovereignty of Pulau Ligitan and Pulau Sipadan* (*Indonesia* v. *Malaysia*) (Report of Judgments, Advisory Opinions and Orders) [2002] ICJ Rep. 139.

58 *Case Concerning Sovereignty of Pedra Branca/Pulau Batu Puteh, Middle Rocks and South Ledge* (*Malaysia* v. *Singapore*) (Report of Judgments, Advisory Opinions and Orders) [2008] ICJ Rep. 168.

59 In accordance with Article 16 of the treaty 'The provisions contained within this chapter (referring to adjudication to the High Council, as established in chapter IV of the treaty) will not be applicable except in the case that the parties to a dispute agree to their application' (Treaty of Amity and Cooperation in Southeast Asia, Indonesia, 14 February 1976; at: www.aseansec.org/1217.htm; accessed 10 December 2009).

The penetration and establishment of international law as a fundamental institution of East Asia's regional order is not surprising in light of the wider experience of international order. International law has been an established part of the European order since the beginning of the nineteenth century, and it was spread to the rest of the world via colonialism, the subsequent decolonization process and then through the construction of the current global order led by the United States; it has thus become one of the first truly universal institutions of contemporary international society.[60] In order to explain the fact that within the regional order of East Asia international law is 'soft', or of low legalisation, we need to focus on the concept of localization formulated by Amitav Acharya. [61] The process of localization does not only refer to the diffusion, reinterpretation or contextualization of an institution or norm in order for it to be applied in a different geographical space; it also includes the norm's 'reconstitution to make an outside norm congruent with a pre-existing local normative order'.[62] This pre-existing local normative order is identified with the constitutional base or structure of the regional order and, as has been previously noted, in the case of East Asia it consists of a developmental hegemonic belief regarding the moral objective of the state, the Westphalian principle of sovereignty and the 'consensual' norm of procedural justice.

Adopting a 'soft' form of international law contributes to its congruence in the regional sphere in at least four complementary ways. First, low legalization reduces the contractual, economic and staffing costs involved in negotiating and supervising legal agreements. States are thus free to commit more resources to promoting economic development and social welfare. Second, the low level of legalization limits the 'sovereignty costs' entailed in any legal agreement between states and, as a result, consolidates the Westphalian concept of sovereignty and reinforces the preference for informality, consensus and conflict aversion in decision-making processes. There are three main sovereignty costs for states: the potential benefits they could obtain if they chose not to cooperate and instead acted as free-riders; the loss of freedom to exercise their authority in certain areas as a result of the commitments they have taken on; and, where there is delegation to a third party or supranational authority, the possible loss of sovereignty arising from present or future decisions that this authority may take.[63] Third, a low level of legalization reduces the homogenizing pressures which generally weigh on participants in

60 Kratochwil (n. 51); Mayall (n. 51); Nardin (n. 52).

61 A. Acharya, 'How Ideas Spread: Whose Norms Matter? Norm Localization and Institutional Change in Asian Regionalism' (2004) 58 *Int'l Org.* 239–75.

62 *Ibid.* 244.

63 The preoccupation with sovereignty costs would also explain why the states of the region have shown themselves to be resistant to the legalization of security agreements, which generally entail higher costs of this type; however, they are somewhat more favourably disposed to the legalization of economic agreements, which traditionally have fewer repercussions on state sovereignty. Abbott and Snidal (n. 54), 440–1; Kahler (n. 54), 567–71.

highly legalized agreements. These pressures tend to highlight a marked level of heterogeneity within the region and – in a context shaped by historic mistrust, power asymmetries and instability – they reinforce the need for consensual processes in decision making. Finally, the low level of obligation, the imprecision and the non-delegation of the commitments taken on all work to reinforce the primacy of the state in regional relations, with the state maintaining its freedom to interpret commitments it has signed up to and also acting as the guarantor that they will be complied with.[64] From the perspective of private national companies, 'soft' international law increases their opportunities for influencing state actions and for maximizing their interests via the exploitation of the imprecisions within commitments and the greater room for states to act according to their own discretion within the framework of the commitments they take on.[65]

It is important that 'soft' international law in East Asia is not understood as a transitional institution on a trajectory towards 'hard' international law, and nor should it be perceived as a reflection of the incapacity of the actors involved in constructing the regional order to establish binding and precise agreements with delegation mechanisms.[66] In fact, this international law with a low level of legalization is the result of a conscious choice and, in terms of the interests of actors and the constitutional structure of the regional order, it provides 'superior institutional solutions'.[67] Two recent trends in the region provide evidence of this. The first is the acceptance by East Asian States of a higher degree of legalization of international law within the framework of international organizations such as the World Trade Organization (WTO), which highlights their capacity to relinquish low levels of obligation, imprecision and non-delegation where their interests or the prevailing circumstances favour this outcome. The second trend refers to the development of different degrees of legalization in regional agreements, these being progressively higher within ASEAN and persistently low or non-existent in other cooperative frameworks, such as the ASEAN Regional Forum and the APEC Forum.[68] These two trends, together with the experience of the last two decades, show that the rise of East Asia should not necessarily be interpreted as a threat to current international law. Without doubt, the new position of the region in the sphere of twenty-first-century international relations will

64 Abbott and Snidal (n. 54), 434–4.

65 *Ibid.* 450–2.

66 For further reading on the concept of international law with a low level of legalization as a step on the path towards 'harder' international law and as a threat to the unity of this institution, see P. Weil, 'Towards Relative Normativity in International Law?' (1983) 77 AJIL 413–42.

67 Abbott and Snidal (n. 54). In a similar vein, Richard Higgott and Shaun Narine have pointed out that the states of East Asia conceive the presence of institutions of order as a means via which to increase their sovereignty and not as a threat to it nor as an objective in itself. R. Higgott, 'De facto and de jure regionalism: the double discourse of regionalism in the Asia-Pacific' (1997) 11 *Global Society* 165–83; Narine (n. 18), 425–6.

68 Kahler (n. 54), 555–9.

influence the form and content of this law, which may 'soften up', but there are no indications that it will be marginalized or displaced as one of the fundamental institutions of the current international order.

12 Post-Soviet states and international law in a multipolar world

Rima Tkatova

The twentieth century was an epoch of international law in a 'divided world' when the stability of international society was guaranteed by bipolarity. It was during this age of bipolarity that Soviet and American doctrines of international law were impregnated by the specificity of interaction between power and law. After the collapse of the Soviet Union, the international community seemed to enter a Fukuyamian 'end of history' and the last decade of the twentieth century was marked by moves towards a more homogeneous and unipolar world order. However, the beginning of the twenty-first century is an age of multipolarity, a concept taken from American international relations theory. International law finds itself closely linked with international policy, the diversity of the legal cultures and civilizations, and the multiplication of sites of power.

There is no doubt that Soviet international law doctrine reflected the division of the world in the twentieth century. The USSR's break-up provoked a revision of the world order and a search for new doctrines of international law in the post-Soviet states. These states are currently searching for their identities and are swinging between 'inertial' applications of Soviet conceptions of international law, difficulties in adapting Western models and a quest for their own 'post-Soviet' ways. Living in this multipolar world, where the 'clash of civilizations'[1] has given way to the cohabitation of different cultures and the diversification of the sites of power in the world, one ponders the place of the Central Asian States in this multipolar and multi-civilizational world. In trying to achieve balance between their Soviet heritage, specific national characteristics, Europeanism, and Eurasianism, these states are creating their own conceptions and visions of the international world order.

Taking into account the major role of Soviet international law doctrine, it is interesting to consider the roles that the post-Soviet states play on the international stage. Can we claim that new international doctrines and practices have appeared in the post-Soviet space? Are we speaking about

1 S. Huntington, *The Clash of Civilizations and the Remaking of World Order* (New York, NY: Simon & Schuster, 1996).

renewal, break or continuity? Did the Russia–Georgia conflict in August 2008 have an influence on the international balance of power?

Before trying to answer these questions, it is important to analyse the historical development of post-Soviet international law. Next, we will consider the renewal of post-Soviet international law. Finally, the role of post-Soviet states in a multipolar world, taking into account the Russia–Georgia conflict in August 2008 will be considered.

12.1 The historical development of post-Soviet international law

In order to understand the uniqueness of Soviet international law, it is important to know the conditions that influenced the creation of international law during the Russian Empire, to define the features of Soviet international law's development as a particular doctrine in a divided world, and to point to how Perestroika changed Soviet international law.

12.1.1 International law during the Russian Empire

The science of international law began in the Russian Empire during the reign of Peter the Great, when the first Russian treaties in law of war and peace were signed during the Northern War (1700–21).[2] The German school of natural law was influential in Russia. International law was initially taught in German at the Academy of Sciences, founded by Peter the Great in 1725, and the University of Dorpat, the most famous school at the time. The first book about international law in Russian was written in 1717 by P. P. Shafirov, a diplomat in Peter the Great's service. In *A Discourse Concerning the Just Causes of the War Between Sweden and Russia*, Shafirov analysed some aspects of international law.[3] However, Russian international law did not really exist at this time because it was steeped in European conceptions of international law and taught in its original languages. In the eighteenth-century works by Grotius Pufendorf, Nettelbladt and Rousseau were translated into Russian, but Vattel's works remained in their original French until the mid-twentieth century.[4] The teaching of international law was introduced in the Russian universities by the University Statute of 1804 as the 'law of nations' and divided into natural law and positive law. However, only natural law was seen

2 K. Grzybowski, *Soviet Public International Law: Doctrines and Diplomatic Practice* (Leyden: AW Sijthoff, 1970), 1; M. Lebedev, 'De l'évolution de la doctrine soviétique et russe de droit international public' (D.Phil. thesis, Université Paris I, 2004), 40. Some authors think international law appeared in Russia as the Russian state formed. See M. de Taube, 'Études sur le développement historique du droit international dans l'Europe orientale' (1926) 11 *Recueil des Cours* 346 and V. E. Grabar, *Materialy k istorii literatury mezhdunarodnogo prava* v. *Rossii* (Izd-vo Akademii Nauk, SSSR Moskva 1958).

3 Grabar (n. 2), 70–5; W. E. Butler, 'Russian International Legal History: A Plea for Revisionism' (2007) 7 *Baltic YIL* 227.

4 Grabar (n. 2), 110–13; L. Mälksoo, 'The History of International Legal Theory in Russia: A Civilizational Dialogue with Europe' (2008) 19 EJIL 219.

as universal law: positive law was treaty law. The discipline was renamed 'international law' by the Statute of 1863.

The real birth of international law in the Russian Empire was in the mid-nineteenth century when a large number of international law texts appeared in Russian. The first Russian textbook, *The Course of International Law* by Professor Kachenovsky was followed by the courses of Kapustin, Kamarovsky, Ivanovsky, Kotlyarevsky and Korkunov.[5] The first Russian international lawyer to become a world-famous scholar was Fyodor Fyodorovich Martens. In 1882 Martens published his monumental course *The Contemporary International Law of Civilized Nations*, which was translated into German, French and Spanish.[6] Martens was an architect[7] of the process of the codification of international law at the Peace Conference at The Hague in 1899. The Martens Clause is still rooted in the history of international humanitarian law.[8] Martens, a committed 'pro-Westerner', saw international law as a project of the Western European 'civilized' nations which included Russia.[9] The 'civilized nations' concept permeated Russian international legal discourse and described European nations as being based on the rule of law and as respecting their international obligations. Antagonism between Slavyanofily (Slavophils) and Zapadniki (Westernizers) marked all of the intellectual Russian debates of the time. The central themes of the dialogue between Slavophils and Westernizers were the role and historical destiny of Russia in the world and the specific place that it occupied between West and East.[10]

The Russian Empire's doctrine of international law and its view of relationships within the international community were deeply liberal and humanistic. Although it was not innovative, Russia contributed to the codification and development of international law. It was at Russia's instigation that the Declaration of St Petersburg, banning weapons that caused excessive suffering, was signed in 1868. The International Peace Conference was convened in 1899 at The Hague on the initiative of Tsar Nicholas II. The

5 N. N. Kirilovskaya, 'Sistema mezhdunarodnogo prava i ego nauki v otechestvennoi mezhdunarodno-pravovoi doktrine XIX-nachale XX v.v. (istoriko-teoreticheskii analiz) (D.Phil. thesis, St Petersburg State University, 2005), 52–9.

6 Lebedev (n. 2), 41–2.

7 W. E. Butler (ed. and tr.), *VV Pustogarov, Our Martens: F.F. Martens, International Lawyer and Architect of Peace* (The Hague: Kluwer Law International, 2000).

8 E. Myles, 'Humanity, Civilization and the International Community in the Late Imperial Russian Mirror: Three Ideas Topical for Our Days' (2002) 4 *Journal of the History of International Law* 310.

9 V. A. Tomsinov (ed.), *FF Martens, Sovremennoe meždunarodnoe pravo civilizovannyh narodov* (Moscow: Zercalo, 2008). Martens defined the tribes of Khiva, Bukhara, Eastern Turkestan and Afghanistan as non-civilized or semi-barbarous peoples: F. F. Martens, quoted in R. Müllerson, *Central Asia: A Chessboard and Player in the New Great Game* (London: Kegan Paul, 2007). However, international relations existed from the creation of the Silk Road and bear witness that Central Asian states acted and existed as subjects of international law: see R. Tkatova, 'Central Asian States and International Law: Between Post-Soviet Culture and Eurasian Civilization' (2010) 9 *Chinese JIL* 205–220.

10 W. E. Butler, *Russian Law* (Oxford: Oxford University Press, 1999), 58–9.

Second Conference at The Hague in 1907 adopted the Convention Respecting the Laws and Customs of War on Land and included the 'Martens Clause'.

12.1.2 The Soviet state and international law

The arrival of the communist regime changed the Russian doctrine of international law. Many outstanding lawyers emigrated because their university chairs were abolished by the Bolsheviks.[11] In characterizing Soviet international law since the 1917 October Revolution, we must consider multiple changes. There were three major periods of development in international law during the Soviet period: the period of transition (1920s–30s), the Stalinist period (1938–55) and the era of peaceful coexistence (1955–85).

In the period of transition, Soviet international law was at the heart of the most disturbed period of the construction of the Soviet system. Observers emphasized the fragility of the new Soviet state and the improbability of its survival. Soviet international lawyers based their arguments on the balance of power between the USSR and the capitalist states and awaited the inevitable decline of their state. This period is bound with the names of two Soviet scholars: E. B. Pashukanis and E. A. Korovin, who tried to find a legal basis for this antagonistic view of the new Soviet diplomacy. Korovin worked out a theory of compromise between the old and new legal systems, as well as a theory of temporary coexistence between states with different social and economic orders until the victory of the revolution on the world scale and its replacement by the inter-Soviet law.[12] Pashukanis modified the theory of compromise in a theory of struggle between the classes and the two systems.[13]

During the Stalinist era, Soviet international law underwent changes and became an instrument of the foreign policy of the USSR. The Second World War played a major role in the transformation of Soviet international law. In order to strengthen its status in the international arena and not to be completely isolated in facing the fascist threat, the Soviet Union was obliged to accept the common and general rules of international law.[14] Nevertheless, according to the Soviet lawyer A. Vyshinski,[15] only those rules of international law, which the Soviet government had recognized, were binding upon the

11 W. E. Butler, 'Russian International Lawyers in Emigration: The First Generation' (2001) *Journal of the History of International Law* 235.

12 E. A. Korovin, *Mezhdunarodnoe pravo perehdnogo vremeni* (Moskva: Gosizdat, 1924); E. A. Korovin, 'La République des Soviets et le droit international' (1925) RGDIP 292ff.; I. Lapenna, *Conceptions soviétiques de droit international public* (Paris: Pédone, 1954), 285–6.

13 J.-Y. Calvez, *Droit international et souveraineté en URSS* (Paris: Armand Colin, 1953), 89; E. B. Pašukanis, *Očerki po meždunarodnomu pravu* (Moskva: Gosizdat, 1935).

14 Moreover, the Soviet Union became a founding member of the United Nations as an act of accommodation, not conviction: A. Z. Rubinstein, 'Moscow's Diplomacy in International Organisations', in R. Clark, F. Feldbrugge and S. Pomorski (eds.), *International and National Law in Russia and Eastern Europe: Essays in Honor of George Ginsburgs* (The Hague: Martinus Nijhoff, 2001).

15 A. Vyshinski stated this view in his report to the Second Conference of the Soviet legal science (16–19 July 1938).

Soviet Union. Vyshinski advocated monism, with national law having primacy over international law, and definitively rejected the superior force of international law upon domestic law. Indeed, the main task of the Soviet science of international law was to destroy what was seen as hostile concepts of international law and to present criticism of all 'mistaken' views. Thus, international law became an instrument of Soviet policy. All studies in the field of international law in the Stalinist period after Vyshinski were written in this spirit.[16] The Soviet vision of international law in the Stalinist era was summarized by the Soviet international lawyer Kozhevnikov: 'among all rules of international law, the Soviet Union recognized those which it could use to achieve its goals and rejected those which in any way impeded this task'.[17]

After the Twentieth Congress of the Soviet Communist Party in 1956, the new leader of the Soviet Union, Nikita Khrushchev, announced a change in the domestic policy of the USSR by launching de-Stalinization, and in its foreign policy by proclaiming peaceful coexistence. This change enabled Soviet jurists, including G. I. Tunkin, to formulate the doctrine of 'peaceful coexistence', which consisted of peaceful competition between socialism and capitalism on the international scene and was a specific form of the class struggle between two systems.[18] In his course at The Hague Academy, Tunkin developed this thesis of peaceful coexistence by asserting that although socialist and capitalist states differ as to the social values which the law had to protect, agreement, and therefore a common legal system, was possible.[19] According to Tunkin:

> international law is the totality of norms, which were developed on the basis of agreements between the states, which govern their relations in the process of struggle and cooperation between them, expressing the will of the ruling classes, and are enforced, in case of necessity, by the pressure applied either collectively or by individual states.[20]

In 1957, the first Soviet Yearbook of International Law was published by the Soviet International Law Association, of which Tunkin was president. This became a member of the International Law Association. By applying the doctrine of peaceful coexistence, the Soviet Union began to participate more actively in the process of the codification and development of international law. It took part in UN Conferences on the Law of the Sea in 1958 and 1960

16 S. I. Krylov, 'Les notions principales du droit des gens. La doctrine soviétique du droit international' (1947) 70 *Recueil des Cours* 432–3; and F. I. Kozhevnikov, *Uchebnoe posobie po mezhdunarodnomu publichnomu pravu (Ocherki)* (Izd-vo Ministerstva Justicii SSSR, Moskva 1947).

17 Kozhevnikov (n. 16); and O. J. Lissitzyn, 'Le droit international dans un monde divisé' (1965) RGDIP 928–9.

18 G. I. Tunkin, 'Mirnoe sosuŝestvovanie i meždunarodnoe pravo' (1957) 7 Sovetskoe Gosudarstvo i Pravo 3.

19 G. I. Tunkin, 'Coexistence and International Law' (1956) *Recueil des Cours* 5.

20 G. I. Tunkin, *Ocherki po mezhdunarodnomu pravu* (Moscow: lzd, 1956).

and the UN Conference on diplomacy in 1961, as well as participating in the work of the UN General Assembly.

Another important point in Soviet international practice was the 'Brezhnev Doctrine' which was born after the 1956 intervention of the USSR in Hungary. It was later explicitly stated by the Soviet leaders in August 1968 during the Soviet invasion of Czechoslovakia by the troops of the Warsaw Pact. This doctrine, also known as the 'doctrine of limited sovereignty', justified interference in the internal affairs of member countries of the Soviet bloc in cases where socialism was threatened.[21] It was also seemingly used in the intervention in Afghanistan in 1979.

12.1.3 Perestroika and international law

In February 1986 Mikhail Gorbachev proclaimed a 'new political thinking'[22] at the Twenty-Seventh Congress of the CPSU. Gorbachev's jus-naturalistic and liberal stance marked a break with the Marxist vision of the world. One of the goals of perestroika was to build a 'socialist rule of law' to constitute with all countries in the world one 'global community of states ruled by law'. The idea of the primacy of international law in international relations became a cornerstone of the new political thinking.[23] The change was reinforced by a sensational event: in 1989, the USSR decided to withdraw the reservations that it had previously made to human rights treaties and recognized the compulsory jurisdiction of the International Court of Justice.[24] This action showed the USSR's new desire to aspire to rule-of-law governance in politics, to recognize the supremacy of international law over domestic law and to acknowledge the importance of all means of peaceful settlement of disputes.

In the 1986 volume of the *Soviet Yearbook of International Law*, Tunkin abandoned the idea of struggle between socialism and capitalism.[25] The 'new thinking of international law' was launched in the USSR:[26] two eminent lawyers who represented this new stream were V. S. Vereshetin and R. A. Müllerson, who focused their works on the new thought in international law

21 G. Fisher, 'Quelques problèmes juridiques découlant de l'affaire tchécoslovaque' (1968) *Annuaire Français de Droit International* 15; and C. Zorgbibe, 'La doctrine soviétique de la "souveraineté limitée"' (1970) RGDIP 873.

22 M. Gorbachev, *Perestroika: New Thinking for Our Country and the World* (London: Collins, 1987).

23 V. S. Vereshetin and R. A. Müllerson, 'The Primacy of International Law in World Politics', in A. Carty and G. Danilenko, *Perestroika and International Law: Current Anglo-Soviet Approaches to International Law* (Edinburgh University Press, 1990); and G. I. Tunkin, 'Remarks on the Primacy of International Law in Politics', in *Le droit international au service de la paix, de la justice et du développement: mélanges Michel Virally* (Paris: Pédone, 1991), 455.

24 P. Bretton, 'L'URSS et la compétence de la Cour internationale de justice en matière de protection des droits de l'homme' (1991) 36 *Annuaire Français de Droit International* 261.

25 G. I. Tunkin, 'Sozdanie vseobiemlûŝej sistemy meždunarodnoj bezopasnosti i meždunarodnoe pravo' (1986) *Sovetskij eželodnik meždunarodnogo prava,* 24.

26 E. McWhinney, 'The "New Thinking" in Soviet International Law: Soviet Doctrines and Practice in the Post-Tunkin Era' (1990) *Canadian YIL* 309.

and the creation of the universal system of international security in an interdependent world.[27] Thus, the Soviet 'New Thinking', influenced by freedom of thought and the end of communist rule, developed a somewhat romantic vision of international law. The ideas of the creation of a common European legal space[28] and of Europe as a 'common home'[29] marked the Eurocentric character of Soviet doctrines at this time.

12.2 Post-Soviet international law: Westernization vs. Eurasianization

The collapse of the USSR provoked a transformative process which affected international law in the post-Soviet states. New approaches in international practice and doctrine appeared. The first metamorphosis, which began with perestroika, tried to overcome Soviet society's stagnation and to democratize the system. This process continued with Westernization and the imitation of the European model of international law. The second change is characterized by the shaping of new models and the formulation of an independent vision and conception of international relations.

12.2.1 New approaches in the international practice of the post-Soviet states in the 1990s: West not East

After the breakup of the USSR, there was an increased willingness among the post-Soviet states to enter into the 'society of civilized nations'. This was demonstrated by their unreserved acceptance of democratic development and the European vision of international law. On 16 December 1991, after the collapse of the USSR, the Declaration on Guidelines on the Recognition of New States in Eastern Europe and in the Soviet Union was adopted by the foreign ministers of European Union members, which made democratic legitimacy a condition for recognizing these states.[30] Consequently, the adhesion of the post-Soviet states to the Council of Europe, and the Organization for Security and Cooperation in Europe, was conditioned by the introduction of rule of law mechanisms in these states. Moreover, the Council of Europe affirmed that the geographical frontiers of Europe could not be fixed and that the Europe of the Council of Europe spreads as far as the principles of

27 V. S. Vereshetin and R. A. Müllerson, 'Novoe myšlenie i meždunarodnoe pravo' (1988) *Sovetskij ežegodnik meždunarodnogo prava,* 8.

28 V. S. Vereŝetin, 'Obŝee pravovoe pole' sovremennogo mira' (1991) 3–4 *Sovetskij ezhegodnik mezhdunarodnogo prava* 3–17.

29 Soviet leaders borrowed this expression from the Vietnamese writer Thanh Hay, who used it to emphasize the unity of North and South civilizations: R. Charvin, 'Le concept de l'humanité et la doctrine soviétique du droit international', in *Humanité et droit international: Mélanges Réné-Jean Dupuy* (Pédone: Paris, 1991), 455.

30 R. Rich, 'Recognition of States: the Collapse of Yugoslavia and the Soviet Union' (1993) 4 EJIL 36.

the organization – rule of law, democracy and human rights – are applied.[31] This 'political conditionality' became the tool for imposing the European model on the post-Soviet space.[32]

In the early 1990s, the Russian Federation advocated the transformation of the post-communist world into a democratic one. Russia also proclaimed the basic elements of its foreign policy. These were partnership and alliance for democracy and a dynamic market economy with countries that share those values, good relations with all neighbouring countries and mutually advantageous cooperation with all the members of the world community.[33] Similar statements were also made by other states of the former Soviet Union, stressing their adherence to European standards, democracy and the rule of law.[34]

'Political conditionality' seemed fulfilled by the post-Soviet states in the 1990s: they strongly supported the creation of the Office of the High Commissioner for Human Rights and actively participated in the World Conference on Human Rights in 1993. The states became full-fledged members of the United Nations, the Council of Europe and the OSCE, and ratified or adhered to the International Covenant on Civil and Political Rights and the International Covenant on Social, Economic and Cultural Rights of 1966 and other international instruments on human rights.[35] The Eurocentric vision of Western international law seemed to be accepted and followed by the post-Soviet states in the 1990s.

12.2.2 New trends in post-Soviet international practice and doctrine, 2000–8: East not West

The new millennium marked a turning point in the post-Soviet states' perception of international law. The euphoria of Westernization passed and these states began to shape their own approaches towards international law. If a certain like-mindedness existed in the post-Soviet states after 11 September 2001, which

31 Council of Europe, Parliamentary Assembly, 'Report on enlargement of the Council of Europe' (16 June 1992) Doc. 6629, Annexe III, para. 1 (at: http://assembly.coe.int).

32 See R. Tkatova 'Les particularités de développement de l'État de droit dans la Communauté des États indépendants', in *L'État de droit en droit international. Colloque de Bruxelles de la Société française pour le droit international* (Paris: Pédone, 2009).

33 UNGA Provisional Record (22 September 1992) UN Doc. A/47/PV.6, 57–8. See also UNGA 'Address by Mr Boris Yeltsin' (28 September 1994) UN Doc. A/49/PV.5, 1.

34 See UNGA Provisional Record (8 October 1991) UN Doc. A/46/PV.14, 33–4 (Ukraine); UNGA Provisional Record (2 October 1991) UN Doc. A/46/PV.11, 62–3 (Belarus); UNGA 'Address by Mr Mircea Ion Snegur' (29 September 1994) UN Doc. A/49/PV.10, 2 (Moldova); UNGA Provisional Record (8 October 1992) UN Doc. A/47/PV.16, 62–4 (Tajikistan); UNGA 'Address by Mr Islam A. Karimov' (5 October 1993) UN Doc. A/48/PV.6 (Uzbekistan); A/49/PV.11, 33 (Kyrgyzstan).

35 Including the Convention Against Torture and Other Cruel, Inhuman or Degrading Treatment or Punishment (1984), the Convention on the Elimination of All Forms of Discrimination against Women (1979), the Convention on the Elimination of All Forms of Racial Discrimination (1965), and the Convention on the Rights of the Child (1989).

consisted in search of collective means in the fight against terrorism,[36] this is in contrast to the diverse approaches taken after the Iraq War in 2003 and the 'velvet revolutions' in 2003–5. We can distinguish three major conceptions in the international practice of the post-Soviet states: international law in a multipolar world, international law as an Occidental model, and international law in a multicultural and multi-civilizational world.

12.2.2.1 Approaches of Russia and Belarus: international law in a multpolar world

'The Foreign Policy Concept of the Russian Federation' of 28 June 2000 aimed at creating a stable, secure, democratic and multipolar world, which could reflect the multiple faces of the contemporary world. The essential role of the United Nations in the formation of this new world order was based on the collective resolution of conflicts, the primacy of law and the democratization of international relations. This conception was emphasized and confirmed in the statement of President Vladimir Putin at the UN World Summit in 2005.[37] At the same Summit, the President of Belarus Alexander Lukashenko emphasized that:

> We must realize that the unipolar world is a world with a single track, a one-dimensional world. We must become aware that the diversity of ways to progress is an enduring value of our civilization, the only one that can ensure stability in this world.[38]

The new foreign policy concept of the Russian Federation was elaborated by President Dmitry Medvedev. It reaffirms the priority of forming a multipolar world and underlines that the:

> balanced and multi-vector character of Russia's foreign policy is its distinguishing feature. This is because of the geopolitical position of Russia as the largest Euro-Asian power, its status as one of the leading

36 UNGA Report of the Secretary-General on the Work of the Organization (24 September 2001) UN Doc. A/56/PV.7, 3, 13 (Russian Federation, Ukraine); UNGA Report of the Secretary-General on the Work of the Organization (25 September 2001) UN Doc. A/56/PV.9, 9 (Belarus).

37 The Foreign Policy Concept of the Russian Federation: Approved by the President of the Russian Federation V. Putin (28 June 2000) (at: www.fas.org/nuke/guide/russia/doctrine/econcept.htm); Statement of the President of the Russian Federation V. Putin at the high-level plenary meeting of the United Nations General Assembly (15 September 2005) (at: www.un.org/webcast/summit2005/statements15/rfe050915eng.pdf).

38 Statement of the President of Belarus A. Lukashenko at the high-level plenary meeting of the United Nations General Assembly (at: www.un.org/webcast/summit2005/statements15/belarus050915eng.pdf).

States of the world and as a permanent member of the UN Security Council.[39]

12.2.2.2 *Approaches of Georgia and Ukraine: the Occidental model of international law*

After the 'velvet revolutions', of the fourth wave of 'democratization',[40] the foreign policy concepts of the Georgian and Ukrainian governments were created with a view to entering the European Union and joining NATO.[41] In its Foreign Policy Strategy of 2006–9, Georgia's goal was to find its place in the common European family by deepening its integration with the EU and joining NATO,[42] while keeping in mind its active participation in regional institutions such as the Community of Democratic Choice (CDC),[43] the Organization for Democracy and Economic Development (GUAM)[44] and the Organization of Black Sea Economic Cooperation (OBSEC).[45]

12.2.2.3 *The approaches of Central Asian states: international law and harmonious multiculturality*

The foreign policies of all the Central Asian States came to be based on the affirmation of national and regional identities and, despite certain disparities,[46] there is a harmony of views within these multi-ethnic and multicultural states. The creation of the Conference on Interaction and Confidence-building Measures in Asia (CICA), the Central Asian Regional Information–Coordination Centre (finalized in 2009), the UN Regional Centre on Preventive Diplomacy (established in December 2007 in Ashgabat) and the 'Bishkek Initiative' (proposed by Kyrgyzstan in 2009)[47] demonstrated a

39 The Foreign Policy Concept of the Russian Federation: Approved by the President of the Russian Federation D. Medvedev (12 July 2008) (at: www.mid.ru/ns-osndoc.nsf/0e9272befa34209743256c630042d1aa/cef95560654d4ca5c32574960036cddb?OpenDocument).

40 According to S. P. Huntington, the first wave took place from 1828 to 1926 and the second from 1943 to 1962 with the decolonization in Africa and Asia. The third began in 1974 with the 'carnation revolution' in Portugal and ended in 1991 with the collapse of the USSR and Yugoslavia. The 'Rose' revolution in Georgia (2003), the 'Orange' revolution in Ukraine (2004) and the 'Tulip' revolution in Kyrgyzstan (2005) were part of the fourth wave: see V. Avioutskii, *Les révolutions de velours* (Paris: Armand Colin, 2006), 3.

41 See the Ministry of Foreign Affairs of the Ukraine website (at: www.mfa.gov.ua).

42 Georgian Foreign Policy Strategy 2006–2009 (at: www.mfa.gov.ge).

43 Created in 2005: Estonia, Georgia, Lithuania, Latvia, Macedonia, Moldova, Romania, Slovenia and Ukraine.

44 Created in 2001: Georgia, Ukraine, Azerbaijan and Moldova.

45 Created in 1999: Albania, Armenia, Azerbaijan, Bulgaria, Georgia, Greece, Moldova, Romania, Russia, Turkey and Ukraine.

46 See Tkatova (n. 9).

47 On 4 March 2009, the President of the Kyrgyz Republic put forward an initiative to establish a permanently acting forum and centre for hosting international conferences on security and stability in Afghanistan and Central Asia in Bishkek, the capital of the Kyrgyz Republic.

community which shared a region-wide concern regarding regional security and stability. The elaboration of the Convention on the Nuclear-Weapon-Free Zone in Central Asia[48] of the Almaty Programme of Action,[49] the submitting of draft resolutions for consideration by the General Assembly called 'On the role of the international community in the prevention of the radiation threat in Central Asia', and 'Sustainable mountain development', and the establishment of 'The International Decade of Action: Water for Life, 2005–2010', reaffirm the willingness of Central Asian States to take into account not only the uniqueness of their region, but their desire to find solutions for the problems of other developing countries. This group of goals is related to the fights against terrorism and drug trafficking, redistribution of water resources, energy management, the Aral Sea disaster and Caspian Sea oil and gas challenges.

12.2.2.4 The approaches of Azerbaijan, Armenia and Moldova: international law and conflictual multiculturality

These three states are affected by 'frozen conflicts' and problems of the self-determination of people. Thus, the problem of the Nagorno–Karabakh conflict, which was an international conflict involving Azerbaijan and Armenia and one of the most violent confrontations at the end of the twentieth century, is the first concern of foreign policies of the two states.[50] If the case of Transdniestria is different in the sense that it is an internal conflict, the foreign policy of Moldova is also constructed around the solving of the conflict.[51]

The call for the renewal of post-Soviet doctrines of international law was launched by Professor Tunkin. Tunkin proposed abandoning the principle of peaceful coexistence and replacing it with a concept of widened international cooperation.[52] In an article written shortly before his death in August 1993, Tunkin stressed the urgent need to continue the progressive development of international law and advocated for the new international order based on the rule of law.[53] The most important figure of Soviet international law thereby

48 Signed on 8 September 2006 and entered into force on 21 March 2009.

49 The complete title is 'Addressing the Special Needs of Landlocked Developing Countries within a New Global Framework for Transit Transport Cooperation for Landlocked and Transit Developing Countries'.

50 Every discourse of Armenia and Azerbaijan at the UNGA from 1991 contained the call for resolving the conflict: see T. Potier, *Conflict in Nagorno-Karabakh, Abkhazia and South Ossetia: a Legal Appraisal* (The Hague: Kluwer Law International, 2001).

51 See the statements of the Republic of Moldova at the UNGA from 1992. See also O. Kamenchuk, 'Complexities of Conflict Prevention and Resolution in the Post-Soviet Space' (2005) 6 *European Yearbook of Minority Issues* 99–116, N. V. Ostrouhov, 'Meždunarodno-pravovye problemy razrešenija vooružennyh konfliktov na postsovetskom prostranstve', dissertation of candidate in law (Moscow, 2005).

52 E. McWhinney and G. Tunkin, *From Coexistence to Cooperation: International Law and Organisation in the Post-Cold War Era* (Dordrecht: Martinus Nijhoff, 1991).

53 G. I. Tunkin, 'Is General International Customary Law Only?' (1993) 4 EJIL 534.

'passed the reins' to the new generation of post-Soviet international lawyers. However, one cannot see between Western-oriented theories and historically conditioned doctrines, specific and clearly defined Russian, Ukrainian, Georgian, Azerbaijani, Kazakh, Uzbek and Kyrgyz models of international law. A significant number of post-Soviet international lawyers still consider themselves as part of one united intellectual space.[54] Only certain trends are detectable in the science of international law in the post-Soviet states: the development of the law of the sea in Azerbaijan,[55] Kazakhstan[56] and Russia,[57] because of the problems of delimitation of the Caspian Sea and the Russian advancement in the Arctic, the study of European law offside-by-side with international law in Russia and Ukraine, and the particular conception of the role of custom in international law developed by some Central Asian scholars.[58] Given that post-Soviet states had always been part of a single state; it has proved difficult to build genuine national identities as well as national doctrines of international law. Furthermore, the common historical heritage cannot so far distinguish a separate doctrine from between these new trends. This is why we include the different approaches in post-Soviet states within the same concept of post-Soviet international legal doctrine.

If defining a legal culture as 'a set of principles, values and concepts, a discourse and a shared practice, maintained by the same methods of teaching and thinking in each country or region of the world in the way that they represent a certain tradition of thought',[59] then the post-Soviet states share the same legal culture. Despite being close to the Roman–Germanic system, the legal systems of these states retain elements of originality that they owe to the socialist period and could be a legal family apart.[60] The language international lawyers use to express themselves is also a factor for a common perception of international law.[61]

54 K. A. Bekjašev (ed.), *Meždunarodnoe publičnoe pravo* (Moskva: Prospekt, 2009), 100.

55 R. Mamedov, *Meždunarodno-pravovoj režim Kaspijskogo morja*, dissertacija kandidata juridičeskih nauk (Baku 1989).

56 A. A. Salimgerej, *Pravovoj status Kaspijskogo morja: problemy teorii i praktiki* (Almaty: KazGJUU 2003).

57 JuG Barsegov, *Kaspij* v. *meždunarodnom prave i mirovoj politike* (Moskva 1998), AN Vylegžanin, *Meždunarodnoe morskoe pravo* (Moskva: Juridičeskaja literatura, 2003).

58 E. M. Abajdeldinov, *Sootnošenie meždunarodnogo i nacionalnogo prava Respubliki Kazahstan (problemy stanovlenija i prioritetnosti)* (Almaty 2006), 70–86.

59 E. Jouannet, 'Les visions française et américaine du droit international: cultures juridiques et droit international', in H. Schmidt (ed.), *Droit international et diversité des cultures juridiques* (Paris: Pédone, 2008), 49.

60 R. Legelais, *Grands systèmes de droit contemporains: approche comparative* (Paris: Litec, 2004), 192; R. David and C. Jauffret-Spinosi, *Les grands systèmes de droit contemporain* (Paris: Dalloz, 2002), 125–202.

61 E. Jouannet, 'Regards sur un siècle de doctrine française du droit international' (2000) *Annuaire Français de Droit International* 2.

12.3 Post-Soviet states in the age of multipolarity: the impact of the Russia–Georgia conflict of August 2008

The Russian President Dmitry Medvedev repeatedly mentioned the concept of multipolarity during the conflict between Russia and Georgia, 'the first war of the multipolar world', in August 2008.[62] This conflict had an impact on post-Soviet international practice as well as on the international order.

12.3.1 The start of the new age of multipolarity: 8 August 2008

At 1 a.m. on 8 August 2008, Georgian military forces launched an 'operation to restore constitutional order' on the territory of Georgia 'in self-defence after repeated armed provocations and with the sole goal of protecting the civilian population and preventing further loss of life among residents of various ethnic backgrounds'.[63] At 1.30 a.m. the tanks of the 58th Russian army entered the territory of Georgia through the Roki Tunnel, justifying this action by a need to stop genocide and protect Russian citizens. During the night of 7 to 8 August, the Georgian army seized a part of Tskhinvali and some Ossetian villages, but was in turn attacked by Russian forces the next morning.[64] On 9 August, Russian bombs hit a residential area of Gori which had three Georgian military bases and launched further air strikes against Georgia, including bombing the port of Poti on the Black Sea, and other targets close to Tbilisi.[65] On 12 August 2008, Russian President Dmitry Medvedev declared an end to the 'coercing Georgia to peace'[66] operation and the same day a draft agreement on settling the conflict, now known as the Medvedev–Sarkozy plan, was developed during negotiations between Medvedev and French President Nicolas Sarkozy, who acted as a mediator in his capacity as President of the European Union.

The events following this conflict divided the international community. The recognition of independence of South Ossetia and Abkhazia by the Russian Federation, the Georgian complaint to the International Court of Justice against the Russian Federation, the involvement of the European Union and the European Court of Human Rights, and the controversies around Georgia's accession to NATO opened debates about the renewal of the

62 P. E. Thomann, 'Russie–Géorgie: première guerre du monde multipolaire' (2008) *Défense nationale et sécurité collective* 34.

63 This Georgian position was expressed at the UN Security Council. UNSC Provisional Record (8 August 2008) UN Doc. S/PV.5951, 5.

64 See 'Russia v Georgia: The Fallout' (22 August 2008) International Crisis Group Rep. 195 (at: www.crisisgroup.org/library/documents/europe/caucasus/195_russia_vs_georgia___the_fallout_russian.pdf).

65 'Géorgie/Russie: Civils en danger' Amnesty International (at: www.amnesty.org/fr/library/asset/EUR56/005/2008/fr/8f6a1015–6947–11dd-8e5e-43ea85d15a69/eur560052008fra.html).

66 See Medvedev's statements (at: www.kremlin.ru/events/chron/2008/08/205061.shtml). R. Allison, 'Russia resurgent? Moscow's Campaign to "Coerce Georgia to Peace"' (2008) 84 *International Affairs* 1145.

world order, the 'world disorder' or the new balance of power in the world. In addition, the debates of the United Nations Security Council from 7 August 2008 were tense and similar to the confrontations of the Cold War era. The Russian representative at the Security Council accused Georgia of genocide and ethnic cleansing against the people of South Ossetia,[67] while the Georgian representative charged Russia with returning to the Soviet doctrine of the 'limited sovereignty'.[68]

The controversial subjects were as set out below.

12.3.1.1 *The number of civilian deaths*

The first controversy created by the conflict focused on the number of dead civilians and refugees in South Ossetia, which varied widely among sources.[69]

12.3.1.2 *The legality of the use of force*

The legality of the use of force by the parties was the main stumbling block to negotiations. Some authors described Russian interference in the internal affairs of Georgia as comparable to the USA's actions in Nicaragua, which were classified by the International Court of Justice as internationally wrongful acts.[70] However, both Georgia and Russia had violated the prohibition of threats of force under Article 2(4) of the UN Charter. Thus, the Independent International Fact-Finding Mission on the Conflict in Georgia concluded that the threats of force issued by Russia and Georgia, and of South Ossetia and Abkhazia were not justifiable under Article 51 of the UN Charter and were illegal.[71]

67 The representative of the Russian Federation at the UN, V. Churkin defended his use of the term 'ethnic cleansing', saying 'How else can we describe it when during the course of today a town of 70,000 inhabitants is being destroyed? What else can we call it when hospitals, schools and residential areas are being destroyed, when scores of thousands of refugees are leaving the Republic?' (UNSC Provisional Record (8 August 2008) UN Doc. S/PV.5952, 10).

68 Georgia's representative at the UN stated: 'all that we were hearing here from the Russian Federation is reminiscent of the statements and propaganda by the Soviet Union when it invaded Afghanistan, Prague and Budapest. The statements were not only based on false information; they were cynical, outrageous and inhuman' (UNSC Provisional Record (10 August 2008) UN Doc. S/PV.5953, 16).

69 The Independent International Fact-Finding Mission on the Conflict in Georgia created on 2 December 2008 by the EU eventually declared that 'Altogether about 850 persons lost their lives, not to mention those who were wounded, who went missing, or the far more than 100,000 civilians who fled their homes. Around 35,000 still have not been able to return to their homes' (Independent International Fact-Finding Mission on the Conflict in Georgia, *Report*, 2009), 5).

70 S. Robert-Cuendet, 'Aspects historiques et juridiques de la crise d'août 2008: des conflits interéthniques à la guerre ouverte avec la Russie' (2008) *Annuaire Français de Droit International* 186–187.

71 The Independent International Fact-Finding Mission identified three armed conflicts: Georgia vs. South Ossetia; Georgia vs. Russia; Georgia vs. Abkhazia.

12.3.1.3 *The legal status and recognition of South Ossetia and Abkhazia*

On 26 August 2008, Russian President Medvedev signed two decrees on the recognition of South Ossetia and Abkhazia as sovereign and independent states.[72] The reactions of states and international organizations to the recognition by Russia of South Ossetia and Abkhazia were prompt. France regretted the Russian decision as it made further negotiations on the agreement on South Ossetia 'extremely difficult'. Italy stressed that 'the decision of the Russian Government has no basis under international law'. The United Kingdom declared that 'military action and Russia's recognition of Abkhazia and South Ossetia by Russia is a unilateral attempt to change the borders of neighbouring countries by the use of force which is totally unacceptable and unjustified'. For Croatia, 'the unfortunate decision to recognize the two Georgian regions is not in accordance with the UN Charter, the Helsinki Final Act, or the previous resolutions of the Security Council'.[73] The extraordinary European Council on the Russian–Georgian crisis, which took place on 1 September 2008, condemned Russia's recognition of South Ossetia and Abkhazia and postponed the conclusion of a partnership agreement with Russia.[74] The North Atlantic Treaty Organization (NATO) also expressed its condemnation of the decision by the Russian Federation to recognize the Georgian regions of South Ossetia and Abkhazia, but was hesitant about Georgia's membership.[75] The Parliamentary Assembly of the Council of Europe declared that the concept of 'protecting citizens abroad' advanced by Russia was unacceptable and disavowed the recognition of two separatist republics as representing the violation of international law and principles of the Council of Europe.[76] States that recognized or expressed a will to recognize South Ossetia and Abkhazia remain a minority. On 3 September 2008, Nicaraguan President Daniel Ortega announced his intention to recognize the two republics proclaimed as 'independent nations' and on 5 September, two decrees endorsed that decision.[77] On 8 September 2008, the President of Belarus, Alexander Lukashenko expressed his country's intention to recognize South Ossetia and Abkhazia.[78] Venezuela and Somalia also supported Russia's recognition of the two entities.[79] The Shanghai Cooperation Organization reacted cautiously without condemning or approving the actions of Russia. At

72 www.kremlin.ru/eng/speeches/2008/08/26/1543_type82912_205752.shtml.

73 UNSC Provisional Record (28 August 2008) UN Doc. S/PV.5969.

74 www.ue2008.fr

75 NATO, Press Release (27 August 2008) (at: www.nato.int/docu/pr/2008/p08–108f.html).

76 www.euractiv.com/fr/elargissement/ue-otan-gardent-pays-distance/article-177763.

77 'Nicaragua joins Russia in recognizing South Ossetia and Abkhazia' (3 September 2008) (at: www.earthtimes.org/articles/show/229515,nicaragua-joins-russia-in-recognizing-south-ossetia-abkhazia.html).

78 http://rian.ru/politics/20080908/151063444.html.

79 'Chavez Backs Russian Recognition of Georgian Regions' (29 August 2008) (at: www.reuters.com/article/gc07/idUSN2945876620080829). Moreover, in December 2009 Nauru recognized the two entities.

its Summit in Dushanbe on 28 August 2008, the Organization expressed grave concern about the situation in South Ossetia and urged the parties to solve their problems peacefully, through dialogue and by facilitating efforts for reconciliation and negotiation.[80]

12.3.1.4 The applicability of international humanitarian law and human rights law

The Independent International Fact-Finding Mission on the Conflict in Georgia analysed the question of the applicability of the rules of both international humanitarian law and international human rights law and found that numerous violations of both had been committed by Georgia, Russia and South Ossetia.[81] It is because of this that two international jurisdictions, the European Court of Human Rights (ECHR) and the ICJ, became involved in the conflict.

12.3.2 After the Russia–Georgia War: a renewed or unbalanced world order?

Analysis of the impact of the Russia–Georgia crisis on the international order is divided. There are two possible results of the crisis: an unbalanced world order, or a renewed world order. In all cases the international community has been disturbed, shaken and/or has shared the crisis.

12.3.2.1 An unbalanced world order

World disorder seems to have settled after the war. The destabilization of the international community was characterized by the controversy around two concepts: international recognition and the responsibility to protect. The argument of the responsibility to protect was put forward by Russia to justify its intervention on Georgian territory. The Russian Foreign Minister Sergei Lavrov stated at a press conference on 9 August 2008 that:

> According to our Constitution there is also responsibility to protect – the term which is very widely used in the UN when people see some trouble in Africa or in any remote part of other regions. But this is not Africa to us, this is next door. This is an area where Russian citizens live. So the Constitution of the Russian Federation, the laws of the Russian Federation make it absolutely unavoidable for us to exercise responsibility to protect.[82]

80 'Shanghai Cooperation Organisation: The Dushanbe summit endorses the Russian action in Georgia' (13 September 2008) *Frontline* (at: www.frontlineonnet.com).

81 See Independent International Fact-Finding Mission (n. 71).

82 www.ln.mid.ru/brp_4.nsf/e78a48070f128a7b43256999005bcbb3/f87a3fb7a7f669ebc32574a1002 62597?OpenDocument.

However, to put the concept of the responsibility of protection into practice, six criteria must be met: just cause, right authority, right intention, last resort, proportionate means and reasonable prospects.[83] In the case of the Russia–Georgia War, evidence for the first criterion could be partially accepted with regard to 'serious and irreparable harm occurring to human beings', even if the number of dead civilians was not clearly established. However, the accusations of genocide or ethnic cleansing were not acceptable. The five other conditions were not met. The Russian intervention took place without United Nations Security Council authorization; this is a prerequisite for any kind intervention. Regarding good intention, military force cannot be used for the alteration of borders or the advancement of a particular combatant group's claim to self-determination. Military intervention must be collective or multilateral, rather than handled by a single country. The criterion of last resort, which requires the exhaustion of all diplomatic means of peaceful resolution of crises, was not met in this case. Finally, sending 20,000 soldiers and 100 tanks into South Ossetia, within a very short time, cannot be regarded as a proportionate means to the initial provocation by Russia.[84] In addition to this, in his declaration about the situation in South Ossetia on 8 August 2008, President Medvedev stated that: 'in conformity with the Constitution and the Russian federal legislation…I have an obligation to defend life and dignity of Russian citizens wherever they are. The logic of our approach at this time is dictated by these circumstances'.[85] The idea of the responsibility to protect is to rescue any citizens in the world who find themselves in difficult situations. The protection of its own citizens on the territory of another state does not relate to the concept of responsibility to protect: it relates to the concept of self-protection.[86] The concept of responsibility to protect was hastily used by Russia and is difficult to accept as valid in the case of Russian–Georgian conflict.

Another controversial subject arose after the adoption of President Medvedev's decrees on the recognition of South Ossetia and Abkhazia on 26 August 2009.[87] International recognition may be explicit or implicit.[88] In this case Russia seems to have opted for an implicit recognition by creating with the decrees a provisional legal basis while awaiting the conclusion of the

83 International Commission on the State Sovereignty, *The Responsibility to Protect* (December 2001) (at: www.iciss.ca/pdf/Commission-Report.pdf, §4.16).

84 International Crisis Group (n. 64).

85 Declaration on the situation in South Ossetia (8 August 2008) (at: www.kremlin.ru/appears/2008/08/08/1522_type63374type63378type82634_205027.shtml).

86 Allison (n. 66), 1152–4.

87 The Decrees of the Russian President on the recognition of South Ossetia No. 1261 and Abkhazia No. 1260 of 26 August 2008 (at: www.kremlin.ru/eng/speeches/2008/08/26/1543_type82912_205752.shtml).

88 J. Salmon, *Dictionnaire de droit international public* (Bruxelles: Bruylant, 2001), 939–40; J. Verhoeven, 'La reconnaissance internationale: déclin ou renouveau?' (1993) *Annuaire Français de Droit International* 18.

agreement of the 'solicited intervention' with South Ossetia to justify the future presence of Russian military forces.[89]

The proclamation of Kosovo's independence on 17 February 2008 and its recognition as a *sui generis* case, 'unique' in some way, served as a stumbling block in discussions about the recognition of South Ossetia and Abkhazia. After the recognition of two republics on 26 August 2008, President Medvedev stated that if the recognition of Kosovo was a *causus sui generis*, so too was the recognition of South Ossetia and Abkhazia. The declaration of Kosovo's independence was based on Security Council resolutions and the Antisaari Plan, and, to date, Kosovo has been recognized by seventy-six states, including a majority of European Union members. South Ossetia's independence was directly recognized by the presidential decrees of Medvedev and is currently recognized by four states. Although the context of the independence of Kosovo and South Ossetia is not the same, the legitimacy of the independence of both entities and their international recognition are controversial subjects which demand clearer and more consistent answers from international law.[90] Sixteen rounds of discussions in Geneva about security in the South Caucasus, which were held in 2008–9 in accordance with the agreement of 8 September 2008, with the representatives of the UN, the EU, the OSCE, Russia, Georgia, the United States and, informally, representatives from South Ossetia and Abkhazia, did not provide clarification on the status of the South Ossetia and Abkhazia. No legally binding document was adopted.

12.3.2.2 *The renewed world order*

The assumption of a renewed global order can be confirmed by the renewal of the approaches of the two concerned states after the crisis. Russia insists on the formation of a multipolar world, while Georgia chooses a world united by democracy. The involvement of international courts in the Russian–Georgian conflict is another factor of renewal, given the historically negative attitude to the judicial settlement of disputes in the countries of the USSR.

Russia clearly expressed its position at the first international forum after the conflict, the 63rd session of the UN General Assembly:

> The illusion of the existence of a unipolar world confused many of us … The all-permissiveness syndrome…went rampantly out of all possible control on the night before 8 August when an aggression was unleashed on South Ossetia. The bombing of the sleeping city of Tskhinval, the

89 P. Weckel and F. Costica, 'Conflit en Géorgie, la portée des reconnaissances prématurées', *Sentinelle de la SFDI* (7 September 2008) no. 158 (at: www.sfdi.org).

90 O. Corten, 'Déclarations unilatérales d'indépendance et reconnaissances prématurées: du Kosovo à l'Ossétie du Sud et à l'Abkhazie' (2008) 4 RGDIP 721. See also R. Müllerson, 'Precedents in the Mountains: On the Parallels and Uniqueness of the Cases of Kosovo, South Ossetia and Abkhazia' (24 January 2009) *Chinese JIL*.

> killing of civilians and peacekeepers trampled under foot all settlement agreements, thus putting an end to the territorial integrity of Georgia… Today, it is essential to analyze the crisis in the Caucasus from the viewpoint of its impact on the region and international community on the whole. The world has changed again. It has become crystal clear that the solidarity expressed by all after 11 September 2001 should be revived through the concepts cleared of geopolitical expediency and built on the rejection of double standards when we fight against any infringements of international law – be it on the part of terrorists, belligerent political extremists or any others. The crisis in the Caucasus proved again that it is impossible and even dangerous to try to resolve the existing problems in the blindfolds of the unipolar world.[91]

Russian aspirations to build a multipolar world, where Russia can play an important role, were reinforced by the proposal of President Medvedev to develop a treaty on Euro-Atlantic security, a kind of 'Helsinki-II', first raised in Berlin on 5 June 2008 and reiterated in his declaration on the conference on world politics in Evian on 8 October 2008.[92]

The Georgian view was expressed by the Georgian President Mikhail Saakashvili at the 63rd session of the UN General Assembly:

> While the crisis poses grave challenges for the entire international community, it creates specific obligations for my own country. I would argue that the answer to that new assault on our shared values is not a closing up or a circling of the wagons, but rather greater openness on many fronts. As a democracy, we have nothing to fear…Despite all the turmoil, my country has endured. That proves the resiliency and irreversibility of our democratic commitment. In short, we will fight the spectre of aggression and authoritarianism with the most potent weapon in our arsenal, namely, our commitment to ever-expanding freedoms within our own borders. That amounts to nothing less than a second Rose Revolution. If our first revolution was about meeting a threat from within by reinventing a failed State riddled by corruption, our second revolution must be even more focused, as we now face an even greater challenge … from the outside. The success of the first Rose Revolution helped save my country. The health of the international order could well depend on the outcome of the second Rose Revolution.[93]

91 UNGA 'Address by Sergei Lavrov Foreign Minister of the Russian Federation' (27 September 2008) UN Doc. A/63/PV.14, 2.

92 D. Medvedev, 'Speech at World Policy Conference' (8 October 2008) (at: www.kremlin.ru/eng/speeches/2008/10/08/2159_type82912type82914_207457.shtml).

93 M. Saakashvili in UNGA Provisional Record (23 September 2008) UN Doc. A/63/PV.6, 26.

The second major factor in the renewal of the world order is the opening of post-Soviet states to international judicial institutions. On 12 August 2008, Georgia instituted proceedings against the Russian Federation before the International Court of Justice for 'its actions on and around the territory of Georgia' as a breach of the 1965 International Convention on the Elimination of All Forms of Racial Discrimination (CERD).[94] Georgia's application also sought 'to ensure that the individual rights' under the Convention 'of all persons on the territory of Georgia are fully respected and protected'.[95] As a basis for the jurisdiction of the Court, Georgia invoked Article 22 CERD. It also reserved its right to invoke Article IX of the Genocide Convention, to which both Georgia and Russia are parties, as an additional basis for the Court's jurisdiction.

Georgia's choice to use the Convention on the Elimination of All Forms of Racial Discrimination and the Convention on the Prevention and Punishment of the Crimes of Genocide is easily explained. In 1989, the USSR recognized the compulsory jurisdiction of the International Court of Justice by deciding to withdraw the reservations it had previously made to human rights treaties. This action showed a new attitude of the USSR with respect to international law, which was characterized by the rule of law in politics, the supremacy of international law over domestic law and the importance of all means of peaceful settlement of disputes. However, the scope of this action was limited because it concerned only six conventions,[96] and only disputes which arose after the date on which the Soviet Union informed the Secretary-General of the withdrawal of these reservations could be submitted to the International Court of Justice.[97]

The European Court of Human Rights also found itself involved in the Russian–Georgian crisis. By 9 October 2008, the ECHR had received some 2,729 applications filed by applicants from South Ossetia. These claimants alleged that, following the intervention of Georgian armed forces in August 2008, they had suffered violations of the rights guaranteed by Articles 2 (right to life), 3 (prohibition of inhuman treatments), 8 (right to respect for private and family life), 13 (right to an effective remedy) and 14 (prohibition of discrimination) of the Convention and Article 1 of Protocol No. 1 (protection

94 See R. Tkatova, 'L'affaire relative à l'application de la Convention internationale sur l'élimination de toutes les formes de discrimination raciale (Géorgie c. Fédération de Russie)' (2009) 3, Journal du CDI 9–12 (at: http://cdi.lyon3.free.fr/cdi.lyon3/Le_Journal_du_CDI.html).

95 'Georgia institutes proceedings against Russia for violations of the Convention on the Elimination of All Forms of Racial Discrimination', ICJ press release 2008/23 (at: www.icj-cij.org/docket/files/140/14659.pdf).

96 Convention on the Prevention and Punishment of the Crime of Genocide of 1948, Convention for the suppression and abolition of the Traffic in Persons and of the Exploitation of the Prostitution of Others 1949, Convention on the Political Rights of Women 1952, Convention on the Elimination of All Forms of Racial Discrimination 1965, Convention on the Elimination of All Forms of Discrimination against Women 1979, Convention against Torture and Other Cruel, Inhuman and Degrading Treatment or Punishment of 1984.

97 Bretton (n. 24), 261–75.

of property). They referred in particular to damage to their health and damage to their property rights.[98] Georgia also wanted International Criminal Court involvement.[99] At the same time, the NGO People in South Ossetia against Genocide filed 2,500 petitions to the ICC about crimes committed by Georgia in South Ossetia.[100] At the ICC, Prosecutor Luis Moreno-Ocampo confirmed on 20 August 2008 that his office was conducting an analysis of the situation in Georgia.[101]

Our century already has some points of reference for the international lawyers of the future: thus 'after 11 September 2001' and 'after the Iraqi War in 2003' are reference points for the international law of the early twenty-first century. Will they also think about the new world order 'after 8 August 2008'?

98 '2,700 requêtes reçues à la Cour par des requérants d'Ossétie du Sud contre la Géorgie', Communiqué du Greffier de la CEDH (10 October 2008) (at: http://cmiskp.echr.coe.int/tkp197/view.asp?item=4&portal=hbkm&action=html&highlight=russie%20%7C%20contre%20%7C%20georgie&sessionid=18818942&skin=hudoc-pr-fr).

99 'Georgia Files Ethnic Cleansing Case against Russian Federation at International Criminal Court' (12 August 2008) Tbilissi's Blog (at: http://tbilisiwebinfo.wordpress.com/2008/08/12/georgia-files-ethnic-cleansing-case-against-russian-federation-at-international-criminal-court).

100 'Up In Flames, Part 5: International Scrutiny of Rights Violations in the Conflict', Human Rights Watch (at: www.hrw.org/en/node/79681/section/31); 'It May Take Years to Investigate Crimes Committed in South Ossetia' *Rossiskaya Gazeta* (11 September 2008) (at: www.rg.ru/2008/09/11/osetia-mucihin.html).

101 'ICC prosecutor confirms situation in Georgia under analysis', ICC press release ICC–OTP–20080820–PR346 (at: www2.icc-cpi.int/menus/icc/press%20and%20media/press%20releases/press%20releases%20(2008)/icc%20prosecutor%20confirms%20situation%20in%20georgia%20under%20analysis).

13 Universality, the UN and the Organization of the Islamic Conference

Single, complementary or competing universal legal orders?

Katja Samuel[*]

13.1 Introduction

The focus of this chapter is on the concept of universality which lies at the heart of the UN's existence and the achievement of its primary Charter purposes and principles. This includes the development of its legal norms, as well as their ultimate acceptance, implementation and enforcement within the UN's membership. However, the attainment of universality can be difficult to achieve in practice because some elements of the UN's membership and core business are, and are likely to remain, multipolar. This may explain why some entities, both states and organizations, may be unwilling or even unable to endorse fully some UN norms which are developing or have been established, such as in the field of human rights. It is important to identify and better comprehend these multipolar tensions, not least as they may require that alternative methods and solutions be developed for approaching traditional law and policy-making issues within the UN system if the UN is to achieve effectively its primary objectives in practice.

This chapter will examine one aspect of this multipolarity, namely an Islamic conception of universality, and how this is being translated into practice by the Organization of the Islamic Conference (OIC) and its membership. From the outset, it is suggested that not only is there a different Islamic conception of universality, but that this has resulted in the existence of parallel and competing Islamic and UN universal legal orders. The OIC is a useful vehicle through which to examine Islamic conceptions and how they may be utilized in practice. While its own membership of fifty-six member states is itself characterized by its heterogeneous nature – representing the spectrum of Islamic beliefs, coupled with *inter alia* geographical, cultural, ethnic, linguistic, historical, political and economic differences – as an international organization the nature of its primary inputs are generally the

* The author's sincere thanks go to Professor Nigel White, Nottingham University, for commenting on earlier drafts, although any errors remain her own.

product of some consensus and, therefore, provide a useful starting point when examining Islamic norms and how they are used in practice.

In terms of general lawmaking, as will be discussed below, the OIC has established itself upon, and seeks to promote, strengthen and implement, Islamic values and norms. This is potentially of great significance within the UN legal order as the OIC's membership represents almost 30 per cent of the UN General Assembly's voting capacity and, therefore, has a potential to influence the development of all General Assembly norms.[1] This is illustrated by the current impasse on agreeing a universal definition of terrorism which is created primarily by the OIC and its membership.[2] However, it is acknowledged that a significant interpretative challenge exists in relation to such an examination of Islamic practice, namely how to differentiate between 'what pertains to religion, what pertains to culture, and what is the political use of both'.[3] As one commentator has observed, '[t]he relationship between the sacred, as announced in the Qur'an, and the political is one of the ongoing, controversial debates within Islamic countries'.[4] This is not assisted by the ambiguities which exist in relation to the exact content and scope of any 'Islamic' justifications cited, which make them more susceptible to politicization.[5] Nevertheless, not least as these challenges are true of any political entity, the current examination is important because it begins a process of identifying the competing understandings of universality operating inside and outside of the UN, and factors which may influence the normative behaviour of some Islamic entities.

Before examining current practice of the OIC, it is necessary first to examine the key UN and Islamic lawmaking building blocks, namely those of a UN conception of universality; an Islamic conception of universality, including the meaning and relevance of the Islamic ummah; and Islamic conceptions of justice and legitimacy. Each of these will be considered in turn.

1 For more information on the OIC, see, for example, S. S. Khan, *Reasserting International Islam: A Focus on the Organisation of the Islamic Conference and Other Islamic Institutions* (Oxford: Oxford University Press, 2001) and the OIC's official website (at: www.oic-oci.org).

2 See for example M. Hmoud, 'Negotiating the Draft Comprehensive Convention on International Terrorism: Major Bones of Contention' (2006) 4 JICJ 1031.

3 M. A. Helie-Lucas, 'The Preferential Symbol for Islamic Identity: Women in Muslim Personal Laws', in V. Moghadem (ed.), *Identity Politics and Women: Cultural Reassertions and Feminism in International Perspective* (Boulder, CO: Westview, 1994), 404. Such interpretative challenges are illustrated clearly by the recent headscarf-hijab debates within Europe. On this, see D. McGoldrick, 'Culture, Cultures, and Cultural Rights', in M. A. Baderin and R. McCorquodale (eds.), *Economic, Social and Cultural Rights in Action* (Oxford: Oxford University Press, 2007), 447–73; D. McGoldrick, *Human Rights and Religion: The Islamic Headscarf Debate in Europe* (Portland, OH: Hart, 2006).

4 D. Littman, 'Universal Human Rights' and 'Human Rights in Islam' (February–March 1999) *Midstream* 3–7.

5 A. E. Mayer, 'Universal Versus Islamic Human Rights: A Clash of Cultures or a Clash with a Construct?' (1994) 15 *Mich.J.Int'l L.* 307.

13.2 UN conceptions of universality

The exact meaning and nature of a UN conception of universality is itself contested, not least because of the religious, legal, cultural and historical diversity of, and competing agendas within, the UN's membership. Although not considered in detail here, the relevance of such cultural relativism debates is acknowledged,[6] not least as values, principles and rules do not operate within vacuums, rather they exist within particular cultures[7] which have different and competing civilizational perceptions, expectations and interpretations of even agreed norms.[8] Wyler and Papaux analogize their relevance to prisms through which any univocal to universal norm is diffracted, received and reappropriated by the various cultures under consideration.[9]

Simma suggests three different conceptions of universality within the UN system. The first is what he terms as the 'classic' understanding whereby non-universal norms, such as at the bilateral and regional levels, are embedded within and are therefore part of a universally applicable and binding body of international law.[10] The second conception is whether international law can be perceived as a coherent legal system rather than merely a random collection of unconnected legal norms, which is developed further in the third conception, namely the perceived necessity by universalists of establishing an integrated global public social order founded on a common legal order.[11]

The first conception is believed to be the most realistic, not least in light of the current discussion of a UN system which is both able to produce its own universally applicable and binding norms, but is able also to accommodate some, but not all, elements of national and regional normative diversity norms under its universal umbrella. As the following examination of Shari'ah norms and obligations will reveal, not only do the second and third conceptions of universality proposed by Simma not exist currently, but they are unachievable objectives. Consequently, the term 'universality' is used here interchangeably to refer to the ability to create hard and soft law norms which are universal in

6 See for example R. Falk, B. Rajagopal and J. Stevens (eds.), *International Law and the Third World: Reshaping Justice* (London: Routledge-Cavendish, 2009); F. Francioni and M. Scheinen (eds.), *Cultural Human Rights* (Leiden: Martinus Nijhoff, 2008).

7 E. Wyler and A. Papaux, 'The Search for Universal Justice', in R. St. J. Macdonald and D. M. Johnston (eds.), *Towards World Constitutionalism: Issues in the Legal Ordering of the World Community* (Leiden: Martinus Nijhoff, 2005), 296.

8 K. Zemanek, 'Basic Principles of UN Charter Law', in R. St. J. Macdonald and D. M. Johnston (eds.), *Towards World Constitutionalism: Issues in the Legal Ordering of the World Community* (Leiden: Martinus Nijhoff, 2005), 402. See also A. A. An-Na'im, *Islam and the Secular State: Negotiating the Future of Shari'a* (Cambridge, MA: Harvard University Press, 2008), 24–5; B. Tibi, 'Human Rights in Islamic Civilisation and in the West: International Morality as a Cross-Cultural Foundation', in Z. D. Abuhusayn and M. I. Waley (eds.), *The West and Islam: Towards a Dialogue* (Istanbul: OIC Research Centre for Islamic History, Art and Culture, 1999), 50.

9 Wyler and Papaux (n. 7), 296.

10 B. Simma, 'Universality of International Law from the Perspective of a Practitioner' (2009) 2 EJIL 265, 267.

11 *Ibid.* 267–8.

the sense that they: produce common rights and obligations throughout the UN's membership;[12] reflect the genuine consensus of at least the vast majority of the UN's membership; are perceived largely as legitimate by UN member states (and international organizations, including regionally); and consequently are generally both implemented and complied with. This approach of identifying significant rather than total adherence to universal norms recognizes that the attainment of absolute and genuine levels of consensus and compliance within such a heterogeneous UN membership is rare in practice.

This understanding of UN universality is located within the Westphalian conception of an international legal system whereby states are the primary actors,[13] and in which the foundational building blocks of international law creation are statehood, sovereignty, sovereign equality and consent.[14] Although a detailed examination of the UN legal order is beyond the scope of the current chapter,[15] it is important to discuss briefly a few key characteristics in order to highlight conceptual differences, and resultant normative tensions, between UN and Islamic conceptions of universality. The first is the centrality of the nation state to international law rights and obligations since the Treaty of Westphalia in 1648,[16] which key characteristics include having: a permanent population; a defined territory; a government; and capacity to enter into relations with other states.[17] As will be examined below in relation to the Islamic ummah, no such conception of a nation state exists with Islam.

An additional significant source of normative tension attributable to the Westphalian system is that ultimate power is vested in the secular framework of sovereign states with independent rulers rather than in higher religious authorities, as had been the case previously.[18] As will be seen, this presents a particular difficulty for Islamic entities with respect to the UN conception of sovereignty, which is foundational to the UN legal order including as an

12 See, for example, H. Kelsen, *Principles of International Law*, ed. and rev. R. Tucker (2nd edn, New York, NY: Rinehart, 1966), 228–9.

13 See, for example, C. Warbrick, 'States and Recognition in International Law', in M. D. Evans (ed.), *International Law* (2nd edn, Oxford: Oxford University Press, 2006), 218, 221.

14 See, for example, *Case of the SS Lotus* (*France* v. *Turkey*) [1927] PCIJ Rep. Series A No. 10, 1, 18–19, which represents the traditional position in international lawmaking of a system of sovereign and equal states which actions are limited only by rules which have been consented to freely as legally binding. See also I. Brownlie, *Principles of Public International Law* (6th edn, Oxford: Oxford University Press, 2003) 3, 57–9, 69–76, 287.

15 See, for example, Warbrick (n. 13), 217; S. C. Neff, 'A Short History of International Law', in M. D. Evans (ed.), *International Law* (2nd edn, Oxford: Oxford University Press, 2006), 35; L. Gross, 'The Peace of Westphalia, 1648–1948' (1948) 42 AJIL 20.

16 See, for example, Neff (n. 15).

17 D. J. Harris, *Cases and Materials on International Law* (6th edn, London: Sweet & Maxwell, 2004), 99, including n. 2. See also R. Higgins, *Problems and Process* (Oxford: Clarendon Press, 1994), 39–42, including on more contested issues relating to statehood such as the recognition of newly created states.

18 Gross (n. 15), 40; R. Falk, 'A New Paradigm for International Legal Studies: Prospects and Proposal' (1975) 84 *Yale LJ* 969, 980–7.

expression of the legal personality and capacity of states,[19] as under Islam ultimate sovereignty resides with Allah and cannot be separated therefore from associated religious duties. Similarly, the concept of sovereign equality, which has been described as 'the linchpin of the whole body of international legal standards, the fundamental premise on which all international relations rest',[20] and which expects that all member states must be treated on the same basis even if their respective rights and duties vary to reflect individual legal obligations, is problematic.[21] In addition to the issue of sovereignty mentioned already, as will be seen, there are some key Islamic concepts which suggest that Muslim and non-Muslim entities, including states, are not regarded as being fully equal within the UN understanding of the term.

13.3 Relevance of the Islamic ummah to the OIC

In order to comprehend more fully Islamic conceptions such as those on universality, it is necessary to consider briefly the foundational concept of the Islamic ummah. The concept, which has no exact English equivalent, refers to a committed group of people sharing the same Islamic ideals, which form a common bond that 'transcend[s] national and tribal loyalties rooted in the accident of birth, and [is] a community of believers, bound together in a brotherhood more vital than that of blood'.[22] Therefore, the term Islamic ummah is used to refer to the worldwide community of Muslim believers, who aspire to create a universal Islamic nation, community or distinguishable political entity based on Islamic ideals,[23] to which all Muslims belong regardless of where they reside physically,[24] and to which ultimate loyalty is owed.[25] It is evident therefore that, unlike the Westphalian system, the normal characteristics of statehood, such as geographical location or fixed territory, are not relevant.[26]

19 See, for example, Brownlie (n. 14), 106; *Western Sahara Case* (Advisory Opinion) [1975] ICJ Rep. 12 [92], which confirmed that the establishment of state sovereignty is inseparably linked to the exercise of authority.

20 A. Cassese, *International Law* (2nd edn, Oxford: Oxford University Press, 2005), 48. See also Warbrick (n. 13), 213; V. Lowe, *International Law* (Oxford: Oxford University Press, 2007), 115; B. Simma (ed.), *The Charter of the United Nations: A Commentary* (Oxford: Oxford University Press, 1994), 87.

21 Warbrick (n. 13), 206.

22 J. A. Williams (ed.), *Themes of Islamic Civilization* (Berkeley, CA: California University Press, 1971), 8–9, cited in Khan (n. 1), 2.

23 A. al-Ahsan, *Ummah or Nation? Identity Crisis in Contemporary Muslim Society* (Leicester: Islamic Foundation, 1992), 7 n. 5; Khan (n. 1), 2–3; M. T. al-Ghunaimi, *The Muslim Conception of International Law and the Western Approach* (The Hague: Martinus Nijhoff, 1968), 62; N. Levtzion, *International Islamic Solidarity and Its Limitations* (Hebrew University, Jerusalem: Magnes Press, 1979), 6; A. A. Kurdi, *The Islamic State: A Study based on the Islamic Holy Constitution* (London: Mansell, 1984) 54.

24 Kurdi (n. 23), citing the Qur'an, al-Anbiyā' 21:92: 'Verily, this nation of yours constitutes one nation and I am your God, therefore worship me [alone]'.

25 *Ibid.* 55.

26 Al-Ghunaimi (n. 23), 64; al-Ahsan (n. 23), 65; Khan (n. 1), 2–3.

Of particular relevance to the current examination of OIC practice, the OIC is founded on the concept and aspirations of the Islamic ummah.[27] One of its key Charter objectives is the attainment of unity, fraternity and solidarity within its membership.[28] The creation of the OIC was itself an institutional attempt to provide a unifying focal point for the Islamic world following the abolition of the Caliphate in 1924.[29] However, the forty-five years of obstacles, including rivalry, distrust, disunity and conflict, prior to the OIC's eventual creation in 1969 reveal some of the historical and ongoing difficulties in achieving such unity in practice.[30]

The ummah identity is reflected in both the OIC's Charter[31] as well as its core outputs such as the resolutions of its heads of state summits and annual meetings of the International Conference of Foreign Ministers, and the Cairo Declaration on Human Rights in Islam 1990 (Cairo Declaration).[32] For example, the intention to adhere strictly to Islamic values and principles was emphasized during the First Islamic Summit Conference in Rabat in 1969, not least as the highest form of practical and ideological protection for Muslims against the dangers confronted by the Muslim world,[33] especially from non-Muslim, Western sources.

Although commentators disagree as to the true extent of the expression of the ummah ideal through the OIC,[34] the concept of ummah is normatively important, including in its relation to the achievement of UN universal ideals, for three principal reasons. First, regardless of the practical difficulties

27 See, for example, G. R. Alibabai, 'OIC: An Overview of its Failures and Achievements', in G. Sarwar, *OIC: Contemporary Issues of the Muslim World* (Rawalpindi: Friends, 1997), 65.

28 OIC Charter, Preamble and Article 1(1). All references to the OIC Charter refer to the March 2008 revised version of the Charter. All OIC documents referred to are available at the OIC's official website (at: www.oic-oci.org).

29 S. G. Haim, 'The Abolition of the Caliphate and its Aftermath', in T. W. Arnold, *The Caliphate* (London: Routledge & Kegan Paul, 1965), 208–10. From the time of the Prophet Muhammad until the abolition of the Ottoman Caliphate in 1924, there were often several, concurrent caliphates claimed by different dynasties, including those of the Umayyads, Abbasids, the Fatimids and the Ottomans, which are described in Arnold's book.

30 See generally M. Krammer, *Islam Assembled: The Advent of the Muslim Congresses* (New York, NJ: Columbia University Press, 1986); Levtzion (n. 23); N. A. Baba, *OIC: Theory and Practice in Pan-Islamic Cooperation* (Karachi: Oxford University Press, 1994); A. L. P. Burdett (ed.), *Islamic Movements in the Arab World 1913–1966*, vol. 4: 1949–1966 (Slough: Archive Editions, 1998).

31 See OIC Charter, Articles 7, 9, 10, 27.

32 See also Islamic Council, Universal Islamic Declaration on Human Rights (UIDHR) 1981 (adopted 19 September 1981) Article XXIII (at: www.ntpi.org/html/uidhr.html; accessed 20 August 2009).

33 Declaration of the Rabat Islamic Summit Conference, 1st OIC Summit 1969. See also al-Ahsan (n. 23), 140, including n. 5; Levtzion (n. 23), 6.

34 Views range from the OIC having little relevance in practice (see, M. El-Sayed Selim and M. B. El-Sayed, 'The Organisation of the Islamic Conference: A General Profile', in M. El-Sayed Selim (ed.), *The Organisation of the Islamic Conference in a Changing World* (Cairo University, Giza: Center for Political Research and Studies, 1994), 4); to it being inspirational (see al-Ahsan (n. 23), 6); to it being the most recent manifestation of the ummah ideal (see, N. A. Baba (n. 30), viii, 24; Khan (n. 1), 4–5, 7).

associated with its realization and related shortfalls,[35] it remains one of the foundational aspirations of the Islamic religion and, having divine characteristics, is a permanent and unchangeable ideal which should influence the practice of Islamic entities. This divine nature, coupled with its potential collective strength, including normatively, is illustrated by the following two quotes from the Qur'an:

> The Muslim is the brother of Muslim: he shall not do him wrong or let wrong be done to him; if he comes to his brother's need, Allah shall come to his needs…and if he shields a Muslim, Allah shall shield him on the day of resurrection.[36]

Therefore, 'Muslims are like a building. Every unit reinforces and is reinforced by others'.[37] A recent example of the physical expression and influence of such ummah identity was the response of outrage by Muslims worldwide to the publication of the Danish cartoons of the Prophet Muhammad.[38]

Second, it introduces a number of other sources of potential normative tension within the UN legal order. One, which has been referred to already, relates to the secular nature of the UN legal order, which is incompatible with Shari'ah and its divine obligations. Another reason relates to the collective rather than individual focus of Islam, whereby the greater good of the former will prevail always over the rights of the latter in the event of any conflict, which can create difficulties especially in relation to international human rights law, which focuses on the individual.[39] Finally here, the concept of the ummah highlights some of the significant differences which exist between UN and Islamic conceptions of universality.

13.4 Islamic conception of universality

The concept of ummah is an integral aspect of an Islamic conception of universality. The latter is linked to the aspired for ideal of the establishment of a universal state,[40] which incorporates the whole of mankind including the

35 See, for example, G. Sarwar, 'OIC – Ideals and Realities', in G. Sarwar, *OIC: Contemporary Issues of the Muslim World* (Rawalpindi: Friends, 1997), 89; S. S. Alam, 'OIC – An Appraisal', in G Sarwar, *OIC: Contemporary Issues of the Muslim World* (Rawalpindi: Friends, 1997), 98; S. Mahmassani, 'The Principles of International Law in the Light of Islamic Doctrine' (1966) 117 *Recueil des Cours* 250; S. A. A'La Mawdudi, *The Islamic Movement: Dynamics of Values, Power and Change*, K. Murad (ed. and tr.) (Leicester: Islamic Foundation, 1984).

36 Prophet Muhammad quoted by Abdullah ibn Umar in Bakhari: 46: 3 cited in Khan (n. 1), 3.

37 Qur'an, al-Ĥujurāt 49:10 cited in Khan (n. 1), 3.

38 See, for example, A. Sari, 'The Danish Cartoons Row: Redrawing the Limits of the Right to Freedom of Expression?' (2005) 16 FYBIL 365.

39 Tibi (n. 8), 53.

40 On the global mission of the Prophet Muhammad from the outset of Islam, see, for example Mahmassani (n. 35), 209.

ummah and non-Muslims,[41] which is premised on a single code of morality, religion and politics,[42] and which is ultimately submitted fully to Allah.[43] However, although the foundational objectives are clear, as with UN conceptions of universality, no single agreed approach or meaning exists in relation to the universality of Shari'ah.[44] In particular, clear divergences of opinion exist between traditional and more liberal interpretations of Shari'ah.

More traditional scholars, such as A'La Mawdudi and Ayatollah Khomeyni, attribute much of the Islamic world's historic and current tribulations to the infiltration of oppressive Western influences which have contaminated Islam. Consequently, they aspire to the attainment of an Islamic state as conceived of in the Qur'an, fully cleansed from all contaminating and alien concepts, such as that of the nation state[45] which violates Shari'ah as loyalty is given to the secular state instead of ultimately to Allah whom Muslims believe to be sovereign.[46] As the exercise of power and leadership in Islam is linked to the attainment of this universal state,[47] any exercise by a state or other entity of power and authority which is inconsistent with Shari'ah is regarded as establishing itself as an illegitimate god against Allah,[48] which clearly has implications for Western states and the UN, including in terms of lawmaking. At the more liberal end of the spectrum, while the Islamic universal conception of the state is recognized also, scholars seek to embed Islamic states within rather than extricate them from the Westphalian conception of statehood.[49] Certainly, the nation state principle, with its secular nationalism, has been embraced in practice by the Islamic world,[50] largely out of economic, political, historical, self-determination, post-colonialism and security-related necessity.[51]

41 S. Dayf, 'The Universality of Islam in the Holy Quran and the Noble Hadith', in Islamic Educational, Scientific and Cultural Organization (ISESCO), *The Universality of Islam* (ISESCO, Rabat 1997) (at: www.isesco.org.ma/english/publications/The%20University%20of%20Islam/Menu.php; accessed 18 August 2009).

42 See, for example, Kurdi (n. 23), 64–5. See too, for example, S. A. A'La Mawdudi, *Witnesses unto Mankind: The Purpose and Duty of the Muslim Ummah*, K. Murad (ed. and tr.) (Leicester: Islamic Foundation, 1986), 32–3.

43 Kurdi (n. 23), 56–7; Alibabai (n. 27), 65; B. Lewis, 'The Return of Islam', in M. Curtis (ed.), *Religion and Politics in the Middle-East* (Boulder, CO: Westview 1981), 9–12.

44 See for example M. A. Baderin, *International Human Rights and Islamic Law* (Oxford: Oxford University Press, 2003), 228.

45 See especially A'La Mawdudi (n. 42); F. Rajaee, *Islamic Values and World View: Khomeyni on Man, the State and International Politics*, vol. 13 (Lanham, MD: University Press of America, 1983), 85.

46 A'La Mawdudi (n. 35), 11, 30; Rajaee (n. 45), 91–2.

47 A'La Mawdudi (n. 35), 11.

48 *Ibid.* 31, 34.

49 M. Khadduri, 'The Impact of International Law upon the Islamic World Order' (1972) 66 ASIL PROC 46, 48–9; Mahmassani (n. 35), 250.

50 Al-Ghunaimi (n. 23), 68–9; An-Na'im (n. 8), 286–7 .

51 For example, Khan (n. 1), 14–15 (on all identified aspects including economics and politics); H. Moinuddin, *The Charter of the Islamic Conference and Legal Framework of Economic Co-operation among Its Member States* (Oxford: Clarendon Press, 1987), 70–1; Burdett (n. 30), 322, 341.

Despite the differences of opinion between Islamic scholars over the exact meaning of Islamic universality, it is evident that significant differences exist between UN and Islamic conceptions of universality. In terms of statehood, as mentioned previously, the concept of ummah differs considerably from that of the nation state within the UN legal order, not least as it is not linked to or dependent upon a fixed or defined geographical territory, with a permanent population. This is illustrated, for example, by the application of personal Islamic laws to all Muslims regardless of whether they live in Muslim or non-Muslim territories.[52]

Significant conceptual differences exist in relation to sovereignty also, with more conservative scholars taking the stance that 'no nation is sovereign since God alone is the only sovereign in Whom all authority vests',[53] such that supreme loyalty should be given ultimately to Allah and not to the nation state as under the Westphalian system of secular nationalism.[54] As sovereignty resides ultimately with Allah, it can be delegated only to man as a divine agent, usually to a single ruler or an institution such as the Imam or Caliph,[55] essentially as personal sovereignty linked to the Islamic constitution (the Qur'an) rather than to territory.[56] Under this conception, the duty of those to whom such sovereignty is delegated is not to create, amend or abolish law, which is the prerogative of Allah alone, but rather to maintain and enforce Shari'ah, which applies equally to the delegated ruler or divine agent.[57]

Similarly, the concept of sovereign equality is problematic under an Islamic conception of universality, not only because of the conceptual differences which exist in relation to sovereignty, but also because of the notion of equality in Islam especially regarding non-Muslim entities. Particularly problematic here are the Islamic doctrines of dhimma and jihad. The doctrine of dhimma refers to the historical classification of all people into one of three main religious categories: Muslims, People of the Book (Christians and Jews), and unbelievers.[58] It introduced thereby the concept of inequality, whereby only

52 Mahmassani (n. 35), 252–3.

53 A. B. K. Brohi, 'Preface', in S. K. Malik, *The Quranic Concept of War* (Lahore: Wajidalis, 1979), viii–ix.

54 al-Ahsan (n. 23), 3, 9, 100; Moinuddin (n. 51), 53; M. H. Kamali, *Principles of Islamic Jurisprudence* (3rd edn, Cambridge: Islamic Texts Society, 2003), 8; B. Lewis, *The Political Language of Islam* (University of Chicago Press, 1999), 30; Kurdi (n. 23), 3, 37; S. Sardar Ali and J. Rehman, 'The Concept of Jihad in Islamic International Law' (2005) 10 JCSL 321, 342; M. Khadduri, *War and Peace in the Law of Islam* (Baltimore, MD: John Hopkins Press, 1955), 287–8; A'La Mawdudi (n. 35), 11.

55 Moinuddin (n. 51). Some Islamic states, such as Saudi Arabia, still believe that Islamic law is a divine constitution which limits the powers of their ruling authority. Mahmassani (n. 35), 233; Kamali (n. 54), 8; Rajaee (n. 45), 67.

56 Al-Ghunaimi (n. 23), 66.

57 Lewis (n. 54), 31. For example, the Qur'an states that 'Verily, the only sovereign is God. He declares the law and He is the best judge' – Qur'an al-An'ām 6:57 referred to by Kurdi (n. 23), 37. See also the Qur'an al-An'ām 6:62; Yūsuf 12:40; al-Qaşaş 28:88; Moinuddin (n. 51), 53; Kamali (n. 54), 8.

58 An-Na'im (n. 8), 130.

Muslims could be full members of an Islamic political community,[59] as well as discrimination towards non-Muslims,[60] such that liberal scholars like An-Na'im have advocated for its repudiation and reform.[61] The other is a conception of jihad[62] which, while not accepted as the basis of normal international relations by many modern Islamic scholars,[63] nevertheless introduces notions of difference and inequality between Muslim and non-Muslim territories which may justify less favourable treatment of the latter.[64]

13.5 Islamic conceptions of justice and legitimacy

In order to comprehend Islamic lawmaking more fully, a discussion of two other core concepts, justice and legitimacy, is needed. Justice is a crucial aspect of all lawmaking, including its subsequent effective implementation and compliance. As Sir Gerald Fitzmaurice observed:

> Justice is very seldom achieved by directly aiming at it: rather it is a by-product of the application of legal rules and principles, a consequence of the general order, certainty and stability introduced into human and international relationships through the regular and systematic application of known legal rules and principles, even if these rules and principles are not always perfect and do not always achieve ideal results in every case.[65]

This requires that legal norms are not only clear and certain, but that they are perceived also as being legitimate and fair in order to be regarded as just and consequently implemented.[66] The UN must adhere to its own foundational values and principles, as indicated in its Charter, which include justice.[67]

59 *Ibid.* 130, 283.

60 *Ibid.* 109.

61 *Ibid.* 131, 134, 136.

62 For an explanation of the concept of jihad see, for example, Mahmassani (n. 35), 250–2.

63 Moinuddin (n. 51), 14, 18–19, 45, 65–6; M. Hamidullah, *Muslim Conduct of State* (7th edn, Lahore: SH Muhammad Ashraf, 1977), 191; M. Khadduri (ed.), *Major Middle Eastern Problems in International Law* (Washington, DC: American Enterprise Institute for Public Policy Research, 1972), 2–3. See also generally Mahmassani (n. 35), 201–328; al-Ghunaimi (n. 23), 65; O. A. A. Abouzeid, 'The Policy of the Organization of the Islamic Conference Towards International Issues that Concern the Islamic World' Profile', in M. El-Sayed Selim (ed.), *The Organization of the Islamic Conference in a Changing World* (Cairo University, Giza: Center for Political Research and Studies, 1994).

64 See, for example, Moinuddin (n. 51), 18.

65 G. G. Fitzmaurice, 'The United Nations and the Rule of Law' (1953) 38 *Transactions of the Grotius Society* 135, 147.

66 O. Yasuaki, 'A Transcivilizational Perspective on Global Legal Order in the Twenty-first Century: A Way to Overcome West-centric and Judiciary-centric Deficits in International Legal Thoughts', in R. St. J. Macdonald and D. M. Johnston (eds.), *Towards World Constitutionalism: Issues in the Legal Ordering of the World Community* (Leiden: Martinus Nijhoff, 2005), 151–2.

67 N. D. White, *The United Nations System: Towards International Justice* (London: Lynne Rienner, 2002), 56.

However, although the value of justice underpins and is reflected throughout the UN system,[68] its significance and normative importance do not equate with an Islamic conception of justice, which is pivotal to understanding lawmaking by Islamic entities. An absolute right at the heart of the Qur'an[69] and a primary objective of its revelation,[70] justice is the supreme and quintessential Islamic value in relation to legal, political and social issues especially.[71] For example, a key objective of justice is to release individuals and society from what is regarded by Islam as domination and subordination,[72] and to replace such injustices with Islamic conceptions of justice, equality, mercy, freedom and brotherhood.[73]

Ultimately, Islamic justice is concerned with the attainment of the Islamic ideal of a well-ordered universe and balanced society premised on Shari'ah values and principles,[74] where ultimate obedience is given to Allah.[75] Consequently:

> Justice in the Quran is symbolised by the al-Mizan (balance or scales), which God tells us is the foundation of the whole universe...The 'setting up of the balance' here denotes the fact of making justice the general law of the creation and of the whole universe. He also makes the scales a concomitant of all laws.[76]

Normatively, it is evident that justice must permeate all aspects of lawmaking, not least as it is regarded as the 'the supreme and overarching value of Islam, integrating all spheres of life within one coherent moral and legal framework, or system, in which, at least according to the Islamists, ethics, morals, and the

68 UN Charter 1945 (adopted 26 June 1945, entered into force 24 October 1945) (UN Charter) Preamble; Universal Declaration on Human Rights (adopted 10 December 1948 UNGA Res. 217 A(III)) (UDHR) Preamble; International Covenant on Civil and Political Rights 1966 (adopted 16 December 1966, entered into force 23 March 1976) 999 UNTS 171 (ICCPR) Preamble; Millennium Declaration (adopted 8 September 2000 UNGA Res. 55/2) (UN Millennium Declaration) paras 1–2, 4, 29–30; World Summit Outcome (adopted 15 September 2005 UNGA Res. 60/1) (World Summit Outcome) paras 5, 77.

69 See, for example, the Qur'an: an-Nisā 4:58, and al-Mā'idah 5:8.

70 M. A. Haleem, 'Human Rights in Islam and the United Nations Instruments', in E. Cotran and A. O. Sherif (eds.), *Democracy, the Rule of Law and Islam* (London: Kluwer Law International, 1999), 436. Refers to the Qur'an, al-Ĥadid 57:25.

71 G. Krämer, 'Justice in Modern Islamic Thought', in A. Amanat and F. Griffel (eds.), *Shari'a: Islamic Law in the Contemporary Context* (Stanford University Press, 2007) 27.

72 UIDHR (n. 32), Preamble.

73 Sheikh Wahbeh al-Zuhili, 'Islam and International Law' (2005) 87 IRRC 269, 271–2.

74 Krämer (n. 71), 24. On the importance of justice within the Islamic political system, see also Kurdi (n. 23), 42, 47.

75 A'La Mawdudi (n. 35), 38–9, 54. See also A. Ahmad, 'The Role of Islamic Law in the Contemporary World Order', in M. A. Baderin (ed.), *International Law and Islamic Law* (Farnham: Ashgate, 2008), 56–7; M. Mumīsa, *Islamic Law: Theory and Interpretation* (Beltsville, MD: Amana, 2002), 177 (Islam aspires for the universe, including all states, to be influenced by the same moral code).

76 S. Dayf, 'Justice', in ISESCO (n. 41).

law are no longer differentiated',[77] with divine[78] and inviolable constitutional qualities foundational to the Islamic state.[79] Unsurprisingly, because of its all-inclusive and divine nature, Islamic justice is believed by Muslims to be superior to any other kind of justice, including its expression in legal norms:[80] 'Islamic justice is something higher than the formal justice of Roman law or any other human law...It searches out the innermost motives, because we are to act as in the presence of Allah, to whom all things, acts, and motives are known'.[81]

Another important characteristic of Islamic justice is that it must be adhered to by believers in all of their actions,[82] including as an expression of faith[83] for which Muslim believers will be judged in the afterlife.[84] This includes a collective, religious responsibility to respond to any injustice or dishonour experienced by Muslims,[85] in a violent or non-violent manner depending on the particular context.[86] Clearly, this may have important ramifications in respect of achieving UN universality more generally.

Justice is linked inseparably with legitimacy, including in terms of lawmaking, not least as only the exercise of power and authority that is based on Islamic values is perceived as being just.[87] Although, as with justice, no general agreement exists as to the exact nature and meaning of legitimacy, it is accepted by most that a strong link exists between the legitimacy of a norm and its ultimate acceptance and compliance, including those of international law.[88] There are two key aspects to UN normative legitimacy, substantive and procedural,[89] which are evident within Shari'ah also.

In terms of Islamic conceptions of substantive legitimacy, this is linked inseparably to the Islamic value of justice as a Qur'anic constitutional principle and to progressing the aspired for ideal of an Islamic universal order as described previously. For example, in relation to the jurisprudence of the ICJ,

77 Krämer (n. 71), 28–9.

78 *Ibid.*

79 *Ibid.* 28, referring to the views of the Egyptian scholar, Farīd 'Abd al-Khāliq.

80 *Ibid.* 30.

81 ARI Doi, *Sharī'ah: The Islamic Law* (Kuala Lumpur: AS Noordeen, 2007) 3, 5; cited in Krämer (n. 71).

82 Kurdi (n. 23), 48; Baderin (n. 44), 100. Referring to the Qur'an, an-Nisā 4:1.

83 Kurdi (n. 23), 48–9. Referring to the Qur'an, an-Nisā 4:135; al-Mā'idah 5:8.

84 *Ibid.* 48–9. Referring to the Qur'an, an-Nahl 16:90.

85 UIDHR (n. 32), Article IV(b) and (c).

86 F. Milani, 'Democracy, Justice and Human Rights: Compatible Values?', and A. Soroush, 'Unmasking Prejudice and Facilitating Understanding', Chatham House Conference 'Is Islam a Threat to the West?' (1–2 June 2005), 45 and 49 respectively (at: www.chathamhouse.org.uk/files/3276_cr-islam0605.pdf; accessed 28 July 2009).

87 A'La Mawdudi (n. 35) 49, referring to the Qur'an, Al-Hadīd 57:25.

88 A. A. An-Na'im, 'Why should Muslims abandon *Jihad*? Human Rights and the Future of International Law', in R. Falk, B. Rajagopal and J. Stevens (eds.), *International Law and the Third World: Reshaping Justice* (London: Routledge-Cavendish, 2009), 82–3; O Yasuaki (n. 66), esp. 177; T. M. Franck, *The Power of Legitimacy Among Nations* (Oxford: Oxford University Press, 1990) 24.

89 I. Scobbie, 'Tom Franck's Fairness' (2002) 13 (4) EJIL 909, 910.

Islamic entities are critical of the limited extent to which Shari'ah principles are reflected within the ICJ's jurisprudence, especially in relation to disputes between Islamic states,[90] not least as Muslim judges are expected to reflect Shari'ah norms within their decision-making processes starting first with the Qur'an as the primary source.[91] Procedural legitimacy is concerned also with fulfilling the requirements of divine justice, especially with ensuring that Allah's ultimate sovereignty is reflected in the expression of any procedural authority, including that relevant Shari'ah norms are complied with.[92] Clearly, such Islamic conceptions of justice and legitimacy have potentially significant implications in terms of UN lawmaking, not least in the development of substantive norms which generally do not reflect Shari'ah values or principles, and which procedurally have been produced by a non-Islamic system.

13.6 Islamic conception of universality and the OIC

It will now be considered if, and to what extent, the Islamic conception of universality described above is reflected within the OIC's core outputs and practice. An initial examination of the OIC's Charter suggests acceptance of the UN legal order, such as affirmation of key UN Charter purposes and principles.[93] This includes specific affirmation of secular nation state principles such as the territorial integrity of all states, their political independence, and their related state sovereignty,[94] which, as described previously, are not characteristics associated with an Islamic conception of the state. Indeed, the OIC and its membership affirm regularly such principles, as illustrated by its opposition to the military intervention in Iraq in 2003.[95]

However, despite such initial affirmation of the UN legal order, an examination of core OIC documents and practice suggests that a parallel and competing Islamic legal order exists also. In terms of significant OIC documents, the starting point is the OIC Charter, which itself limits its initial affirmation of UN legal order norms. First, even in referring to key UN principles, such as in Article 2, the OIC Charter qualifies this by reference to Islamic values for their interpretation, which includes the value of justice with all of its normative consequences as explained previously. More specific is the Charter's interpretation clause at Article 37(2) which states that '[t]he provisions of this Charter shall be

90 C. B. Lombardi, 'Islamic Law in the Jurisprudence of the International Court of Justice' (2007) 8 *Chicago JIL* 85, 87, 91–3.

91 Dayf (n. 76).

92 Lewis (n. 54), 31.

93 OIC Charter, Preamble and Article 2.

94 *Ibid.* Articles 1(3), 1(4), 2(4).

95 For example, UNSC 'Iraq–Kuwait' (Resumption 2) (17 October 2002) UN Doc. S/PV.4625,8; Final Communiqué, 29th OIC International Conference of Foreign Ministers (ICFM) (25–7 June 2002) [36] (at: www.oic-oci.org/english/conf/fm/29/29%20icfm-final-e.htm); Final Communiqué, 30th OIC ICFM (28–30 May 2003) [37] (at: www.oic-oci.org/english/conf/fm/30/30%20icfm-fc-en.htm; accessed 21 August 2009); Final Communiqué Annual Coordination Meeting (ACM) (28 September 2004) [21] (at: www.oic-oci.org/english/conf/fm/acm/ny2004-FC.htm; accessed 21 August 2009).

implemented by the Member States in conformity with their constitutional requirements'. Similarly, the Preamble to the Charter states that human rights, fundamental freedoms, good governance, rule of law, democracy and accountability in member states are to be 'in accordance with their constitutional and legal systems'. While the effect of this interpretative clause will vary between member states because of their different constitutional bases, for those states the constitutions of which are premised on Shari'ah principles, the effect of Article 37(2) is to permit UN norms to be subordinated to the requirements of Shari'ah in the event of any normative conflict.[96]

A similar hierarchy of norms exists within the Cairo Declaration,[97] which is the OIC's most significant human rights document in terms of the articulation of Islamic conceptions of human rights. Although not legally binding on its membership, it is of normative importance, especially as it was adopted at the level of OIC Foreign Ministers. From the outset, the Preamble affirms an Islamic conception of sovereignty, including 'the place of mankind in Islam as vicegerent of Allah on Earth', which, as examined previously, has a number of lawmaking implications such as that Allah's delegated authority must implement divine law and is not permitted to add or take away from it. As with the OIC Charter, the Declaration has qualifying interpretative provisions at Articles 24 and 25 which suggest the normative supremacy of Shari'ah in the event of any normative conflict. Article 24 states that '[a]ll the rights and freedoms stipulated in this Declaration are subject to the Islamic Shari'ah', and Article 25 states that '[t]he Islamic Shari'ah is the only source of reference for the explanation or clarification of any of the articles of this Declaration'.

In terms of its content, many of the Declaration's provisions do not accord with parallel international human rights norms,[98] including through its discriminatory provisions against non-Muslims and women as well as the limitations placed on other fundamental rights, as argued by the then Secretary-General of the International Commission of Jurists, Adama Dieng,

96 For example, Saudi Arabia's constitution is the Qur'an (at: www.servat.unibe.ch/law/icl/sa00000_.html; accessed 13 July 2009); Article 3 of the Constitution of Afghanistan 2004 states that '[i]n Afghanistan, no law can be contrary to the beliefs and provisions of the sacred religion of Islam' (at: www.afghan-web.com/politics/current_constitution.html; accessed 13 July 2009); Article 227 Pakistan Constitution 1973, whereby all existing laws are to be consistent with Islam (at: www.pakistanconstitution-law.com/theconst_1973.asp; accessed 13 July 2009); Article 2(A) Iraqi Constitution 2005 whereby 'no law that contradicts the established provisions of Islam may be established' (at: www.uniraq.org/documents/ iraqi_constitution.pdf; accessed 13 July 2009).

97 Cairo Declaration on Human Rights in Islam (adopted and issued 5 August 1990 19th ICFM Res. 49/19–P) (at: www.oic-oci.org/english/conf/fm/19/19%20icfm-political-en.htm#RESOLUTION%20NO.%2049/19-P (Cairo Declaration)).

98 Mayer (n. 5), 3.

in a statement to the UN Human Rights Commission in 1991.[99] The OIC have sought to justify such deviations on the basis that the Universal Declaration on Human Rights (UDHR) did not reflect adequately an Islamic perspective,[100] and that the Declaration was a complementary rather than competing statement of human rights expressing Islam's unique cultural context.[101] However, the validity of such claims is somewhat dubious, as is discussed below.

Another key documentary source suggesting a competing Islamic universal order is the OIC's resolutions and Final Communiqués. This is illustrated starkly by the outputs in respect of human rights of the most recent OIC Islamic Summit of Heads of State, which took place in Dakar, Senegal 13–14 March 2008. It would appear that since at least 1981, when the Universal Islamic Declaration of Human Rights (UIDHR) was adopted, the OIC has been seeking the development of a parallel Islamic system of human rights the provisions of which are not compatible fully with those of established human rights norms. Although not a formal governmental or OIC initiative, rather that of the Islamic Council in London, the UIDHR was backed and contributed towards by a number of Muslim states, such as Egypt, Pakistan and Saudi Arabia, as well as the Muslim World League, which was a precursor to the creation of the OIC in 1969.[102] Many of its provisions have been reflected and developed further by the Cairo Declaration. Of especial relevance to the current discussion on the existence of Islamic conceptions of universality and an Islamic legal order, the UIDHR Preamble not only affirmed Allah as 'the Sovereign, the sole Guide of mankind and the Source of all Law',[103] and the concept of sovereignty as being limited to power delegated by Allah to man,[104] but also affirmed the duty of Muslims to 'establish an Islamic order'[105] which *inter alia* regulates the exercise of all worldly power.[106]

99 See Written Statement by Association for World Education, 'Question of the Violation of Human Rights and Fundamental Freedoms, including Policies of Racial Discrimination and Segregation, in all Countries, with Particular Reference to Colonial and other Dependent Countries and Territories: Report of the Sub-Commission under Commission on Human Rights Resolution 8 (XXIII) (14 July 2003 E/CN.4/Sub.2/2003/NGO/15) [12] (at: www.unhchr.ch/huridocda/huridoca.nsf/(Symbol)/E.CN.4.Sub.2.2003.NGO.15.En?Opendocument; accessed 29 July 2009).

100 Center for Inquiry, 'Islam and Human Rights: Defending Universality at the United Nations' (21 September 2008) 4 (at: www.centerforinquiry.net/uploads/attachments/ISLAM_AND_HUMAN_RIGHTS.pdf; accessed 3 March 2009).

101 *Ibid.* 5, 8.

102 Mayer (n. 5), 30.

103 UIDHR (n. 32), Preamble [a]. Explanatory note 1 to the UIDHR states that '[i]n the above formulation of Human Rights, unless the context provides otherwise: b) the term "Law" denotes the Shari'ah ie the totality of ordinances derived from the Qur'an and the Sunnah and any other laws that are deduced from these two sources by methods considered valid in Islamic jurisprudence'.

104 *Ibid.* Preamble [b], which refers to 'the Vicegerency (Khilafah) of man who has been created to fulfill the Will of God on earth'.

105 *Ibid.* [g].

106 *Ibid.* [g (vi)].

More specifically, the OIC is seeking: the drafting of an Islamic Covenant on Human Rights and a Covenant on Women's Rights in Islam; the finalizing of the drafting of the Islamic Covenant on the Elimination of All Forms of Racial Discrimination;[107] the development of the Islamic Charter on Human Rights; and the ratification of the Covenant on the Rights of the Child in Islam as soon as possible.[108] Additionally, during the 2008 OIC Heads of State Summit, the OIC endorsed the right of every member state to express reservations on international instruments on human rights, as part of their sovereign rights which, for a number of Islamic states, refers to the ultimate authority of Shari'ah and Allah.[109] Such normative developments do not indicate an affirmation of a UN conception of universality as defined at the outset, including the acceptance and implementation of UN human rights norms; rather it suggests an attempt to move closer to the aspired for ideal of an Islamic universal order premised on Shari'ah norms. Certainly, throughout such efforts, the OIC makes explicit reference to an Islamic conception of sovereignty by continuing to affirm 'the prominent place of Man in Islam as Allah's vicegerent on earth'.[110]

Other practice suggests the existence of an Islamic conception of universality also. For example, following the adoption of the UDHR in 1948, the then UN permanent representative for Iran, Said Raja'I Khorasani, in denying allegations of human rights violations by the Iranian government, stated that Iran recognized no authority apart from Shari'ah law and therefore did not recognize any international instruments or declarations which were contrary to it. In rejecting explicitly any authority of the UDHR, Mr Khorasani stated that the Iranian government would not hesitate to violate its provisions.[111] Interestingly too, even those OIC member states which were original proponents of the UDHR – such as Egypt, Iran, Iraq, Lebanon and Syria – now dispute its universal application and core principles.[112] This may be attributable, at least in part, to the unifying influence of the Islamic ummah through the OIC, which did not exist at the time of the UDHR's adoption. Such opposition remains, including by the OIC itself, which exhorted its membership at its 2008 Islamic Summit to use the opportunity presented by the 60th anniversary of the UDHR to lobby for an Islamic conception of human rights.[113]

A further, and very current example, is the OIC's recent and persistent attempts within the UN, in particular within the UN Human Rights Council, to secure the universal criminalization of what it terms defamation of religions,

107 Final Communiqué, 11th OIC Islamic Summit (13–14 March 2008 Dakar, Senegal) [105] (at: www.oic-oci.org/is11/english/FC-11-%20SUMMIT-en.pdf; accessed 21 August 2009).

108 *Ibid.* [114].

109 *Ibid.* [112].

110 *Ibid.*

111 Center for Inquiry (n. 100), 6; Littman (n. 4).

112 Center for Inquiry (n. 100), 9.

113 11th Islamic Summit (n. 107) [106].

by which it really means blasphemy against Islam, by associating any criticism of Islam or Islamic entities with racism.[114] While this raises a number of concerning issues, one in particular has been the related attempts of the OIC and its membership to change established international human rights norms on freedom of speech and expression away from the protection of individual rights to the protection of religious beliefs and ideologies, specifically Islam. Both the UN Special Rapporteur on Freedom of Opinion and Expression, Mr Ambeyi Ligabo,[115] and the European Union,[116] have resisted such normative developments as being contrary not only to specific human rights protections, but also as being contrary to the foundational assumptions on which international human rights law is premised whereby rights belong to individuals rather than to ideas or institutions.

In response to any criticisms regarding such normative efforts, the OIC and its membership often respond along familiar lines that international human rights law norms do not reflect fully their cultural and religious diversity and requirements, which is not entirely true. It is recognized fully that even though a small number of Islamic states were involved in the drafting and negotiation process of the UN Charter[117] and UDHR,[118] this was at a time when such states were politically weak, including those gaining independence after colonial rule.[119] However, there have been significant opportunities also for the normative input of OIC member states and other former colonized nations since the inception of the UDHR. This includes their involvement with the drafting and negotiation of subsequent significant international law declarations and human rights instruments, which were developed over many years in the General Assembly and which were dominated by Non-Aligned

114 Most recently, on 26 March 2009, the UN Human Rights Council adopted a resolution proposed by Pakistan to provide 'protection against acts of hatred, discrimination, intimidation and coercion resulting from defamation of religions and incitement to religious hatred in general' on *inter alia* the grounds that 'Islam is frequently and wrongly associated with human rights violations and terrorism' (UNHRC, 'Draft Report of the Human Rights Council on its Tenth Session' (12 May 2009) UNHRC Res. 10/22 A/HRC/10/L.11, 78–83).

115 UNHRC, 'Report of the Special Rapporteur on the Promotion and Protection of the Right to Freedom of Opinion and Expression, Ambeyi Ligabo', Seventh Session of the HRC (7 March 2008) UNHRC Rep. A/HRC/7/14) [40].

116 See, for example, Portugal's response on behalf of the European Union to the UN General Assembly Resolution on Combating Defamation of Religions adopted 18 December 2007, referred to by the International Humanist and Ethical Union, 'Islamic Law versus Human Rights' (10 March 2008) (at: www.iheu.org/node/ 2949; accessed 21 August 2009).

117 Egypt, Iran, Iraq, Lebanon, Saudi Arabia, Syria and Turkey (at: www.un.org/en/members/growth.shtml#text; accessed 23 July 1990).

118 Afghanistan, Egypt, Iran, Iraq, Lebanon, Pakistan, Syria and Turkey. See *Yearbook of the United Nations 1948–1949.* (at: www.udhr.org/history/yearbook.htm#(c)%20Adoption%20of%20the%20Declaration; accessed 23 July 2009).

119 On this see, for example, An-Na'im (n. 88), 83.

nations,[120] where the contents of such instruments were affirmed rather than opposed. An example is the International Covenant on Civil and Political Rights 1966,[121] which no state voted against and from which Saudi Arabia was the only Islamic state to abstain,[122] with relatively few reservations being entered on the basis of religious incompatibility.[123] Similarly, the Vienna World Conference on Human Rights in 1993, which resulted in the Vienna Declaration *inter alia* reaffirming that '[t]he universal nature of these rights and freedoms is beyond question', was participated in by 171 states.[124]

13.7 Conclusion: single, complementary or competing universal legal orders?

At the outset, UN universal lawmaking was defined as having four key elements applicable to at least the vast majority of its membership: the ability to develop common rights and obligations; and norms reflective of genuine consensus; which are regarded generally as legitimate; and are therefore implemented and largely complied with.

As far as the overall objective of achieving a single universal UN legal order as defined is concerned, an examination of key Islamic lawmaking conceptions and related practice, especially regarding universality, justice and legitimacy, suggest that its full attainment is highly problematic. In particular, it is evident that the key building blocks of international lawmaking, especially statehood, sovereignty and sovereign equality, either do not have comparable concepts within Islamic doctrine or else have different and incompatible meanings from those of the Westphalian system. It is clear also that this overarching goal of the UN differs considerably from the overarching goal of Islam which is the establishment of a universal Islamic state or other entity which incorporates all of mankind, both Muslim and non-Muslim believers, is premised on Shari'ah, and is submitted fully to Allah. This is contrary to a UN conception of universality for many reasons, not least as the latter is premised on secular principles; has no source of ultimate vertical authority beyond the horizontal authority of its membership; and seeks to be truly universal, including reflecting the cultural, religious and other key values of the spectrum of its diverse membership rather than the values and principles of one source only.

120 S Mirzaee-Yengejeh, 'International Law as a Cultural Perspective: Towards a Convergence of Civilizations: Contributions of Developing Countries to the Formation and Application of International Law Justice', in R. St. J. Macdonald and D. M. Johnston (eds.), *Towards World Constitutionalism: Issues in the Legal Ordering of the World Community* (Leiden: Martinus Nijhoff, 2005), 194–5.

121 Higgins (n. 17), 98; Center for Inquiry (n. 100), 9.

122 Mayer (n. 5), 15.

123 Higgins (n. 17), 96–7.

124 Littman (n. 4).

In terms of the specific elements of UN universality identified, it is suggested that these cannot be met by an Islamic understanding of universality. Firstly, the latter is not concerned with the development of common rights and obligations, rather only those of Shari'ah, which is regarded as the perfect legal, political, social and ethical system to redress many of the world's current injustices and restore balance into the world's order. As such, Shari'ah does not look for the achievement of genuine consensus in its norms, rather for their faithful implementation by man as Allah's vicegerent, who is not authorized to modify its norms. In terms of the element of legitimacy, both procedural and substantive legitimacy are of great importance in Islam. However, because of the quintessential, constitutional nature of Islamic justice, which is interconnected with the achievement of legitimacy, it is difficult to see how UN norms can ever be regarded as being truly legitimate in the Muslim world. Substantively, it is difficult to see how any secular system of government and authority, including the UN, which is not premised on Shari'ah norms can ever be substantively legitimate, as it will be unable to comply with the requirements of Islamic justice, which is such a pivotal aspect of legitimate Islamic lawmaking.[125] Similarly, it is highly questionable whether a non-Muslim person or system may ever truly exercise legitimate power over a Muslim person or system, as the concept of a ruler within Islam is linked to the performance of religious as well as other governing functions[126] based on delegated authority from Allah.[127] Indeed, it was noted that any exercise of power or authority by a state or other entity not premised on Shari'ah norms could be regarded as setting itself up as a false and illegitimate god against Allah.

The next issue to consider, having discounted the possibility of a single universal order, is whether an Islamic conception of universality is complementary to the UN legal order. As was noted above, the OIC has sought to justify historic and current efforts to introduce Islamic norms, such as in relation to the Cairo Declaration, as being no more than complementary action to reflect better the unique nature of Islamic norms. However, the possibility of such actions being merely complementary was discounted primarily as the norms introduced, for example by the Cairo Declaration, were often contrary to and undermined established international human rights law norms.

The final issue, therefore, is whether an Islamic conception of universality is in fact a parallel, competing legal order with that of the UN. As was stated at the outset of this chapter, this is believed to be the most accurate position. Certainly, this is suggested by current OIC efforts to establish Islamic human rights treaties which mirror existing major UN human rights treaties, but which presumably will be more compatible with Shari'ah norms and therefore are likely to violate some established UN human rights norms. In addition to the characteristics of an Islamic universal order described already, one other

125 Lewis (n. 54), 68–70.
126 *Ibid.* 69.
127 *Ibid.* 103.

key factor here is the ultimate normative supremacy of Shari'ah over all other norms, including those of the UN. This is linked partly to the overarching lawmaking function of an Islamic conception of justice, the achievement of which is a divine obligation on all Muslim believers, such that any norms falling short of Islamic justice cannot be just and are therefore not legitimate.

However, not only is the concept of justice reflected within the OIC's Charter, but it was noted above that the supremacy of Shari'ah is evident within the OIC's core documents also, such as Article 37(2) of the OIC Charter, and Articles 24 and 25 of the Cairo Declaration.[128] The existence of a normative hierarchy in which Shari'ah is supreme was suggested also by A'La Mawdudi, who stated that:

> The charter and the proclamations and the resolutions of the United Nations cannot be compared with the rights sanctioned by God; the former are not obligatory on anybody, while the latter are an integral part of the Islamic faith. All Muslims and all administrators who claim to be Muslim have to accept, recognize and enforce them.[129]

This is because of the ultimate loyalty and lordship of Allah over every detail of a Muslim believer's life, including in relation to power, politics and the state.[130]

Clearly all of the above issues raise important issues on not only the development, but also the subsequent implementation and compliance of UN norms, in particular of any norms which are in conflict with Shari'ah. In particular, Islamic conceptions of universality, justice and legitimacy, including the associated normative supremacy of Shari'ah in Islam, challenge significantly Article 103 UN Charter whereby UN norms should prevail in the event of any conflict. Nor is the Islamic conception of universality described here likely to change, as it is premised on divine law and obligations which are both immutable and eternal in nature. It is suggested therefore that full attainment of the UN universality ideal as defined at the outset is an unobtainable goal such that international law is likely to continue to operate within a multipolar world. This is despite the fact that many aspects of the UN legal order are followed in practice by the OIC and its member states, which is at least explicable in part by political, economic and historical realities. However, any such practice which is contrary to Islamic ideals does not render them in any way invalid or of less normative relevance. One consequence of this analysis is that new and imaginative ways may need to be found in the UN's law and policy-making modus operandi but that is a topic for another chapter!

128 See too the UIDHR (n. 32), Foreword and Preamble.

129 S. A. A'La Mawdudi, *Human Rights in Islam* (Markfield: Islamic Foundation, 1993), 16.

130 A'La Mawdudi (n. 35), 30.

14 The development of self-contained regimes as an obstacle to UN global governance

Carmen Draghici

While the absence of a coherent normative and institutional hierarchy has characterized the international community of states at all times, until recently the potential conflicts arising from the fragmentation of international law were mostly relegated to the realm of academic debate.[1] Where they did arise, they typically involved divergent (substantial/procedural) solutions provided for by regional or sectoral agreements on the same matter.[2] The United Nations (UN) Charter norms remained immune from any balancing against particular norms, by virtue of the hierarchical relationship established by Article 103 and of the general acceptance that they codify the international public order. The practical consequences of the fragmentation, and in particular the regionalization, of international law are becoming, nonetheless, appreciable in the light of a series of recent legal developments that redefine the relationship between the UN and the European Union (EU). Such developments were driven by the discrepancy between UN sanctions targeting individuals suspected of terrorist links and the concerns of EU institutions over the infringement of fundamental human rights. The *Kadi* ruling of the

1 On hierarchies in international law, see e.g. P. Weil, 'Towards Relative Normativity in International Law?' (1983) 77 AJIL 413; B. Oxman, 'Complementary Agreements and Compulsory Jurisdiction' (2001) 95 AJIL 277; D. Shelton, 'Normative Hierarchy in International Law' (2006) 100 AJIL 291. On the topic of fragmentation and references to the scholarly debate, see M. Koskenniemi and P. Leino, 'Fragmentation of International Law. Postmodern Anxieties?' (2002) 15 *Leiden JIL* 553; G. Hafner, 'Pros and Cons Ensuing from Fragmentation of International Law' [2004] 25 *Mich.J.Int'l L.* 849; A. Fischer-Lescano and G. Teubner, 'Regime-Collisions: The Vain Search for Legal Unity in the Fragmentation of Global Law' [2004] 25 *Mich.J.Int'l L.* 999. The consequences of the proliferation of international law sources have been examined by a study group of the International Law Commission (ILC) chaired by Martti Koskenniemi in 'Fragmentation of International Law...Report of the Study Group of the International Law Commission Finalized by Martti Koskenniemi' (13 April 2006) UN Doc. A/CN.4/L.682 (hereafter *Koskenniemi Report*). The ILC adopted a shorter text containing 'Conclusions of the Work of the Study Group on Fragmentation' in 'Report of the International Law Commission on the Work of its 58th Session' (1 May–9 June and 31 July–11 August 2006) UN Doc. A/61/10 (2006) (hereafter *ILC Conclusions on Fragmentation*). See M. Matheson, 'The Fifty-seventh Session of the International Law Commission' (2006) 100 AJIL 416, 423ff.

2 See the Mox Plant example of overlapping between functional and geographic special regimes in *Koskenniemi Report* (n. 1), 12–14, [10]–[13]. See also Shelton (n. 1), 293.

European Court of Justice (ECJ)[3] of 3 December 2008[4] and its replications, as well as the subsequent Council Regulation 1286/2009 of 22 December 2009,[5] have challenged the decades-long assumption of the pre-eminence of UN obligations (in particular under Security Council Chapter VII resolutions) over any other international agreements. Starting from these momentous developments, this chapter seeks to address major quandaries in current international law: what relevance and authority does UN law retain in relation to self-contained regimes? Is UN law still conceived as hierarchically superior in case of contrasting obligations, or do the ordinary rules on conflict of norms (i.e. norms of equivalent status) apply?

Section 14.1 discusses the evidence supporting the wide acceptance of the UN Charter as the constitutional framework of the international community. Against this background, section 14.2 examines the emergence of the *Kadi* doctrine rejecting the uncritical execution of UN decisions in the name of non-derogable EU values. The judicial echoes of the *Kadi* ruling, in particular subsequent judgments of both the ECJ and the Court of First Instance (CFI) upholding *Kadi* are also analysed. The institutional follow-up, most notably the recent EU Council regulation reforming the implementation of UN terrorist sanctions, is addressed in section 14.3, with a focus on the impact of EU's conditional acceptance of UN supremacy upon actual global governance. Section 14.4 explores the attempt of the UN Security Council to address the latest challenges to its authority by adopting Resolution 1904 (2009) of 17 December 2009,[6] which introduces an ombudsperson at the core of a new delisting procedure for terrorism suspects. The conclusions highlight the difficulty of achieving UN global governance as long as conspicuous groups of states establish highly homogeneous forms of community on a regional basis and their fundamental rules collide with UN commandments. I argue that the hierarchically superior nature of UN Charter obligations at variance with *lex specialis* finds an exception in the constitutional norms of subsystems such as the EU. Hence the necessity for value-oriented UN reform in order to avoid

3 The Lisbon Treaty, in force since 1 December 2009, renamed the European courts as 'Court of Justice' (formerly 'European Court of Justice') and 'General Court' (formerly 'Court of First Instance'). For the purpose of clarity, this chapter uses the pre-Lisbon denominations throughout.

4 Joined Cases C-402P and C-415/05P *Yassin Abdullah Kadi and Al Barakaat International Foundation* v. *Council of the European Union and the Commission of the European Communities* [2008] ECR I-6351. On the judgment, see e.g. C. Draghici, 'Suspected Terrorists' Rights between the Fragmentation and Merger of Legal Orders: Reflections in Margin of the *Kadi* ECJ Appeal Judgment' (2009) 8 (4) *Wash. U. Global Stud. L. Rev.* 627; 'Plate Tectonics in Luxembourg: the Ménage à Trois between EC Law, International Law and the European Convention on Human Rights Following the UN Sanctions Cases' (2009) 46 (1) CMLR 73; P. de Sena and M. C. Vitucci, 'The European Courts and the Security Council: Between *Dédoublement Fonctionnel* and Balancing of Values' (2009) 20 (1) EJIL 193, 221–8.

5 Council Regulation (EU) 1286/2009 amending Regulation (EC) 881/2002 imposing certain specific restrictive measures directed against certain persons and entities associated with Osama bin Laden, the Al-Qaida network and the Taliban [2009] OJ L346/42.

6 UNSC Res. 1904 (17 December 2009) UN Doc. S/RES/1904.

the risks posed by self-contained regimes to the uniform application of UN law and the recognition of UN primacy itself.

14.1 The United Nations Charter: a constitution of the international community?

The concept of UN global governance is premised on the assumption that the community of states is evolving towards an international constitutional order, centred on the norms enshrined in the UN Charter and on the UN institutional structure.[7] The UN Charter may be *prima facie* construed as a constitution of the world community, in so far as its main principles and purposes (including the prohibition on the threat or use of force, the obligation concerning the peaceful settlement of disputes, cooperation and friendly relations among states and the promotion and protection of human rights) provide the framework of all international rules, and every other treaty regime must be consistent therewith. The ILC conclusions on the fragmentation of international law explicitly underscore the universally accepted 'specialty' of UN Charter norms.[8]

Article 52 of the UN Charter suggests that the expansion of regionalism should be subordinated to UN law[9] and state practice largely confirms this understanding. Express reference to the UN Charter is made in regional treaties, by which they acknowledge the Charter as a framework of international law and a source of legitimacy. One such example is the statute of the North Atlantic Treaty Organization (NATO), which reaffirms in its Preamble the 'faith in the purposes and principles of the Charter', and establishes in Article 1 that the 'Parties undertake, *as set forth in the Charter*... to settle any... dispute...by peaceful means...and to refrain...from the threat or use of force ... *inconsistent with the purposes of the United Nations*' (emphasis added). Moreover, Article 5 of the NATO Treaty refers to the 'right of ... self-defence recognised by Article 51 of the Charter', though self-help is also a well-established institution of general international law.

7 On UN and the constitutionalization of international law, see e.g. P.-M. Dupuy, 'The Constitutional Dimension of the Charter of the United Nations Revisited' (1997) 1 *Max Planck Yearbook of International Law* 1; B. Fassbender, 'The United Nations Charter as Constitution of the International Community' (1998) 36 *Colum.J.Transnat'l L.* 529; S. Kirchner, 'Relative Normativity and the Constitutional Dimension of International Law: A Place for Values in the International Legal System?' (2004) 5(1) *German LJ* 47; S. Breau, 'The Constitutionalisation of the International Legal Order' (2008) 21(2) *Leiden JIL* 545.

8 See *ILC Conclusions on Fragmentation* (n. 1) [36]: 'It is also recognized that the United Nations Charter enjoys special character owing to the fundamental nature of some of its norms, particularly its principles and purposes and its universal acceptance'.

9 See UN Charter Article 52: 'Nothing in the present Charter precludes the existence of regional arrangements or agencies for dealing with such matters relating to the maintenance of international peace and security as are appropriate for regional action, provided that such arrangements or agencies and their activities are consistent with the Purposes and Principles of the United Nations'.

The presumption of UN constitutionalism is further supported by the increasing tendency towards the overlapping of UN law and international law. This stems from the virtually universal UN membership, the expanding scope of multilateral lawmaking within the General Assembly as a privileged forum for the negotiation of international treaties, the general recognition of the 'soft law' value of General Assembly resolutions, and the codification of international law by the UN-established International Law Commission (ILC), resulting in international conventions or authoritative restatements of international norms.[10]

More decisively, the constitutionalist view of the UN is predicated on the position occupied by the Charter in the hierarchy of international norms (other than *jus cogens*). This is mainly, though not exclusively, because of the supremacy clause in Article 103 of the Charter, establishing that in the event of a conflict between obligations under the Charter and obligations 'under any other international agreement', the former 'shall prevail'. Despite the wording of the provision,[11] the ILC suggested that Charter obligations '*may* also prevail' over inconsistent custom, relying, significantly, on 'the constitutional character of the Charter and the established practice of States and United Nations organs'.[12] Regardless of the pre-eminence over custom, the subordination of any international agreement to the Charter undoubtedly confers on the latter a superior normative status.

The exceptional standing of the Charter is also recognized by treaty law as codified by the 1969 and 1986 Vienna Conventions on the Law of Treaties (VCLT). The Preamble to the 1969 VCLT refers to 'the principles of international law embodied in the Charter', and Article 30(1) makes the rules

10 See S. Bleicher, 'The Legal Significance of Re-citation of General Assembly Resolutions' (1969) 63 (3) AJIL 444; C. Joyner, 'UN General Assembly Resolutions and International Law: Rethinking the Contemporary Dynamics of Norm Creation' (1981) 11 *California Western ILJ* 445; B. Sloan, 'General Assembly Resolutions Revisited (Forty Years Later)' (1987) 58 BYIL 39; H. Chodosh, 'Neither Treaty nor Custom: The Emergence of Declarative International Law' (1991) 26 *Texas ILJ* 87; D. Sheltone, *Commitment and Compliance: The Role of Non-Binding Norms in the International Legal System* (Oxford: Oxford University Press, 2000); V. Gowland-Debbas (ed.), *Multilateral Treaty-Making* (The Hague: Martinus Nijhoff, 2000).

11 The wording reflects the intention of the drafters, as proposals to include reference to 'any international obligation' were rejected at the San Francisco conference. See R. Liivoja, 'The Scope of the Supremacy Clause of the United Nations Charter' (2008) 57 ICLQ 583. It can be argued, however, based on Articles 31(3)(b) and 32 of the Vienna Convention on the Law of Treaties, that the *travaux préparatoires* constitute subsidiary means of interpretation, whereas 'subsequent practice' belongs to the general rules of interpretation and, as such, should prevail.

12 *ILC Conclusions on Fragmentation* (n. 1) [35] (emphasis added). It is important to appreciate at the same time that, given the quasi-universal UN membership, the relationship with existing custom presents a theoretical rather than a practical interest. In the event that a norm based on the Charter were to conflict with a customary norm, the Charter-based norm would take precedence as *lex specialis* between the parties. It may be argued, however, that the formation of a new customary norm could prevail over from the Charter as *lex posterior* or 'subsequent practice' in relation to the Charter (for instance, should generalized practice and *opinio juris* arise in connection with humanitarian intervention, this may legitimize an exception from the prohibition of force in derogation of the Charter).

on successive treaties on the same matter 'subject to Article 103 of the Charter'. Article 52 further stipulates that a 'treaty is void if [concluded] by the threat or use of force in violation of the principles of international law embodied in the Charter'. Similarly, Article 65(3) on procedures for treaty termination or annulment establishes that, in case of objections, 'the parties shall seek a solution through the means indicated in Article 33 of the Charter'. The 1986 VCLT includes analogous cross-references; most significantly, Article 30 establishes that 'in the event of a conflict between obligations under the Charter ...and obligations under a treaty, the obligations under the Charter shall prevail'.

Article 103 has thus been apparently incorporated into general treaty law.[13] Unlike any other treaty provision, a state cannot contract out of Article 103 of the UN Charter. This does not mean, however, that the norm contained in Article 103 has a peremptory character.[14] Interestingly, the ILC Conclusions on Fragmentation, while recognizing the constitutional character of the Charter and its specialty, specify that a rule conflicting with Article 103 is not applicable.[15] If Article 103 was intended as a peremptory norm, any inconsistent norm would be void altogether rather than not applicable. Also, the Koskenniemi Report found that in case of contrast with *jus cogens*, UN norms would be invalid.[16] The ILC Conclusions also admitted that, while Charter norms are universally accepted, and it is difficult to contemplate any contradiction with *jus cogens*, problems may arise in connection with UN Security Council resolutions; the Security Council must act according to UN principles (Article 24.2 of the Charter), which include subsequently crystallized *jus cogens*.[17] However, the concept of peremptory norm seems

13 This is without prejudice to the legal position of the (few) non-UN states, and of states not parties to the VCTL, unless we agree that the 1969 VCTL has passed into customary law. In any event, as many as 110 states are currently bound by this instrument (at: http://treaties.un.org/Pages/ViewDetailsIII.aspx?&src=UNTSONLINE&mtdsg_no=XXIII~1&chapter=23&Temp=mtdsg3&lang=en; accessed 6 February 2010). Conversely, the 1986 VCLT between States and International Organizations or between International Organizations is not yet into force; so far it has received 41 instruments of ratification or accession (at: http://treaties.un.org/Pages/ViewDetails.aspx?src=UNTSONLINE&tabid=2&mtdsg_no=XXIII-3&chapter=23&lang=en#1; accessed 6 February 2010).

14 The peremptory nature of Article 103 has found, however, some support in the scholarly literature. See B. Conforti, *Diritto Internazionale* (Naples: ESI, 2006), 166. There are two justifications available for the absolute impossibility to derogate from Article 103. One is that the rights of the remaining parties would be affected, since most UN obligations are of an integral nature, depending on compliance by all parties. Also, *inter se* agreements are prohibited in relation to those provisions derogation from which is incompatible with the effective execution of the object and purpose of the treaty. Article 41(1) VCLT 1969 addresses both situations.

15 *ILC Conclusions on Fragmentation* (n. 1) [41].

16 *Koskenniemi Report* (n. 1), 176–7 [346].

17 *ILC Conclusions on Fragmentation* (n. 1) [40]. See also Judge Lauterpacht, Separate Opinion, *Application of the Convention on the Prevention and Punishment of the Crime of Genocide* (*Bosnia and Herzegovina* v. *Serbia and Montenegro*) (Provisional Measures) [1993] ICJ Rep. 325 [100]. More generally on limits to UNSC discretion, see C. Draghici, 'International Organisations and Anti-Terrorist Sanctions: No Accountability for Human Rights Violations?' (2009) 2 (2) *Critical Studies on Terrorism* 293, 296–9.

reserved to substantive international law, concerned with ethos and public policy (prohibition of genocide, torture and slavery);[18] norms touching upon the functioning of international law, no matter how essential (e.g. *consuetudo est servanda* or *pacta sunt servanda*) are not peremptory, but their constitutional value is undeniable.[19] Therefore, the fact that Article 103 is not *jus cogens* does not affect its quasi non-derogable nature (as between UN states, i.e. in practice under international law tout court).

A further argument in support of UN constitutionalism is provided by international case law, which upholds the view that the international community is verticalized around Article 103. Until the ECJ *Kadi* judgment in 2008, this seemed to be the prevailing opinion of regional and domestic courts.[20] This was, in particular, the stance of the CFI in the *Yusuf and Al-Barakaat*[21] and *Kadi*[22] decisions of 21 September 2005, subsequently confirmed in the *Ayadi*[23] and *Hassan*[24] decisions of 12 July 2006. All these rulings regarded the implementation by EU institutions and member states of UN-imposed sanctions (assets freeze, travel ban) against individuals suspected of (association with) terrorism.[25] A list of suspected individuals and corporations is drawn up by the Sanctions Committee[26] following proposals by member states. The submission of listing proposals is not contingent upon any domestic criminal charge or conviction, as the measures are allegedly preventative rather than punitive. Because the mechanism relies on the surprise effect, suspects are not afforded a prior hearing. However, the mechanism guarantees no right to defence even after the measure has been implemented. At the outset, delisting was possible only if the state of residence or nationality undertook negotiations with the designating state or addressed the Sanctions Committee. Currently, an individual may file a delisting petition with the Focal Point for delisting established pursuant to Resolution 1730 (2006) but re-examination depends on the initiative of a state in the

18 See *ILC Conclusions on Fragmentation* (n. 1) [33]. See also A. Paulus, '*Jus Cogens* in a Time of Hegemony and Fragmentation: An Attempt at a Reappraisal' (2005) 74 *Nordic JIL* 297; Kirchner (n. 7), 212; Shelton (n. 1), 303–17.

19 It is possible to derogate from custom through a treaty (derogation from *consuetudo est servanda*, *inter partes*), but not from *jus cogens*. Also, a treaty in conflict with another treaty will not be void: conflict-of-law principles will apply where possible (*lex posterior*, *lex specialis*), otherwise issues of responsibility will arise, but the validity of the treaty will not be questioned.

20 On the judicial trend pre-dating the ECJ *Kadi* judgment, see, e.g. Draghici (n. 17), 300–3.

21 Case T-306/01 *Yusuf and Al Barakaat* v. *Council and Commission* [2005] ECR II-3533.

22 Case T-315/01 *Kadi* v. *Council and Commission* [2005] ECR II-3649.

23 Case T-253/02 *Ayadi* v. *Council of the European Union* [2006] ECR II-2139.

24 Case T-49/04 *Hassan* v. *Council of the European Union* [2006] ECR II-52.

25 By virtue of emergency powers pursuant to Chapter VII of the UN Charter, the UNSC has adopted financial sanctions directly against named individuals. UNSC Resolutions 1267 (1999), 1333 (2000) and 1390 (2002), as subsequently amended, place an obligation on states to freeze without delay any financial assets or economic resources of the suspects.

26 The Al-Qaida and Taliban Sanctions Committee, established by UNSC Res. 1267 (15 October 1999) UN Doc. S/RES/1267, is one of the three subsidiary bodies of the Security Council addressing terrorism-related issues, and its membership reflects the composition of the Council.

Committee to place the issue on the Committee's agenda. Moreover, the decision is reviewed by the same body which originally imposed the sanction, and following purely intergovernmental consultations. Furthermore, individuals only have access to the portion of their file that the designating state considers to be publicly disclosable and they are at no time entitled to take part in the procedures.[27]

Before the adoption of Council Regulation 1286/2009 in December 2009, EU institutions automatically endorsed the lists, and the measure was implemented without an *ex post facto* hearing, in so far as EU delisting entirely depended upon UN delisting.[28] Targeted individuals challenged the relevant acts before the CFI, on the grounds that they breached, *inter alia*, fair trial rights and the right to an effective remedy. In the aforementioned rulings *Yusuf, Kadi, Ayadi* and *Hassan*, the CFI found that the combined effect of Articles 25 and 103 of the UN Charter gave priority to UN Security Council resolutions adopted under Chapter VII over any conflicting treaty obligation, including human rights treaties or the EC Treaty.[29] The court also considered that Community institutions, bound by the Treaty to further the international obligations of member states, had no autonomous discretion to alter the contents of the UN resolutions; thus, any judicial review of the implementing measures would have amounted to review of the UN sanction itself, which fell outside that court's jurisdiction.[30]

The findings of the CFI were heavily determined by the authority of the UN Charter, and concerns related to the lack of jurisdiction to review Security Council resolutions. In rulings occasioned by analogous sanctions adopted by EU institutions autonomously, such as *Organisation des Modjahedines du peuple d'Iran* of 12 December 2006,[31] and *Sison*[32] and *Stichting Al-Aqsa*[33] of 11 July 2007, the CFI stated that in order for the restrictive measure to comply with respect for defence rights, suspects must be informed of the reasons leading to the measure immediately after its adoption, afforded a hearing if requested, and given access to the information in their file so that they may express their views thereon.

27 See the 'Guidelines of the Committee for the Conduct of Its Work', adopted on 7 November 2002, as amended on 10 April 2003, 21 December 2005, 29 November 2006, 12 February 2007 and 9 December 2008 (at: www.un.org/sc/committees/1267/pdf/1267_guidelines.pdf; [1], [3], [6], [7]).

28 In order to give effect to UNSC's resolutions, the EU Council adopted Common Position 2002/402/CFSP concerning restrictive measures against Usama bin Laden, members of the Al-Qaida organization and the Taliban, and other individuals, groups, undertakings and entities associated with them, implemented by EC Regulation 881/2002 of 27 May 2002, as amended.

29 See e.g. Yusuf (n. 21) [231].

30 *Ibid.* [265], [276].

31 Case T-228/02 *Organisation des Modjahedines du Peuple d'Iran* v. *Council of the European Union* [2007] All ER (EC) 447. See also CFI decision of 4 December 2008, case T-284/08 *People's Mojahedin Organization of Iran* v. *Council of the European Union* [2009] 1 CMLR 44.

32 Case T-47/03 *Sison* v. *Council of the European Union* [2007] 3 CMLR. 39.

33 Case T-327/03 *Stichting Al-Aqsa* v. *Council of the European Union* [2007] ECR II-79.

A posture akin to CFI's analysis of UN dictated sanctions was espoused by the UK House of Lords in *Al-Jedda* in 2007,[34] a case regarding prolonged confinement without trial by British forces in Iraq by virtue of the power to detain conferred by a Chapter VII resolution. The House of Lords found that Security Council resolutions prevail over any other treaty, and therefore UN obligations qualify the individual right to liberty enshrined in Article 5 of the European Convention on Human Rights (ECHR).[35]

Arguably, the practice of UN member states (including judicial practice) has further contributed to the verticalization of the international legal order, subordinating interstate agreements to the Charter and to the undisputed authority of the UN body with the widest mandatory powers.

14.2 The *Kadi* ruling and judicial echoes (*Othman*, *Ayadi* and *Hassan*): de-verticalizing the international community

Despite the wide acceptance of the UN Charter as the foundation of current international relations, its constitutional value and the unrestrained authority of the Security Council demand rethinking in the light of the recent EU reactions to the UN sanctions regime. These reactions indicate that the emergence of institutionalized self-contained regimes might pose a major challenge to UN global governance.

The notion of self-contained regime, coined by the Permanent Court of International Justice (PCIJ) in the *Wimbledon* case,[36] designates an international arrangement based on a set of special rules applying with priority over general law, a 'strong form of *lex specialis*';[37] it encompasses, however, a variety of situations, from a set of secondary norms governing the consequences of a breach of a primary norm in derogation of responsibility law[38] to 'interrelated wholes of primary and secondary rules, sometimes also referred to as "systems"

34 *R (on the application of Al-Jedda)* v. *Secretary of State for Defence* [2007] UKHL 58, on appeal from *R (on the application of Al-Jedda)* v. *Secretary of State for Defence* [2006] EWCA Civ. 327.

35 *Ibid.* [30]–[36].

36 *SS Wimbledon* (1923) PCIJ Series A, No. 1, 23–4. The International Court of Justice (ICJ) identified such a special regime in diplomatic law: 'diplomatic law itself provides the necessary means of defence against, and sanctions for, illicit activities by members of diplomatic or consular missions', therefore violation of diplomatic immunities is not lawful as a counter-measure (see *Case of Tehran Hostages* (*US* v. *Iran*), [1980] ICJ Rep. 38 [83]). For the ICJ the rules on diplomatic protection constitute a 'self-contained regime' (*ibid.* [86]) and based on *lex specialis derogat legi generali* such rules prevail on general rules on counter-measures. The *Koskenniemi Report*, while acknowledging that EU law is sometimes treated as a self-contained regime in so far as 'rules of general international law are assumed to be modified or even excluded in [its] administration' ([129]), discusses EU integration under the regionalization heading, as a 'technique of law-making' (*ibid.* 89, [205]); see specifically, on European integration, *ibid.* 95–6 [218]–[219].

37 *Koskenniemi Report* (n. 1), 55 [123].

38 Article 55 of the ILC Draft Articles on State Responsibility for Internationally Wrongful Acts (2001) acknowledges that the general rules on state responsibility 'do not apply where and to the extent that the conditions for the existence of an internationally wrongful act or the content or implementation of the international responsibility of a State are governed by special rules of international law'.

or "subsystems" of rules that cover some particular problem differently from the way it would be covered under general law'.[39] The definition adopted by the ILC describes the self-contained regime as a 'group of rules and principles concerned with a particular subject matter' and 'applicable as *lex speciali*'.[40] The EU is arguably one of the most advanced forms of subsystem: it is an institutionalized self-contained regime, based on both primary rules and rules of responsibility established by the founding treaty rather than by international law, having its own institutions to administer the relevant rules and monitored by specific tribunals or quasi-judicial bodies. Naturally, no regime is completely self-contained in so far as it depends on general rules to operate (law of treaties, etc.), and where there is no special regulation of a matter, general law still plays a residual role.[41] Also, the EU is still subject to the rules of international law in relation to third parties (e.g. in connection with responsibility for breach of UN law vis-à-vis non-EU states).

The 2008 ECJ *Kadi* judgment redefined the relationship between European and international law from a dualist perspective, with a strong emphasis on the autonomous nature of the EU legal order. The court underlined that 'an international agreement (such as the UN Charter) cannot affect the... autonomy of the Community legal system'.[42] According to the ECJ, the European legal order comprises non-derogable fundamental principles, such as the rule of law and fundamental human rights.[43] Thus, international obligations cannot be accommodated to the extent that they impair those principles that 'form part of the very foundations of the Community legal order'.[44] The system is also endowed with autonomous mechanisms designed to ensure that those principles are enforced, in particular judicial review. Protection of fundamental rights therefore includes for the Court 'the review by the Community judicature of the lawfulness of Community measures as regards their consistency with those fundamental rights'.[45]

Consequently, the ECJ found the power to review the EC regulations giving effect to UN mandatory resolutions within its jurisdiction, in so far as the constitutional guarantee of judicial review 'stemming from the EC Treaty as an autonomous legal system...is not to be prejudiced by an international agreement'.[46] Enquiring whether comparable supervision exists at UN level, so as to justify the court's refraining from review, the ECJ found (despite

39 *Koskenniemi Report* (n. 1), 57 [128].

40 *ILC Conclusions on Fragmentation* (n. 1) [13].

41 *Koskenniemi Report* (n. 1), 77–83 [172]–[190]; 84–5, [192]–[193]. See also B. Simma and D. Pulkowski, *Of Planets and the Universe: Self-contained Regimes in International Law* (2006) 17 EJIL 483.

42 *Kadi and Al-Barakaat* (n. 4) [282].

43 See *ibid.* [303]: '[art. 307] may allow derogations from the primary law in certain instances, those provisions cannot, however, be understood to authorise any derogation from the principles of liberty, democracy and respect for human rights and fundamental freedoms enshrined in Article 6(1) EU as a foundation of the Union'.

44 *Ibid.* [304].

45 *Ibid.*

46 *Ibid.* [316].

announcing that it does not review UN measures) that UN re-examination mechanisms infringe the procedural rights of suspects.[47] As a result, the ECJ annulled the asset-freeze regulation in so far as it concerned the applicant: Security Council resolutions conflicting with non-derogable EC principles cannot be enforced.[48] This amounts to asserting that UN law needs to pass the test of EC legitimacy in order to be implemented in the EU legal space.

The ruling thus challenged the presumption of absolute primacy of UN obligations fostered by Article 103 of the UN Charter. The *Kadi* court did not question the primacy of the UN Charter over any other treaty and recognized the requirement for the EC to 'respect international law in the exercise of its powers'.[49] The court claimed, nevertheless, that compliance with UN law cannot go so far as to interfere with those principles representing the very foundation of the EU. This is ultimately equivalent to a finding that Article 103 does not supersede every conflicting obligation arising under a different treaty. For the ECJ, the norms relating to the protection of human rights or regulating the checks and balances within the EU cannot be displaced.

Arguably, the European subsystem has reached a level of integration such that it has generated its own *jus cogens*. The court's reasoning, distant from any recognition of UN global governance and international public order, is concerned with the intransgressible European public order, based on the rule of law and fundamental human rights.[50] The judgment therefore balances UN law as mere treaty obligation against EU norms as constitutional principles. The court stresses, at the same time, that the power of review only concerns the domestic implementation measures, not the original resolutions, and that such review does not entail any challenge to the supremacy of UN decisions.[51] However, a finding of illegitimacy leading to delisting by the EU institutions in spite of the decision of the Sanctions Committee can only mean that UN law has lost its primacy.

It is important to appreciate that the *Kadi* ruling has not remained in isolation. The recent jurisprudence of the EU courts has already confirmed the revisited relationship between EU and UN law. On the one hand, the CFI has adjusted its jurisprudence to the *Kadi* principles. In its decision *Othman v. Council and Commission* of 11 June 2009,[52] the CFI found that the EU Council 'at no time informed the applicant of the evidence adduced against him',[53]

47 *Ibid.* [319]–[325].

48 *Ibid.* [304]–[309].

49 *Ibid.* [291].

50 The ECJ makes no reference to universal human rights as part of the international *ordre public*. While this can be seen as a reflex of the court's strict definition of jurisdictional boundaries, it may be contrasted with the European Court of Human Rights' recognition that 'the Convention cannot be interpreted and applied in a vacuum' (see *Behrami* v. *France* (2007) 45 EHRR SE10 [71]).

51 See *Kadi and Al-Barakaat* (n. 4) [286]: '[T]he review of lawfulness thus to be ensured by the Community judicature applies to the Community act intended to give effect to the international agreement at issue, and not to the latter as such'.

52 Case T-318/01 *Othman* v. *Council and Commission* [2009] All ER (EC) 873.

53 *Ibid.* [83].

denying him a chance to defend himself and obtain a legal remedy.[54] As did the ECJ in *Kadi*, the CFI annulled the EU regulation in so far as it related to the applicant, and it expressly observed that the applicant found himself 'in a factual and legal situation in every way comparable to that of Mr Kadi'.[55] Again similarly to the ECJ's decision, the CFI noted that, because the grounds for applying the regulation were not disclosed to the court, no review of its lawfulness was possible, which amounted to a violation of 'the fundamental right to an effective legal remedy'.[56] The CFI therefore concluded that the Council adopted the regulation in breach of Mr Othman's fundamental rights, in particular rights of the defence, the right to effective judicial review and the right to property.[57]

Further actions seeking annulment of Article 2 of Council Regulation (EC) No. 881/2002 of 27 May 2002, as amended, are currently under consideration: *Al-Faqih v. Council*,[58] *Sanabel Relief Agency v. Council*,[59] *Abdrabbah v. Council*[60] and *Nasuf v. Council*.[61] These actions, all brought on 5 May 2006, contain the same pleas in law and largely rely on the same main arguments. The applicants allege that Article 2 of Regulation No. 881/2002 as amended infringes fundamental principles of Community law, *inter alia* respect for fundamental rights. Other replicas of *Kadi* can therefore be expected.

On the other hand, the ECJ itself has maintained the approach taken in *Kadi*. The recent judgment in the joint appeal cases of *Ayadi* and *Hassan* issued on 3 December 2009[62] essentially follows the findings in *Kadi*. We can state that by now a consistent pattern of jurisprudence upholding the rule of law and human rights has developed at EU level against the background of authoritative UN counter-terrorism strategies.

The implementation of UN sanctions in the EU was again put to the test by new claims filed with the CFI by Al Barakaat on 30 January 2009[63] and by Mr Kadi on 26 February 2009,[64] seeking to obtain, in so far as they are concerned, the annulment of the Regulation No. 1190/2008 of 28 November

54 *Ibid.* [86].

55 *Ibid.* [82].

56 *Ibid.* [88].

57 The Court recalled that a decision declaring a regulation to be void takes effect only from the date of expiry of the period in which an appeal may be brought before the CFI, two months and ten days from notification of the judgment (or, if an appeal has been brought within that period, as from the date of dismissal of the appeal); the CFI thus considered that the Council would have sufficient time in which to remedy the infringements found by adopting, if appropriate, a new restrictive measure directed against the applicant.

58 App. T-135/06 *Al-Faqih* v. *Council* (15 July 2006) OJ C165, 29.

59 App. T-136/06 *Sanabel Relief Agency* v. *Council* (15 July 2006) OJ C165, 30.

60 App. T-137/06 *Abdrabbah* v. *Council* (15 July 2006) OJ C165, 30.

61 App. T-138/06 *Nasuf* v. *Council* (15 July 2006) OJ C165, 30.

62 Joined Cases C-399/06 P & C-403/06 P *Hassan and Ayadi* v. *Council and Commission* [2009] not yet reported.

63 App. T-45/09 *Al Barakaat* v. *Commission* (4 July 2009) OJ C153, 39.

64 App. T-85/09 *Kadi* v. *Commission* (18 April 2009) OJ C90, 37.

2008 by which the Commission decided to maintain them on the list.[65] The applicants contend that the new regulation violated their defence rights (the right to an effective hearing and the right to effective judicial protection) and failed to remedy the infringements found by the ECJ in its 2008 judgment in that respect. They claim that the contested regulation provides no procedure for communicating the evidence on which the assets-freeze decision was based, or for enabling them to comment meaningfully on that evidence. The applicants further submit that the Commission failed to provide compelling reasons for maintaining the asset freeze, and failed to undertake an assessment of all relevant facts and circumstances in deciding whether to enact the contested regulation.

It remains to be seen if the CFI finds that the substance of the narrative summaries of reasons for listing provided by the Commission contains information sufficiently precise on the alleged collaboration with terrorists for the measure to be compliant with the duty to state reasons and defence rights.[66] If not, the transparency and fairness of the current listing procedure will also be challenged. If the court decides that it needs to perform a full review of the case, assessing the evidence supporting inclusion on the UN list, and if the Sanctions Committee shows itself unwilling to reveal that information because of the sensitive nature of its source (intelligence or police information),[67] the court may decide that it is prevented from reviewing the case, which amounts to a breach of the right to effective remedy. The CFI certainly did not seem persuaded by the confidentiality argument in the 2008 judgment in *People's Mojahedin Organization of Iran* regarding autonomous EU lists: 'the Court considers that the Council is not entitled to base its funds-freezing decision on information or material in the file communicated by a Member State, if the said Member State is not willing to authorise its communication to the Community judicature whose task is to review the

65 The new regulation was adopted after the Commission, following the ECJ's ruling, provided the applicants with the statement of reasons on which the listing by the Security Council was based and an opportunity to present their views. See section 14.3.

66 Res. 1735 (2006), giving publicity to the narrative summaries for designation, was not in place of the time of the initial asset freeze against Kadi and Al Barakaat. However, as is known, the narrative summaries only provide essential publicly available information on which the listing proposal was based.

67 See UN Security Council, 'Ninth Report of the Analytical Support and Monitoring Team' (19 May 2009) UN Doc. S/2009/245 [22]: '[I]f the [CFI] decides to examine the evidence behind the reasons for listing provided by the Committee, or if it decides it must conduct a complete review of the listing decisions, it will give rise to new and more difficult issues. There are limits to the ability of the Committee to reveal the reasons behind its decisions, even to a reviewing body, when these are based on intelligence or law enforcement information which belongs to a particular State. The sensitive nature of information pertaining to persons involved in terrorism and terrorist financing, recognized by the Court of Justice of the European Communities in the Qadi and Barakaat case often inhibits Member States, whether outside or inside the Committee, from sharing this information with others'.

lawfulness of that decision'.[68] The Tenth Report of the Monitoring Team assisting the Sanctions Committee rightly noted with concern the latest legal challenges:

> When the process of judgement and appeal is completed, the resulting decision in these two cases has the potential to create significant difficulties for all member States of the European Union and may alter the terms of the wider discussion of the fairness of the regime and the need for reform.[69]

14.3 Council Regulation 1286/2009 introducing due process provisions: are Security Council blacklisting decisions still mandatory?

The *Kadi* judgment has also triggered unforeseen institutional responses at the EU level. The first reactions to the judgment were rather modest, and left room for speculation as to the intent of EU institutions to safeguard a façade of legality while complying with UN decisions in the same indiscriminating manner. The Presidency of the Council approached the Sanctions Committee, which provided narrative summaries of reasons for listing, and the Commission made them available to Mr Kadi and Al Barakaat. After having considered comments received from the two parties, the Commission passed Regulation 1190/2008 of 28 November 2008, reconfirming their inclusion on the list, and thus deciding to continue the restrictive measures. On the other hand, on 30 December 2008 the European Commission published a notice for the attention of the persons and entities added to the list by the latest EC Regulations to advise them that they may request the grounds for their listing from the Commission, and challenge the regulations concerned before the CFI.[70]

More significantly, on 22 April 2009 the Commission advanced a proposal for amendments to Council Regulation (EC) No. 881/2002 of 27 May 2002, aimed at the inclusion of due process provisions in accordance with the *Kadi* judgment.[71] In the explanatory memorandum accompanying the proposal, the Commission clarifies that the new procedure for implementing UN sanctions is to be based on the procedure applied in the implementation of Council Regulation (EC) No. 2580/2001 of 27 December 2001 concerning the terrorist list drawn up by the EU itself. The reform would thus remove the difference in the treatment of suspected individuals based on the mere origin

68 Case T 284/08 *People's Mojahedin Organization of Iran* [73].

69 UNSC, Tenth Report of the Monitoring Team (2 October 2009) UN Doc. S/2009/502 [36].

70 Commission (EC) 'Notice for the attention of the persons and entities added to the list referred to in… Council Regulation (EC) No 881/2002…by virtue of Commission Regulations (EC) No 1109/2008 and (EC) No 1330/2008' (2008/C 330/09, 30 December 2008).

71 Commission (EC) 'Proposal for a Council Regulation amending Regulation (EC) No 881/2002 imposing certain specific restrictive measures directed against certain persons and entities associated with Usama bin Laden, the Al-Qaida network and the Taliban' (COM(2009)187 final, 22 April 2009).

(EU or UN) of the list.[72] Under the Commission's proposal, upon notification by the UN Sanctions Committee of a new listing decision and receipt of the statement of reasons, the Commission would provisionally freeze the assets of the party concerned, while at the same time sending them a statement of reasons and inviting their views. Finally, aided by an advisory committee, the Commission would examine the views and adopt a final decision confirming or rescinding the provisional freeze.[73]

Council Regulation No. 1286/2009 of 22 December 2009[74] amended Regulation (EC) No. 881/2002 pursuant to the Commission's proposal. Point (9) of the new regulation, inserting a new Article 7(a), is of particular significance for the interplay between the EU and the UN:

> 1. Where the United Nations Security Council or the Sanctions Committee decides to list a natural or legal person...the Commission shall, as soon as a statement of reasons has been provided by the Sanctions Committee, take a decision to include such person...in Annex 1.[75] 2. Once the [Commission's] decision...has been taken, the Commission shall without delay communicate the statement of reasons provided by the Sanctions Committee, to the person, entity, body or group concerned... providing him, her or it an opportunity to express his, her or its views on the matter. 3. Where observations are submitted, the Commission shall review its decision...in the light of those observations...Those observations shall be forwarded to the Sanctions Committee. The Commission shall communicate the result of its review to the person, entity, body or group concerned. The result of the review shall also be forwarded to the Sanctions Committee.

The text is somewhat elusive and does not provide a definitive solution in the event that the Commission does not consider the designation justified, but the Sanctions Committee insists on maintaining the name on the list.

72 As recalled in section 14.2, the CFI had also developed a double pattern of review based on the origin of the list.

73 COM (2009)187 final [8]: 'The following Articles 7a to 7e are inserted: 'Article 7a 1. Where the United Nations Security Council or the Sanctions Committee decides to list a natural or legal person, entity, body or group for the first time, the Commission shall, as soon as a statement of reasons has been provided by the United Nations, take a provisional decision on the amendment of Annex I without delay. 2. Once the provisional decision referred to in paragraph 1 has been taken, the Commission shall without delay communicate the statement of reasons provided by the United Nations, to the person, entity, body or group concerned, either directly or through the publication of a notice, providing him, her or it an opportunity to express his, her or its views on the matter. 3. The Commission shall take a final decision concerning the person, entity, body or group concerned in accordance with the procedure referred to in Article 7b(2)'.

74 Council Regulation (EC) 1286/2009 amending Regulation (EC) No. 881/2002 imposing certain restrictive measures [2009] OJ L346/42.

75 The proposal drafted by the Commission read 'take a *provisional* decision on the amendment of Annex I without delay' (emphasis added).

The implication seems to be, however, that the Commission is the final arbiter of the case: it 'communicates' its decision to the Sanctions Committee after having reviewed the case, and apparently no further action is expected from the Sanctions Committee, nor is there any *navette* system envisaged, allowing the two institutions to reach a concerted decision; the Sanctions Committee is, in fact, merely notified. To put it differently, the decisions of the Sanctions Committee designating suspects and imposing freezing measures are no longer treated as mandatory! The UN listing decisions are considered as *prima facie* appropriate listing proposals, nevertheless open to scrutiny, and the ultimate decision on the merits is reserved to the EU Commission, following an examination of the defence put forward by the suspect. The consequences of the new regulation cannot be overstated: not only is there no automatic compliance with the SC resolutions, but it may lead to a decision to annul a freezing order plainly in contrast with UN Charter obligations.

Clearly, the opposition to a UN sanctions regime insufficiently wary of human rights has now moved from the judiciary to the forefront of EU political institutions. The new Council regulation puts an end to the passive implementation of measures which impinge upon fundamental individual rights as protected by EU law. The possibility to rescind the freezing order demonstrates that the EU is no longer a submissive receptor of UN decisions: the vertical relationship between the EU and the UN is no longer endorsed.

14.4 The ombudsperson and the new delisting procedure in SC Res. 1904 (2009): a disappointing attempt at preserving authority by enhancing acceptance

The latest resolution of the UN Security Council concerning individual sanctions, Res. 1904 (2009) of 17 December 2009, introduces a series of amendments in response to the criticism of the current listing and delisting procedures. As specified in the Preamble, the adoption of this further reform of the sanctions mechanism was partly driven by the legal challenges faced by domestic implementation measures, and the desire to improve the judicial guarantees available to suspects.[76]

Most significantly, the resolution establishes a new delisting mechanism centred on the institution of the ombudsperson, an independent expert

76 See UNSC Res. 1904 (n. 6), Preamble (para. 10): '*Taking note of challenges, both legal and otherwise, to the measures implemented by Member States* under paragraph 1 of this resolution, welcoming improvements to the Committee's procedures and the quality of the Consolidated List, and *expressing its intent to continue efforts to ensure that procedures are fair and clear*' (emphasis added).

appointed on the basis of high professional qualifications and moral integrity.[77] The Office of the Ombudsperson will completely replace the Focal Point for delisting, whose activity will be limited to receiving delisting requests in connection with other sanctions lists.[78] The establishment of an independent body for the review of delisting petitions, as requested by the critics of the existing mechanism,[79] can only be welcomed. Nevertheless, the role assigned to the ombudsperson in the procedure, as defined in the Annex II of the resolution, is utterly disappointing.

The procedure commences with a two-month period of information gathering, extendable to four months if states need additional time to provide information. During this period, the ombudsperson informs the petitioner about the Committee's procedures, forwards the delisting request to the members of the Committee, designating state(s), state(s) of residence and nationality/incorporation, and any UN bodies or other states deemed relevant, asking them to provide any appropriate additional information concerning the delisting request.[80] At the end of the period of information gathering, the ombudsperson presents a written update to the Sanctions Committee on the progress of the case, including details regarding which states have supplied information.

The second phase of the procedure consists of a two-month period of dialogue (also extendable to four months) in which the ombudsperson facilitates the exchange of information between the petitioner, the Sanctions Committee, and the states concerned. The ombudsperson can ask the petitioner questions or request additional information or clarifications that may help the Committee's consideration of the request (including any questions or

77 *Ibid.* [20]: 'Decides that, when considering delisting requests, the *Committee shall be assisted by an Office of the Ombudsperson*, to be established for an initial period of 18 months from the date of adoption of this resolution, and requests the Secretary-General, in close consultation with the Committee, to appoint an *eminent individual of high moral character, impartiality and integrity with high qualifications and experience in relevant fields*, such as legal, human rights, counter-terrorism and sanctions, to be Ombudsperson, with the mandate outlined in annex II of this resolution, and further decides that the Ombudsperson shall perform these tasks in an *independent and impartial manner* and shall *neither seek nor receive instructions from any government*' (emphasis added).

78 *Ibid.* [21]: 'Decides that, after the appointment of the Ombudsperson, the *Office of the Ombudsperson shall receive requests from individuals and entities seeking to be removed from the Consolidated List*, in accordance with the procedures outlined in annex II of this resolution, and that, after the appointment of the Ombudsperson, *the Focal Point mechanism established in resolution 1730 (2006) shall no longer receive such requests*, and notes that the Focal Point shall *continue to receive requests from individuals and entities seeking to be removed from other sanctions lists*' (emphasis added).

79 See *Tenth Report of the Monitoring Team* (n. 69) [41]: 'Most proposals for a panel assume a multiperson expert body with judicial qualifications'.

80 The ombudsperson shall also forward the delisting request to the Monitoring Team, which shall provide within two months: all relevant information available to the Monitoring Team, including court decisions and proceedings, news reports, information that States or international organizations have previously shared with the Committee or the Monitoring Team; fact-based assessments of the information provided by the petitioner; questions or requests for clarifications that the Monitoring Team would like asked of the petitioner regarding the delisting request.

information requests received from relevant states, the Committee and the Monitoring Team), forwards replies from the petitioner back to relevant states, the Committee and the Monitoring Team, and follows up with the petitioner. Upon completion of this period of dialogue, the ombudsperson, with the help of the Monitoring Team, drafts and circulates to the Committee a 'Comprehensive Report' that 'exclusively' summarizes and specifies the sources of all information available (respecting confidential elements of member states' communications with the ombudsperson), describes the ombudsperson's activities with respect to this delisting request, including dialogue with the petitioner, and, based on an analysis of all the information available, lays out for the Committee the principal arguments concerning the delisting request.[81]

The reformed procedure modestly culminates with the 'Committee Discussion and Decision'. After the Committee has had thirty days to review the Comprehensive Report, the delisting request is placed on the Committee's agenda for consideration.[82] The ombudsperson presents the report in person and responds to questions from members of the Committee.[83] Significantly, the decision whether to approve the delisting request is taken by the Committee 'through its normal decision-making procedures'.[84] The ombudsperson is informed of the decision, and in turn informs the petitioner; when applicable, he or she removes the name from the list.[85]

The only substantial improvement introduced by the procedure is that it apparently guarantees the review of the case, regardless of the initiative of a state in the Committee. Other positive developments are enhanced transparency, because of the better coordination of the information exchange between the petitioner, the Committee and any other relevant parties, and the quasi-interlocutory phase (the applicant has an opportunity to respond, indirectly, to the questions addressed by any member of the Committee). That said, the new procedure does not notably alter the decision-making mechanism: the delisting decision is made by the same political body according to the same rules. The ombudsperson's report is not in the form of a decision on the case, as it merely summarizes arguments and evidence, and whatever his or her findings, the report is in no way binding. Also, the presence of the ombudsperson when the Committee considers the case should not be overestimated, because the ombudsperson does not act as defence proxy for the petitioner, but rather as an objective rapporteur.

Compared to the reforms suggested by governmental and independent experts,[86] the amendments introduced by Resolution 1904 (2009) definitely

81 UNSC Res. 1904 (n. 6), Annex II [7].

82 *Ibid.* [8].

83 *Ibid.* [9].

84 *Ibid.* [10].

85 *Ibid.* [11].

86 The Tenth Report of the Monitoring Team quotes: a working document emerged after a seminar sponsored by the Government of the Netherlands on the theme 'Effectiveness and Legitimacy of United

appear unambitious. However, the concern for further adjusting the procedures in the aftermath of important legal challenges to the sanctions regime (in particular the *Kadi* ruling)[87] testifies the Security Council's awareness that non-compliance by major international players will lead to a decrease in UN authority.

14.5 Conclusions: EU and UN, conflict rather than collaboration?

The reality of self-contained regimes is not novel. The ECJ had long established in historical judgments that the EC Treaty is 'more than an international agreement' and has created 'a new legal order',[88] 'its own legal system',[89] 'a Community based on the rule of law inasmuch as neither its member states nor its institutions can avoid a review of the question whether the measures adopted by them are in conformity with the *basic constitutional charter, the Treaty*'.[90] However, the previous case law suggesting the self-contained nature of the EC/EU legal order was inward-oriented, reshaping the obligations of member states and institutions in their mutual relationship and vis-à-vis individuals. The novelty of *Kadi* is the outward-oriented emphasis on the autonomy and specialty of EU law, preventing the operation of international rules with regard to third parties.

What is most striking in *Kadi* and in the subsequent developments in EU legislation is that, while initially designed to accommodate UN obligations, this special regime places itself in conflict rather than continuity with UN law. Article 307 of the EC Treaty was introduced to safeguard the precedence of UN obligations.[91] Also, Article 10A of the Lisbon Treaty explicitly confirms that the EU is expected to function in agreement with the UN Charter:

Nations Targeted Sanctions' (The Hague, May 2009); International Commission of Jurists, 'Assessing Damage, Urging Action – Report of the Eminent Jurists Panel on Terrorism, Counter-terrorism and Human Rights'; Report of the Fourth Freedom Forum and Kroc Institute for International Peace Studies at the University of Notre Dame 'Overdue Process: Protecting Human Rights While Sanctioning Alleged Terrorists'; Report of the Special Rapporteur on the promotion of human rights and fundamental freedoms while countering terrorism (A/63/223); Watson Institute for International Studies at Brown University report 'Strengthening Targeted Sanctions through Fair and Clear Procedures'.

87 The Ninth Report of the Monitoring Team describes the *Kadi* judgment as 'the most significant legal development to affect the [sanctions] regime since its inception' (*Ninth Report* (n. 67), 10, [19]).

88 Case 26/62 *Van Gend en Loos* [1963] ECR 3.

89 Case 6/64 *Costa* v. *ENEL* [1964] ECR 1141.

90 Case 294/83 *Parti écologiste 'Les Verts'* v. *European Parliament* [1986] ECR 1339 [23] (emphasis added).

91 See Art. 307 EC: 'The rights and obligations arising from agreements concluded before 1 January 1958 or, for acceding States, before the date of their accession, between one or more Member States on the one hand, and one or more third countries on the other, shall not be affected by the provisions of this Treaty'.

> The Union's action on the international scene shall be guided by the principles which have inspired its own creation, development and enlargement...democracy, the rule of law, the universality and indivisibility of human rights and fundamental freedoms, respect for human dignity, the principles of equality and solidarity, and *respect for the principles of the United Nations Charter and international law*...[The Union] shall promote multilateral solutions to common problems, *in particular in the framework of the United Nations*. (emphasis added).

Notwithstanding this general outlook, *Kadi* and post-*Kadi* events suggest that the relationship between the UN and self-contained regimes is not necessarily based on the latter's subordination to the former. Despite the conciliatory language of the 2008 *Kadi* judgment, the emerging doctrine sees the relationship between the EU and the UN through the lens of conflict.[92] This tension, widely confirmed by the new Council regulation, suggests that the role of UN law as a constitutional framework for international relations may be little more than a myth. It is yet difficult to predict how the EU reform of the mechanism giving effect to UN sanctions will work in practice. What appears clear is that the actual implementation of UN lists will face a double challenge: the filter of the EU Commission's revision of the grounds for listing, and a possible decision by the EU courts annulling the implementing regulation. Non-compliance with Security Council decisions pursuant to the new EU legislation and/or to CFI rulings on the merits will weaken the authority of UN decisions and, possibly, the collaborative relationship between the UN and other treaty-based regimes. Further instances of defiance are in fact likely to occur based on the same concerns,[93] as the EU example might encourage other legislatures to scrutinize UN decisions, and other courts to renounce judicial self-restraint in cases challenging UN-imposed measures.[94]

92 The court acknowledges that, on the international plane, UN obligations are hierarchically superior, but states that within the EU, fundamental EU principles take precedence. This implies that international obligations will not be given effect unless consistent with EU obligations, which reduces the recognition of UN primacy to a 'theoretical concession' (Draghici (n. 4), 657).

93 See Tenth Report of the Monitoring Team (n. 69) [35]: 'As to the fairness and transparency of the regime, the perception remains in many States that it still lacks appropriate protection of individual rights, despite the publication of narrative summaries of reasons for listing and the Committee's review of the appropriateness of all listings. It is important to deal with the continued criticism of the fairness and transparency of the regime, so as to allow the Committee to turn its attention more fully to countering the threat from Al-Qaida and the Taliban'.

94 A claim brought by Youssef Mustapha Nada Ebada against Switzerland is pending before the European Court of Human Rights, following a ruling by the Swiss Federal Tribunal that upholds the sanctions measures against him based on the UN designation. See Ninth Report of the Monitoring Team 12, [24]. The recent views of the Human Rights Committee in the case of *Nabil Sayadi and Patricia Vinck* v. *Belgium* (Communication No. 1472/2006, 22 October 2008), finding a breach of Articles 12 and 17 of the International Covenant on Civil and Political Rights in relation to the authors' presence on UN terrorist lists, may also induce the Court to take a rights-favourable approach.

The *Kadi* doctrine avows that EU constitutionalism supersedes UN constitutionalism. This contradicts the ILC's findings that, where the principle of harmonious interpretation cannot reconcile an obligation under the Charter with a conflicting treaty obligation, the hierarchically superior norm (the one triggered by the operation of Article 103) prevails.[95] Apparently, where Article 103 enters into competition with the highest-rank principles of a self-contained regime, priority will be given to the 'local' *Grundnorm*, which is closer to the community and protects its fundamental values.[96] For that reason the law of the international community as embodied in UN law and institutions has to attach greater weight to values (human rights, rule of law) if it purports to become an authentic global governance.[97] Otherwise, as the *Kadi* saga proves, subsystems having developed a constitutional dimension based on non-derogable norms may invoke their own *ordre public* to deny compliance with UN resolutions, frustrating UN aspirations to universal governance.

95 *ILC Conclusions on Fragmentation* (n. 1) [42].

96 No choice-of-norm would be possible if Article 103 were recognized as *jus cogens*, in fact special regimes are not allowed to derogate from general law when the latter amounts to *jus cogens* (see *Koskenniemi Report* (n. 1). 84 [191]).

97 Thus, any UN solution to the current crisis of the sanctions regime has to be value oriented. It is unlikely that litigation will discontinue unless the UNSC introduces procedures reflecting international human rights and rule-of-law standards in terms of access to justice and fair trial.

15 The relationship between Community law and international law after *Kadi*

Did the ECJ slam the door on effective multilateralism?

Aurel Sari[*]

15.1 Introduction

Never before has a case generated quite as much excitement and debate among European and international lawyers as the judgment delivered by the European Court of Justice (ECJ) in the joined cases of *Kadi* and *Al-Barakaat* in September 2008.[1] The cases mainly turned on the question of whether the Community courts are competent to exercise their powers of judicial review over Community measures designed to implement sanctions adopted by the Security Council under Chapter VII of the Charter of the United Nations on the ground that these measures are contrary to fundamental human rights protected by Community law.[2] In September 2005, the Court of First Instance (CFI) held that it lacked the authority to annul Council Regulation (EC) No. 881/2002 of 27 May 2002 which imposed sanctions against certain persons and entities associated with Usama bin Laden, Al-Qaida and the Taliban,[3] as doing so would amount to an indirect review of the UN sanctions regime in contravention of both Community law and the UN Charter.[4] Nevertheless, the Court found that it was entitled to subject resolutions of the Security Council to a more limited form of scrutiny by testing their compatibility with *jus cogens* norms. On appeal, the ECJ rejected this line of reasoning and declared that obligations imposed on the member states by the UN Charter cannot prevail over principles that 'form part of the very foundations' of the

* I would like to thank the participants of the 2009 ILA British Branch Spring Conference for comments on an earlier version of this chapter.

1 Joined Cases C-402/05 P & C-415/05 P *Kadi and Al Barakaat* v. *Council and Commission* [2008] ECR I-6351. The ECJ recently confirmed its judgment in Joined Cases C-399/06 P & C-403/06 P *Hassan and Ayadi* v. *Council and Commission* [2009] not yet reported.

2 In addition, the cases also raised questions concerning the legal basis for the adoption of smart sanctions. See T. Tridimas and J. A. Gutierrez-Fons, 'EU Law, International Law, and Economic Sanctions against Terrorism: The Judiciary in Distress?' (2008–9) 32 *Fordham Int'l LJ* 660, 664–79.

3 Council Regulation (EC) No. 881/2002 of 27 May 2002 [2002] OJ L139/9.

4 Case T-306/01 *Yusuf and Al Barakaat* v. *Council and Commission* [2005] ECR II-3533; Case T-315/01 *Kadi* v. *Council and Commission* [2005] ECR II-3649. Below, references will be made only to the CFI's judgment in *Kadi* without referring to the corresponding sections of *Yusuf and Al Barakaat*.

Community legal order.[5] Accordingly, it held that the Community judiciary must ensure the review of 'all Community acts in the light of the fundamental rights forming an integral part of the general principles of Community law, including review of Community measures...designed to give effect to the resolutions adopted by the Security Council'.[6]

According to one pair of commentators, *Kadi* represents 'the most important judgment ever delivered by the ECJ on the relationship between Community and international law'.[7] The case presented the Court of Justice with an opportunity to consider key aspects of this relationship from the perspective of Community law. Among other things, the Court reviewed the legal effect of international agreements within the Community legal system, restated the general duty of the Community to abide by its international obligations and elaborated its understanding of the nature of the Community legal order. The judgment constitutes a rich source of jurisprudence on these matters. However, the Court's conclusions and reasoning raise fundamental questions concerning regime conflict and fragmentation in international law.[8] Since the effectiveness of sanctions imposed by the Security Council depends to a large extent on their implementation in domestic law,[9] the judicial review of such implementing measures at the national or regional level may deprive those sanctions of what the ECJ might otherwise term their '*effet utile*'.[10] Conversely, the lack of judicial remedies available at the international plane to individuals affected by UN sanctions means that the absence of judicial review at the national or regional levels may deprive those individuals of an effective juridical remedy altogether.[11]

The CFI resolved this dilemma in a way that safeguards the effectiveness of the UN sanctions regime, but limits the judicial protection of fundamental rights to a minimum. By contrast, the ECJ emphasized the autonomy of the Community legal order and annulled Council Regulation (EC) No. 881/2002 as being incompatible with fundamental rights guaranteed by Community law. In doing so, the Court upheld the constitutional principles of the Community, but at the same time cast doubts on the authority of the UN Charter and the effectiveness of the UN system of collective security.

Predictably, the decisions of the Community courts in *Kadi* have generated a great deal of debate among, as well as between, European and international

5 *Kadi and Al Barakaat* (n. 1), para. 304.

6 *Ibid.* para. 326.

7 Tridimas and Gutierrez-Fons (n. 2), 661.

8 It is these broader implications, described by some as 'disturbing', of the judgment for the international legal system that seems to explain the extraordinary level of interest taken in the case. See A. Aust, '*Kadi*: Ignoring International Legal Obligation' (2009) 6 IOLR 293, 298.

9 A. Bianchi, 'Assessing the Effectiveness of the UN Security Council's Anti-terrorism Measures: The Quest for Legitimacy and Cohesion' (2006) 17 EJIL 881.

10 See M. Potacs, '*Effet utile* als Auslegungsgrundsatz' (2009) 44 *Europarecht* 465.

11 See M. Gestri, 'Legal Remedies against Security Council Targeted Sanctions: *De Lege Lata* and *De Lege Ferenda* Options for Enhancing the Protection of the Individual' (2007) 17 *Italian YIL* 25; A. Ciampi, 'Individual Remedies against Security Council Targeted Sanctions' (2007) 17 *Italian YIL* 55.

lawyers.[12] In this respect, it has been suggested that any discussion of the two judgments 'is inevitably influenced by preconceptions about national, European, and international law, and how these three levels (should) relate to each other'.[13] Commentators working in these different fields certainly do so subject to their respective structural biases.[14] While one should be wary of underestimating the narrowness of view that scholarly preconceptions may foster, assessing the judgments of the CFI and ECJ on their own terms can nevertheless go some way in bridging these disciplinary divides.[15] In particular, such an analysis reveals the presence of a certain dissonance between what Pasquale De Sena and Maria Chiara Vitucci have usefully termed the formal legal reasoning and the substantive values espoused by the courts.[16] This chapter argues that this dissonance is a key feature of both judgments, although, contrary to what De Sena and Vitucci suggest, it is more pronounced in the judgment of the ECJ. The purpose of the present chapter is to assess the reasoning of the Community courts concerning the relationship between the UN Charter and the EC Treaty with the aim of identifying key points of divergence between their respective formal and value-based arguments and to reconsider the potential impact of *Kadi* on the international legal system from this perspective.

15.2 Framing the dispute

The facts that gave rise to the proceedings in *Kadi* have been widely reported and need not be reiterated here in detail.[17] Beginning with Resolution 1267 of 3 October 1999, the Security Council adopted a series of resolutions under Chapter VII of the UN Charter requiring all states to freeze the funds and other financial resources owned or controlled by Usama bin Laden, Al-Qaida and the Taliban.[18] In late 2001, the Sanctions Committee established under Resolution 1267, added the names of the applicants – Yassin Kadi, Ahmed

12 For a review of the burgeoning literature, see S. Poli and M. Tzanou, 'The *Kadi* Rulings: A Survey of the Literature', in M. Cremona, F. Francioni and S. Poli (eds.), *Challenging the EU Counter-Terrorism Measures Through the Courts* (Florence: European University Institute, 2009), 139.

13 C. Eckes, 'International Sanctions against Individuals: A Test Case for the Resilience of the European Union's Constitutional Foundations' (2009) 15 EPL 351, 352. See also M. Milanović, 'Norm Conflict in International Law: Whither Human Rights?' (2009) 20 *Duke J.Comp.& Int'l L.* 69, 107–10.

14 M. Koskenniemi, 'The Politics of International Law – 20 Years Later' (2009) 20 EJIL 7. See also B. Simma, 'Universality of International Law from the Perspective of a Practitioner' (2009) 20 EJIL 265, 294.

15 Cf. D. Dutton, 'To Understand It on Its Own Terms' (1974) 35 *Philosophy and Phenomenological Research* 246.

16 P. De Sena and M. C. Vitucci, 'The European Courts and the Security Council: Between *Dédoublement Fonctionnel* and Balancing of Values' (2009) 20 EJIL 193.

17 Tridimas and Gutierrez-Fons (n. 2), 661–4.

18 UNSC resolutions relevant to the proceedings include UNSC Res. 1267 (15 October 1999) UN Doc. S/RES/1267, UNSC Res. 1333 (19 December 2000) UN Doc. S/RES/1333 and UNSC Res. 1390 (16 January 2002) UN Doc. S/RES/1390. On the UN sanctions regime, see M. Bulterman, 'Fundamental Rights and the United Nations Financial Sanction Regime: The *Kadi* and *Yusuf* Judgments of the Court of First Instance of the European Communities' (2006) 19 LJIL 753, 754–60; C. A. Feinäugle,

Ali Yusuf and the Al Barakaat International Foundation – to the list of persons and entities subject to restrictive measures pursuant to the relevant Security Council resolutions. On 27 May 2002, the Council of the EU adopted Regulation (EC) 881/2002 to implement these restrictive measures in the territory of the European Community. The applicants subsequently brought two separate actions against the Council and the Commission before the CFI seeking the annulment of Regulation (EC) 881/2002 under Article 230 of the EC Treaty in so far as it concerned them.[19]

The applicants argued that the contested regulation violated their fundamental rights as protected by Community law, in particular the right to a fair hearing, the right to respect for property and the right to effective judicial review. In response, the Council and Commission submitted that the Community is required to act, within its spheres of competence, in such a way as to fulfil the obligations imposed on its member states as a result of their membership of the UN.[20] In particular, the institutions argued that the Community must be regarded, for all practical purposes, as bound by the relevant Security Council resolutions in the same manner as the member states and that the Community institutions therefore enjoyed no autonomous discretion in implementing those resolutions within the Community legal order. Confronted with these arguments, the CFI devoted a significant part of its judgment to examining the nature and scope of the obligations imposed on the member states and the Community by the UN Charter and the EC Treaty. For the Court, the case thus essentially turned on the question of the relationship between the potentially conflicting obligations arising under these two instruments and how that relationship affected its jurisdiction.[21]

On appeal, the arguments of the parties essentially remained the same. Despite the dispute still being therefore framed in terms of a norm conflict, both Advocate General Maduro and the ECJ shifted their attention from the relationship between European and international norms to the broader relationship between the two legal orders. According to Maduro, the key issue raised by the appellants was 'the question of how the relationship between the international legal order and the Community legal order must be described'.[22] For the Advocate General and the ECJ, that question had to be answered from the position of the autonomous nature of the Community legal order. Whereas the CFI decided the case on the basis of the applicable conflict of norms provisions laid down in the UN Charter and the EC Treaty, the Advocate General and the Court of Justice thus reasoned on the level of rules of recognition. The following sections will examine the logic and consistency of these two approaches in more detail.

'The UN Security Council Al-Qaida and Taliban Sanctions Committee: Emerging Principles of International Institutional Law for the Protection of Individuals?' (2008) 9 *German LJ* 1513.

19 See (n. 4).

20 *Kadi* (n. 4), paras. 153–64.

21 *Ibid*. para. 177.

22 *Ibid*. para. 21. The AG adopted the same reasoning in Opinion of AG Maduro, *Al Barakaat* (n. 1).

15.3 A conflict of norms

The CFI's aim in assessing the relationship between the UN Charter and the EC Treaty was to clarify their legal impact on the member states and the European Community. Whereas most aspects of the Court's reasoning have been criticized extensively in the literature, it appears that at least some of that criticism was misdirected.

15.3.1 The position of the member states

Concerning the member states, the Court rightly held that their obligations under the UN Charter prevail over their obligations arising under any other international agreement in accordance with Article 103 of the Charter.[23] As a matter of international law, the member states' duty to implement the sanctions regime established by the relevant Security Council resolutions thus takes precedence over their conflicting obligations under the EC Treaty.[24] The CFI also found that the Charter obligations of the member states enjoy primacy as a matter of Community law. The Court here pointed to Article 297 EC, which implicitly recognizes that the member states may adopt measures which affect the functioning of the common market in order to carry out obligations they have accepted for the purpose of maintaining peace and international security. According to the Court, Article 297 EC was introduced into the EC Treaty specifically to guarantee the primacy of Charter obligations.[25] The CFI also invoked the first paragraph of Article 307 EC, which provides that the rights and obligations arising from agreements concluded by the member states with third countries before the former became bound by the EC Treaty are not affected by the provisions of that treaty.[26] As the ECJ has held on successive occasions, the purpose of this provision is to ensure that the EC Treaty does not affect the member states' duty under international law to comply with their pre-existing treaty obligations and to respect the corresponding rights of third countries.[27]

Little fault can be found with the CFI's conclusion concerning the purpose of Articles 297 and 307 EC. Indeed, most commentators have not taken issue with this part of the judgment, but directed their criticism at the effects the Court ascribed to these provisions. Piet Eeckhout, among others, has suggested that Articles 297 and 307 EC merely permit the member states to derogate

23 *Kadi* (n. 4), para. 183. See R. Bernhardt, 'Article 103', in B. Simma, A. Paulus and H. Chaitidou (eds.), *The Charter of the United Nations: A Commentary* (2nd edn, Oxford: Oxford University Press, 2002) 1292; R. Liivoja, 'The Scope of the Supremacy Clause of the United Nations Charter' (2008) 57 ICLQ 583.

24 Cf. *Lockerbie Case* (*Libya* v. *UK*) (Provisional Measures) [1992] ICJ Rep. 3, para. 39; *Lockerbie Case* (*Libya* v. *US*) (Provisional Measures) [1992] ICJ Rep. 114, para. 42.

25 *Kadi* (n. 4), para. 188.

26 On the special position of Germany, see *ibid.* para. 187.

27 Case 10/61 *Commission* v. *Italy* [1962] ECR 1; Case 286/86 *Deserbais* [1988] ECR 4907 para. 17.

from their Community law obligations, but do not require them to do so.[28] This may be so, yet from the member states' perspective this question has little practical significance. The outcome is the same in both cases precisely because Articles 297 and 307 EC are engaged only when the member states are subject to an international obligation.[29] The member states are required to give effect to their Charter obligations irrespective of whether Articles 297 and 307 EC impose on them a corresponding duty of compliance as a matter of Community law or merely permit them to abide by those international obligations in the face of conflicting Community norms.[30] This lack of discretion at the international level is of course what according to the CFI distinguished the present case from cases involving autonomous sanctions lists drawn up at the level of the EU.[31]

15.3.2 The position of the European Community

The CFI went on to consider whether the European Community was bound by the UN Charter separately from its member states. In line with existing case law,[32] it denied that the Community was directly bound by the Charter either in its own right or as a possible successor to the rights and duties of its member states. Adopting the logic of *International Fruit Company*,[33] the Court nonetheless found that 'the Community must be considered to be bound by the obligations under the Charter in the same way as the Member States, by virtue of the Treaty establishing it'.[34]

The Court reached this conclusion in two stages. First, it held that the Community is subject to a negative duty not to 'impede the performance of the obligations of Member States which stem from [the] Charter'.[35] The Court here appeared to embrace what German writers have termed the mortgage theory (*Hypothekentheorie*). In essence, the theory postulates that the member states could not transfer more powers onto the Community than they possessed at the time of its creation and that the Community therefore lacks the legal

28 P. Eeckhout, *Does Europe's Constitution Stop at the Water's Edge?* (Gröningen: Europe Law Publishing, 2005), 23. See also C. Eckes, 'Judicial Review of European Anti-Terrorism Measures: The *Yusuf* and *Kadi* Judgments of the Court of First Instance' (2008) 14 ELJ 74, 83; N. G. Vitzthum, 'Les compétences législatives et juridictionnelles de la Communauté européenne dans la lutte contre le terrorisme – l'affaire "Kadi"' (2008) 11 *Zeitschrift für Europarechtliche Studien* 375, 409.

29 Case C-324/93 *Evans Medical* [1995] ECR I-563, para. 32.

30 See also P. Pescatore, 'Les relations extérieures des communautés européennes: contribution à la doctrine de la personnalité des organisations internationales' (1961) 103-II *Recueil des Cours* 1, 160–1.

31 E.g. Case T-228/02 *OMPI* [2006] ECR II-4665, at paras. 99–108; Case T-327/03 *Al-Aqsa* [2007] not yet reported; Case T-47/03 *Sison* [2007] not yet reported, at paras. 153–5. See C. Eckes, 'Sanctions against Individuals – Fighting Terrorism within the European Legal Order' (2008) 4 *EUConst*. 205.

32 Case T-184/95 *Dorsch Consult* [1998] ECR II-667, para. 74.

33 Case 24-72 *International Fruit Company* [1972] ECR 1219.

34 *Kadi* (n. 4), para. 194.

35 *Ibid.* para. 197.

capacity to act contrary to the UN Charter. As has been argued before,[36] this theory suffers from excessive formalism.[37] The transfer of legal capacities onto international organizations is not a zero-sum process.[38] States do not alienate their sovereign competences and may do collectively what they are not capable of unilaterally.[39] Contrary to what the mortgage theory assumes, overlaps in the competences of states and international organizations are not only possible, but the very existence of Article 103 of the UN Charter is testimony to the fact that they do occur in practice.[40] However, these shortcomings do not invalidate the first step of the CFI's reasoning, as the Community's duty not to hinder the member states in the performance of their Charter obligations can be deduced from Articles 297 and 307 EC independently of the mortgage theory.[41]

In a second step, the Court went on to argue that in so far as its member states have conferred onto the Community powers necessary for carrying out their Charter obligations, the Community is bound to exercise those powers in such a way as to enable the member states to comply with their obligations.[42] In this sense, the Community has become indirectly bound by the Charter obligations of the member states by way of 'functional succession'.[43] The CFI seemed to conflate two distinct questions here: is the Community bound to assist the member states in complying with their Charter obligations and, if so, what is the extent of this duty?

The Court answered the first question with reference to Article 48(2) of the UN Charter, which provides that decisions of the Security Council shall be carried out by the members of the UN 'directly and through their action in the appropriate international agencies of which they are members'. Since the Community must respect international law in the exercise of its powers,[44] the Court inferred that Community law must be interpreted, and its scope limited, in such a way as to enable the Community to give effect to Article

36 K. Osteneck, *Die Umsetzung von UN-Wirtschaftssanktionen durch die Europäische Gemeinschaft* (Berlin: Springer, 2004), 224–6.

37 Essentially, it reflects a constitutionalist outlook. Cf. J. Erne, 'Conferral of Powers by States as a Basis of Obligation of International Organisations' (2009) 78 NJIL 177, 181–2.

38 See J. Klabbers, *An Introduction to International Institutional Law* (2nd edn, Cambridge: Cambridge University Press, 2009), 308–11.

39 For the *locus classicus* on the first point, see *SS Wimbledon* (1923) PCIJ Series A, No. 1, 25; for the second point, see *Reparations for Injuries Suffered in the Service of the United Nations* (Advisory Opinion) [1949] ICJ Rep. 174, 185. See also R. Barents, *The Autonomy of Community Law* (The Hague: Kluwer, 2004), 156–9.

40 H. G. Schermers and N. Blokker, *International Institutional Law* (4th edn, The Hague: Martinus Nijhoff, 2003), § 1707.

41 See also C. Tomuschat, 'Note on Cases T-306/01 and T-315/01' (2006) 43 CMLR 537, 542.

42 *Kadi* (n. 4), paras. 198–203.

43 Cf. M. Nettesheim, 'UN Sanctions against Individuals – A Challenge to the Architecture of European Union Governance' (2007) 44 CMLR 567, 584; N. Lavranos, 'UN Sanctions and Judicial Review' (2007) 76 NJIL 1, 10–13; Eckes (n. 28), 84.

44 Case C-286/90 *Poulsen and Diva* [1992] ECR I-6019, para. 9; Case C-162/96 *Racke* [1998] ECR I-3655, para. 45.

48(2) of the Charter. This argument is based on the assumption that Article 48(2) of the UN Charter purports to bind international organizations. However, practice demonstrates that this is not the case.[45] Moreover, the Community's duty to respect international law does not extend to the provisions of international agreements to which it is not a party, such as the UN Charter.[46] While a duty of assistance therefore cannot be derived from the notion that the Community is indirectly bound by the Charter obligations of its member states,[47] such a duty is nevertheless implicit in certain provisions of the EC Treaty, including Article 301 EC, which directs the Council to take the necessary urgent measures to implement economic sanctions decided within the framework of the Common Foreign and Security Policy.[48] Since the adoption of economic sanctions under Article 301 EC must be considered a Community objective,[49] it follows that the member states and the institutions are bound by the principle of mutual cooperation laid down in Article 10 EC in the implementation of UN sanctions.[50]

Concerning the extent and possible limits of the Community's duty of assistance, the CFI held that the member states' intention to comply with their Charter obligations, as reflected in particular in Article 301 EC, compels the Community to 'adopt *all* the measures necessary' to enable them to perform those obligations,[51] even if these contravene Community law. This conclusion is difficult to justify. The Court ignored the fact that Article 301 EC directs the Council to adopt economic sanctions in order to implement common positions or joint actions, which in turn may not affect the EC Treaty pursuant to Article 47 TEU.[52] Given that the conformity of measures adopted under Article 301 EC with Community law is a condition of their validity, that provision does not evince an intention that the Community should assist the member states in carrying out their Charter obligations even by breaching its own constituting treaty. More fundamentally, the CFI relied on the concept of functional succession to extend the legal effect of Article 103 of the UN Charter to the Community. While it may seem intuitive to consider the

45 B.-O. Bryde and A. Reinisch, 'Article 48', in B. Simma, A. Paulus and H. Chaitidou (eds.), *The Charter of the United Nations: A Commentary* (2nd edn Oxford: Oxford University Press, 2002), 775.

46 In *Poulsen and Diva* (n. 44), the ECJ relied on such agreements only 'in so far as they codify general rules recognized by international custom' (para. 10). See also *Racke* (n. 44), para. 24. Nothing suggests that Article 48(2) of the Charter is such a provision.

47 For another view, see R. H. Lauwaars, 'The Interrelationship between United Nations Law and the Law of Other International Organizations' (1984) 82 *Mich.L.Rev.* 1604, 1610–11; A. von Arnauld, 'UN-Sanktionen und gemeinschaftsrechtlicher Grundrechtsschutz' (2006) 44 *Archiv des Völkerrechts* 201, 206.

48 See P. Koutrakos, *EU International Relations Law* (Oxford: Hart, 2006), 428–41.

49 *Kadi and Al Barakaat* (n. 1), para. 227.

50 See, by analogy, Case C-308/06 *Intertanko* [2008] ECR I-4057, para. 52. The same argument has been made without recourse to Article 301 EC (see S. Bohr, 'Sanctions by the United Nations Security Council and the European Community' (1993) 4 EJIL 256, 267–8).

51 *Kadi* (n. 4), para. 204 (emphasis added).

52 Case C-70/94 *Werner* [1995] ECR I-3189, paras. 10–11.

Community as the member states' successor in those areas where it enjoys exclusive competence,[53] it is nevertheless questionable whether the formal requirements of functional succession laid down in *International Fruit Company* are satisfied in the case of the UN Charter.[54] Even if they were, the application of Article 103 to the Community by analogy would confer primacy on the Community's Charter obligations solely over obligations arising from any international agreement it has concluded. It would not require the Community to act contrary to the EC Treaty, just as it does not require members of the UN to act contrary to their constitutions.

15.4 Legal ontology: the autonomy of the community legal order

In contrast to the CFI, Advocate General Maduro and the ECJ approached the relationship between the UN Charter and the EC Treaty from a legal systems perspective. According to the Advocate General, the logical starting point of the discussion should be the case of *Van Gend en Loos* in which the ECJ proclaimed the autonomy of the Community legal order.[55] For Maduro, the independent character of the Community law as a 'municipal legal order' meant that it fell to Community courts to 'determine the effect of international obligations within the Community legal order by reference to conditions set by Community law'.[56] The Court of Justice based itself on the same constitutional premise. It first recalled that the Community is based on the principle of the rule of law and declared that obligations imposed by an international agreement cannot have the effect of prejudicing the constitutional principles of the Community.[57] It then examined whether in the present case, either the principles governing the relationship between the international legal order and the Community legal order, or the provisions of the EC Treaty nevertheless excluded the exercise of judicial review over the contested measure.[58] It found that judicial review was not so excluded for two key reasons.

15.4.1 A conflict of norms? What conflict?

A conflict of norms exists only between rules operating on the same plane.[59] In the CFI's assessment, such a conflict existed in the present case

53 L. M. Hinojosa Martínez, 'Bad Law for Good Reasons: The Contradictions of the *Kadi* Judgment' (2008) 5 IOLR 339, 339–41.

54 Osteneck (n. 36), 260–91; P. Eeckhout, *External Relations of the European Union* (Oxford: Oxford University Press, 2005), 438–9.

55 Case 26-62 *Van Gend en Loos* [1963] ECR 1.

56 *Opinion of AG Maduro* (n. 22), para. 23.

57 *Kadi and Al Barakaat* (n. 1), paras. 281–9.

58 *Ibid.* paras. 290–9, 300–9.

59 Milanović (n. 13), 102.

because the Charter obligations of the member states produced effects within the Community legal order both for the member states themselves as well as for the Community. The Court of Justice denied that this was the case. It adopted what has widely been described as a dualist position, maintaining that international agreements cannot prejudice the constitutional principles of the EC Treaty. From the perspective of Community law, the obligations incurred by the member states on the plane of international law are incapable of affecting the Community legal order because they operate on a different level from that of Community law. Consequently, the obligations that arise for the member states under the UN Charter are of no concern to the Community courts for the purposes of testing the internal legality of Community measures.[60] This explains why the ECJ did not waste a single word on discussing the legal effects of Article 103 of the Charter. This was also the position of Advocate General Maduro, who expressly argued that the annulment of the contested regulation is without prejudice to the rules of state responsibility and Article 103 of the UN Charter.[61]

Despite the constitutionalist terminology employed by the Court of Justice, the fact remains that the Community legal order originated in public international law.[62] In *Van Gend*, the ECJ famously described Community law as 'a new legal order of international law'.[63] While the Court may have conceived Community law as a self-contained regime, in those early days it regarded it as a self-contained regime of international law.[64] The Advocate General's reference to Community law as 'a municipal legal order of transnational dimensions',[65] and the apparent endorsement of this view by the Court of Justice, suggests that in their view Community law today no longer occupies the same '*espace juridique*' as public international law. This raises a range of interesting questions, including how this transformation has come about and what the concept of a municipal order of transnational dimensions entails.

For present purposes, the point to bear in mind is that even if Community law has now morphed from an international/supranational into a 'municipal' legal order, the founding text of the Community still retains its character as

60 This is to say that Charter obligations are of no concern under any circumstance. See *Kadi and Al Barakaat* (n. 1), paras. 294–6.

61 Opinion of AG Maduro (n. 22), para. 39.

62 J. H. H. Weiler and U. R. Haltern, 'The Autonomy of the Community Legal Order: Through the Looking Glass' (1996) 37 *Harv.Int'l LJ* 411, 417ff.

63 *Van Gend en Loos* (n. 55), 23.

64 Generally, see B. Simma and D. Pulkowski, 'Of Planets and the Universe: Self-contained Regimes in International Law' (2006) 17 EJIL 483.

65 Opinion of AG Maduro (n. 22), para. 21.

an instrument of international law.[66] The dual status of the EC Treaty as an international agreement and primary Community law means that the divorce between international law and Community law is not quite as perfect as the Advocate General and the ECJ have suggested. On the one hand, the continued existence of the EC Treaty as an international agreement means that the conflict of norms provisions of international law, including Article 103 of the UN Charter,[67] cannot be ignored or dismissed as something completely irrelevant and extraneous to Community law. On the other hand, the Court's attempt to deny the legal effects of the UN Charter by invoking the principle that 'an international agreement cannot affect the allocation of powers fixed by the Treaties or, consequently, the autonomy of the Community legal system' is not persuasive.[68] In the past, the ECJ has employed this 'no effects' principle to limit the impact within Community law of international agreements to which the Community was a party.[69] In *Kadi*, the Court not only extends the principle to agreements concluded solely by the member states, but it now appears to exclude categorically the possibility that *any* international agreement could affect the EC Treaty.[70] Extending the 'no effects' principle to the UN Charter in this manner disregards the special relationship that the first paragraph of Article 307 EC establishes between certain international agreements and the EC Treaty.

The place that the Court assigned to the UN Charter within the hierarchy of Community norms suggests that this was indeed the ECJ's strategy. According to the Court, if Article 300(7) EC were applicable to the UN Charter, the latter would have primacy over secondary Community legislation, but not over primary law.[71] This is a peculiar argument. Article 300 EC regulates the conclusion of international agreements by the Community and as such does not apply to the UN Charter. Why did the Court choose to argue by way of hypothesis and consider the Charter in the context of Article 300 EC? One possible explanation is that the ECJ relied on this provision to respond to the functional succession argument put forward by the CFI:[72] even

66 J. Boulouis, 'Le droit des Communautés européennes dans ses rapports avec le droit international général' (1992) 235-IV *Recueil des Cours* 9, 38; T. Schilling, 'The Autonomy of the Community Legal Order: An Analysis of Possible Foundations' (1996) 37 *Harv.Int'l LJ* 389, 403; T. Hartley, 'The Constitutional Foundations of the European Union' (2001) 117 LQR 225, 226; B. de Witte, 'International Law as a Tool for the European Union' (2009) 5 *EUConst.* 265, 267–72. Cf. R. Schütze, 'On "Federal" Ground: The European Union as an (Inter)national Phenomenon' (2009) 46 CMLR 1069, 1082–3.

67 See ILC, 'Fragmentation of International Law: Report of the Study Group of the International Law Commission Finalized by Martti Koskenniemi' (13 April 2006) UN Doc. A/CN.4/L.682.

68 *Kadi and Al Barakaat* (n. 1), para. 282.

69 E.g. Opinion 1/91 *European Economic Area* [1991] ECR I-6079, para. 35; Case C-459/03 *Mox Plant* [2006] ECR I-4635, para. 123.

70 See also Lavranos (n. 43), 11–12.

71 *Kadi and Al Barakaat* (n. 1), paras. 305–9.

72 Lavranos (n. 43), 11; M. Payandeh and H. Sauer, 'European Union: UN Sanctions and EU Fundamental Rights' (2009) 7 ICON 306, 311.

if the Community were bound by the UN Charter, the latter could not prevail over primary law because of Article 300 EC. This explanation is not persuasive. Not only did the CFI deny that the Community became bound by the UN Charter directly, but the central message of its argument was that the Community was in the same position as the member states in that the legal effects of the Charter prevailed over its conflicting obligations under the EC Treaty. Pointing to Article 300 EC does not counter these arguments. Considering the general wording of the relevant passages, the more likely explanation, therefore, is that the ECJ relied on Article 300 EC in order to equate the legal effects of the Charter with the legal effects of agreements concluded by the Community and thereby avoid recognizing that the obligations of the member states under the Charter prevail over the EC Treaty pursuant to the first paragraph of Article 307 EC.[73] While some commentators have rightly chastised the CFI for turning the traditional hierarchy of norms in Community law on its head,[74] the ECJ may be criticized in similar terms. Not only has the Court of Justice overlooked the legal consequences that flow from the continued existence of the EC Treaty as an international agreement, in particular the applicability of Article 103 of the UN Charter, but it also refused to recognize, to all intents and purposes, that Article 307 EC accords a special status to the UN Charter within Community law.

15.4.2 The 'no derogation' thesis

The Court of Justice also denied that an internal conflict of norms could exist between Articles 297 and 307 EC on the one hand and the general principles of Community law on the other hand. Both the Advocate General and the ECJ postulated what can be termed the 'no derogation' thesis, whereby Articles 297 and 307 EC cannot be understood to permit derogations from principles that form part of the very foundations of the Community legal order. The Court's reasoning is rather laconic on this point. While it acknowledged that Articles 297 and 307 EC permit certain exceptions to primary law, it provided no further reasons why general principles, in particular the protection of fundamental rights and judicial review, are excluded from the scope of these exceptions.[75] The opinion of the Advocate General offers more detail, though not much more clarity.

73 See also C. Tomuschat, 'The *Kadi* Case: What Relationship between the Universal Legal Order under the Auspices of the United Nations and the EU Legal Order?', in M. Cremona, F. Francioni and S. Poli (eds.), *Challenging the EU Counter-Terrorism Measures Through the Courts* (Florence: European University Institute, 2009), 11, 15; P. J. Cardwell, D. French and N. White, '*Kadi* v. Council of the European Union (C-402/05 P)' (2009) 58 ICLQ 229, 234–5.

74 N. Lavranos, 'Judicial Review of UN Sanctions by the Court of First Instance' (2006) 11 *European Foreign Affairs Review* 471, 477–80; G. Harpaz, 'Judicial Review by the European Court of Justice of UN "Smart Sanctions" against Terror in the *Kadi*' (2009) 14 *European Foreign Affairs Review* 65, 76–7.

75 *Kadi and Al Barakaat* (n. 1), paras. 301–4.

Regarding Article 297 EC, Advocate General Maduro suggested, with reference to the *Centro-Com* case,[76] that any measures the member states adopt outside the Community framework in order to comply with their obligations under the UN Charter must be consistent with Community law.[77] This seems to miss the underlying issue. The thrust of the Article 297 EC argument is that this provision recognizes, implicitly, that the member states may derogate from the EC Treaty in order to comply with the obligations they have accepted for the purpose of maintaining peace and international security. To declare that the member states must comply with Community law when acting under the CFSP or outside the context of the treaties simply states the default position: the point of Article 297 EC is that it creates an exception to this ordinary state of affairs.[78] While it is clear that Article 297 EC is subject to certain limits and, as a whole, must be read in a restrictive fashion,[79] its core meaning and scope cannot be simply wished away.

The *travaux préparatoires* of what is now Article 297 EC confirm that its purpose is to protect the functioning of the common market as well as the interests of the member states. Specifically, the *travaux* suggest that Article 297 EC was meant to safeguard not only obligations arising under Chapter VII of the UN Charter, but also obligations undertaken in regional collective security mechanisms.[80] Moreover, unlike the other exceptions recognized by Article 297 EC, a derogation on the grounds of complying with obligations accepted for the purpose of maintaining international peace and security does not depend on the subjective assessment of the member states,[81] but on the objective existence of a conflict between an international obligation and a rule of Community law.[82] Clearly, the obligations imposed on the member states by the relevant Security Council resolutions fall squarely within the scope of Article 297 EC and entitle them to derogate from conflicting norms of Community law. There is no textual support for the view that Article 297 EC is inapplicable to the present case.

As regards Article 307 EC, the UN Charter plainly satisfies the two preconditions for the application of that provision:[83] the Charter is a pre-existing treaty and third countries can derive rights from it, which the member

76 Case C-124/95 *Centro-Com* [1997] ECR I-81.

77 Opinion of AG Maduro (n. 22), para. 30.

78 See Opinion of AG Cosmas, C-423/98 *Alfredo Albore* [2000] ECR I-5965, paras. 22–36.

79 Case 222/84 *Johnston* [1986] ECR 1651, para. 26. See P. Koutrakos, 'Is Article 297 EC a "Reserve of Sovereignty"?' (2000) 37 CMLR 1339.

80 The draft at one stage referred to obligations undertaken 'au titre de la Charte des Nations-Unies ou des accords régionaux de défense conclus au sens de l'article 52 de ladite Charte ou d'accords conclus avec les pays auxquels l'unissent des liens particuliers'. The deletion of this qualification suggests that the remaining text was meant to be interpreted broadly. See 'Propositions de la délégation française relatives à la défense nationale' CM3/NEGO-261 (8 January 1957) in *Négociations du traité la CEE et la CEEA* (Historical Archives of the European Communities) MAE48 f-d/57, 1.

81 Opinion of AG Jacobs, Case C-120/94 *Commission* v. *Greece* [1996] ECR I-1513, para. 54.

82 Cf. Eeckhout (n. 54), 442–4.

83 Joined Cases C-364/95 & C-365/95 *T. Port GmbH* [1998] ECR I-1023, para. 61.

states must respect.[84] Why, then, did the Advocate General and the ECJ suggest that the first paragraph of Article 307 EC is inapplicable in the present case? According to Advocate General Maduro, the notion that Article 307 EC could permit a possible derogation from the principle of respect for fundamental rights enshrined in Article 6(1) TEU would be contrary to Article 49 TEU, which renders accession to the Union conditional on respect for the principles set out in Article 6(1) TEU. It would also contradict the 'established case-law of this Court, according to which the Community guarantees a complete system of judicial protection in which fundamental rights are safeguarded in consonance with the constitutional traditions of the Member States'.[85] In Maduro's view, nothing suggests that Article 307 EC has a special status of this nature.

This argument puts the cart before the horse. The ECJ has held consistently that Article 307 EC 'is of general scope and applies to any international agreement, irrespective of subject-matter, which is capable of affecting the application of the Treaty'.[86] If the applicability of Article 307 EC does not depend on the subject matter of the international agreement concerned, it cannot depend on the subject matter of the provisions of the EC Treaty either. In other words, Article 307 EC must apply to norm conflicts regardless of the substantive content of those norms.[87] Rather than it being necessary to prove that the first paragraph of Article 307 EC permits a derogation from fundamental rights, what requires proof is that it does not permit this derogation. Neither the Advocate General nor the Court of Justice have offered such evidence. Moreover, if the international obligations assumed by the member states for the purpose of maintaining international peace and security cannot justify a derogation from the fundamental principles of the Community on the basis of Articles 297 and 307 EC, it is difficult to see why they should justify any derogation, even a proportionate one, on the combined basis of Articles 60, 301 and 308 EC.[88] The fundamental principles of the Community legal order either embody absolute values from which no derogation is possible at all, or they do not. The ECJ cannot have it both ways.

84 Article 2(2) of the UN Charter requires all members to 'fulfil in good faith the obligations assumed by them in accordance with the present Charter'. EU member states thus owe an obligation to other members of the UN to fulfil their Charter obligations. For confirmation of the vertical operation of Article 2(2), see *Land and Maritime Boundary* (*Cameroon* v. *Nigeria*) (Preliminary Objections) [1998] ICJ Rep. 275, paras. 37–9. Cf. *Documents of the United Nations Conference on International Organization*, vol. 6 (London: United Nations Information Organizations, 1945), 71–80.

85 Opinion of AG Maduro (n. 22), para. 31.

86 Case 812/79 *Burgoa* [1980] ECR 2787, para. 6; Case C-158/91 *Levy* [1993] ECR I-4287, para. 11; Case C-84/98 *Commission* v. *Portugal* [2000] ECR I-5215, para. 43; Case C-466/98 *Commission* v. *UK* (*Open Skies*) [2002] ECR I-9427, para. 23.

87 In this, Article 307 EC mirrors Article 103 of the UN Charter.

88 Case C-84/95 *Bosphorus* [1996] ECR I-3953, paras. 21–5; *Kadi and Al Barakaat* (n. 1), paras. 357ff.

15.5 Making sense of Kadi

According to De Sena and Vitucci, the formal legal arguments employed by the CFI are so weak that they lack credibility.[89] They suggest that the Court's reasoning cannot be understood without considering what *real* objectives it pursued in its judgments. In their view, a careful analysis of the CFI's arguments reveals that it was motivated by an overriding desire to ensure the effectiveness of the relevant Security Council resolutions. By finding that the obligations arising under the Charter prevail over conflicting norms of Community law, the Court chose to uphold the substantive values reflected in those resolutions at the expense of protecting fundamental human rights. This interpretation seems to overestimate the dissonance between the formal and substantive aspects of the CFI's judgments. Section III has argued that the Court's reasoning is not at all as 'spurious' as some commentators have suggested.[90] There is nothing strained about asserting that the Community may not hinder member states in complying with their Charter obligations or that it must assist them in performing those obligations in accordance with Article 10 EC. Both propositions can be justified by formal legal arguments. However, the same cannot be said about the notion that the Community is bound by the obligations arising from the UN Charter in the same way as the member states because it inherited their functions. In the absence of compelling formal arguments or subsequent practice, the conclusion that the Community institutions must give precedence to the UN Charter over the EC Treaty does require a leap of faith or indeed an overriding desire – some might call it a teleological approach – to ensure the effectiveness of the UN collective security system.

Whereas De Sena and Vitucci at first sight find the formal legal arguments of the ECJ more credible than those of the CFI, they detect 'significant traces of a "value oriented approach"' in its judgment too.[91] In essence, they suggest that the dualism of the Court was incomplete: the ECJ not only gave a nod to the primary role of the Security Council in maintaining international peace and security, but it also considered the Commission's argument that it should refrain from exercising its powers of judicial review in the light of recent improvements in the UN sanctions regime on the merits, rather than dismissing it, in true dualist fashion, as irrelevant for the purposes of the internal review of the lawfulness of Community acts. In their view, the Court thus followed the Advocate General and held open the door for a *Solange* compromise should the Security Council enhance the human rights safeguards

89 De Sena and Vitucci (n. 16), 199–202.

90 R. Schütze, 'EC Law and International Agreements of the Member States – An Ambivalent Relationship?' (2007) 9 CYELS 387, 405.

91 De Sena and Vitucci (n. 16), 224.

of the UN sanctions regime in the future.[92] This is a compelling analysis, except that it seems to accept the constitutionalist position adopted by the ECJ as a formal, rather than a value-based, feature of its reasoning.

15.5.1 A hierarchy of substantive values?

Nothing the ECJ said about the autonomous nature of the Community legal order in *Kadi* can be regarded as truly novel. Nevertheless, the Court did more than just reiterate its earlier case law. First, rediscovering the language of *Les Verts*, the Court put constitutional considerations at the centre of its argument by recalling that the EC Treaty serves as the 'basic constitutional charter' of the Community.[93] Second, it declared in sweeping terms that international agreements 'cannot affect the allocation of powers fixed by the Treaties or, consequently, the autonomy of the Community legal system'.[94] Third, building on this, it asserted categorically that Articles 297 and 307 EC do not permit any derogations from principles that form part of the 'very foundations of the Community legal order'.[95] Section IV sought to demonstrate that this line of reasoning cannot be justified by formal legal arguments: indeed, the Court seemed to arrive at its conclusions despite what the provisions of the EC Treaty require. Was the Court led by value-based arguments instead? If so, what values?

It is useful at this point to revisit the 'no derogation' thesis, as it holds a clue as to what did not motivate the Court. The 'no derogation' thesis suffers from an apparent contradiction: if Articles 297 and 307 EC cannot be understood to authorize any derogation from the fundamental principles of the Community legal order, including human rights, why are such derogations permissible on the basis of other provisions, such as Article 36 EC or Articles 60, 301 and 308 EC jointly? The fact that these provisions clearly do permit certain derogations from fundamental human rights guaranteed by Community law suggests that the Court's reasoning in *Kadi* could not have been based on the idea that the fundamental principles of the Community legal order enjoy some sort of supra-constitutional status amounting to a Community *jus cogens* from which no deviation is allowed under any circumstances.[96] A second clue may be found in the structure of the judgment itself. The sole reason why the ECJ examined the relationship between the UN Charter and the EC Treaty was to determine whether or not that

92 Not everyone shares this view. See D. Halberstam and E. Stein, 'The United Nations, the European Union and the King of Sweden: Economic Sanctions and Individual Rights in a Plural World Order' (2009) 46 CMLR 13, 60–1. See also K. S. Ziegler, 'Strengthening the Rule of Law, but Fragmenting International Law: The *Kadi* Decision of the ECJ from the Perspective of Human Rights' (2009) 9 HRLR 288, 298–302.

93 Case 294/83 '*Les Verts*' [1986] ECR 1339, para. 23.

94 *Kadi and Al Barakaat* (n. 1), para. 282.

95 *Ibid.* para. 304.

96 Cf. Ziegler (n. 92), 297–8.

relationship had the effect of limiting its powers of judicial review as the CFI had held. Tellingly, at the outset of the pertinent section of the judgment, the ECJ recalled that:

> an international agreement cannot affect the allocation of powers fixed by the Treaties or, consequently, the autonomy of the Community legal system, observance of which is ensured by the Court by virtue of the exclusive jurisdiction conferred on it by Article 220 EC, jurisdiction that the Court has, moreover, already held to form part of the very foundations of the Community.[97]

It will be remembered that Article 220 EC directs the Court to ensure that in the interpretation and application of the EC Treaty the law, rather than the autonomy of the Community legal order, is observed. The two are not necessarily the same thing. Equally remarkable is the circularity of this paragraph: the exclusive jurisdiction of the Court guarantees the autonomy of the Community legal order which in turn guarantees the exclusive jurisdiction of the Court.

Consequently, the Court's main concern in *Kadi* was to assert its own jurisdiction in response to the challenge mounted by the Council and the Commission to its competence to review the contested Regulation.[98] This is not to say that defending and expanding its judicial function was the only substantive value that motivated the Court. Evidently, other values are at work in its judgment, in particular the need to preserve the autonomy of the Community legal order, to protect fundamental human rights and to guarantee judicial review as a reflection of the rule of law on the one hand, and the need to observe international undertakings and to respect the primary responsibility of the Security Council for the maintenance of international peace and security on the other. Rather, it is to suggest that the ECJ relied on these different values principally as arguments for and against the exercise of its judicial review powers, rather than to balance them directly and in their own right.[99] In other words, the need to reconcile the protection of individual rights with the demands of collective security was not the Court's central preoccupation in *Kadi*.[100]

15.5.2 Limited implications?

Three key observations may be made in the light of the foregoing. First, the ECJ's judgment displays a considerable dissonance between the formal legal

97 *Ibid.* para. 282.

98 This is explicit throughout the Court's reasoning, see e.g. *Kadi and Al Barakaat* (n. 1), paras. 280, 290 and 317.

99 Cf. *R (Al-Jedda)* v. *Secretary of State for Defence* [2007] UKHL 58, 394–5.

100 See also G. de Búrca, 'Three Replies to Pasquale De Sena and Maria Chiara Vitucci' (2009) 20 EJIL 853, 857.

arguments employed by the Court and the substantive values that motivate its reasoning. This dissonance indicates that the dualism embraced by the Grand Chamber was not inevitable but was rather value based and ultimately political[101] in the choices it made on how to respond to the challenge to its jurisdiction. Several commentators have noted that the formal legal context offered ample room for alternative discourses and solutions.[102]

Second, since the ECJ's arguments are not based on considerations of international law, its judgment actually makes no direct contribution to the various questions of international law it raises. Thus, the judgment adds little to the debate concerning the balancing of human rights and international security, other than in the closed framework of the Community legal order.[103] Indeed, the ECJ seems determined to avoid addressing this question at the level of international law altogether: in *Hassan and Ayadi*, it recently declined an invitation to consider whether the Security Council offered protection equivalent to that of the European Convention on Human Rights.[104] Similarly, whereas the CFI relied on *jus cogens* to test the validity of Security Council resolutions,[105] the ECJ made it known in so many words that it was not the function of the Community courts under Article 220 EC to review the conformity of the acts of an international body with international law. This may be understood as a sign of judicial self-restraint of the *forum non conveniens* type. However, the Court's message may be more general: while it will refer to norms and values of public international law when necessary to interpret rules of Community law,[106] it is not prepared to apply and adjudicate upon the relationship between one rule of international law and another. In other words, it has no appetite to engage in a Scelleian *dédoublement fonctionnel*.[107]

Finally, on reflection, the precedential value of *Kadi* may be more limited than commonly thought. The fact that the ECJ approached *Kadi* from a legal

101 Cf. S. Besson, 'European Legal Pluralism after *Kadi*' (2009) 5 *EUConst.* 237, 261–2; *Cardwell, French and White* (n. 73), 239.

102 See S. Griller, 'International Law, Human Rights and the European Community's Autonomous Legal Order: Notes on the European Court of Justice Decision in *Kadi*' (2008) 4 *EUConst.* 528, 542–54; A. Gattini, 'Joined Cases C-402/05 P and 415/05 P, *Yassin Abdullah Kadi, Al Barakaat International Foundation* v. *Council and Commission*, Judgment of the Grand Chamber of 3 September 2008, nyr' (2009) 46 CMLRev 213, 224–35.

103 *Kadi and Al Barakaat* (n. 1), paras. 342–4. Cf. E. de Wet, 'The Role of European Courts in the Development of a Hierarchy of Norms within International Law: Evidence of Constitutionalisation?' (2009) 5 *EUConst.* 284, 305.

104 See (n. 1), para. 50.

105 This has been much criticized. See, e.g. M. Payandeh, 'Rechtskontrolle des UN-Sicherheitsrates durch staatliche und überstaatliche Gerichte' (2006) 66 ZaöRV 41, 52–7. For a positive assessment, see H. P. Aust and N. Naske, 'Rechtsschutz gegen den UN-Sicherheitsrat durch europäische Gerichte? Die Rechtsprechung des EuG zur Umsetzung "gezielter Sanktionen" aus dem Blickwinkel des Völkerrechts' (2006) 61 ZÖR 587.

106 Case 70/87 *Fediol* [1989] ECR 1781, para. 20; *Bosphorus* (n. 88), para. 26. See the chapters by C. Tietje, A. Rosas and P. J. Kuijper, in J. Wouters, A. Nollkaemper and E. de Wet (eds.), *The Europeanisation of International Law* (The Hague: TMC Asser, 2008).

107 As argued by De Sena and Vitucci (n. 16).

order perspective makes it tempting to read the judgment as a fundamental reassessment of the relationship between Community law and international law. Whereas the logic of constitutional dualism embraced by the Court certainly has the potential to serve as a catalyst for such a reassessment, the Court did not travel very far down this road in *Kadi*. As far as the effects of customary international law within Community law are concerned, it reaffirmed its earlier jurisprudence without change. While the Court appears to have extended the principle that an international agreement cannot affect the allocation of powers fixed by the treaties to all international agreements, not just those concluded under Article 300 EC, its aim in doing so may have been to curb the effects of Articles 297 and 307 EC. In this respect, it is interesting to note that the ECJ's traditional approach is to accept the applicability of Article 307 EC, but to limit its impact by way of an expansive interpretation of the duty its second paragraph imposes on the member states to take all appropriate steps to eliminate the incompatibilities established between their pre-existing agreements and the EC Treaty.[108] This approach may be inappropriate in the case of the UN Charter, since requiring the member states to renegotiate or withdraw from the Charter may prove politically unacceptable. It may well be that the Court chose to declare Articles 297 and 307 EC inapplicable in the present case by subjecting them to an exception not present in the text of the EC Treaty – the need to respect the principles that form part of the very foundations of the Community legal order – in order to avoid having to make such a determination. If correct, this analysis suggests that the Court's reasoning in *Kadi* was conditioned by the fact that the case turned on the legal effects of the UN Charter and that its value as a precedent may be limited largely to this context.[109]

15.6 Conclusion

Without doubt, *Kadi* is a significant case. However, the challenge it presents to the international legal system is tactical, not strategic. D'Aspremont and Dopagne have spoken of the ECJ's judgment in *Kadi* as a reminder of the elementary divide between legal orders.[110] Certainly, international law entitles an autonomous legal order to dualism. As the preceding sections have suggested, it was perfectly legitimate for the ECJ to annul the contested regulation as being incompatible with Community law, as neither the UN Charter nor the EC Treaty requires the institutions to act contrary to that treaty. Nevertheless, the ECJ's dualism is problematic. From an internal perspective, it may be queried whether it is for the Court and its Advocate

108 C.N.K. Franklin, 'Flexibility vs. Legal Certainty: Article 307 EC and Other Issues in the Aftermath of the *Open Skies* Cases' (2005) 10 *European Foreign Affairs Review* 79, 91–103; J. Klabbers, *Treaty Conflict and the European Union* (Cambridge: Cambridge University Press, 2009), 115–49.

109 Cf. Hinojosa Martínez (n. 53), 343.

110 J. d'Aspremont and F. Dopagne, '*Kadi*: The ECJ's Reminder of the Elementary Divide between Legal Orders' (2008) 5 IOLR 371.

General to proclaim that the Community legal system has reached the pinnacle of its constitutionalist evolution by transmuting into a municipal legal order entitled to dualism. From an external perspective, dualism administered in small doses appears to do the international legal system little harm. However, its effects may become altogether more corrosive if dualism is applied as a more frequent remedy.[111] In a piece published in the *Wall Street Journal* shortly after the ECJ rendered its decision in *Kadi*, Jack Goldsmith and Eric Posner referred to that judgment as evidence that 'Europe's commitment to international law is largely rhetorical. Like the Bush administration, Europeans obey international law when it advances their interests and discard it when it does not'.[112]

The answer to *Kadi* ought to come on two fronts. On the international level, the Security Council must live up to the pressures of reform and offer meaningful remedies to individuals affected by its sanctions regimes.[113] The ECJ seems to have indicated its willingness, in principle, to abstain from exercising its judicial review powers should the UN protect fundamental rights at a level equivalent to that guaranteed within Community law. However, the Court's dualism suggests that it is likely to view equivalent protection as requiring an approximation of UN conduct to European constitutional standards, rather than as a search for common ground on the basis of universally applicable human rights norms.[114] Other national and international courts, such as the European Court of Human Rights, may be swayed to cooperate with the Security Council more readily. Closer to home, the member states would be well advised to assert their rights under Articles 297 and 307 EC in response to the 'no derogation' thesis developed by the Court. Where the institutions are unable to assist the member states in complying with their Charter obligations because the necessary Community measures cannot be adopted without breaching Community law, the member states should adopt those measures collectively, with reference to Articles 297 and 307 EC, by way of systematic cooperation outside the framework of the EC Treaty.

111 The Human Rights Committee seems to have applied its own equivalent of the 'no derogation' thesis in *Sayadi and Vinck* v. *Belgium*, CCPR/C/94/D/1472/2006 (29 December 2008). See M. Milanović, 'The Human Rights Committee's Views in *Sayadi* v. *Belgium*: A Missed Opportunity' (2009) 1 *Goettingen JIL* 519.

112 J. Goldsmith and E. Posner, 'Does Europe Believe in International Law?', *Wall Street Journal* (25 November 2008).

113 See A. Reinisch, 'Should Judges Second-Guess the UN Security Council?' (2009) 6 IOLR 257, 284–90; L. van den Herik and N. Schrijver, 'Eroding the Primacy of the UN System of Collective Security: The Judgment of the European Court of Justice in the Cases of *Kadi* and *Al Barakaat*' (2008) 5 IOLR 329, 337–8.

114 Cf. Halberstam and Stein (n. 92), 63–4.

Index

Page numbers in **Bold** represent figures.
Page numbers followed by n represent endnotes.